INFORMATION SYSTEMS

An Introduction to Informatics in Organisations

OTHER TITLES BY THE SAME AUTHOR

Information Systems Development, 3rd edn (1998)
Database Systems, 2nd edn (2000)

INFORMATION SYSTEMS

An Introduction to Informatics in Organisations

Paul Beynon-Davies

palgrave
macmillan

First published 2002 by
PALGRAVE MACMILLAN
Houndmills, Basingstoke, Hampshire RG21 6XS and
175 Fifth Avenue, New York, N. Y. 10010
Companies and representatives throughout the world

PALGRAVE MACMILLAN is the new global academic imprint of St. Martin's Press LLC Scholarly and Reference Division and Palgrave Publishers Ltd (formerly Macmillan Press Ltd).

ISBN-10 0–333–96390–3
ISBN-13 978–0–333–96390–6

This book is printed on paper suitable for recycling and made from fully managed and sustained forest sources.

A catalogue record for this book is available from the British Library.

Typeset by Ian Kingston Editorial Services, Nottingham, UK

10   9   8   7   6   5   4
11   10   09   08   07   06

Printed and bound in China

For my father, David Beynon-Davies, who has been a continuous inspiration

CONTENTS

PREFACE

'When I use a word', Humpty Dumpty said in a rather scornful tone, 'it means just what I choose it to mean – neither more or less'.

Lewis Carroll: *Through the Looking Glass*, Chapter 6

 INFORMATION SYSTEMS AND INFORMATICS

A sign of any developing discipline is a clear definition of the terms used for explicating and understanding phenomena. The author had some difficulty in deciding a title for this work in that there is a lack of precise terminology in its area of coverage. After much thought we decided to use the term *information systems*, as adopted by other texts in this area as a working title (Backhouse *et al.*, 1991). However, the term *information systems* is a difficult one to define, precisely because it is used in a number of different ways. It is used to refer:

- to a *product*, essentially a system of communication between members of some human group. In modern settings such a system of communication is likely to utilise various forms of information technology.
- to an *academic field of study*. Over the last three decades the field of information systems has become established in many centres of higher education around the world. Information systems has become established as an area of teaching and of research.
- to an area of *industrial practice*. The planning, management and development of information systems for organisations is a thriving part of most economies in the Western world. The effective operation of such systems has become increasingly important for the competitive position of modern organisations.

In this work we have attempted to distil the essence of information systems as a product, as an academic discipline and as an area of practice. However, we wish to emphasise a number of important distinctions that preclude us from using the same term in a number of different ways. For example, we make a clear distinction between an information system and an information technology system in this work. Information systems have existed for thousands of years. Only recently has modern information technology (hardware, software, data and communications technology) been used to support such systems.

For this reason we have chosen to use the term *informatics* to refer to the academic discipline and area of professional activity and reserve the term *information system* for a system of communication within some organisation. Informatics is a bridging discipline. It is fundamentally interested in the application of information, information technology and information systems within organisations – hence the subtitle of this work.

The book is based on the author's experience of teaching various undergraduate, postgraduate and commercial courses in the area of organisational informatics for nearly two decades. It is also based on the author's consulting and professional practice of informatics.

MISSION

The book has the following mission:

- *Core material*. The aim of this work is to provide coverage of essential core material in the area of informatics for use on both academic and commercial courses. We have attempted to distil the essence of what one needs to know about the area.

- *Clear definition of terms*. Following on from the discussion in the previous section, we have attempted to utilise a more precise vocabulary than competing texts for explaining the area. We have also attempted to demonstrate how a more coherent account of the field follows from this greater precision in the use of terminology.

- *Stronger theory*. Over the last two decades, informatics has achieved a greater degree of coherence as a discipline. However, most introductory and intermediate texts on the subject tend to de-emphasise the coverage of theory. Here, we aim to provide a stronger theoretical foundation than competing texts. Foundation concepts discussed in earlier chapters are used throughout the text to provide coherence to the description of the current practice of organisational informatics.

- *Holistic emphasis*. Part of the exercise in creating this text has been to provide a more integrated and holistic account of the discipline of organisational informatics. Informatics is not a series of interesting but independent technological issues. It is a seamless web of computing application in organisations.

- *Practical emphasis*. Having stronger theory does not mean less relevance to practice. In fact, we would argue the opposite. A strong theoretical foundation gives a clearer practical emphasis to the coverage of material. It becomes clearer to identify good practice when directed by strong theory.

- *Integration with other texts. Information Systems: an Introduction to Informatics in Organisations* acts as a companion volume to my two other texts, also published by Palgrave: *Information Systems Development* and *Database Systems*. The current text acts as an introduction to the material covered in more detail in these two other texts

◎ STRUCTURE OF THE BOOK

The book is organised in 10 major parts. Each part forms a component element of an informatics model that is introduced in the first chapter of the book. The aim of this form of presentation is to emphasise the necessary multi-faceted and interconnected nature of the domain.

Each part of the book consists of a number of chapters, and each chapter has been written as a notebook on a key topic within informatics. Although each chapter can be read independently, the reader is able to follow links to other chapters to gain a sense of the interconnectedness of the subject.

Each chapter begins with a set of learning outcomes and ends with a written summary. The main text of each chapter is divided into a discussion of key concepts and a number of boxed examples. Examples are used to specifically highlight the concept just discussed. We provide a balance of recent and historical examples in the text and would argue that the utilisation of seminal historical examples is important for building knowledge within the discipline.

Each chapter contains a section of revision questions, exercises and student projects:

- *Questions*. Revision questions are designed to test the reader's understanding of the contents of each chapter and their ability to recall appropriate answers. Answers to the questions can be obtained by re-reading the relevant chapter.

- *Exercises*. Exercises are opportunities for the reader to take what has been learnt and extend knowledge or apply it to some other situation. They are deliberately open-ended and may be used in tutorials or other learning opportunities to structure more extensive learning about the topic under discussion.

- *Projects*. A student research project is a larger piece of work in terms of both effort and duration than a student exercise. Typically it will involve some form of independent investigation including the activities of formulating a project proposal, producing a plan of work, conducting some form of data collection and analysing and presenting results. Ideally, a research project should display elements of independent/critical thinking. It should be noted that the suggestions are expressed merely in the form of some interesting research questions. They will demand much further work to develop into a working research proposal.

A combined glossary and index is included, making it easier to skim search for coverage of particular topics.

◎ SPIDER DIAGRAMS

Each part and chapter begins with a spider diagram. Spider diagrams were originally developed by Tony Buzan (1982) as an effective method of note-taking within study which utilises the natural ability of humans to associate. The idea of a spider diagram is simply to relate concepts together using free-form lines. The centre of the diagram is used to locate the orienting concept. Associated concepts are drawn radiating outwards. Any concept on a spider diagram may act as an orienting concept on its own spider diagram. In this way, most of the structure of the book can be observed in the set of spider diagrams.

Spider diagrams are primarily used as a method of summarising the organisation of information contained in this work. However, we hope that the student of the area will also find them useful as a revision aid and the lecturer or instructor will find them useful as a way of summarising key elements of the domain.

ROUTES THROUGH THE MATERIAL

The text has deliberately been constructed to be as flexible as possible, both for the reader and for use by the lecturer or instructor.

Some suggested ways of including material from the book in various modules delivered at first, second or third year levels of undergraduate courses in information systems, business studies, software engineering or computer science are included below. Clearly the level at which such modules may be delivered will vary depending upon the scheme of study.

The domain chapter could be used within each module to provide a 'fish-eye' or holistic view of the domain and locate more clearly the area of coverage.

Module covering the fundamentals of information, systems and organisations
  Part 1 – *Information and systems* and Part 4 – *Organisations*

Module covering the fundamentals of information technology and information systems development
  Part 2 – *Information technology* and Part 6 – *Information systems development*

Module covering the effects of information technology and information systems
  Part 3 – *Use and impact of information systems* and Part 5 – T*he information systems environment*

Module covering the planning and management of information technology and information systems
  Part 7 – *Informatics planning* and Part 8 – *Informatics management*

Module covering E-business and E-commerce
  Part 9 – *E-business*; Parts 1–8 should be covered as prerequisite material

Module covering the profession and discipline of informatics or information systems
  Part 10 – *Informatics discipline*

WEB SITE AND TEACHING PACK

A Web site including a teaching pack for lecturers/instructors has been produced to accompany the book and can be accessed at:

http://www.palgrave.com/resources

ACKNOWLEDGEMENTS

My thanks to the anonymous reviewers and to Tracey Alcock at Palgrave for support in the production of this work.

REFERENCES

Buzan, A. (1982). *Use Your Head*. BBC Books, London.

Backhouse, J., Liebenau, J. and Land, F. (1991). On the discipline of information systems. *Journal of Information Systems*, **1**(1), 19–27.

CHAPTER 1

THE INFORMATICS DOMAIN

LEARNING OUTCOMES

After reading this chapter, you will be able to:

- Define a number of key concepts in the domain of informatics
- Explain the relationship between these key concepts in terms of an interaction model
- Outline the major structural elements of the book

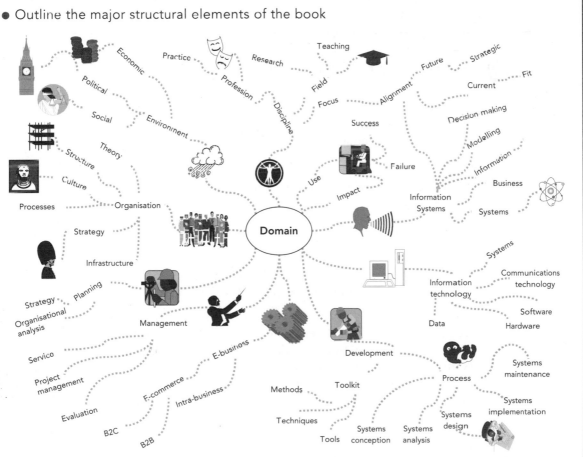

1.1 ⊚ INTRODUCTION

In this chapter we shall use a model to discuss the key elements of informatics as a domain. The model is founded on the premise that the effects of an information system for an organisation emerge over time as the result of the interaction of the system with its organisational context. Understanding the nature of this interaction is therefore central to obtaining the benefits of information systems as well as avoiding the hazards that information systems can hold for organisations (Silver *et al.*, 1995). This focus on the application of information systems within organisations we take to be the fundamental basis on which the discipline of informatics as an academic field of study and as an area of industrial practice is founded.

A word of caution. This serves as an orienting chapter for the book, since it provides a high-level view of the informatics terrain and provides the structure for the ten major parts of the text that follow. The reader is not expected to assimilate all the concepts discussed here in one pass, but should feel free to follow links to further chapters at any time. The chapter can be used at some later point as a way of reviewing the material covered.

1.2 ⊚ ELEMENTS OF THE DOMAIN

The model in Figure 1.1 depicts the major elements of the informatics domain and also forms the basic structure for the book. Each of the component elements contained in the model is covered in more detail as a part of the book:

- The information system (Parts 1 and 2)
- The use and impact of information systems (Part 3)
- The organisation (Part 4)
- The external environment of the organisation (Part 5)
- The IS development process (Part 6)
- The process of informatics planning (Part 7)
- The process of informatics management (Part 8)

Within this chapter we consider each of these elements in turn, then summarise the interrelationships between components in terms the overall criteria of 'fitness for purpose'. Informatics as a practical discipline (Part 10) has the overall aim of trying to improve the fit between information systems and organisations. In its most recent guise organisational informatics is critical to the areas of electronic business (e-business) and electronic commerce (e-commerce) (Part 9).

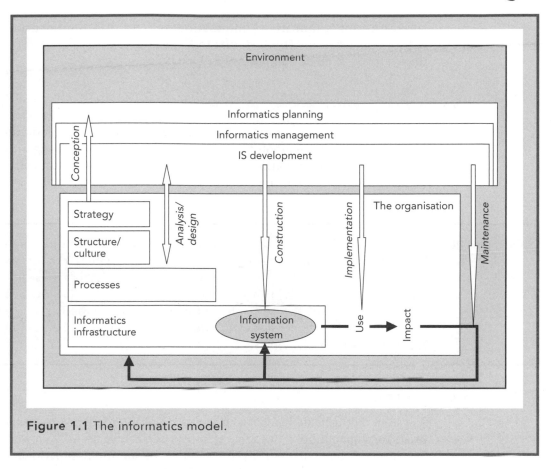

Figure 1.1 The informatics model.

1.3 (◎) KEY TERMS

In this section we define a number of essential key terms that form the bedrock of the informatics model.

1.3.1 INFORMATICS

Informatics is the study of information, information systems and information technology applied to various phenomena. The term has been used repeatedly by various branches of the European Union to encompass the application of information technology in support of the information society. In Germany the term *informatik* and in France the term *informatique* are much used.

The term has also been extremely popular within the health and biological sciences fields, as is evident in the common use of such terms as *health informatics*, *medical informatics* and *bio-informatics*. Some have used the term to elevate traditional information management (librarianship) concerns to a new plane founded in information technology. Here we use the term in the sense implied by Kling and Allen (1996). They use the term *organisational informatics* to encompass the application of information, information systems and information technology within organisations. This is similar to Kling and Scaachi's (1982) interest in what they call the 'Web of Computing'.

1.3.2 INFORMATION

Information is data interpreted in some meaningful context. A datum, a unit of data, is one or more symbols that are used to represent something. Information is interpreted data. Information is data placed within a meaningful context. The use of the term information therefore implies a group of people doing interpretation (Chapter 2).

Example ▐▐▐➡ Consider the string of symbols 43. Taken together these symbols form a datum, but by themselves they are meaningless. To turn these symbols into information we have to supply a meaningful context. We have to interpret them. This might be that they constitute an employee number, a person's age, or the quantity of a product sold. Information of this sort will contribute to our knowledge of a particular domain. It might add, for instance, to our understanding of the total number of products of a particular type sold.

1.3.3 SYSTEM

A system might be defined as a coherent set of interdependent components that exists for some purpose, has some stability, and can be usefully viewed as a whole. Systems are generally portrayed in terms of an input–process–output model existing within a given environment. The environment of a system might be defined as anything outside the system that has an effect on the way the system operates. The inputs to the system are the resources it gains from its environment or other systems. The outputs from the system are those things which it supplies back to its environment or other systems. The process of the system is the activity which transforms the system inputs into system outputs. The systems concept has been applied both to technology and to human activity (Chapter 3).

1.3.4 INFORMATION SYSTEM (IS)

An information system is a system of communication between people. Information systems are systems involved in the gathering, processing, distribution and use of information. Information systems support human activity systems (Chapter 4).

1.3.5 HUMAN ACTIVITY SYSTEM (HAS)

A human activity system (HAS) is a social system – sometimes referred to as a 'soft' system. A human activity system is a logical collection of activities performed by some group of people. A human activity system will have a distinct goal or goals that it fulfils. Another term now used as a synonym for a HAS is *organisational process*.

Example ⦀➡ Information systems are frequently called after the human activity system they support. Hence we find people referring to the finance information system (for the finance HAS) or the order-processing information system (for the order-processing HAS).

1.3.6 STAKEHOLDERS

The group of people to which an information system is relevant is normally that group known as the system's users. Another group of people may be involved in building an information system. These are the developers of the information system. There may also be a number of other groups involved with some information system. Each such group is a stakeholder in the information system.

1.3.7 INFORMATION TECHNOLOGY (IT)

Information technology is any technology used to support information gathering, processing, distribution and use. Information technology provides means of constructing aspects of information systems, but is distinct from information systems. Modern information technology consists of hardware, software, data and communications technology (Part 2).

It is important to recognise that information systems have existed in organisations prior to the invention of IT, and hence IS do not need modern IT to exist. In Chapter 4 we consider some historical forms of IT such as writing on clay tablets. However, in the modern, complex organisational world, most IS rely on hardware, software, data and communications technology to a greater or lesser degree because of the efficiency and effectiveness gains possible with the use of such technology.

The supporting relationships between human activity systems, information systems and information technology are illustrated in Figure 1.2.

1.3.8 INFORMATION TECHNOLOGY SYSTEM (ITS)

An information technology system is a technical system (Chapter 12). Such systems are frequently referred to as examples of 'hard' systems in the sense that they have a physical existence. An information technology system is an organised collection of hardware, software, data and communications technology designed to support aspects of some information system. An information technology system has data as input, manipulates such data as a process and outputs manipulated data for interpretation within some human activity system.

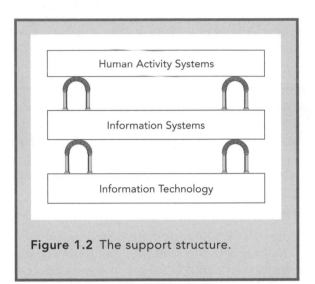

Figure 1.2 The support structure.

Example ▐▐▐▶ Take an order-processing IT system. In such a system the data entered will describe the properties of orders. The manipulation comprises the processing of orders probably in relation to other data collected, such as that on customers. The manipulated data in the system constitutes the processed orders.

The order-processing IT system will support that activity concerned with the effective sales of products or services to customers. Without effective and efficient performance of this activity the organisation is unlikely to survive in its marketplace.

1.3.9 SOCIO-TECHNICAL SYSTEM

Most systems in organisations are examples of socio-technical systems. A socio-technical system is a system of technology used within a system of activity. Information systems are primary examples of socio-technical systems. Information systems consist of information technology systems used within some human activity system. They therefore bridge between information technology and human activity. Part of the human activity will involve the use of the information technology system. The information provided by the information technology system will also drive decision-making leading to further action within the organisation. Some of the key elements of such socio-technical systems are illustrated in Figure 1.3.

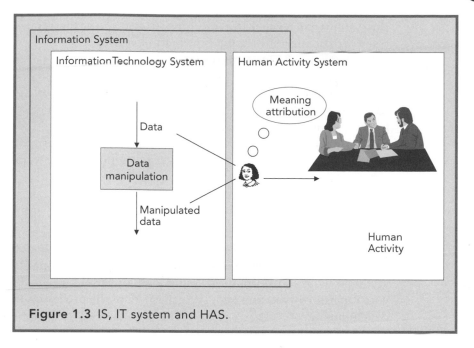

Figure 1.3 IS, IT system and HAS.

Example ▐▐▐▶ A group has three members. Each member of the group delivers leaflets to houses in specified areas: this is the human activity of the group. To support this activity the group notes on a regular basis which leaflets have been delivered to which houses. They need to do this because they are paid on the basis of how many leaflets they deliver to houses in an area. This comprises their information system. Initially it is a manual information system in that details of leaflet deliveries are noted in a paper file. Eventually, as the business expands in terms of the volume of leaflets handled and the complexity of the instructions for delivery from their customers, the manual system becomes cumbersome. They eventually purchase a personal computer and store the delivery information on a database system. This constitutes the information technology in support of the information system. Part of the activity of the information system now involves using the database system. But it still supports a similar human activity system.

1.4 ◎ PROPERTIES OF AN INFORMATION SYSTEM

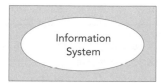

Information systems have to be designed in the sense that the key features of such systems need to be determined prior to the construction and implementation of the systems. Such key features or properties are critical ways in which we can assess the worth or success of some information system.

Traditionally, design features of an information system fall into one of two categories: functionality – what the system does; and usability – how the system is used. One should note that both functionality and usability are inherently related to the place of the information system within the context of some human activity system. Hence to functionality and usability we should add utility. Utility or efficacy is an important but neglected feature of an information system. Utility concerns the contribution the IS makes to supporting the human activity of some organisation.

1.4.1 FUNCTIONALITY

The functionality of some information system is normally determined by a close examination of organisational requirements. The functionality of an information system is what an information system does or should be able to do. Specifying the core functionality of an IS is a critical aspect of the process of information systems development.

1.4.2 USABILITY

Usability is evident in the way in which an IS embeds itself within human activity. An information system's usability is how easy a system is to use for the purpose for which it has been constructed. Usability is evident at the human–computer interface – that place where the user interacts with the IT system.

1.4.3 UTILITY

Whereas functionality defines what a system does and usability defines how a system is used, utility defines how acceptable the system is in terms of doing what is needed. Utility refers to the worth of an information system in terms of the contribution it makes to its human activity system and to the organisation as a whole.

Functionality is primarily a feature of the information technology system. Utility is primarily a feature of the human activity system. Usability is a mediating feature between the technical system (the information technology system) and the social system (the human activity system) and is evident at the interface.

Example ||||➡   • *Functionality.* Some aspect of the functionality of an IS is normally contained in the name usually given to an IS. For instance, if we describe some system as being an order-processing system, then we are indicating that the system in some way captures, stores and manipulates data associated with the processing of orders, probably from customers.

- *Usability.* In terms of an order-processing system, the systems' usability will be determined by how easy it is for users such as order clerks to input data about orders into the system and to extract data about orders from the system.

- *Utility.* The utility of an order-processing system might be defined in terms of the contribution it makes to the efficient handling of orders made by customers of the organisation. An IT system may contribute significant cost savings in order processing. It may also contribute to improvements in organisational effectiveness. For instance, it may have positive implications for the level of customer satisfaction experienced.

By IS development we mean the process devoted to the construction of an IS. The focus within IS development has historically been on issues of functionality. The concern has been and still is to produce well-engineered systems, in the sense that they do the job specified for them. But well-engineered systems are insufficient in themselves. They must also be usable. Hence much work has been undertaken in improving the user interfaces associated with IT systems.

However, traditionally IS have been built to merely automate existing patterns of work – particularly to replicate manual functions of existing human activity systems. There is evidence to suggest that the utility of such systems, however important, is limited in the sense of offering only incremental improvement. Hence, increasingly, IS are being used to design new ways of working in an attempt to gain greater leverage in terms of utility for organisations.

Functionality, usability and utility are thus three necessarily interdependent variables that serve to define the interaction between the design of an information system and the human activity it is meant to support or enable. Clearly, the design of an IS can affect this interaction in various subtle ways.

Examples ▶ Shoshanna Zuboff (1988) illustrated how computer systems can be designed in which users are placed outside of the system, engaged in merely monitoring the work process. The alternative is that the computer system can be defined such that work becomes more visible and workers are given close involvement in the work process. Zuboff calls this the choice between automating on the one hand and informating on the other.

This is similar to the work of Mumford (1996), in which the emphasis is on the design of work in parallel with the design of IT systems. As an example, an information system may be designed to continually monitor the work of insurance clerks, or support and enable the individual work and teamwork of clerks.

1.5 INFORMATION SYSTEMS USE

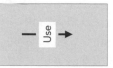

After an information system is introduced into an organisation, the IS begins to have effects on that organisation. We may distinguish between the first-order effects and second-order effects arising from such introduction. First-order effects concern issues of use. Second-order effects concern the impact of IS on the activities of individuals, groups and the organisation as a whole.

Use is primarily a usability concern. However, we must recognise that many systems may not actually get used; they may be abandoned before they become used. This we call use failure (see Chapter 13).

Example ▌▌▌▶ The experiences of the Spanish air traffic control system (SACTA) demonstrate a clear case of use failure (Salabert and Newman, 1995). The system was implemented, but became subject to the difficulties inherent in an environment in which air traffic controllers were in wage dispute with their employers. The system was used by the controllers in ways that demonstrated the worth of controller activity. However, the use also clearly served to demonstrate the limitations of the system. One clear tactic employed was to overload the system with use to such a point that it became unworkable. This led to the eventual abandonment of the system.

Secondly, we must recognise that if a system is used, it may be used in ways unintended in terms of its original design. Such unintended use may be positive, as in the case when a decision support system serves not only as a tool for enhancing decision-making, but also as a tool for improving customer relations. The unintended use may also be negative, as when an executive information system is used to intimidate subordinates and stifle creativity rather than to enhance managerial processes.

1.6 INFORMATION SYSTEMS IMPACT

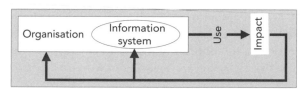

Organisational impact is a utility concern (Chapter 14). Business organisations overtly invest in information systems for one of two reasons: to be more efficient, usually by increasing productivity, or to be more effective. This normally equates to attempts to increase the market share of a business.

As far as commercial organisations are concerned, both efficiency and effectiveness are strategies to make more money, i.e. to increase profitability. But the introduction of an information system does not always have these effects. Evidence suggests that there are some inherent paradoxes/contradictions involved with the introduction of IS into organisations.

Second-order effects, or what we have called impact on Figure 1.1, may be distinguished in terms of their impact on the individual, on groups and on the organisation as a whole.

Example ▐▐▐▶ In terms of impact on the individual and group one may cite the shifts in power and influence that may arise after the introduction of some information system. For example, substantial shifts of this nature were experienced in relation to the position of office workers such as secretaries when information systems were first introduced to replace typical secretarial skills such as typing. In contrast, job enrichment or greater degrees of worker empowerment may become feasible with the introduction of an IS.

In terms of impact on the organisation as a whole the relationship between information systems and productivity is one of the most hotly debated. One key reason organisations use IS is the expectation that employing such systems will raise the productivity of the workforce. However, over a number of years, this link between IS usage and productivity has been questioned.

1.7 ORGANISATION

The Organisation

Strategy

Structure/
Culture

Processes

Informatics
Infrastructure

Generally speaking the discipline of informatics is interested in human activity within organised groupings of individuals – organisations. Organisations are social collectives, but not all social collectives are organisations. Organisations are social collectives in which formal procedures are used for coordinating the activities of members in the pursuit of joint objectives. The concept of organisation arises from our general readiness to treat as a meaningful entity the abstract notion of a body of people having a form independent of the people that compose it.

Defining the precise nature of organisation is a difficult task (Chapter 16). In this work we focus on five critical aspects of organisation that affect decisions about the effective place of information, information systems and information technology: structure, culture, processes, strategy and infrastructure.

1.7.1 ORGANISATION STRUCTURE

Structure (Chapter 17) refers to the formal aspects of an organisation's functioning: division of labour; hierarchical authority; job descriptions; etc. Structure impacts on the choice of IS, the design of IS and the deployment of IS. Traditionally, IS support existing organisation structure in the sense that information systems tend to emulate the current structural divisions in organisations. However, IS may also contribute to organisational restructuring and may be means for flattening organisational structures in various ways by removing managerial layers.

1.7.2 ORGANISATION CULTURE

Culture (Chapter 18) refers to a common set of shared basic assumptions or meanings held by groups of people. A number of dimensions of organisational culture can be identified such as whether an organisation values individuality or teamwork, whether it favours bigger or smaller organisational units, and whether it favours risk taking or risk aversion in decision-making.

Organisational cultures influence the development, adoption and use of information systems in various ways. For instance, different organisations may value information technology differently. Information systems may also impact on organisational culture in various ways. Information systems are frequently used as ways of introducing attempted changes to organisation culture by managerial groups.

1.7.3 ORGANISATION PROCESSES

Organisations can be viewed as systems of human activity and critical to the concept of system is that of a process (Chapter 19). Organisations can be seen to be made up of a number of human activity systems or processes. An organisational process is a set of activities cutting across the major functional boundaries of organisations by which organisations accomplish their missions, particularly the key one of delivering value to the customer.

A key recent emphasis within informatics is to design IS around processes rather than structures or functions. Processes are the means by which value is delivered to a customer. Developing information systems around so-called value chains has the potential to deliver radical improvements in organisational performance.

1.7.4 ORGANISATION STRATEGY

Strategic decision-making is focused on the future and the environment of the organisation. Organisation strategy (Chapter 20) is a detailed plan for future action and comprises the general direction or mission of an organisation. Planning is the process of formulating strategy; management is the process of implementing strategy.

A key principle is that organisation strategy should drive informatics strategy. Informatics planning is the process of developing informatics strategy. Informatics management is the process of implementing informatics strategy.

1.7.5 INFORMATICS INFRASTRUCTURE

Most organisations either have an explicit or implicit informatics infrastructure (Chapter 21). An informatics infrastructure equals the set of organisational resources that give the organisation the capacity to generate new IT systems. An informatics infrastructure includes not only physical resources such as existing hardware, software, data facilities and communications, but also non-physical resources such as knowledge, plans, people and skills.

An informatics infrastructure can be seen to be made up of three interdependent levels:

- Information infrastructure
- Information systems infrastructure
- Information technology infrastructure

It must be recognised that an informatics infrastructure is both enabling and constraining. Any application of information systems can leverage or extend the existing informatics infrastructure. A given IS leverages the infrastructure when it draws upon the resources the existing infrastructure offers. IS extends the infrastructure by contributing physical or non-physical resources that can be drawn upon by other applications.

However, an infrastructure may also be a constraining influence. For instance, legacy systems – large and ageing corporate support systems – generally constrain the organisation in the sense that they determine the way in which much corporate data must be collected, manipulated and distributed. They also restrict available upgrade paths for information technology.

1.8 ENVIRONMENT

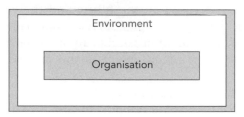

An organisation is a human activity system, or more accurately a series of interdependent human activity systems that is affected by forces found within its environment. Organisations are not isolated entities, but are open systems that build information systems to cope with environmental pressures and constraints. Hence the success of any organisation will depend on how well it integrates with aspects of its environment (Part 5).

By environment we normally mean anything outside of the organisation. The global environment can be considered in terms of an interaction between three major environmental systems: an economic system, a social system and a political system. The external environment comprises a network of activities and relationships in each of these environmental systems between the organisation and other agencies.

The external environment in each of these systems will exert an impact on the information systems activities of some organisation, group or individual. Likewise, the information systems activities of individuals, groups and organisations are likely to impact on social, economic and political systems. Also information technology and information systems will have a significant impact on the shape of economic, social and political systems.

1.8.1 ECONOMIC ENVIRONMENT

An economic system is the way in which a group of humans arrange their material provisioning. It essentially involves the coordination of activities concerned with such provisioning. An organisation's economic environment is defined by activities and relationships between economic actors and the organisation (Chapter 22). The economic environment is particularly concerned with the performance of national and international commerce and trade and is influenced by such factors as levels of taxation, inflation rates and economic growth.

Example ▐▐▐▶ Regulatory changes frequently impact on the logic of an organisation's transaction processing and reporting systems. An example here is the way in which European Monetary Union has forced a level of standardisation amongst financial information systems in the European Union.

1.8.2 SOCIAL ENVIRONMENT

The social environment of an organisation concerns the cultural life of some grouping, such as a nation state. The social system consists of a series of cultural activities and relationships (Chapter 23) and concerns ways in which people relate to organisational activity. It concerns issues of fashion, taste and ethical and moral considerations.

> Example ||||➡ Information systems are used to collect vast amounts of data on individuals. Many countries have therefore initiated data protection legislation to ensure rights to personal privacy. Information systems developed within such countries must conform to the data protection legislation.

1.8.3 POLITICAL ENVIRONMENT

The political environment or system concerns issues of power. Political systems are made up of sets of activities and relationships concerned with power and its exercise (Chapter 24). The political environment is particularly concerned with government and legislation and is a major constraining force on organisational behaviour in the area of informatics. Likewise, informatics has been an influential force in the recent trends in electronic government and tele-democracy.

> Example ||||➡ Many Western governments are using information technology to facilitate greater levels of communication between government representatives and the general populace. This trend is generally referred to as tele-democracy.

1.9 INFORMATION SYSTEMS DEVELOPMENT

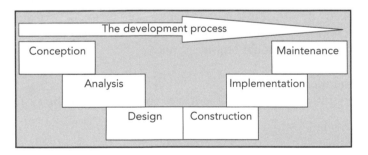

Information systems development (Part 6) is a key organisational process for many organisations. It is a process and hence can be considered as a system in itself. The key inputs into the process are information technology resources and developer resources. The key outputs are some information system and some associated human activity system. A number of key activities are involved in the development process including conception, analysis, design, construction, implementation and maintenance. A toolkit of methods, techniques and tools is required by the developer to engage in these activities.

1.9.1 INFORMATION SYSTEMS DEVELOPMENT PROCESS

The process of information systems development (Chapter 25) of whatever form involves the following activities.

Conception
Conception (Chapter 27) is the phase in which an organisation develops the key business case for an information system. An organisation evaluates the information system strategically and assesses its feasibility. The organisation also attempts to estimate the degree of risk associated with a project to construct the proposed information system. An information systems project which succeeds the strategic evaluation and feasibility assessment will pass on to a process of systems analysis.

Analysis
Systems analysis (Chapter 28) involves two primary and interrelated activities – requirements elicitation and requirements representation. Requirements elicitation is the process of identifying requirements for new systems. Requirements specification is the process of documenting identified requirements.

Design
Design (Chapter 29) is the process of planning a technical artefact to meet requirements established by analysis. Such a design or system specification acts as a blueprint for systems construction.

Construction
This phase involves the actual construction (Chapter 30) of the information system. This may either be conducted by a team internal to the organisation or undertaken by an outside contractor (a form of construction known as outsourcing). Many information systems are now also bought in as a package and tailored to organisational requirements.

Implementation
Implementation (Chapter 31) involves the delivery of the system into its context of use.

Maintenance
This is the feedback process (Chapter 32) that involves changes to information systems and to elements of the organisation. It must be acknowledged that information systems rarely stand still. They may change for a number of reasons:

- In the process of using information systems errors may be found in such systems or changes may be proposed. Fixing errors (bugs) and changing systems is normally classed as maintenance.

- At some point in time a system may be abandoned or need to be re-engineered to fit new organisational circumstances.
- Changes also occur over time in terms of adjustments made to the way both the IS and its context of use works.

Example ▐▐▐➤ How the system is used, its perceived consequences for performance and people, will affect the organisational context over time. For instance, it may lead to organisational restructuring. There is much evidence of the way in which the development and use of an IS can act as major vehicles for organisational learning (Zuboff, 1988). An organisation may utilise an information system as a major vehicle for learning about its organisational processes and for planning changes to such processes.

1.9.2 INFORMATION SYSTEMS DEVELOPMENT TOOLKIT

To undertake any development effort the information systems developer needs a toolkit (Chapter 26). Such a toolkit will consist of methods, techniques and tools:

- *Methods*. These constitute frameworks which suggest, sometimes in great detail, the tasks to be undertaken in a given development process.
- *Techniques*. These form the component parts of methods in that they constitute particular ways of undertaking given parts of the process, particularly analysis and design.
- *Tools*. By tools we primarily mean here available hardware, software, data and communication facilities for engaging in some part of the internal project development process or its set of associated external activities.

1.9.3 DOMAIN-DEPENDENT SYSTEMS

The way in which a system is developed can affect system acceptance. Giddings (1984) characterises information systems as domain-dependent software. Information systems are domain-dependent because there is a necessary interdependence between the system and its universe of discourse, typically the organisation which sponsors the development of the IS. Such systems are characterised by an intrinsic uncertainty about the universe of discourse. In particular, the use of the system may change the nature of the universe of discourse and hence the nature of the problem being solved.

Conventional approaches to IS development tend to treat this feature of the development process as something of an aberration that has to be worked around in the context of a development project. In this book we treat this phenomena as a fundamental premise of IS development that must be accommodated within the development process itself. We believe that this uncertainty is a reflection of the organisational learning focused in the introduction of information technology. However, to achieve such accommodation demands a critical reflection on the way in which information systems are conventionally developed.

1.10 ⊚ INFORMATICS PLANNING

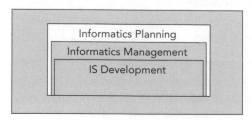

Besides poor productivity there are numerous other negative effects that arise from the introduction of IT systems. Some people have argued, for instance, that IS/IT has been largely used not to enhance effectiveness but to increase job loss, deskilling and a consequent loss of morale amongst the workforce of many organisations. IT systems have also been particularly used as a way of closely monitoring and hence controlling the behaviour of workers. Many IS/IT projects have also either been abandoned at great expense, or have failed to deliver expected benefits in use (Chapter 15).

So IS do not always have intended benefits. How then can we ensure that: failure does not occur, that negative effects do not occur and that positive effects do occur? The main point is that we cannot do this by directing attention and resources solely at the IS itself. We must consider IS in the context of its organisation, and the organisation in the context of its environment. Perhaps a better way of putting this is that IS in some way contributes to the success of some organisation within its environment. But what makes a successful organisation?

Peter Drucker's (1994) *Theory of the Business* attributes organisational success to three factors:

- Businesses understanding their external environments
- Businesses undertaking missions (developing strategies) consistent with their external environments
- Businesses developing core competencies needed to accomplish their missions

Organisational success is predicated in part on IS success. Effective informatics planning and management are seen to be necessary conditions for ensuring IS success. Planning and management are necessary to ensure that information systems are aligned with organisational strategy.

Informatics planning (Chapter 34) is the process of deciding upon the optimal informatics strategy for some organisation. The general principle established in the literature is that informatics strategy should be aligned with organisation strategy. Organisation strategy may initiate organisational analysis. Informatics strategy may be involved in the identification of the strategic application of information systems that may influence organisation strategy.

1.10.1 ORGANISATIONAL ANALYSIS

We use the term organisational analysis (Chapter 33) to mean the analysis of the human activity systems of organisations with the intent of redesigning key aspects of such processes. Information technology is seen to be a key enabler of such redesign.

1.10.2 INFORMATICS STRATEGY

An informatics strategy (Chapter 35) includes detailing expectations as to the architecture in the following three areas:

- *Information architecture*. This consists of activities involved in the collection, storage, dissemination and use of information within the organisation.
- *Information systems architecture*. This consists of the information systems needed to support organisational activity in the areas of collection, storage, dissemination and use.
- *Information technology architecture*. This consists of the hardware, software, communication facilities and IT knowledge and skills available to the organisation.

The objective of informatics planning is to develop strategy in each of these three areas. The practical output of informatics planning is a document set which describes strategy in these three areas. An informatics strategy can be described as being the structure within which information, information systems and information technology are applied within the organisation. Such a strategy should establish an organisation's long-term infrastructure that will allow information systems to be designed and implemented efficiently and effectively. An informatics strategy is particularly directed at avoiding fragmentation, redundancy and inconsistency amongst information systems in the organisation. The strategy should also be directed at ensuring an effective 'fit' between an organisation and its information systems.

Example ||||➤ Take the example of a university. As part of its information architecture the university will need to establish precisely what data it needs to collect, manipulate and disseminate on its students. To enable this information strategy the institution establishes personnel and procedures for the collection, manipulation and dissemination of this data. To improve the efficiency and effectiveness of processes such as enrolment, assessment and grading the university decides to implement a student management information technology system.

1.10.3 STRATEGIC INFORMATION SYSTEMS

A strategic information system (Chapter 36) might be defined as any information system which directly assists an organisation in achieving its organisation strategy. Strategic information systems are outward looking, acting as bridges into the environment of the organisation. Strategic IS frequently create new markets for the organisation.

Example ▐▐▐▶ A key example of a strategic IS is the way in which the Republic of Singapore's extreme reliance on foreign trade led it to develop an IS (Tradenet) that significantly reduced the time required for shippers to clear customs. The objective was to give Singapore a competitive advantage over other ports in the Far East.

1.11 INFORMATICS MANAGEMENT

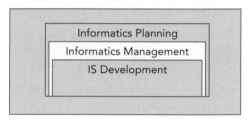

Informatics Planning
Informatics Management
IS Development

Planning is the process of determining what to do over a given time period. Managing is the process of executing, evaluating and adapting plans in the face of contingencies.

Michael Earl has distinguished between three forms of management relevant to informatics (Chapter 37): information systems management, information technology management and information management. This is clearly closely related to the three levels of informatics strategy:

- *Information management* is concerned with the overall strategic direction of the organisation and the planning, regulation and coordination of information in support of this direction.
- *Information systems management* is concerned with providing information handling to support organisational activities.
- *Information technology management* is concerned with providing the necessary technical infrastructure for implementing desired information handling.

For many organisations information, information systems and information technology services will be organised in one function. This function, service or department will be particularly involved in setting up and managing development projects. It will also be critically involved in evaluating information technology systems for the organisation in various ways.

1.11.1 THE INFORMATICS SERVICE

Most medium to large-scale organisations employ people specifically in informatics work. The informatics service (Chapter 40) is that specialist function of an organisation devoted to activities such as planning, management, development and maintenance.

1.11.2 PROJECT MANAGEMENT

A project is any concerted effort to develop an information technology system. The initiation of projects will be done as part of an organisation's IS planning and IS management processes. Project management (Chapter 38) will interact with the development process.

The issue of project management can be divided into three interrelated areas: project planning, project organisation and project control. Project planning involves determining as clearly as possible the likely parameters associated with a particular project. Project organisation concerns how to structure staff activities to ensure maximum effectiveness. Project control concerns ensuring that a project remains on schedule, within budget and produces the desired output.

1.11.3 INFORMATION SYSTEMS EVALUATION

A number of questions have been frequently voiced by general management within organisations in relation to information systems and information technology:

- Do we know how much is currently spent on IS?
- What value results from this spending?
- How should IS alternatives be justified/prioritised/financed?

IS evaluation (Chapter 41) is an attempt to provide answers to some of these questions. IS evaluation should be a necessary part of the management of IS and an intrinsic phase within any planning for information systems. We may distinguish between three main types of evaluation:

- *Strategic evaluation.* Sometimes referred to as pre-implementation evaluation, this type of evaluation involves assessing or appraising an IS/IT investment in terms of its potential for delivering benefits against estimated costs.
- *Formative evaluation.* Formative evaluation involves assessing the shape of an IS whilst in the development process itself. Formative evaluation may be used to make crucial changes to the design of an information system or to make critical decisions concerning the degree of project abandonment.
- *Summative evaluation.* This type of evaluation occurs after an IS has been implemented. For this reason it is sometimes referred to as post-implementation evaluation. Ideally, summative evaluation involves returning to the costs and benefits established in strategic evaluation after a period of use of the IS.

1.12 ⓒ E-BUSINESS AND E-COMMERCE

Much has been recently published on the topics of e-business and e-commerce. Business can be considered either as an entity or as the set of activities associated with a commercial organisation. E-business is the utilisation of information and communication technologies (ICT) to support all the activities of business. Commerce constitutes the exchange of products and services between businesses, groups and individuals. Commerce or trade can hence be seen as one of the essential activities of any business. E-commerce focuses on the use of ICT to enable the external activities and relationships of the business with individuals, groups and other businesses.

Both e-business and e-commerce are modern facets of organisational informatics. In a sense, Part 9 involves us in using the concepts established in previous parts of the book to explain this modern phenomenon. Fundamentally, e-business and e-commerce focus around organisational value chains. Organisations can be seen as consisting of a series of interdependent chains that deliver value. Three chains are significant for most businesses:

- The *internal value chain* consists of a series of processes by which the organisation delivers a product or service.
- The *supply chain* consists of those processes by which an organisation obtains goods and services from other organisations.
- The *customer chain* consists of those processes by which an organisation delivers value to its customers.

The trend to use ICT to restructure aspects of the internal value chain of organisations has been ongoing for a number of decades. Recently, increasing interest has been expressed in using ICT to re-engineer aspects of the organisation customer and supply chain.

Business-to-business (B2B) e-commerce has been undertaken for a number of decades in that businesses have used electronic records to transfer documentation in terms of standards in the area of electronic data interchange or EDI. More recently the Internet and its associated technologies have been used to transfer data between companies engaged in a trading relationship. Business-to-customer (B2C) is a relatively new feature of electronic commerce. It is only comparatively recently with the rise of technologies underlying the Internet that direct connections between customers and businesses have been made possible.

1.13 ⓒ THE DISCIPLINE OF INFORMATICS

We have used the term informatics to refer to that discipline (Part 10) concerned with information, information systems and information technology. Many would use the term *information systems* to refer to the same area. We have avoided this in an attempt to provide a more precise terminology that suggests the true multi-faceted and interdisciplinary nature of the domain.

Informatics is a valid academic field, a thriving area of industrial practice and an interesting and productive area for research.

1.13.1 INDUSTRIAL PRACTICE

Informatics has become a central part of most organisations and many specialist roles are now available in the planning, management and development of information systems (Chapter 46). In terms of informatics practice there has been a substantial debate about whether the vast array of jobs and roles available in the area can reasonably be considered a profession.

1.13.2 PROFESSION

Concern has been expressed over the regulation and control of informatics activities in organisations, societies and economies. Work in informatics has some characteristics of professional status but currently lacks significant traits characterising established professions such as law and medicine. There are also significant barriers in the way of the professionalisation process for informatics work (Chapter 47).

1.13.3 ACADEMIC FIELD

Informatics is a maturing academic field (Chapter 48). This is evident in that:

- There are currently a substantial community of scholars both within the UK and throughout the world who work in the area of informatics.
- Within the UK there are numerous academic departments which teach informatics type modules and courses.
- There are a number of established conferences for the discipline.
- A number of journals exist for publishing the results of research in this area.
- A number of bodies exist to foster communication, cooperation and collaboration for academics in this area.

1.13.4 INFORMATICS RESEARCH

The major question is what makes informatics distinctive from other fields such as management science, computer science and software engineering. It might be argued that it is impossible to build a well-founded academic field without a coherent body of well-established research. There are a number of established approaches for conducting informatics research, a review of which is provided in Chapter 49.

1.14 KEY ISSUES

This text is particularly interested in the application of informatics within organisations. There are a number of elements contained within this definition that will be discussed in more detail throughout the various chapters of this text:

- That informatics concerns itself with information in general as well as the more specific topics of information systems and information technology. The definition of what information constitutes and how information is related to effective decision-making and human action is a key concern for informatics.

- That an information system need not necessarily be computerised; that the processes of gathering, processing, storing and distributing information have been undertaken in human societies for many thousands of years with various information technologies. Computer and communication technology is only the latest, if highly ubiquitous, example of such 'information technology'.

- That the idea of information and an information system cannot be understood properly without a description of its context. Usually the level of context is an organisation or part of an organisation within which such systems are placed. Sometimes, the level of markets, societies and economies are important, as is the case for instance with systems making up the financial infrastructure of a nation. More recently, the focus has shifted up to the global scale in the case of such an 'information system' as the Internet.

- The central idea is that an information system must 'fit' its organisational context: the organisation, its strategy, its processes and its environment. Information systems that do not fit are likely to be resisted, underused, misused or sabotaged. Information systems that do not fit are likely to have negative effects on organisational performance

1.15 SUMMARY

- Informatics is the study of information, information systems and information technology applied to various phenomena. We are primarily interested in the application of informatics in organisations and society.

- Information is data interpreted in some meaningful context.

- A system is a coherent set of interdependent components which exists for some purpose, has some stability, and can be usefully viewed as a whole. The systems concept has been applied both to technology and to human activity.

- An information system is a system of communication between people.

- Information technology provides means of constructing aspects of information systems, but is distinct from information systems. Information technology supports information systems.

- Information systems support human activity systems.

- A human activity system is a logical collection of activities performed by some group of people.
- Information systems are socio-technical systems. A socio-technical system is a system of technology used within a system of activity.
- Design features of an information system fall into three categories: functionality, usability and utility.
- The process of IS development can be seen as being made up of a number of generic phases: conception, analysis, design, construction, implementation and maintenance.
- Many information systems may not actually get used; they may be abandoned before they become used. If a system is used, it may be used in ways unintended in terms of its original design.
- Information systems are domain-dependent because there is a necessary interdependence and uncertainty between the system and its domain or universe of discourse.
- Organisations invest in information systems overtly to increase efficiency and/or effectiveness. There is substantial evidence that these overt aims are often not achieved.
- Organisational success is predicated in part on IS success mediated through changes to human activity. Effective informatics management and planning are seen to be necessary conditions for ensuring IS success.
- The success of an information system can be judged in various ways – functionality/ usability and utility – is largely defined in terms of its contribution to the success of an organisation in its environment.
- An organisation's strategy, structure and culture may influence the design of information systems as well as the success of these IS.
- An informatics infrastructure equals the set of organisational resources that give the organisation the capacity to generate new IT applications.
- Of particular interest to information system practitioners is the development of information systems that may impact upon the competitive position of the organisation within its environment.
- The contemporary interest in e-business and e-commerce is a reflection of the increasing importance of informatics to organisational performance both in terms of its internal processes and in terms of its external relations with customers and suppliers.
- The discipline of informatics focuses on the application of information, IS and IT within organisations and is particularly interested in improving the fit between organisations and its information, IS and IT resources.

1.16 ⊚ QUESTIONS

(i) Why is an interaction model important for describing the domain of informatics?

(ii) List the major elements involved in the interaction between information systems and organisations.

(iii) Define the term *informatics*.

(iv) Distinguish between information, information systems and information technology.

(v) Distinguish between functionality, usability and utility/efficacy.

(vi) Are the consequences of introducing some information system always positive?

(vii) Distinguish between organisational structure and culture.

(viii) Is an organisational process the same as a human activity system?

(ix) List some of the features of the external environment of an organisation.

(x) List the main phases of the process of information systems development.

(xi) List the three levels of an informatics architecture.

(xii) Why is it important to evaluate information systems?

(xiii) In what way is e-business simply organisational informatics in a new guise?

(xiv) What do we mean when we say that the domain of informatics is interested in the fit between information technology and organisations?

1.17 ⊚ EXERCISES

(i) Consider a university as an organisation. Utilise the interaction model discussed in this chapter to describe a higher education institution known to you. Define the key elements of the environment of the university. Describe the organisation in terms of its strategy, processes (human activity systems), structure, culture and IT infrastructure.

(ii) Select one information system known to you in an organisation. Attempt to develop a 'natural history' of its development and attempt to map this history on to the phases of conception and initiation, analysis, design, implementation and adaptation discussed in this chapter.

(iii) Investigate the use of the term informatics and generate a list of its application.

1.18 PROJECTS

(i) Investigate the relevance of the informatics model by applying it to one or more organisations.

(ii) Determine whether the informatics model can be used as a tool in the planning or management of information systems in organisations.

(iii) Investigate an area such as health informatics or bio-informatics and determine the level of overlap with the elements of the informatics model.

(iv) Investigate the relevance of the informatics model to e-business.

1.19 REFERENCES

Drucker, P. F. (1994). The theory of the business. *Harvard Business Review*, **72**(5), 95–104.

Giddings, R. V. (1984). Accommodating uncertainty in software design. *Communications of the ACM*, **27**(5), 428–434.

Kling, R. and Allen, J. P. (1996). Can computer science solve organisational Problems? The case for organisational informatics. In *Computerisation and Controversy: Value Conflicts and Social Choices* (ed. R. Kling). Academic Press, San Diego.

Kling, R. and Scaachi, W. (1982). The web of computing: computer technology as social organisation. *Advances in Computers*, **21**, 1–90.

Mumford, E. (1996). *Systems Design: Ethical Tools for Ethical Change*. Macmillan, London.

Salabert, D. and Newman, M. (1995). Regaining control: the case of the Spanish air traffic control system – SACTA. *European Conference on Information Systems* (ed. G. Doukidis), Athens, Greece, pp. 1171–1179.

Silver, M. S., Markus, M. L. and Beath, C. M. (1995). The information technology interaction model: a foundation for the MBA core course. *MIS Quarterly*, **19**(3), 361–390.

Zuboff, S. (1988). *In the Age of the Smart Machine: the Future of Work and Power*. Heinemann, London.

PART 1

INFORMATION AND SYSTEMS

It is a very sad thing that nowadays there is so little useless information.

Oscar Wilde (1854–1900)

Everybody gets so much information all day long that they lose their common sense.

Gertrude Stein (1874–1946)

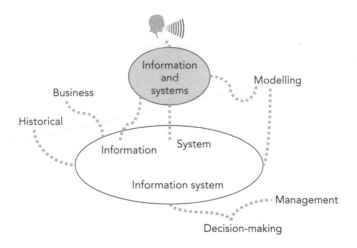

In this part we examine some of the fundamental or foundation concepts of the discipline of organisational informatics.

- The topic of information is introduced in terms of the area of semiotics to help us understand its multi-faceted nature.

- A detailed description of the component elements of systems thinking, arguably one of the most pervasive influences on modern informatics.

- We utilise both these foundation concepts in an examination of two historical information systems. This historical analysis enables us to make a clear distinction between information systems and information technology.

- We consider some generic information systems underlying modern business activity. This forms the information systems infrastructure of many modern commercial organisations.

- Information systems are used to enable effective decision-making, particularly management decision-making. A class of information systems – management information systems – are built to support this need.

- We consider the importance of modelling to information systems work and examine three different approaches to information systems modelling. We utilise each of these three approaches in further chapters.

INFORMATION

Where is the life we have lost in living?

Where is the wisdom we have lost in knowledge?

Where is the knowledge we have lost in information?

T. S. Eliot: *The Rock* (1934)

LEARNING OUTCOMES

After reading this chapter, you will be able to:

● Define the relevance of semiotics to the concept of information

● Relate issues concerning the pragmatic level of sign-systems

● Define elements at the semantic level of sign-systems

● Recognise elements at the syntactic level of sign-systems

● Describe issues relating to the empiric level of sign-systems

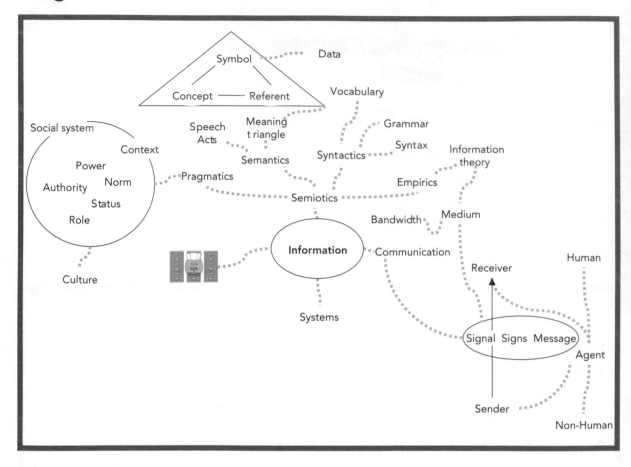

2.1 ⊚ INTRODUCTION

Although the concept of information is clearly critical to the discipline of informatics, the concept is frequently treated as an unquestioned supposition of informatics work. We openly use the word in terms such as information technology, information systems and information society. Part of the problem with the concept of information is that it is an extremely vague one, open to many different interpretations. In this chapter we use an area of work known as semiotics or semiology to organise our discussion of the concept of information. This enables us to consider the wide variety of concerns associated with information on four different but interdependent levels.

2.2 ⊚ SEMIOTICS

Liebenau and Backhouse (1990), following Stamper (1973, 1985) have discussed information in terms of an area known as semiotics or semiology.

Modern semiotics developed in linguistics and the philosophy of language. Ferdinand de Saussure is normally seen to be one of its founding fathers in his pioneering work on general linguistics published in 1916. The area was given more sophistication in the work of the American philosopher Charles Morris. In anthropology the use of semiotic approaches was commonplace in the work of Claude Levi-Strauss in the late 1950s. More recently it has been applied to literary criticism and also contributed to literature itself. Umberto Eco's *The Name of the Rose* is perhaps the most popular recent example of this form of literature.

Semiotics or semiology is the study of signs. Signs are seen as the component elements of communication. Communication is a process that has the following characteristics:

- It involves two or more parties.
- One or more of the parties in a communication process will be the sender with intentions to convey.
- The intentions of the sender will be expressed in a message.
- The message will be transmitted by the sender in terms of signals along some medium.
- One or more of the other parties will be a receiver. Receivers have the ability to interpret the signals.

Example ▐▐▐▶ In face-to-face conversation humans communicate largely using the medium of spoken language, transmitting sounds through the medium of air. In a telephone conversation we still utilise spoken language, but the medium is now electromagnetic signal transmission along telephone lines. In electronic mail (e-mail) the medium changes to written language and may involve asynchronous interaction – i.e. there need not be short-term and interleaved interactions between sender and receiver.

Clearly, since communication involves human intentions and interpretation, it is a social phenomenon. Effective communication takes place when there is a high degree of correspondence between the sender's intention and the interpretation of the message supplied by the receiver. We take as evidence of effective communication having taken place that the receiver can provide an account of the content of a message which closely corresponds with that provided by the sender.

Note that the two parties involved in communication need not be humans. Take the example of an alarm clock. The alarm on the clock sounding is a signal that is interpreted as a message by a person to indicate some significant time. The message is also likely to trigger some response by a human being, such as getting out of bed. Clearly communication has occurred here and information has been transmitted.

2.2.1 SIGNS

Information is embodied in the concept of a sign.

A sign is anything that is significant. In a sense, everything that humans do is significant to some degree. The world within which humans find themselves is resonant with sign-systems. A sign-system is any organised collection of signs. Everyday spoken language is probably the most readily accepted and complex example of a sign-system. Signs, however, exist in most other forms of human activity, since they are critical to the process of human communication and understanding.

Example ▐▐▐▐➤ Humans communicate through non-verbal as well as verbal sign-systems. We colloquially refer to such non-verbal communication as 'body language'. Hence humans can impart a great deal in the way of information by facial movements and other forms of bodily gesture. Such gestures are also signs.

Note the link between the words *sign* and *significant* in English. These words clearly have the same root. The concept of the significance of signs cannot be divorced from people. Different people find different things significant. Many such differences in interpretation are due to differences in the context and culture of communication.

2.2.2 LEVELS OF SIGNS

Signs and sign-systems can be considered in terms of four interdependent levels (Stamper, 1973): pragmatics, semantics, syntactics and empirics. These constitute the four main branches of semiotics.

Pragmatics

Pragmatics is the study of the general *context and culture* of communication or the shared assumptions underlying human understanding. For communication to occur between human beings signs must exist in a context of shared understanding. As we shall see, there must be agreed expectations between the symbols and the referents or concepts they signify. Pragmatics is the study of such mutual understanding. Much of pragmatics can be considered as the study of culture – the common expectations underlying human communicative behaviour in a particular context.

Semantics

Semantics is the study of the *meaning* of signs – the association between signs and behaviour. Semantics can be considered as the study of the link between symbols and their referents or concepts; particularly the way in which signs relate to human behaviour embodied in norms.

Syntactics

Syntactics is the study of the logic and *grammar* of sign systems. Syntactics is devoted to the study of the physical form rather than the content of signs.

Empirics

Empirics is the study of the *physical characteristics* of the medium of communication. Empirics is devoted to the study of communication channels and their characteristics, e.g. sound, light and electronic transmission.

In terms of a communication process, pragmatics concerns the issue of intentions, semantics the meaning of a message, syntactics the formalism used to represent the message and empirics the signals used to code and transmit the message.

Pragmatics and semantics study the purpose and content of communication. Syntactics and empirics study the forms and means of communication. Pragmatics and semantics clearly impinge upon other disciplines such as sociology and politics. Syntactics and empirics impinge upon the domain of psychology and indeed even electronics.

2.3 PRAGMATICS

As we have indicated above, communication is a social phenomenon. Hence the study of the general *context and culture* of communication demands a recognition that all communication occurs within a background of social systems, culture, roles, status, power and authority.

2.3.1 SOCIAL SYSTEMS

Signs are only significant in terms of some social system. A social system provides the context for the interpretation of signs. A number of concepts borrowed from social science are useful in understanding signs and their relationship to social systems: culture, norm, role, power and status. These concepts are important in understanding human behaviour in organisations and hence will recur in the discussion of the chapters that follow.

2.3.2 CULTURE

A *culture* is the set of behaviours expected in a social group. A *social group* is any collection of people who regularly interact with one another. It is a truism that any long-standing social group develops its own expected set of behaviours. Such expectations are known as *norms* of human behaviour in the jargon of social science, to distinguish them from deterministic rules. A norm is an expectation that people will behave in a certain way in a certain social situation. If a person infringes the norms of some social situation then frequently sanctions will be exercised against that person by members of the social group.

Example ▶ Consider the case of a lecture in a university as a social situation. The persons participating in the lecture can be seen as constituting a social group in that they are likely to have interacted with each other over a period of time. As a social situation a lecture will also have some established norms of behaviour. For instance, it is normally expected that one person – the lecturer – will do most of the talking and will be the person who controls the scheduling of activity within the lecture. If one or more persons infringe this expectation by perhaps persistently standing up and singing at the top of their voice they are likely to be ejected from the lecture, or other sanctions may be exercised.

2.3.3 ROLES

People behave in social situations. But people package behaviour in collections which social scientists call social *roles*. The analogy here is clearly with acting on the stage. To paraphrase Shakespeare – 'All the world is a stage, and we are merely players'. In other words, we all take on a number of different roles throughout our lifetime, and for each role different expectations are involved.

Example ▶ The author plays a multitude of roles in his everyday life such as son, father, lecturer, consultant, researcher, colleague, and so on. Each of these social roles demand different expectations of him.

2.3.4 STATUS

A complementary concept to that of social role is that of social status. A person's status implies some form of position in a social hierarchy. The formal hierarchy of an organisation may not be the most important one for organisational members. There are frequently one or more informal hierarchies that may be more effective in organisational terms.

2.3.5 POWER AND AUTHORITY

Power is not a good or a commodity, it is a relationship. Power is the ability of a person or social group to control the behaviour of some other person or social group. Authority is legitimated power in that those over whom it is exercised accept the exercise of power. Organisational politics is the embodiment of the exercise of power within some organisation.

In many organisations there will be a mismatch between naked power and authority. Manager A may be the person in whom formal power is invested. Manager B, however, has the recognised authority, and it is this manager who actually controls staff.

There is a tendency to conceptualise power as a commodity owned by a particular individual or group. Power and authority are, however, not static entities.

Power and authority are relationships between individuals and groups. They are fluid entities that are continually negotiated and re-negotiated within organisations. Some individuals or groups may currently exercise significant amounts of power but in the future may lose such ability.

2.3.6 SIGNS AND SOCIAL SYSTEMS

All of the concepts discussed in relation to social systems above are clearly related to the concept of a sign:

- If culture consists of shared understanding, such understanding must be communicated via a body of signs. In acting appropriately in a given context people signify their acceptance of organisational norms. Sanctions such as ostracism from the group may be exercised for infringement of norms and serves to signify such infringement.

- A person's role and indeed social status are frequently made apparent through signs. Corporate executives, for instance, will frequently signify their status in the organisation via a panoply of status 'symbols' such as expensive company cars, large offices and expensive furnishings.

- Power has to be exercised through communication. People gain an idea of a person's authority through the significance of their ability to control the behaviour of others.

2.4 SEMANTICS

Semantics is the study of what signs refer to. Communication involves the use and interpretation of signs. When we communicate the sender has to externalise his or her intentions in terms of some signs. In face-to-face conversation this will involve the use of linguistic signs. The receiver of the message must interpret the signs. In other words, he or she must assign some meaning to the signs of the message. Semantics is concerned with this process of assigning meaning to signs.

A simple model of semantics is one in which a sign can be broken down into three component parts which are frequently referred to collectively as the meaning triangle (Sowa, 1984) (see Figure 2.1):

- The *symbol* (or *symbols*), sometimes referred to as the signifier. That which is signifying.

- The *referent*, sometimes known as the signified. That which is being signified.

- The *concept*. The idea of significance.

Examples ▌▌▌➤ The symbols 43 constitute the signifier. A possible referent is a collection of products. The concept is the quantity of a product sold.

The symbols M and F might be significant in some informatics context. To speak of information we must supply some concept and/or referent for the symbols. M might have as its referent the male population; F might have as its referent the female population. Taken together, the meaning of these symbols is supplied by the concept of human gender.

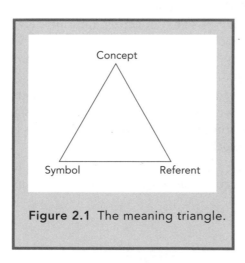

Figure 2.1 The meaning triangle.

Symbols are equivalent to data in the classic language of information systems. A datum, a single item of data, is a set of symbols used to represent something.

The meaning triangle should not be taken to mean that signs have an inherent meaning. A sign can mean whatever a particular social group chooses it to mean. The same sign may mean different things in different social contexts. As interpreters of signs, humans are extremely proficient at assigning the correct interpretation for a sign in a particular context.

Example ▌▌▌➤ In the Welsh language the same verb *dysgu* (pronounced dusgey) is used both for *to teach* and *to learn*. Hence the same sentence – *Rydw i'n dysgu* – can mean either *I am learning* or *I am teaching* depending on the context supplied usually by elements such as the rest of the conversation.

Signs are used in various ways in human life. In terms of informatics we are interested in the way in which signs are used to generate action. The American philosopher Charles Morris created a more sophisticated model of semantics that is founded in the notion of action. More recently another American philosopher

John Searle has built on Morris's work and has built a detailed theory of so-called speech acts.

For Morris, semiosis – the process of using signs – is a five-term relation, expressed by the letters V, W, X, Y and Z. V is a sign which sets up in W (the interpreter) the disposition to react in a certain kind of way X (the interpretant) to a certain kind of object Y (the signification) under certain conditions Z (the context).

Example ▐▐▐▶ Take the sign in Figure 2.2. The visual image is the sign. The interpreters of this sign are any persons in the place in which the sign is displayed, say an office. The interpretant of the sign is the disposition to abstain from smoking. The signification is refraining from smoking. The office provides the context and defines the area in which the prohibition is or should be effective.

Figure 2.2 A sign.

Example ▐▐▐▶ Take the sign 030500. Given context we interpret this as a date. However, in Britain we would interpret the significance of the sequence of digits differently from those in the USA. In Britain the first two digits represent the day of the month. In the USA the first two digits represent the month.

The term universe of discourse (UoD) or domain of discourse is sometimes used to describe a context within which a group of signs (usually linguistic terms) is used continually by a social group or groups. For informatics work it is important to develop a detailed understanding of the structure of these terms. In database work (see Chapter 10) this structure is known as a schema. A schema is an attempt to develop an abstract description of some UoD.

2.5 SYNTACTICS

The most important category of sign-system used in human communication is that of language. Syntactics concerns itself with all these representational aspects of language. All languages consist of the following elements:

- *Vocabulary*. A complete list of the terms of a language
- *Grammar*. Rules that control the correct use of a language
- *Syntax*. The operational rules for the correct representation of terms and their use in the construction of sentences of the language

We may distinguish between two broad categories of languages: natural languages and formal languages. Natural languages are those used for everyday communication and include languages such as English, French and Welsh. Natural languages have evolved over time in particular linguistic communities, and indeed continue to evolve. As such they tend to be extremely rich and complex in terms of vocabulary, grammar and syntax. Formal languages are artificial languages normally constructed for some defined purpose. As such they tend to have much simpler vocabularies, grammar and syntax. Informatics work abounds with a variety of such formal languages. All the existing programming languages, such as C++ or Java, are examples of formal languages.

Some of the most well-developed examples of formal languages are those developed in formal logic, including propositional and predicate logic. These languages are useful as ways of representing restricted UoDs and developing reasoning about their properties. Many of the formal languages used to build information systems, such as structured query language (SQL) (see Chapter 10), are founded in formal logic.

2.6 ⓔ EMPIRICS

The level of empirics is normally associated with the work of Claude Shannon. Shannon (1949) is known for his work on the *statistical theory of signal transmission* – generally called information theory – something of a misnomer because it works with a restricted view of information in that it considers only signal transmission. In this section we adapt an example of the application of information theory originally discussed in Stamper (1973) to illustrate the fundamental principles of empirics.

Shannon was concerned with the physical problems involved in transmitting messages and the properties of the communication channels used for such transmission. Within information theory, messages are carried in some form of 'carrier' signal and information is equated with variety or modulation in some signal. If we are unable to modulate the pattern of a signal then no information can be communicated between transmitter (sender) and receiver. Once we can vary the signal then it becomes possible to code certain messages using variations in the signal. Most communication channels nowadays use a form of binary coding (conceived as 0s or 1s similar to the dots and dashes of Morse code) and hence are binary communication channels.

Example ▐▐▐▌➤ Let us suppose that we wish to transmit some message from a factory in London to a factory in Cardiff. We use some form of unspecified communication channel to transmit this message. The message is carried in a signal travelling down this communication channel. Initially, these signals are restricted to always having the same pattern. So what information can be transmitted using this signal? The answer is none at all. The signal is just a steady stream of energy.

It is only when we can modulate the signal in some way that we can transmit information. Suppose we can make the signal in the example either emulate a 'dot' (a zero) or a 'dash' (a one) (familiar in the Morse code). Now we have the ability to code messages as signals.

Suppose we have two lines of products identified by the letters A, B, C, D and W, X, Y, Z of the alphabet. At the start of every working day an administrative worker at the London factory reads through a pile of orders. On each order only one product type is indicated. The administrator sends one message for each order. To do this each product is coded in terms of zeros and ones. The codes for products A, B, C, and D are given below:

A	B	C	D
11	10	01	00

This means that each message out of the four possible needs just two signals. Assuming that each signal takes one second to transmit, the message can be transmitted at the rate of one every two seconds. Thus, 30 messages can be transmitted per minute.

However, 30 messages per minute may not be the capacity of this communication channel. For instance, we may find from an analysis of past orders that statistically certain product types in the second line of products are ordered a lot more frequently than others. Let us assume that a half of all orders are for W, a quarter for X and an eighth each for Y and Z. This statistical analysis enables us to formulate a more efficient code for this product line using shorter codes for the most popular letters and longer codes for the least popular letters. A possible code is indicated below:

W	X	Y	Z
1	10	100	1000

This coding enables us to send more than 30 messages per minute. Shannon's theory actually allows us to compute the capacity of a communication channel in terms of transmission of the most economical form of coding for messages. His theorems are defined in terms of the concept of entropy – the degree of uncertainty associated with a message. Fundamentally this is a measure of probability based on the relative frequency of messages. The more infrequent a message, the more information it conveys.

The important point of Shannon's theory is that it led to the definition of a number of generic properties of all communication channels including writing, human speech and modern digital communication lines. These include noise, distortion, speed, redundancy and bandwidth. Information theory can thus be seen to be the foundation of modern communications engineering (Chapter 11).

2.7 ⊚ SUMMARY

- Information can be seen as embodied in signs and the process of signification, essential elements of the area known as semiotics.
- Semiotics or semiology is the study of signs. Semiotics consists of four sub-areas: pragmatics, semantics, syntactics and empirics.
- Pragmatics is the study of the general *context and culture* of communication or the shared assumptions underlying human understanding.
- Semantics is the study of the *meaning* of signs.
- Syntactics is the study of the logic and *grammar* of sign systems.
- Empirics is the study of the *physical characteristics* of the medium of communication.
- Signs are the component elements of communication. Communication involves senders, receivers, communication channels and messages.
- Signs can be considered in terms of three constituent elements: the symbol or that which is signifying, the referent or that which is being signified and the concept or the idea of significance.
- Symbols are equivalent to data. A datum, a single item of data, is a set of symbols used to represent something.

2.8 ⊚ QUESTIONS

(i) What does the term semiotics mean?

(ii) Describe the major elements in any communication process.

(iii) On how many levels can we consider a sign? Name the levels.

(iv) Social systems can be said to consist of norms, roles, power and authority. Define each of these terms.

(v) Define the three elements of the meaning triangle.

(vi) How does grammar differ from syntax?

(vii) Distinguish between natural and formal languages and give examples of both.

(viii) Why is the area of information theory misnamed?

(ix) In information theory the concept of information is inherently associated with the issue of uncertainty. Explain why this is the case.

2.9 EXERCISES

(i) Consider contemporary facilities on the Internet, such as chat rooms and discussion boards, in terms of the classic elements of a communication.

(ii) All the inputs into and outputs from information systems can be regarded as signs. Give some examples of semantic problems that might arise in interpreting signs from information systems. Discuss the problems involved in individuals and groups misinterpreting certain of these signs.

(iii) In what way is the Highway Code a sign system?

(iv) Analyse written communication in terms of the distinction between pragmatics, semantics, syntactics and empirics.

(v) Investigate the way in which various forms of logic are formal languages.

(vi) Various signs have been invented within email systems, such as –:) , to attempt to provide emotional content via this communication medium. Investigate the range and use of such symbols and analyse them in terms of semiotic concepts.

2.10 PROJECTS

(i) What consequences does a semiotics view of information have for informatics?

(ii) Investigate the ways in which signs are used to perpetuate aspects of social systems such as power and authority.

(iii) Determine the relevance of speech act theory to informatics.

(iv) Investigate the relevance of information theory to information systems work.

(v) Electronic mail is becoming pervasive in many organisations. What consequences does the increasing use of this form of communication have for organisations?

2.11 REFERENCES

Liebenau, J. and Backhouse, J. (1990). *Understanding Information: An Introduction*. Macmillan, London.

Sowa, J. F. (1984). *Conceptual Structures: Information Processing in Mind and Machine*. Addison-Wesley, Reading, MA.

Shannon, C. E. (1949). *The Mathematical Theory of Communication*. University of Illinois Press, Urbana.

Stamper, R. K. (1973). *Information in Business and Administrative Systems*. Batsford, London.

Stamper, R. K. (1985). Information: mystical fluid or a subject for scientific enquiry? *The Computer Journal*, **28**(3).

SYSTEMS

Observe how system into system runs,
What other planets circle other suns.

Alexander Pope: *An Essay on Man* (1733), Epistle 1

After reading this chapter, you will be able to:

- Relate some of the fundamental history of the systems concept
- Define some of the fundamental elements of systems thinking
- Describe some of the disciplines that developed from systems thinking
- Discuss some of the influences of systems thinking on the information systems discipline

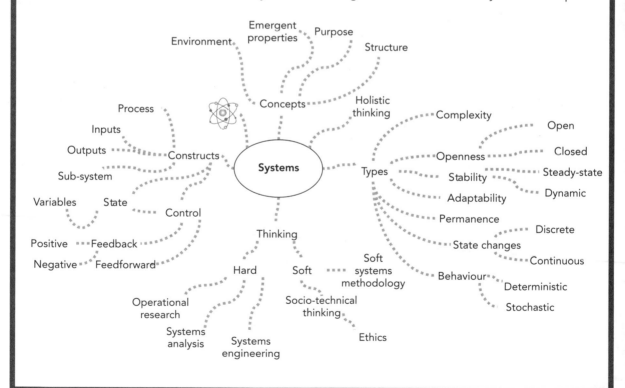

3.1 INTRODUCTION

We are surrounded by systems. Our bodies are made up of various systems, such as a digestive system and a central nervous system. We live on a planet that is part of the solar system. We engage with people in groups that form social, political and economic systems. We are educated in the use of number systems. Modern organisations would collapse without information systems.

At first sight these varied systems appear to have little in common. However, on closer examination we see that all these phenomena are collections of things that are interrelated through defined relationships. Systems theory or systems thinking is the attempt to study such generic features of all systems. In this chapter we introduce some of the basic elements of systems thinking – we discuss the concept of a system and define some of its generic features.

3.2 HISTORY

Elementary systems thinking emerged in the work of the Gestalt psychologists, a collection of psychologists who emphasised the study of the mind as a whole unit, rather than as a collection of psychological parts. This approach they described as holistic thinking (Ellis, 1938).

The idea of using the concept of a system to understand phenomena is normally attributed to work in the 1930s conducted by Ludwig von Bertalanffy, a German biologist. He gave the name general systems theory to a discipline devoted to formulating principles that apply to all systems (Bertalanffy, 1951).

Following Bertalanffy's pioneering work systems thinking began to be applied to numerous fields, leading eventually to the creation of the Society for General Systems Research, a group including Bertalanffy, Rapaport, Boulding and Gerard. Boulding's work (Boulding, 1956) in particular highlighted certain phenomena as being present in many disciplines such as populations, individuals in environments, growth, information and communication. This established some of the fundamental principles of general systems theory.

Systems ideas have had their greatest impact in the field of organisational/ management science (Churchman *et al.*, 1957; Emery and Trist, 1960; Katz and Kahn, 1966; Maurer, 1971). It is from the adaptation of the systems idea within thinking about organisations that much of the thrust for contemporary information systems can be seen to derive.

3.3 FUNDAMENTAL CONCEPTS

There are a number of fundamental concepts that form the elements of systems thinking.

3.3.1 SYSTEM

Systems thinking employs the concept of a system: an organised whole in which parts are related together, which generates emergent properties and has some purpose.

3.3.2 HOLISTIC THINKING

Systems thinking maintains Aristotle's dictum that *the whole is more than the sum of its parts*. Systems thinking proposes that it is important to investigate and understand complex phenomena holistically. The early ideas in systems thinking can be seen as a reaction against the reductionism inherent in the scientific method, i.e. the conventional approach to scientific investigation which involves dissecting a problem into its smallest parts.

Example ||||➡ In studying digestion in the body as a system we are interested in studying the properties that arise from the interaction of a number of organs of the body.

3.3.3 SUBJECTIVE DEFINITION

Systems are clearly a human conceptualisation. They do not exist independently of the observer in the sense that it is the human observer that views something as a system. There may be some agreement amongst a group of people about the shape of or properties of a system, in which case there is an inter-subjective consensus about the definition of the boundaries, components and relationships present in the system.

Example ||||➡ Most people would agree on the general properties of the basic number system and most doctors would agree on the general properties of the digestive system. However, different groups may have different perspectives on the structure and particularly the purpose of economic and social systems.

3.3.4 ORGANISATION

Systems are organised. Systems are different from aggregates or collections of things.

Example ||||➡ A collection of bicycle parts constitutes an aggregate. Only when such parts are arranged in a particular way can we speak of the system of a bicycle.

3.3.5   PURPOSE

To say a system displays organisation implies that a system is organised to do something. Teleology is an important part of systems thinking – the position that systems are organised to achieve some goals. The defined purpose of some system will normally determine how we intend to measure the performance of some system.

Example ▐▐▌➡ The purpose of a system of drains underlying a major city might be defined as the dispersal of water from the city's streets. In terms of this defined purpose we could measure the performance of the drainage system in terms of how long it takes to disperse a particular volume of water.

3.3.6   EMERGENT PROPERTIES

Systems have emergent properties. A system is a complex entity that has properties which do not belong to any of its constituent parts, but emerge from the relationships or interaction of its constituent parts.

Example ▐▐▌➡ In a traffic network a bottleneck experienced at some road intersection is the result of the interactions of a large body of components (cars) interacting in particular ways. A bottleneck is not a property of any one component (car), it is only a property of the system as a whole.

3.3.7   ENVIRONMENT

In thinking about a system we necessarily define a boundary that separates those things that are part of the system from those things outside of the system. Those things outside of a system constitute the system's environment.

Example ▐▐▌➡ If we consider an organisation as a system then we define its boundary in terms of activities performed by its members. We might prohibit the consideration of activities of its customers and suppliers as forming part of the system. These activities would form part of the system's environment.

3.3.8   PROCESS/TRANSFORMATION

Most systems are involved in some transformation of something – changing the state of something into something else.

Example ‖‖⟩ A transportation system can be considered as a system that satisfies the demand for travel by moving people around some space. A flower can be conceived of as a system that transforms water, carbon dioxide and light into carbohydrates and oxygen.

3.3.9 INPUTS AND OUTPUTS

A system communicates with its environment in terms of inputs to and outputs from the system. A system transforms inputs into outputs. In Figure 3.1, processes are represented as boxes and inputs and outputs as arrows. The environment of some system is defined in terms of a number of agents or agencies that interact with the system (represented as rounded shapes on the diagram).

Example ‖‖⟩ A manufacturing firm considered as a system transforms raw materials (inputs) from its suppliers (agent) into finished products (outputs) for its customers (agent).

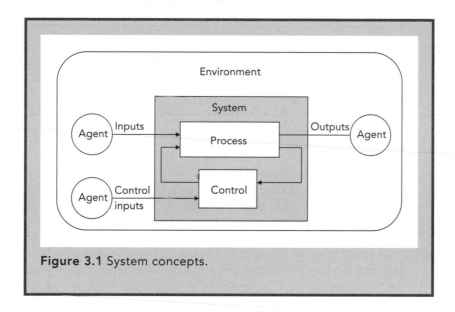

Figure 3.1 System concepts.

3.3.10 SUBSYSTEMS

Systems can generally be seen as being composed of subsystems (Figure 3.2). Hierarchy seems to be an inherent property of most systems.

Example ▐▐▐▶ An automobile can be viewed as being composed of subsystems such as the elec-
trical subsystem and the transmission subsystem. Alternatively, the human body
consists of a number of subsystems such as the nervous system, the circulatory
system, the digestive system etc.

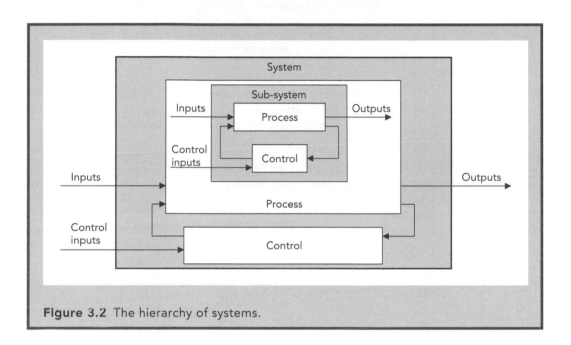

Figure 3.2 The hierarchy of systems.

3.3.11 STATE

The behaviour of a system can be defined in terms of the notion of state. The state
of a system is defined by the values appropriate to the system's attributes or state
variables. At any point in time a value can be assigned to each of a system's state
variables. The set of all values assumed by the state variable defines a system's state.

3.3.12 TYPES OF SYSTEM

There are a number of ways in which we may define types of system. Such types are
normally expressed in terms of bipolar properties that usually express the ends of
some dimension. Table 3.1 presents some of the common types of systems
discussed in the literature.

3.3.13 CONTROL

Open systems normally adapt to changes in their external environments. Hence
the discipline of ecology utilises the concept of open systems to explain the

Table 3.1 Types of system.

System property		
Complexity	Simple systems include those such as a chair which integrate several non-moving parts together.	Complex systems are those such as social systems that are made up of a multitude of parts and relationships.
Openness	A closed system is one in which there is no interaction between the system and its environment.	An open system is one in which there are interactions between the system and its environment.
Stability	The state of some systems demonstrate the property of equilibrium. These are referred to as steady-state systems.	The state of other systems fluctuate rapidly. Such systems are described as dynamic systems.
Adaptive/non-adaptive	Some systems adapt to changes in their environments. They are adaptive systems.	Other systems fail to adapt to changes in their environment. They are non-adaptive.
Permanence	Systems may exist for a substantial period of time. They are permanent systems.	Other systems exist only for a short period of time. They are non-permanent systems.
Discrete/continuous	In some systems the changes between system states are discrete, i.e. occur at defined intervals.	In other systems change is continuous throughout some period.
Deterministic/stochastic	In a deterministic system the behaviour of the system is predictable in every detail.	In a stochastic system behaviour is affected by random inputs

adaptations that animals and plants make to changes in the physical environment – their habitat.

Control is the mechanism that implements adaptation in most systems. Systems generally exhibit some form of control that enables the system to adapt to changes in its environment. Control can be viewed in terms of a monitoring subsystem that regulates the behaviour of other subsystems. This monitoring or control subsystem ensures defined levels of performance for the system through imposing a number of control inputs upon the system. Such control inputs will normally be in the form of decision rules or a decision strategy. The rules are initially supplied to the control subsystem from outside of the system and are used to steer a system in a desired direction by supplying control signals to the process of the system (Figure 3.1). The discipline of cybernetics (hence 'cyberspace') is founded on the study of such control systems (Wiener, 1948).

3.3.14 PERFORMANCE

Control is normally exercised in terms of some defined measures of performance. A monitoring subsystem may only work effectively if there are defined levels of performance for the system. Such performance levels will be defined by higher-level systems.

Example ⫸ In terms of a physical system such as a thermostat a performance measure will be defined in terms of a temperature level.

There are three main types of performance measures: efficacy or utility, efficiency and effectiveness.

- *Effectiveness*. Effectiveness is a measure of the extent to which a system achieves its intended transformation.
- *Efficiency*. Efficiency is a measure of the extent to which the system achieves its intended transformation with the minimum use of resources.
- *Efficacy*. A measure of the extent to which the system contributes to the purposes of a higher-level system of which it may be a subsystem.

Example ⫸ Consider the concept of an information technology system as discussed in Chapter 1. The efficiency of the system could be measured in terms of features such as the time it takes to respond to a user's query. The effectiveness of the IT system could be measured in terms of the degree to which it improves information flow in the organisation. The efficacy of the IT system could be measured in terms of the degree to which it contributes to the human activity system which it supports.

3.3.15 FEEDBACK

Control is normally exercised within a system through some form of feedback. Outputs from the process of a system are fed back to the control mechanism. The control mechanism then adjusts the control signals to the process on the basis of the data it receives. Feedback has two major forms: positive and negative feedback.

3.3.16 NEGATIVE FEEDBACK

Control is normally exercised through a negative feedback loop (Figure 3.3). The monitoring subsystem monitors the outputs from the system and detects variations from defined levels of performance. If the outputs vary from established levels then the monitoring subsystem initiates some actions that reduce the variation.

Examples ▶ In a thermostat, if the temperature falls below some specified level then the thermostat initiates an action such as opening some hot water valve.

In a company, maintaining cash flow can be conceived of as a system with negative feedback in which the cash balance continually influences company decisions on expenditure and borrowing.

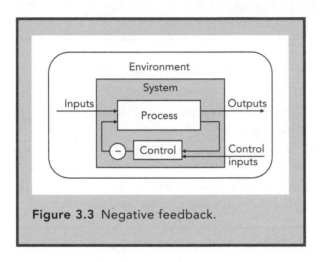

Figure 3.3 Negative feedback.

3.3.17 POSITIVE FEEDBACK

Positive feedback is a deviant version of control evident in many systems (Figure 3.4). Commonly known as a 'vicious circle' it involves the monitoring subsystem increasing the discrepancy between desired and actual levels of performance.

Examples ▶ The 'arms race' that occurred during the 'Cold War' period is a classic example of a system characterised by a positive feedback loop. The USA increased its level of armament to improve its security. This prompted the USSR to increase its level of armament because of a perceived greater threat to its security. The USA responded by increasing its levels of armament, and so on.

A variation on this theme also occurs in the world of informatics. In large information systems development projects there is a tendency to escalate decision-making (Chapter 15) such that more resources are thrown at an ailing project in the hope of preventing failure. What tends to happen is that costs escalate demanding even more resources to be thrown at the project.

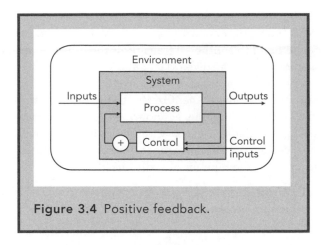

Figure 3.4 Positive feedback.

3.3.18   FEEDFORWARD

Feedback is a reactive form of control. Feedforward is a proactive form of control. Feedforward controls predict how changes in inputs are likely to affect system behaviour and send control signals to the system that will maintain such behaviour as close as possible to the desired course.

Example ⫸   Most organisational planning is a form of feedforward control. For instance, managers attempt to predict the likely short term future for areas such as orders for their products and on this basis may decide to increase or decrease stock levels of their products.

3.3.19   SYSTEM LAGS

In most systems there is a time lag in the exercise of control. Lag is a delay between the issuing of a control signal and the adjustment of the system process to the signals.

Example ⫸   Take the case of a shower in which a human controls the temperature of the water by turning a tap. Usually there is a perceivable lag between turning the tap and experiencing the required water temperature.

Examples of systems ⫸
A network of roads as well as the traffic on such roads can be considered as a system. The system is made up of various types of roads with different properties such as carrying capacity. The roads are related together in the sense that they occupy some geographical space and they connect together at intersections, forks

and interchanges. The traffic network has a purpose in enabling the transportation of people from one point to another. It transforms the inputs of traffic at given originating locations into traffic at given destination locations. The traffic system of some country may contain a number of subsystems comprising motorways, city networks, and so on. The environment of the traffic network might be defined in terms of people, vehicles and the economy. The emergent properties of this system may be of particular interest to a traffic engineer. He or she will study this system in terms of certain performance measures such as the rate of traffic flow, the number of hold-ups and the number of traffic accidents.

A sawmill may be considered as various types of system. An industrial engineer may view it as a production system, a management scientist as a profit-maximising system.

The industrial engineer will be interested in the performance of the system in transforming logs into finished products using particular resources such as plant and machinery. The purpose of studying a sawmill in this way would be to determine effective procedures for controlling the production process. This might concern the physical placement of machinery, the way in which products are handled, and so on.

The management scientist would probably not be interested in the physical activities of the sawmill. He or she would be interested in the financial consequences of such activities. The sawmill may be conceived of as a series of subsystems such as a log handling and storage subsystem, a finished goods and warehousing subsystem, a marketing subsystem and a financial control subsystem. The main interest of the management scientist is in the way in which each subsystem communicates its needs to other subsystems and how the flow of goods and information affects the financial performance of the firm. The system's environment in this case consists of the market for logs, the market for finished wood products and other elements such as the financial, labour and legal environment of the firm.

3.4 DISCIPLINES THAT DEVELOPED FROM GENERAL SYSTEMS THEORY

General systems theory influenced the development of a number of disciplines. The three disciplines which have contributed most to the formation of the modern informatics domain are probably systems engineering, systems analysis, and operational research. These are all what Peter Checkland has called 'hard' systems approaches (Checkland, 1978). They are 'hard' not in the sense of being any more difficult than other systems approaches. They are 'hard' in the sense that they involve using system concepts as a means of investigating complex situations and taking rational action with the objective of achieving what are seen to be defined, unquestioned and frequently unproblematic goals.

3.4.1 SYSTEMS ENGINEERING

Systems engineering emerged as an endeavour during the 1940s and 1950s. The primary focus of systems engineering was on the production of complex physical artefacts such as large-scale integrated manufacturing plants or the design of industrial plant such as petrochemical plants. Systems engineering focused on problem-solving. It assumed that the problem to be solved has already been identified and in some way defined. On the basis of this problem definition the systems engineer decides what must be done to achieve the defined goal selecting appropriate techniques to achieve it.

3.4.2 SYSTEMS ANALYSIS

Systems analysis arose particularly in the 1950s at the RAND Corporation in the USA. This form of application of systems thinking became particularly influential during the 1970s and 1980s with the attempt to develop specialised methods for information systems development (Part 6). The aim of such methods or methodologies was to enhance processes of rational decision-making in relation to IS development.

3.4.3 OPERATIONAL RESEARCH

Operational research (OR) arose in wartime studies which considered such issues as at what height anti-submarine aircraft should fly to have the best chance of locating their targets. Broadly speaking, operational research conceived of itself as the application of the methods of science to the problems of management. One of the key insights of operational research is that what at first sight appear distinct problems within organisational life have the same underlying systemic structure. For instance, the abstract concept of a queue appears in a number of industrial situations. OR developed a number of ways of analysing queues and optimising their performance.

3.5 ⊚ SYSTEMS THINKING AND ITS INFLUENCE ON THE DISCIPLINE OF INFORMATICS

Clearly the idea of a system has had a profound influence on the domain of informatics. The term system is inherently embedded within the label we apply to the major focus of the discipline and provides a substantial amount of the traditional world-view of the discipline.

The disciplines of systems analysis and engineering contributed to the development of modern information technology in the sense that they heavily influenced the design of devices we now experience as the modern computer (Chapter 8). These disciplines also influenced the creation of the communications revolution that underpins the modern 'information highway'.

The broad thrust of systems analysis as an endeavour has been the fundamental underpinning of IS interventions within organisations. Analysis (Chapter 28) forms a distinct and important activity within most IS development projects.

The equating of organisation with the system idea has been highly prevalent within informatics (Chapter 16). This 'metaphor' is particularly prominent in modern approaches to not only information systems, but also management science – the assumption that organisations can be designed by modelling them in system terms and implementing new processes within organisations.

3.5.1   SOFT SYSTEMS

Human activity systems are soft systems. They are collections of people undertaking activities to achieve some purpose. Human activity systems are soft because:

- The boundaries or scope of the human activity system may be fluid.
- The purpose of the system may be problematic and certainly open to interpretation.
- It may be difficult to precisely define exact measures of performance for the human activity system.

The consequence of this is that the analysis of soft systems must necessarily involve problem-setting as well as problem-solving. Hard systems analysis is concerned with determining the best way of achieving a predetermined aim. Soft systems analysis must first be involved in determining options in terms of aims that might wish to be achieved. Organisational analysis, described in Chapter 33, is a form of soft systems analysis.

Because, as we have argued in Chapter 1, information systems utilise information technology and information systems exist in the context of human activity systems, work in informatics has both hard and soft systems aspects. In terms of technology, the informatics worker must attempt to optimise performance of the IT system in terms of some defined parameters – this is a hard systems problem. On the other hand, the informatics worker has to concern herself with the effective utilisation of information technology and the related question of how human activity changes with the application of such technology – this is a soft systems problem.

3.6 ⊚ SUMMARY

- The concept of a system is fundamental to the discipline known as systems thinking or system theory.
- Systems theory studies the general characteristics of all systems.
- A system is an organised collection of things with emergent properties and with some defined purpose.

- The definition of the characteristics of some system is a subjective, sometimes an inter-subjective, endeavour.
- Critical features or components of all systems are subsystems, input-process-output, an environment, control.
- Systems may be classified in various ways, including open, closed systems and adaptive systems.
- Systems thinking stimulated a number of distinct disciplines, including systems engineering, operational research and systems analysis.
- Informatics work involves both hard systems analysis and soft systems analysis.

3.7 QUESTIONS

(i) The key elements of any system are inputs, outputs and what else?

(ii) What is meant by control in systems theory and how is it achieved?

(iii) Distinguish between an open and closed system.

(iv) Describe the three types of measure that we may use to assess the performance of some system.

(v) Distinguish between feedforward and feedback.

(vi) Distinguish between positive and negative feedback.

(vii) Distinguish between hard and soft systems.

(viii) Relate some of the ways in which informatics has been influenced by systems thinking.

3.8 EXERCISES

(i) Annotate the system diagram in Figure 3.1 with the high-level components of a personal computer. What constitutes input, output, process and control?

(ii) At a high level consider a university as a system. Identify its inputs, outputs, processes and possible subsystems.

(iii) Find one example of feedback and feedforward in some real-world systems.

(iv) Consider some real-world phenomenon as a system. Consider what type of system it constitutes in terms of the typology of systems described in this chapter.

(v) Draw a system diagram to represent a thermostat, the cash flow of some company and the arms race.

(vi) Trace the contribution of one of the hard systems thinking fields to informatics in more detail.

3.9 PROJECTS

(i) Apply systems thinking to a non-trivial problem in business or commerce and analyse the efficacy of using this approach.

(ii) Investigate the degree to which it is appropriate to use a systems model for describing and understanding organisations.

(iii) The whole is greater than the sum of its parts or the system is greater than the sum of its subsystems. What do you think is meant by this in terms of information systems? Provide some cases to examine in what ways it represents some notion of truth in organisations.

(iv) Investigate Checkland's concept of a soft system and its appropriateness for informatics work.

3.10 REFERENCES

Bertalanffy, L. V. (1951). General Systems Theory: a new approach to the unity of science. *Human Biology*, **23**(Dec.), 302–361.

Boulding, K. E. (1956). General Systems Theory – the skeleton of a science. *Management Science*, **2**(April), 197-208.

Checkland, P. B. (1978). The Origins and nature of 'hard' systems thinking. *Journal of Applied Systems Analysis*, **5**(2), 99-110.

Churchman, C. W., Ackoff, R. L. and Arnoff, E. L. (1957). *Introduction to Operations Research.* Wiley, New York.

Ellis, W. D. (1938). *A Source Book of Gestalt Psychology.* Routledge and Kegan Paul, London.

Emery, F. E. and Trist, E. L. (1960). Socio-technical systems. In *Management Science, Models and Techniques* (eds. C. W. Churchman and M. Verhulst). Pergamon, New York.

Katz, D. and Kahn, R. L. (1966). *The Social Psychology of Organisations.* Wiley, New York.

Maurer, J. G. (1971). *Readings in Organisation Theory: Open Systems Approaches.* Random House, New York.

Wiener, N. (1948). *Cybernetics.* Wiley, New York.

CHAPTER 4

INFORMATION SYSTEMS

Life was simple before World War II. After that, we had systems.

Grace Hopper, 1987

LEARNING OUTCOMES

After reading this chapter, you will be able to:

- Discuss two case studies of historical information systems
- Distinguish between human activity systems, information systems and information technology
- Distinguish between types of information system

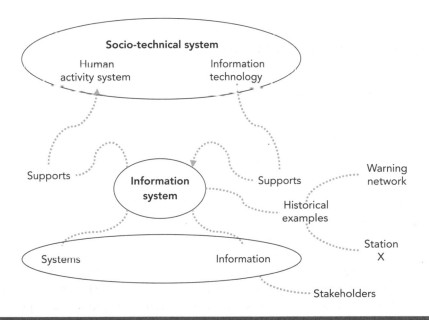

4.1 ⊚ INTRODUCTION

In this chapter we consider two historical information systems that contributed to allied victory during the Second World War: the warning network of the Royal Air Force (RAF) and the intelligence activities of the code-breaking establishment, Station X.

During the summers of the late 1930s the Royal Air Force's Fighter Command created an information system that eventually contributed to victory in a decisive battle against the German Luftwaffe – the Battle of Britain – in 1940 (Holwell and Checkland, 1998a,b). Since control of the skies was an essential pre-condition of a successful sea-borne invasion, this victory caused Hitler to abandon the planned invasion of Britain and turn his attention eastwards to Russia. This, in turn, made it possible for the invasion of continental Europe by the Allies in 1944.

Station X at Bletchley Park in the UK became the largest code-breaking and intelligence establishment of the Second World War. Efficient decoding of messages from the German war machine gave the Allied forces a significant edge in military campaigns.

The reason for discussing these historical information systems is that their remoteness in time enables us to consider the issue of what constitutes an information system in a fresh light. A consideration of these systems particularly helps us to understand some of the important differences between information systems and information technology.

4.2 ⊚ THE WARNING NETWORK

During the early 1930s, accepted military strategy for air defence was to fly so-called 'standing patrols' on flight paths likely to intercept bombing raids by an enemy. This constituted an extremely expensive military strategy in that aircraft had to be kept permanently in the skies. Not surprisingly, this strategy was eventually replaced with the use of interceptor flights that could take off quickly and attack incoming bomber raids. However, the key question remained: how was an air force to determine the precise position of incoming enemy aircraft in sufficient time to enable effective interception?

The key solution to this problem involved the utilisation of radio technology to detect aircraft – a technology that became known as radar. Both the Germans and British had access to this technology, and indeed German radar was technically superior to its British equivalent at the time. The crucial difference was that the British were better able to utilise the technology. The British were able to gain what would be known in modern management jargon as competitive advantage (Chapter 20) from this technology.

The first step in this process of achieving advantage was British Fighter Command constructing a chain of radar stations around the British coast. This was supplemented with a chain of posts manned by persons observing incoming aircraft, known as the Observer Corps.

The second crucial step was the creation of an effective system in which the 'information technology' could be utilised. During the summers between 1936 and 1939, a series of teams formed from physicists, engineers and RAF personnel engaged in a series of practical exercises with the aim of solving the fundamental problem of turning raw data from radar and observer posts into information for pilots to fly to the precise point at which to intercept enemy raids. The eventual information system that was created allowed an initially under-strength RAF to successfully compete with a numerically greater force of enemy aircraft.

4.2.1 THE SYSTEM

It is interesting that this system was not originally called an information system. It was given a series of different names such as warning and control system, early warning network or the control and reporting system.

The early warning network was a system in the sense that it had inputs, processes and outputs. The key inputs to the system involved a continually changing stream of data from radar stations and Observer Corps posts. The key process of the system involved the timely collection, integration and evaluation of this data at a number of head-quarter stations. The key outputs from the system were instructions to appropriate fighter squadrons to take off, given directions by radio telephone to meet incoming bombers, and then fly back to base.

Information technology was utilised in support of the information system, but not in the form we currently now it. There were actually two chains of radar stations: one for detecting high-flying aircraft and one for detecting low-flying aircraft. Over a thousand observer posts and fighter airfields were also connected to headquarters by dedicated Post Office teleprinter and telephone lines.

The main headquarters of RAF Fighter Command at Bentley Priory, north of London, had overall strategic control of operations. The organisation of Fighter Command was divided into four geographical groups covering major parts of the country. Each group was in turn divided into sectors with a Sector HQ at each of the airfields. Group HQ had tactical control within their area and Sector HQ had control of pilots when airborne.

The operation of the system is represented in Figure 4.1. Data from the two chains of radar stations were telephoned to Fighter Command HQ. This data went first to a filter room where the quality of the data was assessed. Filtered data was then passed on next door to the Fighter Command Operations Room. Filtered data and classified plots were recorded by members of the Women's Auxiliary Air Force (WAAF) with the movement of wooden blocks or counters against a large-scale map of the UK. These counters indicated the height, strength and direction of the enemy raids. In addition, a display (a slotted blackboard) called the 'tote' recorded enemy raids and the state of readiness of RAF squadrons (available 30 minutes, five minutes, take-off readiness two minutes or in the air) – indicated by a series of lights. Changes to the positioning of counters and updates to the tote were conducted simultaneously at headquarters, group and sector levels.

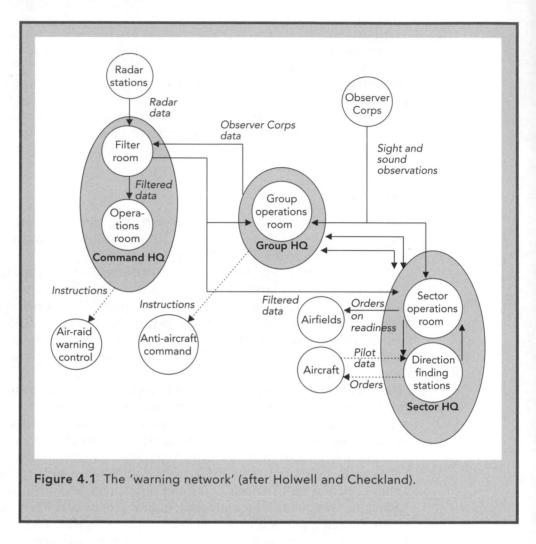

Figure 4.1 The 'warning network' (after Holwell and Checkland).

The operations room at group and sector levels worked in the same way except that the maps used represented group and sector areas respectively. Group HQs received information from the Observer Posts, which was passed on to command and sector HQs.

The sector room was set up with one unit duplicating the picture at command and group level. The second unit plotted on the map the exact location of their own planes from their radio transmissions. From here aircraft were assigned to a particular raid and their interception courses were continually plotted using compass, ruler, pencil and paper. The sector operations controller scrambled selected aircraft on command from the group HQ. Once in the air, command passed over to the flight leader until combat was over.

There were also links from the system to Anti-Aircraft command, the Observer Corps, the BBC and civil defence organisations such as those sounding air-raid warnings.

4.2.2 THE SYSTEM IN USE

The information system described above proved its worth in action during the period from July to the end of October 1940. On Sunday 15 September the system was severely tested. One hundred German bombers crossed the Kent coast at 11:30 that day. Seventeen squadrons from three groups of the RAF went to intercept them. At 14:00 the same day a second wave came in and was met by 31 squadrons (over 300 planes in all). At the end of the day RAF losses were 27 aircraft with 13 pilots killed. The Luftwaffe lost 57 aircraft.

4.3 STATION X

Another key information system was the intelligence provided by the cryptanalytic work conducted at Bletchley Park in the UK during the Second World War. This code-breaking and intelligence establishment was referred to as Station X (Channel 4, 1999).

This unit was set up in the first few months of the war and became the largest code-breaking establishment of its kind. At its height it employed over 10,000 people. It recruited some of the best minds in Britain at the time. Alan Turing, one of the founding fathers of computing, worked at this code-breaking establishment for a number of years and one of the first programmable computers, the Colossus, was built at Bletchley Park.

The Second World War was a wireless war. The fast military movement of machinery, men and equipment demanded constant intercommunication between units generally using transmission by Morse code. All such military messages were encrypted by the Germans using a complex electro-mechanical device known as the Enigma machine. This machine transposed the letters of the words of a message into other apparently random configurations of letters depending on the way the coding machine was configured. The sender of the message typed the message letter by letter into the machine using a keyboard, and a display indicated the transposed letter. The message was then sent to the receiver by radio using Morse code. The receiver typed the transposed message into a second machine to get the decoded message.

Effective communication was reliant on both sender and receiver configuring their machines in the same manner. Therefore, each day units in the German military forces were given instructions on how they should configure their Enigma machines. This configuration involved changing a number of rotors on the machine and plugging connections between pairs of letters on its front. The Germans believed at the time that the astronomical number of different ways in which the machine could be configured would ensure that it was impossible for the code to be cracked quickly enough by the Allies for effective action.

Receiving stations situated around the world picked up encrypted radio signals from the German war machine. This task was performed by thousands of wireless intercept officers, known as the Y service. The messages were passed on from the Y service by teleprinter to station X. Here the teleprinter tape was pasted on to sheets of paper and passed to the code-breaking units.

Station X was organised in terms of a number of pairs of huts, each pair specialising in communications from a major segment of the German forces. For example, Hut 8 was the German U-boat Enigma decrypt hut and Hut 4 was its associated naval intelligence unit. Once a message had been deciphered in the code-breaking hut it was literally pushed into its associated intelligence hut along a connecting corridor.

Early decryption of the messages passed on from the Y service relied on manual code-breaking and some security mistakes in the use of the Enigma machine by the German forces. Later decryption relied on the development of an electro-mechanical device known as a Bombe that was designed by Alan Turing. This device enabled the automatic rejection of millions of incorrect possibilities very quickly. A typical Bombe 'run' took something of the order of 15 minutes. These machines were given instructions in what was known as a 'menu' constructed by the code-breakers. The menu was configured in a Bombe machine by the physical movement of component elements performed by members of the women's contingent of the Royal Navy. In essence this constituted programming the code-breaking machine.

Just before the Allied invasion of France the first programmable computer, known as Colossus, was installed at Station X. Eventually, 10 machines were to be installed there. Consisting of large arrays of thermionic valves, these machines enabled the cracking of complex codes in a matter of a few minutes.

In essence, the decryption process involved translating the signals into referents such as German U-boat positions and movements. To do this, a large amount of data from many thousands of messages had to be cross-referenced using a large card indexing system. The information gleaned was then incorporated into the total knowledge available to allied intelligence on military movements and strategy. This was the key output from the system.

The intelligence provided by Station X was critical to the human activity system of military operations on land, on the sea and in the sky. It contributed to the successful protection of Allied ship convoys, the defeat of Rommel's army in the North African desert and the successful planning of the invasion of Europe by the Allies.

Example ▐▐▐➡ The encryption and decryption of messages is clearly a human activity system reliant on information (Singh, 2000) as is its counterpart code-breaking. Figure 4.2 illustrates the essential elements of this system. A plain text message is first encrypted using a particular algorithm (or method for producing something – see Chapter 9) and an appropriate key that specifies the exact details of a particular encryption. At the receiver end the algorithm is applied as a decryption method using another key. This reveals the plain text message to the receiver.

One of the simplest forms of encryption employs the substitution of letters of the alphabet with the letters from some cipher alphabet. The cipher alphabet is the key to a message. The encryption and decryption algorithms involve the mere substitution of symbols between alphabets. For instance, suppose we have the plain alphabet and cipher alphabets below:

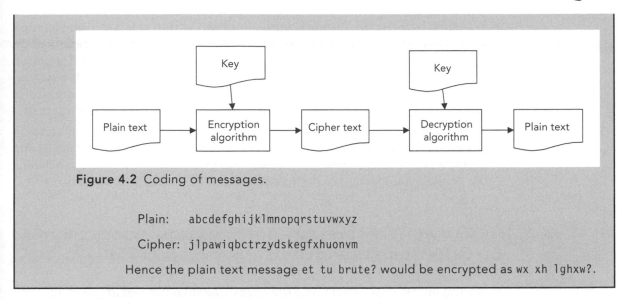

Figure 4.2 Coding of messages.

Plain: abcdefghijklmnopqrstuvwxyz

Cipher: jlpawiqbctrzydskegfxhuonvm

Hence the plain text message et tu brute? would be encrypted as wx xh lghxw?.

4.4 ◎ HISTORICAL INSIGHTS

Besides their critical historical importance, the examples discussed in this chapter are extremely useful in offering key insights into the characteristics of information systems in general:

- Both the Warning Network and Station X can clearly be seen as systems. They can be seen to be made up of a number of interdependent parts. They had clearly delineable inputs, processes and outputs and the behaviour of the systems was reliant on the effective performance of their parts.

- Both systems were clearly concerned with data generation, dissemination and use. They were clear examples of information systems.

- Information systems are distinct from information technology. We have provided here examples from the past in which the 'information technology' was subtly different from modern information technology. The analysis of historical information systems of this nature can offer key insights into the characteristics of information systems in general.

- The information system was reliant on technology – particularly the telephone and radio communications. However, the core of this system was not the technology; rather, it was the way in which the technology was used to support purposeful action that proved the key – its key benefit was its utility.

- Good information systems are critical to effective human action. The information system set up by the RAF enabled them to beat off the mass raids of the German Luftwaffe. Station X provided valuable intelligence on which strategic decisions were made about military deployment of Allied forces. Hence the key utility of both systems was established in relation to the effectiveness of action reliant upon it. The totality of this human action we have described previously as a human activity system.

- The effective place of 'information technology' within the larger information system has to be designed with the aid of system stakeholders. The identification and participation of key stakeholders in the development of some information system are key factors in the successful construction and use of such a system. For example, the Warning Network was designed with the participation of a number of stakeholder groups, including aircraft engineers, pilots and scientists.
- Information systems and information technology do not stand still. They continually evolve. For instance, within Station X a number of code-breaking strategies and organisations were attempted over the six years of the Second World War, including the eventual introduction of electro-mechanical and electronic equipment.

4.5 HUMAN ACTIVITY SYSTEMS, INFORMATION SYSTEMS AND INFORMATION TECHNOLOGY

Historical information systems like the ones we have considered in this chapter are therefore useful in highlighting differences between human activity systems, information systems and information technology.

Human activity systems are social systems. They consist of people engaging in coordinated and collaborative action. In the case of the warning network the human activity system consisted of the command and control of the fighter aircraft of the RAF. In the case of Station X the human activity system consisted of the decryption of German military communications and the generation of military intelligence on the basis of these communications.

Information systems are forms of human activity system. Information systems are systems of communication. They involve people in producing, collecting, storing and disseminating information. The information system of the warning network involved collecting data from radar, organising this data for military decision-making and the dissemination of both decisions and data to airfields.

Information technology is any collection of artefacts used to support aspects of an information system. Information technology during the Second World War involved elements like radar, telephone communications and the use of maps and tote devices. The need to analyse massive possible coding combinations in Enigma-encrypted messages eventually led to some of the earliest electronic computing devices.

An information system is a socio-technical system. It consists of both information technology and human activity. Lyytinen (1985) defines information systems as 'linguistic communication systems only technically implemented'. In other words they constitute communication systems designed to support human activity with the aid of technology. Table 4.1 provides some other historical examples of the distinctions between information, information technology, information systems and human activity systems.

Table 4.1 Examples of historical information, information systems, information technology and human activity systems.

Period	Human activity system	Information	Information system	Information technology
Approximately 4000 BC	Taxation collection and administration in the royal courts of Sumeria	Royal assets and taxes	Asset and taxation recording	Writing on stone tablets
1890	US census production	US population characteristics	Census data collection, processing and reporting	Punched cards and tabulating machines
1940	'Warning Network': RAF command and control of fighter aircraft	Radar data, observation data, telephone communications	Collecting data from radar, organising this data for military decision-making and the dissemination of both decisions and data to airfields	RADAR, telecommunications, totes
2000	University registry	Students, modules, assessments	Student and assessments information system	Computer hardware, software, data and communications technology

4.6 TYPES OF INFORMATION SYSTEM

Information systems can be classified in various ways. In general we may classify information systems along a vertical dimension and a horizontal dimension. Vertically we make a distinction in terms of three levels of human activity and decision-making that the information systems support. Horizontally we make a distinction in terms of the types of organisation in which the information systems are applied. These two dimensions are illustrated in Figure 4.3.

4.6.1 HORIZONTAL INFORMATION SYSTEMS

Much of the modern literature focuses on information systems relevant to private sector organisations or businesses. Such systems are discussed in more detail in Chapter 5. However, information systems are equally important to organisations in the public sector. A classic example here is the information systems needed to support the activities of the UK National Health Service (NHS).

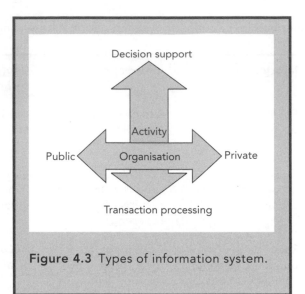

Figure 4.3 Types of information system.

Example ▐▐▐▶ Information systems are important within the National Health Service (NHS) in:

Supporting clinical decisions

- assessing a patient's medical history for relevant problems

- aiding the management of a patient's visit or stay

- assisting with tasks such as producing order forms and discharge letters

- sharing information about the care and progress of the patient with other health care professionals

Monitoring clinical performance

- providing information for audit of individual clinical cases and for quality assurance relating to services and outcomes

- providing information for research studies into best care practices

Evaluating clinical performance

- monitoring the quality of care against standards specified in contracts

- monitoring costs and taking measures to reduce them where appropriate

- ensuring that bills are raised for services provided

- making statutory returns to government and international bodies

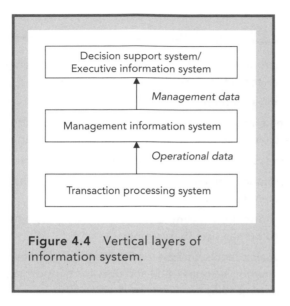

Figure 4.4 Vertical layers of information system.

4.6.2 VERTICAL INFORMATION SYSTEMS

One of the conventional typologies distinguishes between three major types of system: transaction processing systems (TPS), management information systems (MIS) and decision support systems (DSS)/executive information systems (EIS) (see Figure 4.4). As you will see from Figure 4.4, each of these systems builds upon the other. DSS/EIS rely on data from MIS that in turn relies on data from TPS.

- *Transaction processing systems.* These are the operational information systems of the organisation. In a business organisation examples include order entry, accounts payable and stock control systems. They process the detailed data generated in the operations of the business. The detailed data are normally referred to as transactions and include customer orders, purchase orders, invoices etc. This data is essential to support the day-to-day operations that help a company add value to its products and/or services. TPS are sometimes referred to as the life-blood of the organisation because they are so critical to effective activity within the organisation.

- *Management information systems.* These are used particularly by some operational layers of management to monitor the state of the organisation at any one time. From such a system or level of systems managers would be expected to retrieve data about current production levels, number of orders achieved, current labour costs and other relevant managerial data.

- *Decision support/executive information systems.* Whereas MIS are generally used to enable effective short-term tactical decisions about the operation of the organisation, DSS and EIS are generally expected to support longer-term strategic decision-making. DSS/EIS will utilise the management data generated by MIS to model short-term and long-term scenarios of company performance. These scenarios are used to ask 'What if?' questions of business planning and to generate policy decisions in the area of business strategy.

4.7 ⊚ SUMMARY

- The analysis of historical information systems is an extremely useful exercise for highlighting the essential features of information systems
- Information systems are communication systems.
- Information systems are distinct from information technology. Information technology supports communication within the information system.
- Good information systems are critical to efficient and effective action.
- The place of information technology within an organisation has to be determined with the aid of system stakeholders.
- Information and information technology systems rarely stand still. They evolve to support changes to human activity systems.
- There are three major levels of systems: transaction processing systems (TPS), management information systems (MIS) and decision support systems (DSS)/executive information systems (EIS).
- We may also distinguish information systems in terms of the organisation in which they are applied; those in the public sector differ from those which are applied in the private sector.

4.8 ⊚ QUESTIONS

(i) Describe in what ways the warning network can be considered an information system.

(ii) In what ways can the intelligence work performed by Station X be regarded as an information system?

(iii) Why is it important to study historical cases of information systems?

(iv) Distinguish between a human activity system, an information system and an information technology system.

(v) Distinguish between transaction processing systems, management information systems and decision support/executive information systems.

(vi) In terms of the distinction between public and private sector information systems, give some examples of systems in each sector.

4.9 ⊚ EXERCISES

(i) Consider some historical information system and build a case description of its use. Some possible cases include Herman Hollerith's invention and use of his tabulating machine for running the US national census, the management of railway ticketing in the 19th century, and the operation of Lloyd's insurance.

(ii) Distinguish between the information system and the information technology in each historical case.

(iii) In terms of some organisation, identify its key EIS, MIS and TPS.

(iv) Investigate the distinction between EIS, DSS and MIS in more detail.

4.10 PROJECTS

(i) Build a detailed case study of some historical information system and clearly delineate elements such as the information system, the 'information technology' and the human activity system.

(ii) Construct a detailed map of some organisation's information systems. Include both computerised as well as non-computerised information systems.

(iii) Investigate the degree of integration between information systems in some organisation.

(iv) Distinguish between transaction processing systems and management information systems in some company and assess their effectiveness.

4.11 REFERENCES

Channel 4 (1999). *Station X*. Channel 4 TV programme, UK.

Holwell, S. and Checkland, P. (1998a). *Information, Systems and Information Systems*. John Wiley, Chichester.

Holwell, S. and Checkland, P. (1998b). An information system won the war. *IEE Proceedings Software*, **145**(4), 95–99.

Lyytinen, K. J. (1985). Implications of theories of language for information systems. *MIS Quarterly*, March(9), 61–74.

Singh, S. (2000). *The Science of Secrecy*. Fourth Estate, London.

CHAPTER 5

BUSINESS INFORMATION SYSTEMS

Drive thy business or it will drive thee.

Benjamin Franklin (1706–1790)

LEARNING OUTCOMES

After reading this chapter, you will be able to:

- Define some key transaction processing information systems experienced in business organisations

- Describe the relationship between information systems and human activity systems in commercial organisations

- Discuss the distinction between supplier-facing and customer-facing IS

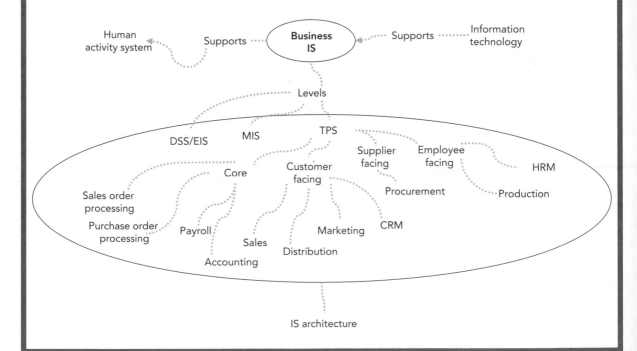

5.1 INTRODUCTION

In this chapter we develop a generic description of some key information systems in modern business. We utilise the system diagramming tools described in the previous two chapters to enable us to do this. Some of the important reasons for outlining generic IS models are also discussed.

In Chapter 4 we discussed three major levels of information systems relevant to modern organisations: transaction processing systems (TPS), management information systems (MIS) and decision support systems (DSS)/executive information systems (EIS). We will generally concentrate on explicating transaction processing systems in this chapter because they form the bedrock for the two other types of information system. Management and executive information systems are considered in Chapter 6.

5.2 GENERIC INFORMATION SYSTEMS MODELS

Clearly each business is different. This may be partly due to different environments in the sense that obviously different organisations are in different sectors of the economy – retail, manufacturing, education – to name but a few. However, even organisations in the same industrial sector will operate differently. Part of the reason for this may be to achieve something of a competitive advantage over their competitors in the market-place. Competitive advantage may be achieved in a number of ways: through differentiation in human activity, effectiveness in human activity and/or efficiency of human activity (Chapter 20).

The consequence of this is that each company's collection of IS will necessarily be different. Hence organisations may implement different operational procedures or may parcel up the basic elements of transaction processing in terms of different units. We refer to the entire makeup of an organisation's information systems as its IS architecture or infrastructure (Chapter 21).

Having said this, there are a number of core information systems that, at a high level, most businesses have in common. Financial data is the life-blood of most business organisations and is subject to a vast range of external regulation in the sense that companies must prepare their financial reports in well-established ways. Therefore it is no surprise to find that, in most business organisations, information technology was first applied in the accounting department, and financial information systems form the core around which a number of other information systems are located.

Generic IS models are also useful in that they help us to distinguish between the information systems architecture of some organisation and its supporting information technology architecture. Generic software packages have been developed which attempt to automate key business functions and in a sense supply an IT architecture for companies. Models such as these also help us to demonstrate the key place of contemporary initiatives such as electronic commerce and electronic business (Part 9).

Some segments of the information systems of some organisation may conform more closely to the generic model than others. This is normally because there is some external regulation of the practices in a particular business area. Payroll is a case in point. Such IS areas may be the most appropriate for outsourcing to an external supplier (Chapter 40). There is probably little advantage in having a different payroll system from your competitors.

Although most manufacturing organisations are likely to utilise elements of an architecture similar to the model discussed here, organisations are likely to differ in the degree to which information technology is applied in key areas. For instance, some organisations may still have a manual information system to support stock control. Deciding where IS are key to the organisation is a key aspect of informatics planning (Chapter 34).

5.3 CORE INFORMATION SYSTEMS

Many businesses that sell products are founded around the following key information systems:

- Sales order processing
- Purchase order processing
- Accounting
- Payroll

Businesses which sell services will operate differently in the sense of having different human activity systems, and hence will have core information systems in similar areas, but these will operate differently from that described in this chapter. Figure 5.1 illustrates some of the flows of data (represented by labelled arrows) between these four major transaction processing systems.

Note the symmetrical nature of two of these information systems: sales order processing and purchase order processing. This is because relationships between customers and suppliers normally form chains in a given economic market-place. Figure 5.2 illustrates the fact that a supplier to a particular company will regard that company as one of its customers. Hence its sales order processing system will regard the order from this company as a sales order, and so on. Company B is therefore a customer of C and in turn A is a customer of B.

The links to its customers are normally referred to as a company's customer chain. In recent electronic commerce literature, customer chains are normally referred to as B2C – business to customer. The links to a company's suppliers are normally referred to as the company's supply chain, or B2B – business to business (Chapter 22).

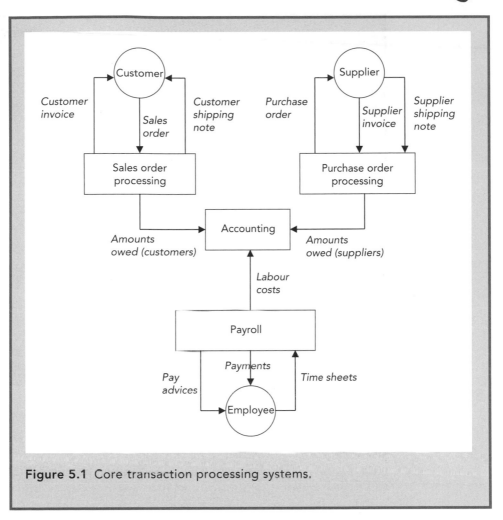

Figure 5.1 Core transaction processing systems.

5.4 SALES ORDER PROCESSING

Figure 5.3 indicates a decomposition of the elements of the process box *Sales order processing* in Figure 5.1. Hence sales order processing can be seen to be a subsystem of the transaction processing system of some company and in turn sales order entry can be seen as a subsystem of sales order processing.

Note that this system assumes that goods will be dispatched to customers with an invoice for payment. A payment from the customer will be made to the company at some time after receipt of the invoice. This is the usual state of affairs when the company and its customer are in a so-called trusted relationship. In other words, the company has established in some way that payment will be made at some later date and is therefore willing to effectively award credit to a customer.

In many sectors of business customers are usually members of the general public. In such situations orders and payments are normally expected to arrive at the same

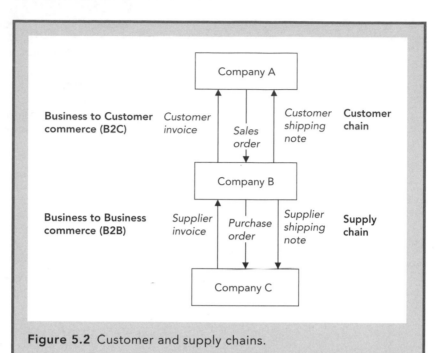

Figure 5.2 Customer and supply chains.

time. The customer notification effectively serves as a record of the transaction between the company and the customer.

A suggested decomposition of the order entry subsystem is given in Figure 5.4. Note that we have provided some constructs known as data stores on this diagram. A data store is a repository of data. For example, in a manual information system this might constitute a filing cabinet or a card index. In an information technology system a data store would probably constitute a database (Chapter 10) of some kind. A data store is represented on a system diagram by an open box. This is to indicate the important reliance of actual information systems on organised repositories of data such as that kept on a company's products or customers.

Order entry is a key process that interfaces to the organisation's customers. Order entry captures the key data needed to process a customer order. Traditionally, orders might be expected to arrive through the post or over the telephone line. More recently orders may be sent electronically and come over electronic data interchange (EDI) links or via the Internet (Chapter 42).

Normally the order entry system would make an enquiry of the stock control system to check that suitable quantities of the desired item are available. If an order item cannot be filled then a substitute item might be suggested or a back order generated. This back order will be filled later when stock is replenished. A notification of a confirmed, partially filled or back order would be supplied to the customer.

Orders processed by the order entry system will then be passed to a shipment planning system. This is a particularly important system for medium to large

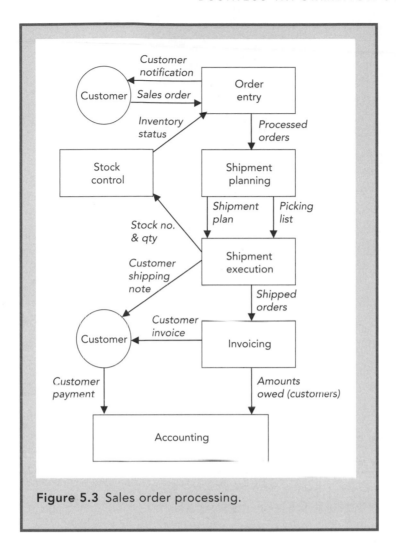

Figure 5.3 Sales order processing.

companies with lots of customers, minimal stock and many points of distribution. This system determines which orders will be filled and from which location they will be shipped. The system produces two outputs: a shipment plan which indicates how and when each order is to be filled and a picking list which is used by warehouse staff to select the desired goods from the warehouse.

Shipment execution supports the work of the shipping function and is used to coordinate the flow of goods from the business to customers. The system will produce a shipping note that is attached to each despatch of goods. It also passes on details of the shipment to invoicing.

Invoicing systems take the data supplied on shipping and produce invoices to customers using data stored about customers, orders, products and prices. Invoices may be sent at time of shipment or some time thereafter.

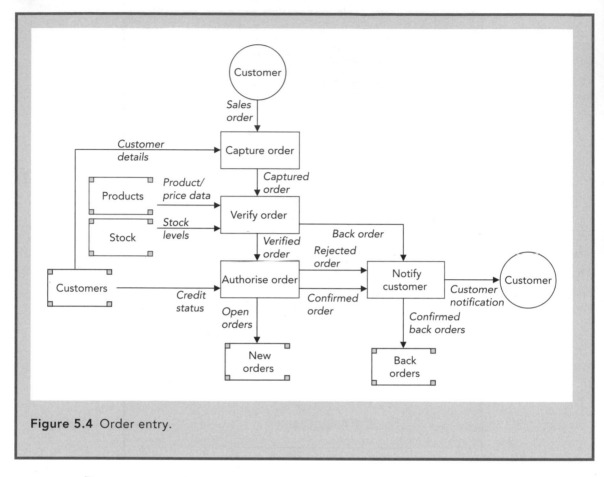

Figure 5.4 Order entry.

5.5 PURCHASE ORDER PROCESSING

Figure 5.5 represents elements of a standard purchase order processing subsystem.

Most businesses have several forms of stock or inventory. These include raw materials, materials for packing, finished goods and parts for maintenance of products. Stock control or inventory control systems are designed to manage data about this material. The objective for most businesses is to minimise the amount of stock held whilst ensuring optimal performance of other systems such as manufacturing.

Minimal stock levels are a crucial element of a modern business philosophy known as just in time (JIT) manufacturing. Providing facilities for storing stock of raw materials needed for manufacture is a critical cost to the business. The more stock held the greater the costs incurred. JIT aims to store only enough stock to meet the short-term needs of production. Warehouses are replenished with raw materials *just in time* to ensure efficient production.

Purchases may be generated in two ways. The stock control system itself may generate an automatic purchase order if the level of a stock item falls below a certain level. Most medium to large organisations will have a purchasing or procurement unit. Staff in this unit will be generating purchase orders on the basis

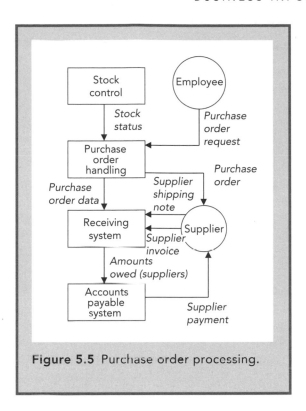

Figure 5.5 Purchase order processing.

of orders it receives from the stock control system or from requests from staff for those items not included within the general remit of stock control.

Purchase orders will be produced by purchase order handling and then sent to relevant suppliers. This data will then be used to update a receiving system that will check the data it has on purchase orders against invoices it receives from suppliers.

If the goods received from suppliers match purchase order information then financial information about the amounts owed to suppliers is passed on to a major subsystem within accounting – accounts payable.

5.6 ACCOUNTING

Figure 5.6 represents elements of a standard accounting system.

Most accounting systems are divided up into three major subsystems: accounts receivable, accounts payable and general ledger. The data store used by the accounts receivable system is generally called a sales ledger because it records financial details of all amounts owed by customers to the organisation. The data store used by the accounts payable system is sometimes called the purchase ledger because it stores details of all monies owed to suppliers by the organisation.

A third accounting system called a general ledger system is used to record details of all the financial transactions relevant to an organisation: income, expenditure

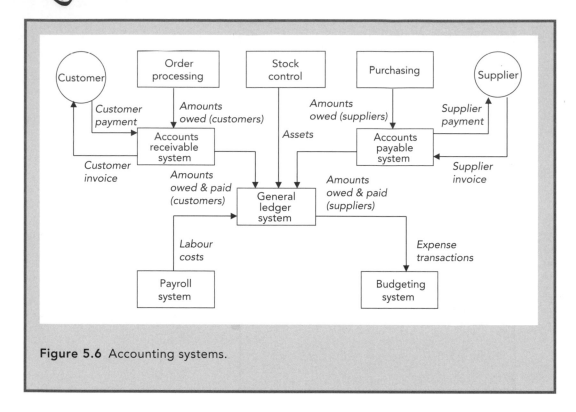

Figure 5.6 Accounting systems.

and assets. It hence receives data from accounts payable, accounts receivable and stock control systems.

The accounts receivable system is essential for managing the cash flow of the company. When goods are shipped to customers a record of the amount owed by customers is passed on to the accounts receivable system. This leads to the customer's account being updated. When customers send payments to the company the credit balance of the customer is reduced by the appropriate amount. The data about customer credit and amounts paid is regularly used to update the general ledger system.

The accounts payable system is also essential for managing the cash flow of the company. When goods are ordered from suppliers a record of the amount owed to suppliers is passed on to the accounts payable system. This leads to the supplier's account being updated. When the organisation makes payments to its suppliers the credit balance owed to suppliers is reduced by the appropriate amount. The data about credit owed to suppliers and amounts paid is regularly used to update the general ledger system.

The third key input into a general ledger system is a payroll system. The payroll system will regularly update the general ledger with the costs incurred in paying staff. There will also be an input into the general ledger from the stock control system detailing the current financial position of assets held by the company.

5.7 ⊚ PAYROLL

Figure 5.7 represents elements of a standard payroll subsystem.

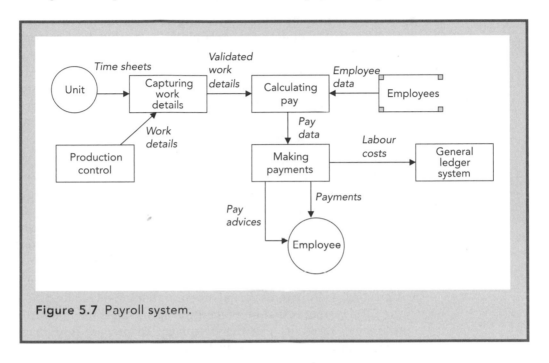

Figure 5.7 Payroll system.

Payroll produces two primary outputs: some payment to the employee, and a record (payslip or pay advice) of the details of the payments made. The key input into a payroll system is some data of the work undertaken during a given time period such as a week or month. These details may be collected on time-sheets sent on from operational departments or may be automatically generated from a production scheduling and control system. The payroll system will need to access data stored on each employee, such as pay rates and tax details to produce given pay advices. Periodically, the payroll system will update the general ledger system with the financial costs of labour.

5.8 ⊚ OTHER TRANSACTION PROCESSING SYSTEMS

These four information systems of order processing, purchasing, payroll and accounting form the core of most businesses' IS architecture. On this foundation a large number of other information systems are normally built. These may be other transaction processing systems that interface to a company's customers, suppliers or employees or forms of management information system.

In terms of TPS we may distinguish between such information systems on the basis of which agency they are interfacing with: customers, suppliers or employees.

5.8.1 CUSTOMER-FACING TPS

Typical customer-facing TPS include sales, customer relationship management, marketing and distribution systems.

- *Sales*. In some companies, particularly those associated with high-value products such as automobile sales or industrial equipment, customers would not normally fill out orders themselves. They are more than likely to interface with some sales force in relation to making orders. Hence a sales system is a common component of the information systems architecture of such organisations. This system will record the activities of the sales force in terms of what sales have been made, to whom, by whom and when. This data will frequently be used to calculate commission owed to sales people on products sold.

- *Customer relationship management (CRM)*. A customer is likely to interact with a company in a number of other ways besides making orders. Customer relationship management has become a popular philosophy in the recent management science literature. Winning new customers and keeping existing customers happy is seen to be a key to organisational success. A customer relationship management system would ideally track all customer interactions with a company from initial enquiries through making orders to the whole range of after-sales services that might be offered to and consumed by the customer.

- *Marketing*. A key organisational function that is likely to feed off data gathered by the CRM system is that of marketing. Marketing is likely to utilise the information held about its existing customers to prepare and manage advertising campaigns for company products and services.

- *Distribution system*. Critical aspects of this system will be concerned with optimising the use of delivery channels to customers. In the retail sector for instance large food retailers are likely to have fleets of vehicles involved in the delivery of goods to stores. These vehicles may have to make up to 100 deliveries in any given working week. Clearly, effective and efficient systems are needed to plan and schedule routes for the vehicles to deliver foodstuffs.

5.8.2 SUPPLIER-FACING TPS

Typical supplier-facing TPS include procurement and supplier relationship management systems.

- *Procurement*. This system will be concerned with managing the process of procuring the goods, services and raw materials needed by the company to operate effectively. It will interact with both the purchase ordering system and the supplier relationship management system.

- *Supplier relationship management (SRM)*. This is the sister system to the customer relationship management system. It keeps track of all supplier interactions with the company.

5.8.3 EMPLOYEE-FACING TPS

Typical employee-facing TPS include human resource management and production control systems.

- *Human resource management.* A company is likely to need to build systems to record, process and maintain large amounts of information about its employees. Payroll data is only one facet of this data. Companies will also want to maintain detailed histories of the employment of their employees.

- *Production system.* This system will be involved in scheduling future production, monitoring current production and interfacing with the stock control system in terms of requisitioning raw material for production and replenishing supplies of finished goods.

Figure 5.8 illustrates some of the data flows that relate these various additional systems to the core IS we have discussed. Note that we have introduced five generic

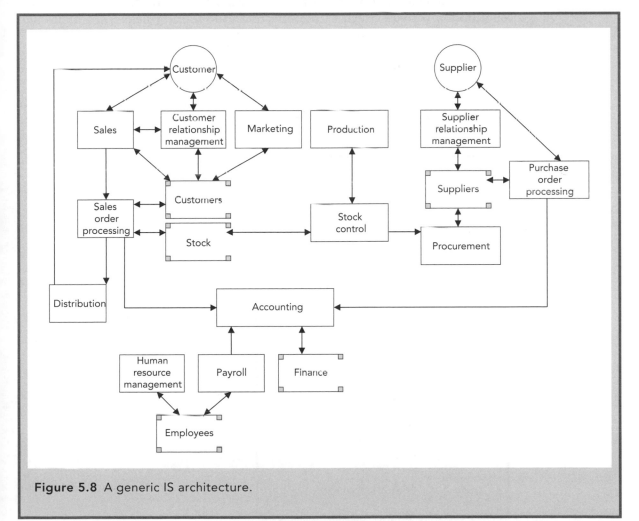

Figure 5.8 A generic IS architecture.

data stores that form crucial links between these information systems: customers, suppliers, employees, finance and stock. This indicates the importance of large corporate data sets as integration links within the information systems architecture. As we shall see, such data sets are likely to be implemented in an information technology architecture as a series of large corporate databases or data warehouses (Chapter 10).

5.9 ⊚ INFORMATION SYSTEMS AND HUMAN ACTIVITY SYSTEMS

Information systems are of course not the only operations of companies. For most companies, information systems do not normally deliver value to a company in themselves. It is important to emphasise that information systems support human activity systems. An information system will frequently be named after the human activity system it supports. Hence the distribution information system will support distribution activities such as the effective utilisation of delivery vehicles and warehouse facilities in the delivery of goods to customers.

To emphasise this linkage between information systems and human activity systems it is useful to include another symbol on system diagrams to represent the physical flow of goods and/or services. For this we utilise a broad labelled arrow.

Hence an economic market-place is made up of businesses with goods, services and information flowing between them. Particularly important is the notion of the

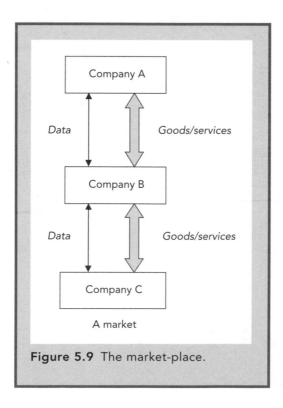

Figure 5.9 The market-place.

global economy in which goods and services flow across national boundaries over vast distances. Data is essential to the effective performance of a market-place, particularly on the global scale, because it enables the effective management and control of the flow of goods and services. This is illustrated in Figure 5.9.

5.10 SUMMARY

- Each business organisation's information systems will necessarily be different. However, there are similarities across organisations in the same business sector. Hence it is possible to develop generic descriptions of a number of key business information systems.
- Key business information systems include sales order processing, purchase order processing, accounts and payroll.
- Other key transaction processing systems may be distinguished in terms of whether they are supplier-facing, customer-facing or employee-facing.
- Customer-facing TPS include sales, customer-relationship management, marketing and distribution.
- Supplier-facing TPS include procurement and supplier-relationship management.
- Employee-facing TPS include human resource management and production management.
- Information systems support the flow of goods and services between organisations in some market.

5.11 QUESTIONS

(i) Why are generic IS models useful?

(ii) List the four core information systems of many organisations.

(iii) Describe the difference between the supply chain and the customer chain.

(iv) Name some customer-facing TPS.

(v) Name some supplier-facing TPS.

(vi) Name some employee-facing TPS.

(vii) Why are information systems important to the idea of an electronic market-place?

5.12 EXERCISES

(i) Find a company close to you. Take along one or more of the generic information systems models discussed in this chapter. Compare the operations of the company to those described on the model. How closely do they match? In what ways are they different?

(ii) Consider a future situation in which corporations become involved in mining asteroids within the solar system. Would the informatics architecture of such corporations be different from the one discussed in this chapter?

(iii) Produce a description of the customer-facing information systems of some company.

(iv) Produce a description of the supplier-facing information systems of some company.

(v) Produce a description of the employee-facing information systems of some company.

5.13 🌀 PROJECTS

(i) Investigate the relevance of the distinction between management information systems and transaction processing systems in some organisation. Identify clearly the current users of such systems.

(ii) Draw a detailed map of the information systems used within some business organisation known to you. To what extent do they map onto the systems described in this chapter?

(iii) Develop a case study of the historical development of information systems and information technology systems in relation to one company.

CHAPTER 6

MANAGEMENT AND DECISION-MAKING

So much of what we call management consists in making it difficult for people to work.

Peter Drucker

No sensible decision can be made any longer without taking into account not only the world as it is, but the world as it will be...

Isaac Asimov (1920–1992)

LEARNING OUTCOMES

After reading this chapter, you will be able to:

- Describe the activity of decision-making
- Identify the relationship between rationality and decision-making
- Distinguish between three levels of management
- Recognise differences between management information systems and executive information systems

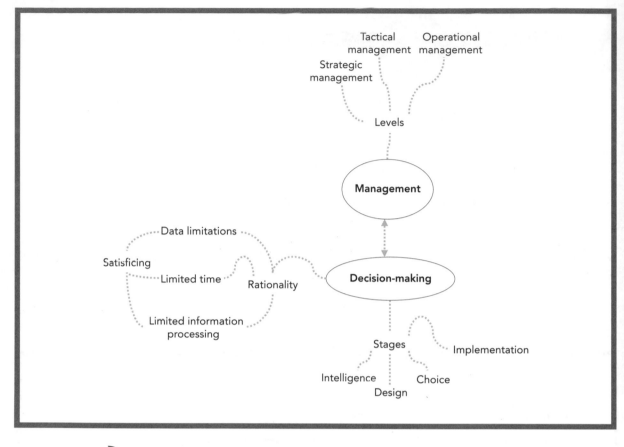

6.1 INTRODUCTION

Information supports human activity in the sense that it enables decisions to be made about appropriate actions in particular circumstances. Decisions and decision-making therefore mediate between information and action and are a critical aspect of the domain of informatics (Figure 6.1). In this chapter we consider the issue of decision-making as a process and compare a rational model of this process against some of the practicalities of the human experience of decision-making.

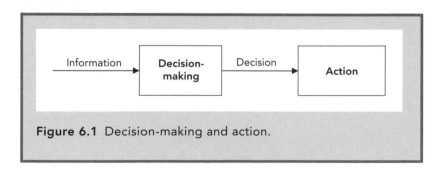

Figure 6.1 Decision-making and action.

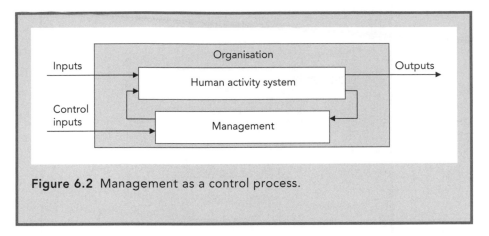

Figure 6.2 Management as a control process.

Management can be seen as a control process within organisations (Figure 6.2). Management is a human activity system that controls other human activity systems. The primary activity of management is making decisions, particularly those at the strategic and tactical levels concerning organisational action (Chapter 20). Effective management decision-making is reliant on good information. It is for this reason that we consider these three issues of management, decision-making and information in this chapter.

6.2 THE PROCESS OF DECISION-MAKING

One of the primary activities of management is decision-making. Decision-making is the activity of deciding on appropriate action in particular situations. Decision-making is reliant on information in the sense that information is seen as reducing uncertainty in decision-making (Chapter 2).

Information is data interpreted in some context by some particular person or group. Since information relies on data, the general assumption is that good decision-making is reliant on good data. This prompts the question: what is good data? Some possible features of good data are:

- *Accuracy*. Is the data expressed to a suitable level of accuracy?
- *Age*. Is the data current?
- *Time horizon*. Is data suitably timely?
- *Level of summarisation*. Is the data summarised to an appropriate level of aggregation?
- *Completeness*. How completely does the data cover the domain?
- *Accessibility*. Is the data accessible?
- *Relevance*. Is the data relevant to the decision to be made?

Clearly most of these properties depend upon the context within which a decision is made. But on what basis does decision-making take place? Simon (1960) argues that there are four general stages in any decision-making process, as illustrated in Figure 6.3:

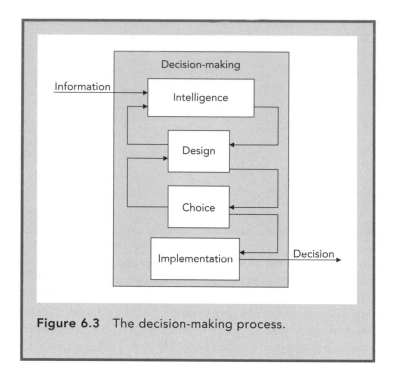

Figure 6.3 The decision-making process.

- *Intelligence*. In this phase data in the decision-making area are examined. Examination of this data may lead to the specification of a problem to be solved or some recognition of an opportunity for the organisation.
- *Design*. The problem is formulated; solutions are developed and tested for feasibility.
- *Choice*. Selection is made amongst alternatives.
- *Implementation*. The chosen alternative is implemented and substantiated to stakeholders in the organisation.

The decision-making model illustrated in Figure 6.3 has a number of explicit feedback loops. This suggests that most decision-making is iterative. For instance, at the design phase additional questions may arise that demand further intelligence gathering.

Example IIII➡ Consider an academic school at a university making decisions as to which new modules to run. The intelligence phase will involve gathering data about possible staff interests and skills, modules run by other institutions and the requests made by commerce and industry. In the design phase a number of key module descriptions may be written and assessed in terms of the feasibility of the school running them. A choice will then be made amongst the alternative modules, and the chosen modules will then be passed on to other organisational processes such as validation.

6.3 RATIONALITY

Classic models of decision-making assume it to be a rational process. Rational decision-making is characterised by the following features:

- *Intelligence.* In rational decision-making the decision-maker must gather *all* relevant data and interpret it in an unbiased manner.
- *Design.* The decision-maker must identify *all* feasible alternatives and identify an explicit set of criteria for selecting between them.
- *Choice.* The decision-maker should choose amongst alternatives based on a *systematic assessment* using explicit weightings of the importance of key criteria.

Close studies of actual human decision-making reveal that most such activity within organisations diverges substantially from this rational ideal. This is not surprising when one realises that rational decision-making requires unlimited time within which to make a decision, all the information relevant to the problem and an information processor that is able to handle all of the information and alternatives.

Therefore most human decision-making appears to be satisficing rather than rational behaviour. Satisficing decision-making describes how humans make decisions in a limited amount of time, based on limited information and with limited ability to process information.

- *Limited time.* Most management decision-making has to be done in a finite amount of time.
- *Limited information.* In most practicable situations it is impossible to gather all the possible data relevant to the problem because of limited resources.
- *Limited information-processing capability.* The decision-making process is constrained by the limitations of human information processing. For instance, information is interpreted and human interpretation is subject to non-rational emotive influences. Also, human beings display limitations of short-term memory. Most humans can handle on average only seven items of information at any one time.

6.4 LEVELS OF MANAGEMENT

Decision-making is a key activity of management but decision-making is performed at a number of levels within organisations. In terms of management decision-making we may identify three levels of management: strategic management, tactical management and operational management (Figure 6.4).

These three levels of management can be distinguished on the dimensions of:

- *Decision-making characteristics.* The higher we travel up the management hierarchy the less structured problems and decisions become. Structured decisions are frequently called algorithmic decisions in that an explicit procedure can be

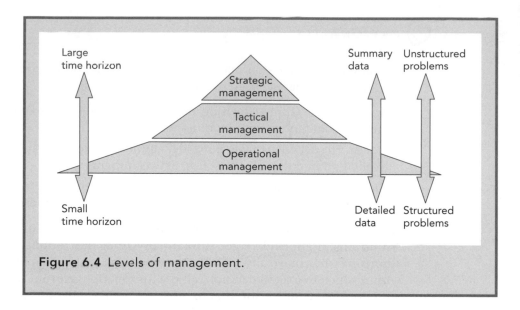

Figure 6.4 Levels of management.

represented and implemented for making such decisions. Unstructured decisions are frequently called heuristic decisions in that no set procedure can be established, but some 'rules of thumb' can be suggested as to ways of approaching the problem.

- *Data needs*. The higher we travel up the management hierarchy the greater the need for summary data and data concerned with the external environment. Operational management need detailed data on the operational activities of the organisation. Strategic management needs data which summarises aspects of organisational performance and compares this against competitors.

- *Time horizon*. The higher we travel up the management hierarchy the larger the time horizon of both decisions and information. Operational managers need data to help them make decisions on an hour-by-hour basis. Strategic managers are more likely to think in time-frames of months and years.

6.5 MIS, DSS AND EIS

The key interest in management and decision-making fostered particularly by the literature in the area of organisational behaviour (Chapter 16) led to the development of a number of specialised information systems for management: MIS, DSS and EIS.

MIS generally are proposed for providing data in support of structured decision-making. A decision is structured if the decision-making process can be described in detail before the decision is made. Tactical decision-making is therefore likely to be of a structured form. Examples of structured decisions are deciding on appropriate stock levels and pricing normal orders.

DSS and EIS generally are proposed for providing data in support of unstructured decision-making. A decision is unstructured if the decision-making process cannot be described in detail. This may be because the problem has not arisen before, is characterised by incomplete or uncertain knowledge, or uses non-quantifiable data. Examples of unstructured decision-making are selecting personnel and determining investment.

Example ▐▐▐▶ In Chapter 5 we identified four major data sets – employees, customers, finance and stock – important to the information systems architecture of our model organisation. These four major data sets are likely to form the key inputs into a management information system for some organisation (see Figure 6.5). Using such a system, operational managers can continually monitor the state of the organisation. This is indicated in Figure 6.5 as one large management information system. In practice it may form a number of integrated MIS, perhaps for particular business areas. One of the key outputs from the MIS will be summarised data on major trends affecting the company such as labour costs, current levels of assets and current levels of spending. This data may be written to a planning data store for use by an executive information system. The EIS is likely to be used to formulate high-level strategic decisions affecting the company.

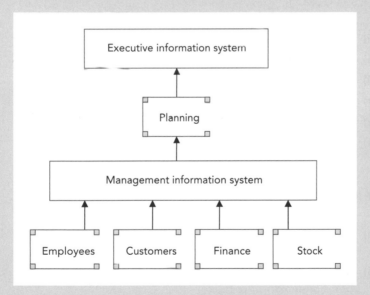

Figure 6.5 EIS, MIS and data stores.

6.6 ⊙ SUMMARY

- Decisions and decision-making mediate between information and action.
- Good decision-making is reliant on 'good' information. Information reduces uncertainty in decision-making.
- Characteristics of 'good' data include accuracy, relevance, timeliness, accessibility and completeness.
- We may identify three levels of management: strategic management, tactical management and operational management. There are clear differences in information needs and forms of decision-making appropriate to the three levels of management.
- Simon identifies the following stages in any decision-making: intelligence, design, choice and implementation.
- Most human decision-making is satisficing rather than rational.
- MIS, EIS and DSS have all been developed with the aim of supporting management decision-making in organisations.

6.7 ⊙ QUESTIONS

(i) Define the process of management in systems terms.

(ii) List some of the features of good data.

(iii) What are the features of rational decision-making?

(iv) Explain why human decision-making is satisficing rather than rational.

(v) Distinguish between the three levels of management.

(vi) Distinguish between MIS, DSS and EIS.

6.8 ⊙ EXERCISES

(i) Generate the information appropriate to some decision. What action results from the decision?

(ii) Dissect some decision-making in terms of the phases of Simon's model of the decision-making process.

(iii) Provide three examples of accurate, timely and complete data.

(iv) Give an example of human decision-making suffering from limited time and information.

(v) Consider some organisation known to you. Classify the managerial divisions in the chart of the organisation in terms of the distinctions made between levels of management.

(vi) Investigate some organisation to determine whether they have any management information systems and what precisely they are used for.

6.9 PROJECTS

(i) Investigate the applicability of the three-layered management model to some organisation.

(ii) Investigate the utility of Simon's model of decision-making by gathering detailed observational material on decision-making within project management.

(iii) Determine the level of use of MIS, DSS and EIS in some industrial sector.

6.10 REFERENCE

Simon, H. (1960). *The New Science of Management Decisions*. Harper & Row, New York.

INFORMATION SYSTEMS MODELLING

'What is the use of a book', thought Alice, 'without pictures or conversation?'

Lewis Carroll: *Alice's Adventures in Wonderland* (1865), Chapter 1

LEARNING OUTCOMES

After reading this chapter, you will be able to:

- Relate why modelling is an essential element of information systems work
- Identify the importance of abstraction to effective modelling
- Describe three alternative forms of information systems modelling

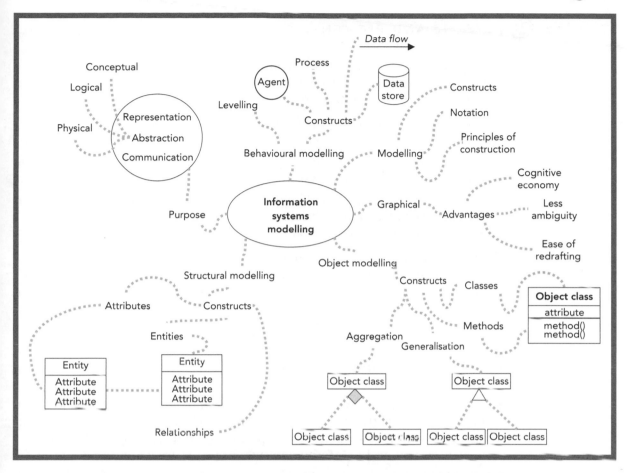

7.1 INTRODUCTION

Systems are complex entities. To understand the structure and behaviour of systems we have to model them. We have implicitly used some graphical models of systems in general and information systems in particular in previous chapters (Chapters 3, 4 and 5). In this chapter we consider the use of such models in greater detail and provide some preliminary notation for undertaking modelling.

Clearly modelling can be done on a number of levels. We can build general systems models, information systems models and models of information technology systems. In this chapter we focus primarily on the issue of information systems modelling. Further techniques for information technology systems modelling are discussed in further chapters (Chapters 27, 28 and 29). The reader is referred to Beynon-Davies (1998) for more details of these approaches.

7.2 🌀 PURPOSE AND ELEMENTS OF MODELLING

Any model can be seen as a sign system (Chapter 2) – a collection of signs used by some social group. The construction of such sign-systems is the process of modelling and is undertaken for three reasons:

- *Communication*. The primary use for a model is as a medium of communication between some group of persons.
- *Representation*. A model is used to represent common understandings about some real-world phenomena amongst this group of persons.
- *Abstraction*. Modelling generally implies some form of simplification of the real world. The modeller uses a model to focus on what are seen to be the important features of some real-world situation.

Although modelling is an essential element of information systems work, there is no agreement about the most appropriate way of modelling systems in general or information and information technology systems in particular. In this chapter we portray at a high level some of the key elements of most accepted approaches to information systems modelling.

Any modelling of whatever form needs three elements:

- *Constructs*. By constructs we mean the component elements of the modelling approach.
- *Notation*. By notation we mean the form of representation employed for the constructs within the modelling approach. Such a notation can be textual, graphical and/or mathematical. Graphical notations are probably the most frequently employed in information systems work because of ease of use.
- *Principles of construction*. By principles we mean the formal and informal rules for correctly constructing models.

7.3 🌀 PROCESS OF MODELLING

In the world we are, as human beings, confronted by a vast range of phenomena. To help us understand phenomena we abstract. Abstraction is the process of recognising similarities between phenomena and ignoring differences. An abstraction is therefore a group of phenomena covered by similar properties. Other commonly used words for an abstraction are *concept* and *sign*. A simple view of the process of modelling therefore sees it as a form of mapping between concepts in a model and the real world domain or universe of discourse under consideration (Figure 7.1). This corresponds to the three-way division of signs discussed in Chapter 2:

- The *extension* of a concept refers to the range of phenomena that the concept in some way covers. Another word for the extension of a concept is its referent.
- The *intension* of a concept is the collection of properties that in some way characterise the phenomena in the extension.

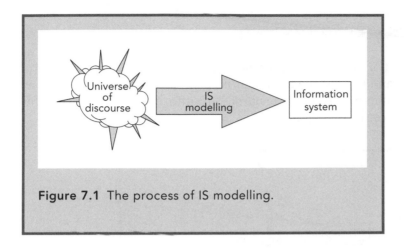

Figure 7.1 The process of IS modelling.

- The *designation* of a concept is the collection of symbols by which the concept is known.

The important part of the definition of the extension of a concept provided above is the phrase 'in some way'. In classic Aristotelian logic the intension of a concept is a collection of properties that may be divided into two groups: the defining properties that all phenomena in the extension must have; and the properties that the phenomena may or may not have. The nature of the defining properties is such that it is objectively determinable whether or not a phenomenon has a certain property. In classical logic, such properties are designated by predicates. Hence defining properties in this view determine a sharp boundary between membership and non-membership of a concept.

Having said this, there is a tendency in the literature to assume that the process of developing a model using some notation is an unproblematic process. The major philosophical position taken in much of information systems development is that of objectivism (Chapter 49). The assumption is that there is some objective reality, elements of which can be captured and represented (hence the tendency to use terms such as requirements *capture* (Chapter 28)). Although this position works well in relation to the physical world, where the objects can be seen, touched and smelt, this position is problematic when applied to the social world, of which organisational reality is a part. A more appropriate philosophical position in relation to this world might be described as a subjectivist or interpretive position. The assumption here is that organisational reality is not a given; reality is socially constructed in the process of human interaction (Chapter 16).

Any modelling is therefore more accurately viewed as a process of negotiation between stakeholder groups within organisations. Such stakeholder groups must reach some inter-subjective agreement about the form and interpretation of various models constructed. Information systems modelling is hence the process of reaching some inter-subjective agreement about the properties of some information system and representing these properties in some form of notation. Models are critically used in the analysis and design (Chapter 28 and 29) phases of IS development for this purpose.

7.4 A TYPOLOGY OF MODELLING

It is useful to distinguish between two dimensions for modelling work. On the one hand there is the level of abstraction at which we choose to model. On the other hand there is the coverage of some information system that the model attempts to encapsulate (Figure 7.2).

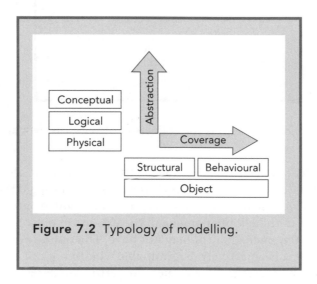

Figure 7.2 Typology of modelling.

In terms of abstraction the mapping between the Universe of Discourse and models is normally discussed on three levels. In other words, there are three levels of abstraction at which we may develop models:

- *Conceptual models*. This is the highest level of abstraction. A conceptual model represents some UoD but contains little or no implementation detail.
- *Logical models*. These models seek to encapsulate key elements of the universe of discourse and bridge between conceptual and physical models.
- *Physical models*. These are close to a description of reality and contain detailed plans for implementation.

> Example ||||▶ Consider models built of the data required by some information system. A conceptual model of the data will describe the broad collections of data required and the relationships between these collections. A logical model will structure the data in terms of concepts such as tables and keys (Chapter 10). A physical model will comprise the actual structures used within some database system such as files and indexes.

In terms of coverage we may distinguish between:

- *Behavioural modelling*. This form of modelling focuses on the activities of some information system and the dynamics of data flow.

- *Structural modelling.* This form of modelling focuses on the structure of data needed to support an information system.
- *Object modelling.* This form of modelling attempts to integrate behavioural and structural viewpoints around the central idea of objects.

7.5 BEHAVIOURAL MODELLING

In a sense we have already used a form of behavioural modelling in Chapters 3, 4 and 5. Behavioural modelling is an attempt to represent the dynamics or behaviour of some system. Behavioural modelling for information systems can be undertaken using four main constructs:

- *Agent.* An agent is something (usually a person, group, department or organisation, but possibly some other information system) that is a net originator or receiver of system data. It is represented on a diagram by some form of rounded shape – circle or oval – with an appropriate name. Generally we use agents to indicate something lying outside a system that serve to define the key boundaries of the system.
- *Data flow.* A data flow is a pipeline through which packets of data of known composition flow. Data flow is represented on a diagram by a labelled directed arrow. Double-headed arrows mean that a process is both passing data to another process or data store and receiving data from another process or data store.
- *Data store.* A data store is a repository of data. For example, in a manual information this might constitute a filing cabinet or a card index. In an information technology system a data store would probably constitute a database (Chapter 10) of some kind. A data store is represented on a diagram by an open box.
- *Process.* A process is a transformation of incoming data flow(s) into outgoing data flow(s). A process is represented on a diagram by a labelled square or rectangle. The label should obviously be some meaningful encapsulation of the key purpose of the process.

Figure 7.3 illustrates the graphical notation for each of these behavioural modelling constructs.

This is clearly a very simple notation. However, it can be used to conduct a substantial amount of modelling of system dynamics. An extended notation for behavioural modelling is formulated in Chapter 33.

Most real-life systems are too involved to represent as a single diagram. In representing systems, we therefore usually approach the problem in a top-down manner and decompose a system into subsystems, sub-subsystems, and so on. Each process on a system diagram could be considered as a subsystem and at least theoretically could be modelled by its own system diagram. This is the approach we took in Chapter 5 in portraying some of the major information subsystems in a generic IS architecture for a typical business organisation.

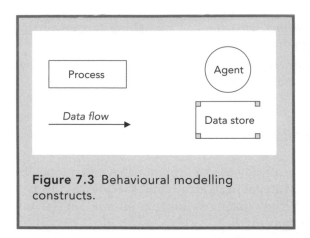

Figure 7.3 Behavioural modelling constructs.

Example ▐▐▐▶ Figure 4.1 uses only two constructs to model the warning network: agents and data flows. As such it constitutes a conceptual model of this information system. We can clearly model more of the information dynamics of the warning network by utilising the two other system modelling constructs, processes and data stores. To do this we need to generalise the key processes and data repositories of the system. This would constitute a logical model for the warning network as is represented in Figure 7.4.

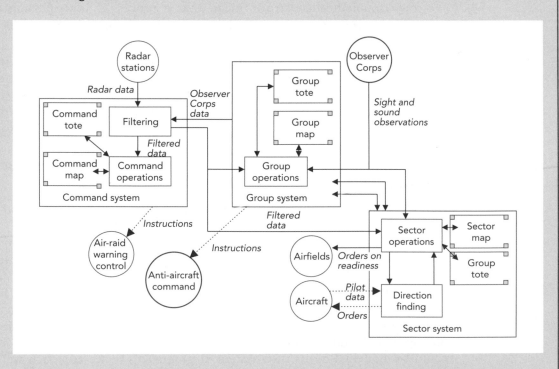

Figure 7.4 Logical model of the warning network (after Holwell and Checkland).

7.6 STRUCTURAL MODELLING

Behavioural modelling gives us a way of understanding and representing the activities of data manipulation and the data flow through information systems. Another crucial element of any information system is the way in which data is structured or organised. Structural modelling gives us the means for understanding and representing this issue of data structure.

A common approach for representing data structure is by using the constructs of entities, relationships and attributes:

- *Entity*. An entity is a thing of interest from some domain about which we wish to store data.
- *Relationship*. A relationship is an association between two or more entities.
- *Attribute*. An attribute is a property of some entity.

Figure 7.5 illustrates a graphic notation for each of these structural modelling constructs. Entities are represented by labelled boxes, attributes by labels within the entity box and relationships by lines drawn between boxes.

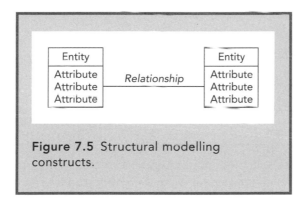

Figure 7.5 Structural modelling constructs.

Two sets of rules may be attached to relationships to model some of the business rules in an information system:

- *Cardinality*. Cardinality establishes how many instances of one entity are related to how many instances of another entity. A relationship may be one-to-one, one-to-many or many-to-many.
- *Optionality*. Optionality establishes whether all instances of an entity must participate in a relationship or not.

Example III➡ Consider the relationship *teaches* between a lecturer and a module. A lecturer may teach many education modules and each module may be taught by more than one lecturer. Hence the cardinality of this relationship is many-to-many. The optionality of the lecturer entity in the teaches relationship is probably mandatory. This means that every lecturer must teach on at least one module. The optionality of the module entity in this relationship is probably also mandatory in the sense that all modules must have an assigned lecturer to teach them.

Figure 7.6 illustrates a possible graphic notation for representing cardinality and optionality. The asterisk (*) in each set of brackets indicates a many state for cardinality.

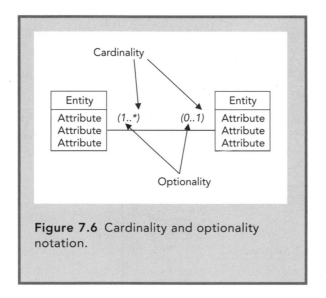

Figure 7.6 Cardinality and optionality notation.

Example ▐▐▐▶ Figure 7.7 illustrates a simple structural model for a student information system at a university. Take the relationship between the entity student and the entity course.

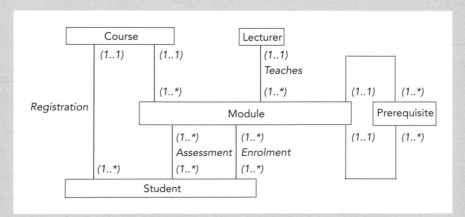

Figure 7.7 Structural model of a student information system.

The optionality represented indicates that a course must have at least one student and a student must register on a course. In terms of cardinality the relationship is one-to-many, indicating that many students take a course, but that a given student may register only for one course at one time.

7.7 OBJECT MODELLING

There is an obvious relationship between the forms of behavioural and structural modelling described above in the sense that a structural model will give us greater detail on the relationship between and structure of data stores on a behavioural model. Hence there is a correspondence between the data stores on a behavioural model and the entities, attributes and relationships on a structural model. However, this integration is quite loose and is reliant on the system modeller making such relationships explicit.

Object modelling developed as an attempt to integrate in one modelling approach both the dynamics of data and issues of data structure. An object model consists of a collection of objects. Objects can be seen as extended entities – entities with some behaviour specified. Object modelling works with the following constructs:

- *Object*. An object is anything having an independent existence from some UoD which we choose to model.
- *Object class*. An object class is an abstraction of the common features of a group of objects. Objects may have attributes, relationships and/or methods in common. Objects are not normally indicated on object models but their classes are.
- *Attribute*. An attribute is a property of some object class.
- *Relationship*. A relationship is some connection between object classes.
- *Method*. A method establishes some behaviour expected of an object class.

Figure 7.8 illustrates a possible graphic notation for each of the constructs of object modelling. We again use boxes for object classes and establish two

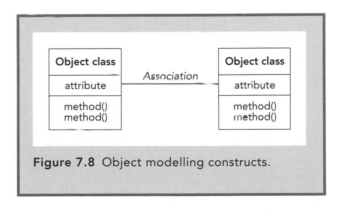

Figure 7.8 Object modelling constructs.

partitions within the box for attributes and methods. Lines are again used to represent relationships of association between classes.

In object modelling a relationship may be of one of three types:

- *Association*. An association relationship establishes a connection between the instances of classes and is defined by cardinality and optionality. Hence association relationships are commonplace on structural models as described in the previous section.

- *Generalisation*. This type of relationship establishes levels of abstraction between object classes. Generalisation is the process of extracting common features from a group of object classes and suppressing the detailed differences between object classes. In practice, generalisation allows us to declare certain object classes as sub-classes of other object classes.

- *Aggregation*. This type of relationship serves to collect together a set of different classes into one unit or aggregate. An aggregation relationship occurs between a whole and its parts. An aggregation is an abstraction in which a relationship between objects is considered as a higher-level object. This makes it possible to focus on the aggregate while suppressing low-level detail.

Examples ||||➡ In the UoD of the Stock Exchange, Stock and Share might be seen as sub-classes of a Security object. In a personnel UoD employee could be seen as a super-class of a manager and a technician class.

A financial portfolio can be considered as an aggregate of securities, insurance policies, and savings accounts. A country can be considered an aggregate of regions that are aggregates of counties which are aggregates of districts, and so on.

A graphical notation for generalisation and aggregation relationships is given in Figure 7.9. A triangle placed on a relationship indicates generalisation and a diamond indicates aggregation.

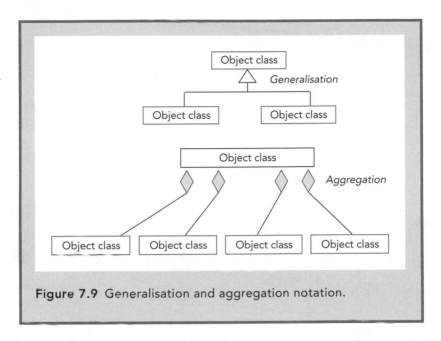

Figure 7.9 Generalisation and aggregation notation.

Example ⫸ Figure 7.10 illustrates a possible object model for share dealing on the Stock Exchange. Most of the relationships on this diagram are association relationships.

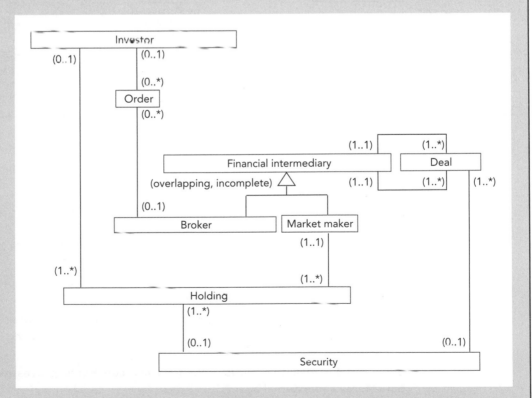

Figure 7.10 Stock Exchange object model.

One example of generalisation is given. A financial intermediary is said to be a super-class of a broker class and of a market maker class.

Behavioural abstraction is included in an object model in terms of methods. The difference between an entity and an object class lies in the specification of methods associated with an entity. We turn an entity into an object class by first drawing an interface around it. Then we write within the interface the names of the most important methods defined for the object.

Example ▐▐▐➡ Consider two object classes, BankAccount and Customer, in Figure 7.11. Six methods are defined for these classes: enrolCustomer, deleteCustomer, openAccount, creditAccount, debitAccount and closeAccount. These labels represent the so-called signatures for the methods. The actual behaviour of each method will have to be specified elsewhere.

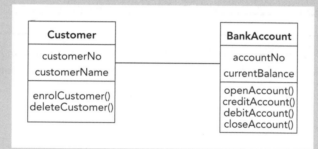

Figure 7.11 Methods on an object model.

7.8 ⊚ SUMMARY

- Modelling is an essential element of information systems work.
- Any modelling needs three elements: constructs, notation and principles of construction.
- Modelling is normally undertaken for three reasons: representation, communication and abstraction.
- Modelling approaches can be distinguished in terms of levels of abstraction: conceptual models, logical models and physical models.
- Modelling approaches can also be distinguished in terms of their coverage of particular aspects of an information system: structural modelling, behavioural modelling and object modelling.
- Behavioural modelling consists of the following constructs: processes, data flows, data stores and external agents.

- Structural modelling consists of the following constructs: entities, relationships and attributes.
- Object modelling consists of the following constructs: objects, classes, attributes and methods.

7.9 QUESTIONS

(i) Explain why modelling is important as an exercise.

(ii) Describe the major elements of a model.

(iii) Explain why graphical models are useful.

(iv) Distinguish between the extension, intension and designation of a concept.

(v) In what way do conceptual models differ from logical and physical models?

(vi) Distinguish between structural, behavioural and object modelling.

(vii) List the major constructs of structural modelling.

(viii) List the major constructs of behavioural modelling.

(ix) List the major constructs of object modelling.

7.10 EXERCISES

(i) Take a modelling approach such as one of those discussed in this chapter and separate out the issues of constructs, notation, and principles of construction.

(ii) Analyse the concept of a computer in terms of the ideas of extension, intension and designation.

(iii) Conceptual modelling is a particular phase of database development. Investigate the use of this term in the database area.

(iv) Develop a high-level behavioural model of an information system known to you.

(v) Develop a high-level structural model of an information system known to you.

(vi) Develop a high-level object model of an information system known to you.

7.11 PROJECTS

(i) Investigate the importance of the process of abstraction to successful information systems modelling work.

(ii) Compare two approaches to information systems modelling in terms of criteria such as coverage and ease of use.

(iii) Object modelling seems to be used much more frequently than data and process modelling to document systems. Investigate why this might be the case.

(iv) Investigate the suitability of object modelling for documenting organisation processes.

7.12 REFERENCE

Beynon-Davies, P. (1998). *Information Systems Development: an Introduction to Information Systems Engineering*, 3rd edn. Macmillan, London.

PART **2**

INFORMATION TECHNOLOGY

Any sufficiently advanced technology is indistinguishable from magic.

Arthur C. Clarke: *Technology and the Future*

- Software
- Hardware
- Data

- Communications technology
- Information technology system

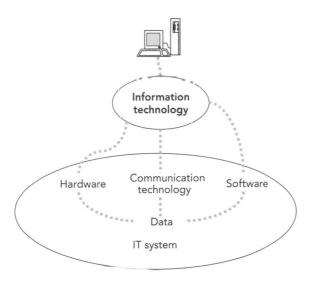

Information technology comprises artefacts for the collection, storage, dissemination and manipulation of data. As we have argued in Chapter 4, there are a variety of historical forms of IT. Modern IT is focused on the computer and related technologies.

Modern information systems are very reliant on information technology for their effective functioning. In this part we consider the four major elements of contemporary information technology:

- *Computer hardware*. This comprises the physical (hard) aspects of information technology consisting of processors, input devices and output devices (Chapter 8).

- *Computer software*. This comprises the non-physical (soft) aspects of information technology. Software is essentially programs – sets of instructions for controlling computer hardware (Chapter 9).

- *Data*. This constitutes a series of structures for storing data on peripheral devices such as hard disks. Such data is manipulated by programs and transmitted via communication technology (Chapter 10).

- *Communication technology*. This forms the interconnective tissue of information technology. Communication networks between computing devices are essential elements of the modern IT infrastructure of organisations (Chapter 11).

These four elements are component parts of most information technology systems (Chapter 12). Information technology systems are component elements of information systems.

CHAPTER 8

H A R D W A R E

Where a calculator on the ENIAC is equipped with 18,000 vacuum tubes and weighs 30 tons, computers in the future may have only 1,000 vacuum tubes and perhaps weigh 2 tons.

Popular Mechanics, March 1949

LEARNING OUTCOMES

After reading this chapter, you will be able to:

● Describe the history of the computer and the Turing machine

● Define the key elements of computer hardware

● Outline some of the ways of defining the capacity of a computer system

● Relate some of the developments in hardware

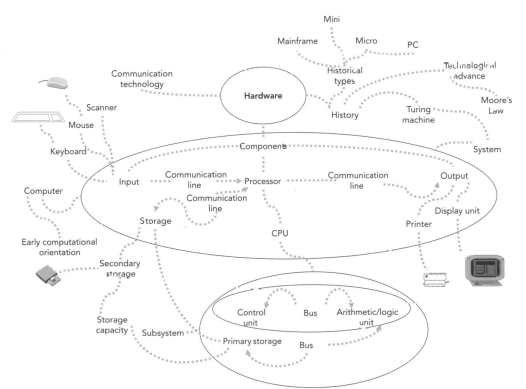

8.1 ⊚ INTRODUCTION

The term *hardware* is generally associated with electronic digital computers. The modern computer is a general-purpose machine for running computer software (Chapter 9). It stores data (Chapter 10), communicates with other devices (Chapter 11) and forms a critical element of a modern IT system (Chapter 12). A computer can be considered as a 'hard' system with its foundation in a theoretical machine known as a Turing machine. In this chapter we discuss the major elements of a computer system. We also discuss various types of computer system and some of the contemporary developments in hardware.

8.2 ⊚ HISTORICAL CONTEXT

The modern computer is an electronic device with the following critical properties:

- *Digital device*. The computer is a machine that works in discrete stages and stores data in discrete coding.
- *General-purpose*. The computer is a device designed to be used in a variety of situations.
- *Programmable*. As a consequence of its general-purpose nature, a computer must be programmed to behave appropriately in specific situations.

Like any technology, the modern computer emerged in a historical context. The earliest programmed digital machine was the punched-card loom invented by Jacquard in 1801. This device permitted the automatic digital process control of the production of woven figure fabrics. Charles Babbage applied the punched-card idea to program his 'Analytic Engine' in 1833, which contained all the elements of a truly automatic computer, but was never completed. In 1886 Herman Hollerith developed a successful electro-mechanical punched-card machine for tabulating census data at the US Bureau of Census.

Although the principles inherent in the modern computer were established in the 19th century it was only after the Second World War that rapid development occurred in building stored-program computers. Many attribute the developments in this area to the foundation of the Turing machine.

A modern-day computer is a physical implementation of an abstract machine known as a Turing machine, so called because it was proposed by Alan Turing in the 1930s. Turing conjectured that a Turing machine possesses the power to solve any problem that is solvable by computational means. Hence Turing machines are generally described as being 'universal' machines.

A Turing machine is made up of two parts: a control mechanism and an input medium. The control mechanism can be in one of a finite number of states at any time. One of these states is deemed to be the initial state and another the halt state of the machine.

The input medium was originally characterised as an infinitely long piece of paper tape. The machine is equipped with a tape head that is used to both read and write symbols on the paper tape. A machine can move the tape both backwards and forwards through the tape head.

The individual actions that can be performed by a Turing machine consist of write actions and move actions. A write operation consists of replacing a symbol on the tape with another symbol and then shifting to a new state. A move operation consists of moving the tape head one cell to the right or one cell to the left and then shifting to a new state. Which action will be performed at a particular time depends on the current symbol in the cell visible to the tape head as well as the current state of the machine's control mechanism.

Turing's original 'machine' was a human acting with pencil and paper. It was only with the advent of electronic equipment that the idea of Turing machines could be practically realised. However, the important point is that the theoretical computational abilities of the system remain the same regardless of the technology. In fact, Turing's model is more general than today's electronic computers, since a Turing machine is never restricted by lack of storage space (it uses a tape of infinite length), whereas an actual machine must employ finite storage, however great.

The other important characteristic of a Turing machine is that it demonstrated that any computational process can be 'programmed'. That is, a set of instructions can be given to such a machine to determine its behaviour. Alan Turing worked at Bletchley Park (Chapter 4) during the Second World War and contributed to the design of the early computing machines both there and subsequently at the University of Manchester.

The first large-scale fully automatic electro-mechanical digital computer was produced by IBM between 1937 and 1944 and became known as Mark 1. The first truly electronic digital computer – the Electronic Numerical Integrator and Calculator (ENIAC) was constructed between 1942 and 1945 at the University of Pennsylvania.

ENIAC went commercial in 1951. Called the UNIVAC-1 it proved successful in processing the 1950 US census. This led to an explosion of commercial machines leading to the dominance of the IBM 360/370 mainframe computer in 1964.

The invention of micro-electronics in the early 1970s led eventually to the fall of the corporate mainframe. First minicomputers were introduced during the 1970s, offering powerful computing at more affordable pricing. Then microcomputers (renamed personal computers) were introduced during the 1980s, offering computer power on the desktop.

8.3 THE COMPONENTS OF HARDWARE

A modern computer can be considered as a system with four main subsystems: input, processing, storage and output (Figure 8.1).

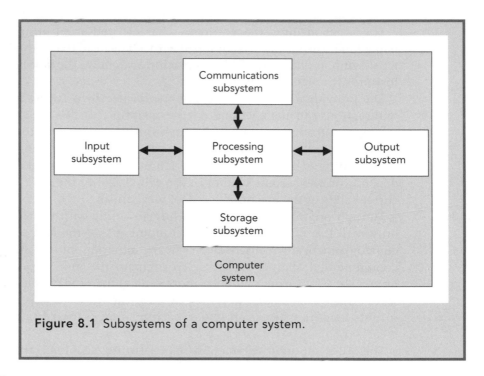

Figure 8.1 Subsystems of a computer system.

8.4   INPUT SUBSYSTEM

Input to a computer is achieved through a variety of input devices. Such input devices make up the input subsystem of a computer system. As a result of digital convergence there have emerged a proliferation of input devices able to connect to computers. Devices are clearly specialised in terms of the type of data being captured. Computers are now able to capture data from multiple media: character-based data, sound, images, graphics and movement.

- *Character-based input devices* include keyboards and point of sale (POS) devices.
- *Image-based input devices* include digital cameras and scanners.
- *Sound-based input devices* include microphones and voice-recognition devices.
- *Movement-based input devices* include computer mice, touch-sensitive screens and joysticks.
- *Graphics-based input devices* include graphics tablets.

8.5   PROCESSING SUBSYSTEM

The processing subsystem is known as the central processing unit (CPU). This subsystem is the workhorse of a computing system. The central processing unit can be subdivided into the following components (Figure 8.2):

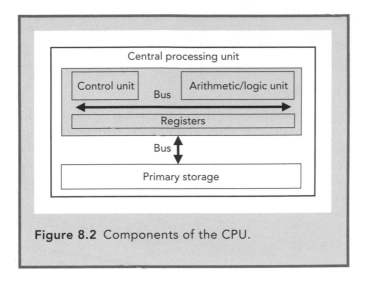

Figure 8.2 Components of the CPU.

- The *Control Unit* directs and coordinates the rest of the system in carrying out program instructions.
- The *Logic Unit* calculates and compares data, based on instructions from the controller.
- The *Primary Storage Unit* holds data for processing, instructions for processing and processed data waiting to be output.
- *Registers* are high-speed storage areas used to temporarily hold small units of program instructions and data immediately before, after and during execution of the processing unit.
- Communication between these three components is effected by physical connections known as *buses*.

Computers are instructed by programs. Programs are composed of a sequence of instructions. A computer operates by taking each instruction in turn and executing the instruction. Operation therefore involves two phases: an instruction phase and an execution phase. In the instruction phase the computer's control unit fetches the instruction from memory. Then the instruction is decoded to enable the central processor to understand what is to be done. In the execution phase the logic unit does what it is instructed to do, making either an arithmetic computation or a logical comparison. The results of the execution are then stored in the registers or in memory. A machine cycle constitutes the combination of the instruction and execution phases.

8.6 STORAGE SUBSYSTEM

The storage subsystem is used as a repository for data used by the processing subsystem. Data is stored in the storage subsystem for short-term or long-term use.

Data for short-term use is stored in so-called primary storage. Data for long-term use is stored in secondary storage.

8.6.1 PRIMARY STORAGE

Primary storage is sometimes referred to as main memory. Primary storage includes media that can be directly acted upon by the central processing unit (CPU) of the computer, such as main memory or cache memory. Primary storage usually provides fast access to relatively low volumes of data. Main memory is referred to as volatile memory because the data is lost when the power supply of the computer system is switched off.

8.6.2 SECONDARY STORAGE

Secondary storage cannot be processed directly by the CPU. It hence provides slower access than primary storage, but can handle much larger volumes of data. Secondary storage is referred to as non-volatile storage because it persists after power loss.

A number of hardware devices are used for secondary storage:

- *Magnetic tape*, similar in nature to that used in audio cassettes.
- *Magnetic disks*, such as so-called 'hard' disk drives and 'floppy' disk drives – thus named because the magnetic media used in these devices were originally made of hard and soft materials respectively.
- *Optical discs* such as Compact Disc Read-Only Memory (CD-ROM) drives and DVD (digital versatile disc) drives.

The most basic unit of data stored on a storage device is the bit (0 or 1). To code information, bits are grouped together in bytes – a fixed length of 8 bits. A word is a multiple of bytes and varies in length from one computer to another – typically 16, 32 or 64 bits making up a word. The capacity of a storage device is typically expressed as the number of bytes it can store. Disk capacities are normally described in terms of kilobytes (kbyte: approximately 1 thousand bytes), megabytes (Mbyte: approximately 1 million bytes), gigabytes (Gbyte: approximately 1 billion bytes) or terabytes (Tbyte: approximately 1 trillion bytes).

8.7 OUTPUT SUBSYSTEM

Output from a computer is achieved through a variety of output devices. Such output devices make up the output subsystem of a computer system. As a result of digital convergence there have emerged a proliferation of output devices able to connect to computers. Devices are clearly specialised in terms of the type of data being output. Typical output devices include:

- *Sound-based output devices*, such as speakers
- *Movement-based output devices*, such as robotic devices or other forms of moving machinery
- *Character-based, image-based and graphics-based output devices*, such as monitors and printers

8.8 COMMUNICATION SUBSYSTEM

The communications subsystem is a specialised form of input/output subsystem concerned with connecting a computer system to computer networks (see Chapter 11). Connection may be made by using a standard telecommunications infrastructure, such as the telephone network, or a dedicated network.

8.9 CAPACITY OF A COMPUTER SYSTEM

A number of concepts are used to indicate the performance or capacity of some computer system:

- *Machine cycle time*. This is the time in which a machine cycle occurs. It is typically measured in fractions of a second – microseconds (one-millionth of a second), nanoseconds (one-billionth of a second) or picoseconds (one trillionth of a second). Cycle time is also measured in terms of millions of instructions per second, or MIPS.
- *Clock speed*. Each CPU produces a series of electronic pulses at a predetermined rate called the clock speed. The clock speed affects the cycle time. Clock speed is usually measured in megahertz (MHz) – a hertz is one cycle per second.
- *Word length*. The word length is the number of bits that a computer can process at one time. It is a characteristic of a computer's CPU. Typically this is 16 bits, 32 bits or, more recently, 64 bits. A 32-bit CPU will process 32 bits of data in one machine cycle.
- *Storage capacity*. The capacity of both primary and secondary storage is usually defined in terms of the number of bytes that can be stored. A typical floppy disk will store from kbytes to Mbytes of data, hard disks for personal computers typically hold from Mbytes to Gbytes of data, and disk packs used in mini and mainframe systems typically store Gbytes to Tbytes of data.

The capacity in each of these areas has increased dramatically over the period from the invention of the modern computer after the Second World War. In the 1960s, Gordon Moore, the chairman of the board of Intel (a processor manufacturer) formulated what is now known as Moore's Law. Basically this states that processor density – the number of switching devices on a silicon chip – will double every 18 months. This has held true for over four decades and is likely to continue for a few years yet.

8.10 ⊚ COMPUTER SYSTEM TYPES

Broadly speaking we may distinguish between three major types of computer system:

- *Personal computers*. These were originally called microcomputers and now are frequently referred to as desktop computers because of their primary use as an individual work tool. Processor speeds for personal computers generally lie in the range 5–20 MIPs. The main memory capacity of such machines generally fall in the range 16–128 Mbyte.

- *Minicomputers*. The term *minicomputer* has now fallen into disuse. The term *midrange computers* indicates their use as collaboration tools for a department or a small organisation. Typical processor speeds generally lie in the range 25–100 MIPs. Main memory capacities fall in the range 32–512 Mbyte.

- *Mainframe computers*. Mainframe computers are now also referred to as superservers to emphasise their main use as a major collaboration tool for an organisation. Processor speeds for mainframes generally lie in the range 40–5000 MIPs. Main memory capacity falls in the range 256–1024 Mbyte.

8.11 ⊚ SUMMARY

- A computer system has a history in a theoretical concept known as a Turing machine.
- A computer system is made up of five major subsystems: an input subsystem, an output subsystem, a processing subsystem, a storage subsystem and a communications subsystem.
- The input subsystem consists of a number of devices which capture data for the computer system.
- The processing subsystem is the workhorse of the computer system.
- The output subsystem consists of a number of devices which output data from a computer system.
- The communications subsystem is a specialised form of input/output subsystem concerned with connecting a computer system to computer networks.
- The capacity of a computer system can be defined in terms of such factors such as cycle time, clock speed, word length and storage capacity.
- Broadly speaking we may distinguish between three major types of computer system: personal computers, midrange computers and mainframe computers.

8.12 ⊚ QUESTIONS

(i) Describe the three high-level properties of the modern computer.

(ii) List the five component subsystems of a computer system.

  (iii) Describe the component elements of a central processing unit.

  (iv) Define the terms cycle time, word length and storage capacity.

   (v) Distinguish between primary and secondary storage.

  (vi) List the major forms of input and output device.

 (vii) Distinguish between personal computers, midrange computers and mainframe computers.

8.13 EXERCISES

   (i) The Turing machine is frequently described as an abstract machine. Investigate the precise meaning of the term *abstract machine*.

  (ii) Find a description of some computer. Describe the computer in terms of its major input, processing and output systems.

 (iii) Describe some computer system known to you in terms of features such as its cycle time, word length and storage capacity.

  (iv) Identify the range of computers in some organisation and classify them in terms of the levels discussed in this chapter.

8.14 PROJECTS

   (i) Conduct an assessment of the hardware used by a particular organisation. Develop policy guidelines for a standard hardware profile for the organisation.

  (ii) Smart cards are now being used as a key data capture device for transactional data. Investigate the increasing use of smart cards for this purpose.

 (iii) Investigate the idea of pervasive computing and determine its likely impact on organisational informatics.

  (iv) Investigate the current predictions for processing power over the next decade in terms of its impact on organisational informatics.

SOFTWARE

All programmers are playwrights and all computers are lousy actors.

Anonymous

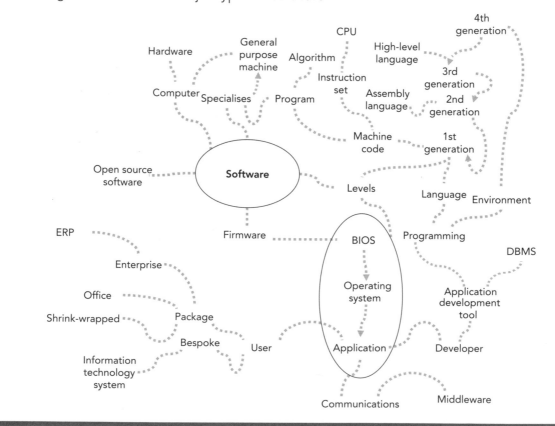

9.1 INTRODUCTION

The term *software* is generally used to describe computer programs. A computer program is a series of instructions for hardware. Computer programs transform the universal machine embodied in hardware (Chapter 8) into a machine specialised for some task. Programs are written using a formal language (Chapter 2). Suites of programs designed for specialised tasks form the software architecture of some IT system (Chapter 12). In this chapter we consider some of the major types of software run on computer systems.

9.2 CHARACTER SETS AND INSTRUCTION SETS

A program is a sequence of instructions given to a computer. Programs must be written in some formal language (see Chapter 2) known as a programming language. All software is essentially programs.

Instructions need a scheme for representation in a computer system. A representation scheme equates to a character set. Since the modern computer is a digital machine, a character set is effectively a way of coding certain symbols into a string of bits. Symbols are called characters and consist of letters, digits, punctuation and non-printing characters such as control characters. One of the standard character sets is ASCII – American Standard Code for Information Interchange. This constitutes a standard coding system for characters adopted for most computer systems.

Example ||||➡ In ASCII the capital A is represented by the binary string 10100001.

The binary string 10100001 constitutes a word. A word is a group of bits that a computer's CPU treats as a single unit. The standard size of a word depends on the computer system. Typically the modern computer would have a word length of 32 bits.

Along with a character set a computer system needs an instruction set. An instruction set constitutes a complete set of instructions used by a particular type of processor.

Example ||||➡ A common instruction is the *fetch* instruction. This causes the processor to retrieve the next machine language instruction from main memory and load it into the instruction register in the control unit.

9.3 PROGRAMMING LANGUAGES

Programming languages are used to describe algorithms – i.e. sequences of steps that lead to the solution of a well-defined problem. Programming languages are broadly classified into two groups: low-level languages and high-level languages. Low-level languages are close to machine languages. They demonstrate a strong correspondence between the operations implemented by the language and the operations implemented by the underlying hardware. High-level languages in contrast are closer to human natural languages. Each statement in a high-level language will be equivalent to many statements of a low-level language. The key advantage offered by high-level languages is therefore abstraction. As the level of abstraction increases the programmer needs to be less and less concerned about the hardware on which a program runs and more and more concerned with the problems of the application. Hence the trend has been to build more and more abstraction into programming languages.

We may therefore distinguish between three levels of programming language in terms of abstraction capability:

- *Machine code.* This is the earliest form of programming language, only one step removed from the binary code used by the machine to perform instructions. Hence it is also known as a first generation language.

- *Assembly language.* This was the first attempt to abstract out detail of the machine and provide the programmer with a more powerful set of symbolic instructions with which to write programs. Assembly languages are second generation languages.

- *High-level languages* (also known as third generation languages). These are meant to be general-purpose programming languages further removed from machine implementation. Such languages can be divided into further groupings such as procedural languages (FORTRAN, COBOL, C), functional languages (LISP), logic programming languages (PROLOG), and object-oriented languages (Smalltalk, C++, Java). Procedural languages are by far the most widely used for information systems development, although object-oriented languages in particular are beginning to have some influence in the development domain.

Example ⫸   Most procedural programming languages are built out of two constructs: statements and control structures:

Statements are the basic instructions of high-level languages. Statements are command lines built from a mixture of keywords, variables and constants. For example:

```
balance := balance + credit;
READ (credit);
WRITELN ('Balance is', balance);
```

The first statement assigns the summation of the values held in the two placeholders or variables, balance and credit, to the placeholder on the left of the := sign. The second statement reads a value from a file into a variable. The third statement writes a string to the terminal screen.

Control structures are used to control the flow of execution of statements. Control structures come in three major forms: sequences, conditions and loops.

Sequences are logical sets of statements. Many imperative languages encase sequences in the keywords BEGIN and END to form a block. For example:

```
BEGIN
   balance := balance + credit;
   WRITELN ('Balance is', balance);
END;
```

Conditions allow selection among alternatives. For example:

```
IF credit > 0 THEN balance := balance + credit;
```

Loops are the mechanisms of iteration. For example, in a countable loop the iteration is performed a specified number of times, as below:

```
FOR count := 1 to 10 DO
   BEGIN
      READ (credit);
      balance := balance + credit;
      count := count + 1
   END;
```

There are also a range of specialised formal languages used for particular information technology purposes. One of the most important types of such languages for information systems is the so-called database sub-language. These are not full programming languages, but are designed for managing access to databases (Chapter 10).

Example ▐▐▐▶ The most commonplace example of a specialised IT language is SQL – structured query language. This database sub-language forms the standard interface to relational database systems. An example of a query written in SQL is given below:

```
SELECT *
FROM Modules
WHERE courseCode = 'CSD'
```

This query retrieves data from all the columns in a table named modules where the courseCode for the module matches the code CSD.

9.4 ⊚ TYPES OF SOFTWARE

In terms of a typical IT system it is useful to delineate three major levels of software. This forms the software architecture of some IT system (see Figure 9.1):

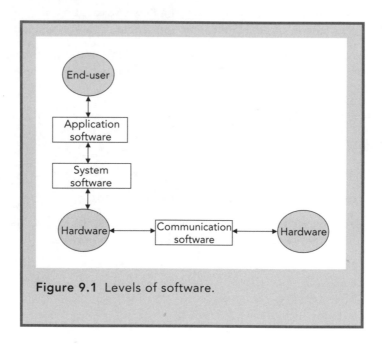

Figure 9.1 Levels of software.

- *System software.* System software refers to that collection of programs which coordinate the activities of hardware and all programs running on the computer system. System software acts as an interface between application software and hardware. The most important type of system software is the operating system. This is a piece of software that supervises the running of all other programs on some hardware. The operating system undertakes tasks such as scheduling the running of programs, controlling input and output to programs, and managing files on secondary storage.

- *Communication software.* This is a special type of software used to enable inter-communication between different computing devices in a network (Chapter 11).

- *Application software.* A software application or application system is normally used as another term for an information technology system. An application system is a system, normally written using some language or tool-set, and designed to perform a particular set of tasks for some organisation.

9.5 SYSTEM SOFTWARE

System software is that software that manages the computer system's resources. System software includes operating systems, programming language compilers and utility programs such as virus protection software.

An operating system is a complex program that controls the execution of other programs. It also manages the use of other resources such as data storage within a computer system.

In terms of processing an operating system will:

- Run several tasks simultaneously taking into account the priorities assigned to each task
- Service many different users working on-line at the same time and prevent interference between these multiple users
- Interface to communication software enabling it to connect with other computers and computing devices such as peripherals

In terms of data the operating system will:
- Maintain file systems for the storage of data and programs
- Ensure the consistency of access to file systems
- Control access to data and programs

9.6 COMMUNICATION SOFTWARE

One of the key objectives of most computer networks is to achieve high levels of connectivity. Connectivity is the ability of computer systems to communicate with each other and share data. For connectivity, standards must be defined to enable communication between sender and receiver. Such standards are embodied in communication software.

One approach to developing higher connectivity amongst systems is by using the idea of open systems. Open systems are built on public domain operating systems, user interfaces, application standards and networking standards. One of the oldest examples of an open systems model for communications is TCP/IP (The Transmission Control Protocol/Internet Protocol). This was developed by the US Department of Defense in 1972. TCP/IP is the communications software model underlying the Internet. A protocol is a statement that explains how a specific networking task should be performed. TCP/IP divides the communication process into five layers of network tasks:

- *Application*. The application layer is that closest to the network user. The application layer provides data entry and presentation functionality to the end-user of the network.

- *Transport/TCP.* This layer breaks application data up into TCP packets known as datagrams. Each packet consists of a header comprising the address of the sending computer, data for reassembling the data and error-checking data.

- *Internet protocol.* This layer receives datagrams from the TCP layer and breaks the packets down further. An IP packet contains a header with an address and carries TCP information and data in the body of the packet. The IP layer routes the individual packets from the sender to the receiver.

- *Network.* This handles addressing issues, usually within the operating system, as well as providing an interface between the computer and the network. Each device on a network will normally have a unique ID (an IP number) assigned to it – represented in the network interface of each device.

- *Physical.* Defines the basic characteristics of signal transmission along communication networks.

Two different computer systems using TCP/IP are able to communicate with each other even though they may be based on different hardware and software platforms. Data sent from one computer passes down through the five layers. Once the data reaches the receiving computer it travels up through the layers. If the receiving computer finds a damaged packet it requests the sending computer to send again. This process is illustrated in Figure 9.2.

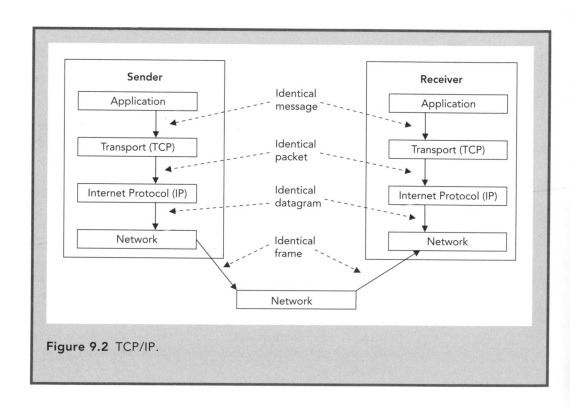

Figure 9.2 TCP/IP.

9.7 APPLICATION SOFTWARE

Application software can be distinguished in terms of the number of people that use the software:

- *Personal productivity software*, such as word processing packages, is software designed for individual use.
- *Workgroup software* (sometimes known as groupware) such as electronic mail systems is designed to be used by groups of users working together on some task.
- *Enterprise software* is designed to be used across the major part of the organisation or the entire enterprise. Classic accounting systems are examples of this type of software. Enterprise resource planning software is an integrated suite of enterprise software.

We can also distinguish between software that has been produced for the mass market, so-called *shrink-wrapped software*, and software that has been produced specifically for the purposes of some organisation, so-called *bespoke software*. Falling between these two poles is the class of software known as *packaged software*. This is software which is written to handle some generic organisational function such as order processing, but which is tailorable to the specific needs of some organisation.

Some software is designed for use by development practitioners such as programming languages (Chapter 26). Much software is produced for various groups of users. Some is specialised software such as that used for computer-aided design/engineering.

9.8 SOFTWARE DISTRIBUTION AND PRICING

There are a number of different models for software distribution and pricing:

- *Direct purchase*. Software is packaged and sold as a unit with a fixed price. This is normally used for shrink-wrapped software.
- *Leasing*. Here the software is paid for as used. The software remains the property of the software vendor but is hired from the vendor for use. This is normally appropriate for substantial cost enterprise software.
- *Application Service Provision (ASP)*. A software service is provided as an application. The ASP runs the application for the customer. This is normally used for the provision of standard software services, such as payroll.
- *Freeware*. Some software is available free from suppliers. Programmers develop this software out of interest and distribute it free, usually via the Internet. The Open Source software movement is a pressure group challenging cost models of software distribution.

Examples ▐▐▐➤ The classic example of direct purchase models is the range of shrink-wrapped software supplied by Microsoft. The classic example of freeware is the operating system Linux, which relies on a world-wide consortium of dedicated and enthusiastic developers for its development and maintenance.

9.9 ⊚ SUMMARY

- Computers need instruction sets and character sets.
- Programming languages are used to implement programs – a specification of some algorithm in the instructions of some formal language.
- There are three levels of programming language: machine code, assembly language and high-level language.
- We may also distinguish between three major levels of software: system software, communication software and application software.
- Application software is either personal productivity software, workgroup software or enterprise software.
- Software can be provided by direct purchase, through leasing, in terms of application service provision or as shareware.

9.10 ⊚ QUESTIONS

(i) Why is software programs?

(ii) Distinguish between a character set and an instruction set.

(iii) Describe the three levels of programming language.

(iv) What is meant by a database sub-language?

(v) Distinguish between system software, communication software and application software.

(vi) What is meant by personal productivity software, workgroup software and enterprise software?

(vii) Describe the major forms of software distribution.

9.11 ⊚ EXERCISES

(i) EBCDIC is another well-known character set. Investigate how this character set differs from ASCII.

(ii) Some computer processors are described as RISC, or reduced instruction set, processors. Investigate what this means.

(iii) Investigate the primary differences between procedural programming languages and object-oriented programming languages.

(iv) Consider some computer environment known to you. Find out what systems, communications and applications software runs in the environment.

(v) Investigate what software is available under the Open Software movement.

9.12 PROJECTS

(i) Conduct an inventory of the software used in an organisation known to you. Categorise the inventory in terms of the distinctions made in this chapter.

(ii) Investigate the degree of standardisation of software amongst a range of organisations. How important is standardisation to a successful IT infra-structure?

(iii) Investigate the total cost of ownership problem in relation to a chosen organisation.

(iv) Determine the likely success of the open software movement.

CHAPTER 10

DATA

It is a capital mistake to theorise before one has data. Insensibly one begins to twist facts to suit theories, instead of theories to suit facts.

Sir Arthur Conan Doyle (1859–1930): *A Scandal in Bohemia* (1891)

LEARNING OUTCOMES

After reading this chapter, you will be able to:

- Relate the issue of data representation
- Describe the concepts of data types and multimedia data
- Discuss the issue of data storage
- Define the functionality of a software system known as a DBMS

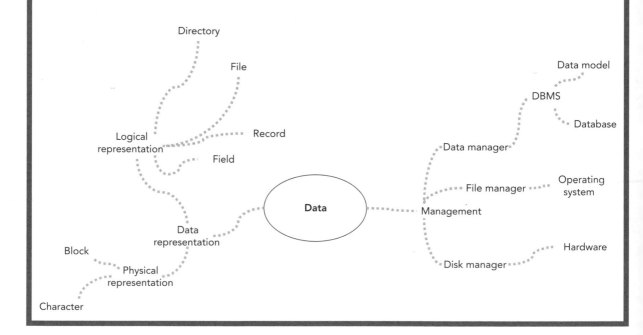

10.1 INTRODUCTION

Most information system applications are typified by reasonably straightforward processing of large amounts of structured data. So-called databases are therefore a common component of IT systems. In this chapter we consider how data is represented and structured on computing devices. We consider how operating systems organise and store data and how a special piece of software known as a DBMS is centrally important to modern IT systems. More detail on data technology is provided in Beynon-Davies (2000).

10.2 DATA REPRESENTATION

Data is symbols (Chapter 2). Data has to be represented in some way for storage and manipulation by computer hardware and software and for transmission by communication technology. We may distinguish two levels of data representation: logical representation and physical representation. Logical representation of data is used primarily by computer software. Physical representation of data is used primarily by computer hardware.

10.2.1 LOGICAL DATA REPRESENTATION

Logical data representation is that form of representation used by system and application software (Chapter 9). In terms of operating systems such as Microsoft Windows, data is represented using constructs such as records, files, file types and folders or directories. In terms of database management systems or DBMS (see below) data may be represented in terms of constructs such as databases, tables and rows.

Data is usually stored logically in the form of the data structures of some operating system or DBMS. Each data structure consists of a collection of data elements. A data element is a collection of related data values or data items. Each data item will be of a given data type. A data type amounts to a format for data items. Figure 10.1 illustrates this hierarchy of logical data structures.

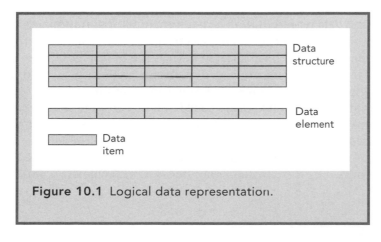

Figure 10.1 Logical data representation.

Example ▐▐▐▶ One of the most popular forms of logical data representation is that used in relational databases. The one and only data structure in a relational database is the table. Each table is made up of a number of data elements called rows and each row is made of a number of data items known as columns. Each row in the table is identified by values in one or more columns of the table and is called the table's primary key. Values in columns may also act as links to data contained in other tables. Such columns are called foreign keys.

Two tables are contained in the database below. Both the modules and the lecturers tables have two columns each. ModuleName is the primary key of the modules table and staffNo is the primary key of the lecturers table. The modules table contains a foreign key staffNo that references the primary key of the lecturers table.

Modules	
moduleName	staffNo
Relational Database Systems	234
Relational Database Design	234
Relational Database Design	234
Deductive Databases	345

Lecturers	
staffNo	staffName
234	Davies T
345	Evans R

10.2.2 PHYSICAL DATA REPRESENTATION

Physical data representation is that form of representation used by computer hardware. The computer is a digital electronic device. The base form of representation in a computer and its associated devices is a binary notation. At its lowest fundamental level symbols are coded as strings of 0s and 1s in an information technology system. Therefore data, just like instructions (Chapter 9), is represented in a computer by character strings coded in terms of some character set. A character set is a uniform type of coding scheme for computing devices. The symbols coded are referred to as characters, words or bytes and consist of letters, digits, punctuation and non-printing characters, such as control characters. The length of a word is determined by a particular computer system. Typically a word will consist of 32 bits.

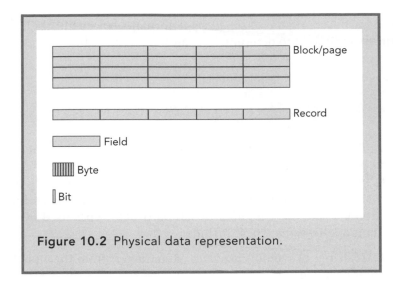

Figure 10.2 Physical data representation.

The capacity of some storage device is frequently expressed in terms of the maximum number of bytes it can store. A byte consists of 8 bits. Capacities are normally described in terms of kilobytes (kbyte: 1 approximately thousand bytes), megabytes (Mbyte: approximately 1 million bytes), gigabytes (Gbyte: approximately 1 billion bytes), or terabytes (Tbyte: approximately 1 trillion bytes).

The main unit of physical storage is the block or page (Figure 10.2). A block is a contiguous area of space on some storage device. Operating systems will generally use an intermediate construct of a file to manage data. Files are made up of a number of records and records are made up of a number of fields.

Files and records have to be mapped onto blocks, since blocks are the physical unit of transfer between hardware and software. Usually, the record size will be less than the block size, meaning that many records will be stored in each block (Figure 10.3). Consequently, a file will be made up of many blocks, frequently, but not

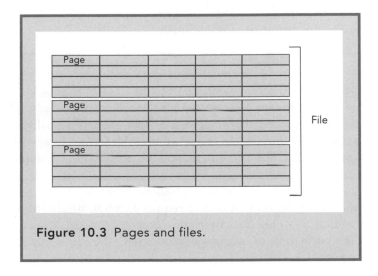

Figure 10.3 Pages and files.

necessarily, contiguous. Each file will normally have a file header. This will contain information used to determine the addresses of file blocks and information about the structure of records.

10.3 DATA TYPES AND MULTIMEDIA DATA

Most data needed in commercial information systems is what we might call standard data. Standard data is defined in terms of a number of standard data types. A data type acts as a categorisation of data and defines not only the format of some data item but also the allowable set of operations we may perform on the data in the item. There are a number of standard data types used by most information systems applications. These include:

- *Text*. Strings of symbols made up of characters from the alphabet and a range of other characters.
- *Numbers*. These include integer, decimal and real numbers.
- *Units of time*. These include dates, seconds, minutes and hours.

Example ⫸ Clearly it is important for a computer system to know the type of data it is dealing with. For instance, it makes sense to add two integers such as 1 and 2 together. It makes very little sense to add the character A to the character B. Hence a number data type will allow addition, but a text data type will disallow it.

Information systems are now being used to capture, store and manipulate far more complex data types than the standard data types discussed above. This is to enable such systems to handle different media. Such complex data types include:
- *Images*. Graphics and photographic images
- *Audio*. Various forms of sound data
- *Video*. Various forms of moving image

Example ⫸ These forms of complex or multimedia data need different coding schemes or formats to enable the representation of this data in digital form. For instance, images are coded in terms of pixels. A pixel is a picture element. A high-resolution computer monitor can be considered as a 1024×768 grid in which each cell of the grid is a pixel. To represent an image we therefore need to store for each pixel in the image its colour. For a complete monitor over 700,000 pixels are needed.

Information systems are now also required to handle complex data structures as well as well as complex data items or elements. Organisations want to be able to define the structure of documentation that they use for communication. A document such as an invoice or a contract is a complex data structure in that it may be made up of text, numeric data and images. Also different organisations may use different formats for such documents. Hence there is pressure on organisations in the same industrial sector to develop standards for such documentation. Such standards are being specified using a formal language know as XML – extensible markup language. XML is a variant of the Internet language HTML (Chapter 11) and is discussed in more detail in Chapter 45.

10.4 DATA MANAGEMENT

Traditionally, data management in information technology systems has been the domain of the file system managed by the operating system. During the 1970s a type of software started being used for the higher-level management of data: database management systems or DBMS. DBMS are software systems for managing databases.

10.4.1 DATABASE

A database is an organised repository for data having the following properties:

- *Data sharing*. A database is normally accessible by more than one person, perhaps at the same time.
- *Data integration*. One major responsibility of database usage is to ensure that the data is integrated. This implies that a database should be a collection of data that has no unnecessarily duplicated or redundant data.
- *Data integrity*. Another responsibility arising as a consequence of shared data is that a database should display integrity. In other words, the database should accurately reflect the universe of discourse that it is attempting to model.
- *Data security*. One of the major ways of ensuring the integrity of a database is by restricting access; in other words, securing the database. The main way this is done in contemporary database systems is by defining in some detail a set of authorised users of the whole, or more usually parts, of the database
- *Data abstraction*. A database can be viewed as a model of reality. The information stored in a database is usually an attempt to represent the properties of some objects in the real world.
- *Data independence*. One immediate consequence of abstraction is the idea of buffering data from the processes that use such data. The ideal is to achieve a situation where data organisation is transparent to the users or application programs that feed off data.

10.4.2   DBMS

A database management system (DBMS) is an organised set of facilities for accessing and maintaining one or more databases. A DBMS is a shell which surrounds a database and through which all interactions with the database take place. The interactions catered for by most existing DBMS fall into four main groups:

- *Structural maintenance*: adding new data structures to the database; removing data structures from the database; modifying the format of existing data structures.
- *Transaction processing*: managing logical units of work: inserting new data into existing data structures; updating data in existing data structures; deleting data from existing data structures.
- *Information retrieval*: extracting data from existing data structures for use by end-users; extracting data for use by application programs.
- *Database administration*: creating and monitoring users of the database; restricting access to data structures in the database; monitoring the performance of databases.

10.4.3   DBMS, FILE MANAGER AND DISK MANAGER

The module of software concerned with the management of pages on disk is sometimes known as the disk manager. That module of software concerned with the management of files for the operating system is sometimes known as the file manager. When a file is created, the file manager needs to request a set of blocks from the disk manager. For instance, suppose we work in an environment in which the blocks are fixed at 4 kbyte (4K). A 60K file will therefore need 15 blocks, and therefore the file manager requests a set of 15 blocks from the disk manager. The set of blocks is given a logical identifier – blocksetID – and each block within the set is assigned a logical ID, usually just its position within the block set. The file manager knows nothing of the physical storage of data on disk. It merely issues logical block requests (consisting of blocksetIDs and blockIDs) to the disk manager.

The disk manager translates the logical block requests from the file manager into physical blockIDs. The disk manager will usually maintain information about the correspondence between logical and physical blockIDs and will contain all the code used to control the disk device.

Figure 10.4 illustrates the process by which a DBMS communicates with an operating system's file manager, which in turn issues requests to the disk manager. The DBMS has to translate requests against the constructs of a particular data model (e.g. tables) into requests for files from disk.

10.4.4   DATA MODELS

Any database and DBMS adheres to a particular data model. A data model is an architecture for data. It describes the general structure of how data is organised.

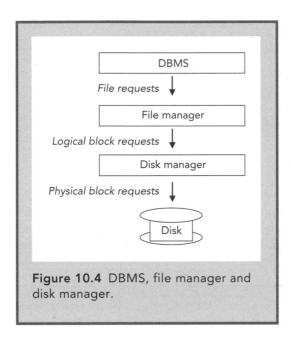

Figure 10.4 DBMS, file manager and disk manager.

Probably the most popular of the data models is the relational data model. A data model is generally held to be made up of three components:

- *Data definition*. This comprises a set of data structures. In the relational data model there is only one data structure – the table, or relation.
- *Data manipulation*. This comprises a set of data operators for the insertion of data, the removal of data, the retrieval of data and the amendment of data in data structures. The relational data model has a collection of such operators known as the relational algebra.
- *Data integrity*. This comprises a set of integrity rules that must form part of the database. Integrity is enforced in a database through the application of integrity constraints or rules. In the relational data model there are three types of such rules: entity integrity rules, referential integrity rules and domain integrity rules.

Example ▐▐▐▶ As far as the modules and lecturers tables described above are concerned, data definition corresponds to specifying the structure of these tables. Data manipulation involves entering a new module or lecturer, deleting a module or lecturer row or amending the data in one of the columns of the tables.

Entity integrity merely states that every table should have a primary key such as staffNo in lecturers. Referential integrity states that every foreign key value, such as for staffNo in the modules table, must refer to a primary key value in the database.

10.5 TYPES OF DATABASE APPLICATION

As we have indicated above, databases are arguably the most important contemporary component of an information technology system. In such systems databases serve three primary purposes: as production tools, as tools for supporting decision-making and as tools for deploying data around the organisation.

10.5.1 PRODUCTION DATABASES

Such databases are used to collect operational or production data. Production databases are used to support standard organisational functions by providing reliable, timely and valid data. The primary usage of such databases include the creating, reading, updating and deleting of data – sometimes referred to as the CRUD activities.

Example ▐▐▐▶ In terms of a university, a production database will probably be needed to maintain an ongoing record of student progression.

10.5.2 DECISION-SUPPORT DATABASES

Such databases are used as data repositories from which to retrieve information for the support of organisational decision-making. Such databases are read-only databases. They are designed to facilitate the use of query tools or custom applications.

Example ▐▐▐▶ In terms of a university, a decision-support database may be needed to monitor recruitment and retention patterns amongst a student population.

A data warehouse (Chapter 39) is a type of contemporary database system designed to fulfil decision-support needs. However, a data warehouse differs from a conventional decision-support database in a number of ways. First, a data warehouse is likely to hold far more data than a decision-support database. Volumes of the order of 400 Gbytes to terabytes of data are commonplace. Second, the data stored in a warehouse is likely to have been extracted from a diverse range of application systems, only some of which may be database systems. Third, a warehouse is designed to fulfil a number of distinct ways (dimensions) in which users may wish to retrieve data.

A data mart is a small data warehouse. Whereas a data warehouse may store of the order of 400 Gbytes of data, a data mart may store something of the order of 40 Gbytes of data. A data mart is also likely to store data representing a particular business area rather than representing data applicable to the entire organisation.

10.5.3 MASS-DEPLOYMENT DATABASES

Such databases are used to deliver data to the desktop. Generally such databases are single-user tools running under some PC-based DBMS, such as Microsoft Access. They may be updated on a regular basis either from production or decision-support databases.

Example ⦀▶ In terms of a university, a mass-deployment database will be needed by each lecturer to maintain an ongoing record of student attendance at lectures and tutorials.

10.5.4 INTEGRATION OF DATABASES

Ideally we would like any database system to fulfil each of these purposes at the same time. However, in practice, medium- to large-scale databases can rarely fulfil all these purposes without sacrificing something in terms of either retrieval or update performance. Many organisations therefore choose to design separate databases to fulfil production, decision-support and mass deployment needs and build necessary update strategies between each type (Figure 10.5).

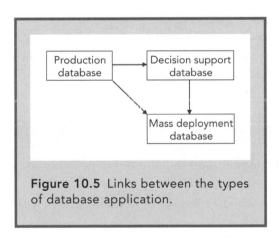

Figure 10.5 Links between the types of database application.

10.6 ⦿ SUMMARY

- Data has to be represented in some way for storage and manipulation by computer hardware and software. We may distinguish two levels of data representation: logical representation and physical representation.

- Logical data representation is that form of representation used by systems and applications software and consists of directories and files.

- Physical data representation is that form of representation used by computer hardware and consists of blocks and records.

- Various levels of software must map between logical and physical forms of data representation.
- Modern information technology systems tend to use databases and DBMS.
- A database is an organised repository for data.
- A database management System (DBMS) is an organised set of facilities for accessing and maintaining one or more databases.
- Any database and DBMS adheres to a particular data model.
- Databases are generally used as production databases, decision-support databases or mass-deployment databases.

10.7 QUESTIONS

(i) Distinguish between logical and physical data representation.

(ii) Define the concept of a data type.

(iii) Distinguish between standard and complex data types.

(iv) Explain the relevance of XML to data representation.

(v) Distinguish between a database and a DBMS.

(vi) List the primary characteristics of a database system.

(vii) Define the concept of a data model.

(viii) Distinguish between production, decision-support and mass-deployment database applications.

10.8 EXERCISES

(i) Investigate the logical representation of data within some operating system known to you.

(ii) Consider some secondary storage device and determine the block or page size used on the device.

(iii) Consider some IT system known to you. Attempt to estimate the volume of data stored in the system.

(iv) Image data are stored in a limited range of formats. Investigate the formats available.

(v) Investigate the range of contemporary DBMS used in some organisation.

(vi) Determine the forms of production, decision-support and mass-deployment databases used in some organisation known to you.

10.9 ◎ PROJECTS

(i) Investigate the likely importance of XML to the interoperability of database systems.

(ii) Most information systems projects utilise database technology. Investigate why this is the case.

(iii) Genetic sequences are now able to be determined and represented as data. Determine the precise characteristics of such data and the features of databases needed to handle such complex data.

(iv) Investigate the prevalence of data warehousing as an organisational technology.

(v) Develop a map of the production, decision-support and mass deployment databases in a range of organisations and develop policy as to the optimal distribution of these types of database application.

10.10 ◎ REFERENCE

Beynon-Davies, P. (2000). *Database Systems*. Palgrave, London.

COMMUNICATIONS TECHNOLOGY

Take care of the sense, and the sounds will take care of themselves.

Lewis Carroll: *Alice's Adventures in Wonderland* (1865) Chapter 9.

LEARNING OUTCOMES

After reading this chapter, you will be able to:

- Explain the position of communications technology as a branch of empirics
- Define the concept of a communication channel
- Distinguish between telecommunications media, devices and carriers
- Discuss the Internet as the current context for communications technology

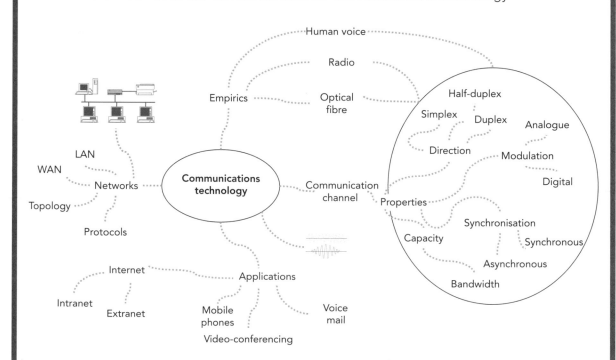

11.1 INTRODUCTION

Modern-day computers are seldom purely standalone devices. Most computers, particularly in business organisations, are connected to other machines via short-haul or long-haul communication connections of various forms. A collection of machines connected by communication connections is known as a computer network. Computer networks are a major component in the prevalent strategy of distributed computing, i.e. siting computer power where it is needed within the organisation. In its basic form distribution permits output devices such as printers or storage devices such as high-capacity disk drives to be shared across the network. In its more sophisticated form, processing and/or data will be distributed across the network. Some have even argued that for modern organisations the computer is the network.

11.2 EMPIRICS

Communication technology comes under the area of empirics in terms of semiotics. Empirics concerns the characteristics of the physical characteristics of communication. Generally speaking we can distinguish between three component elements of any communication (Chapter 2):

- A *sender* that transmits some message as a signal
- A *communication channel* or medium along which the message is transmitted
- A r*eceiver* which interprets the signal as a message

In normal face-to-face conversation both sender and receiver are humans and the communication channel is air. The signal involves the transmission of sound through air. For information technology systems so-called telecommunications are more relevant. Telecommunication refers to the electronic transmission of signals for communications usually at a distance. In fact, IT systems generally utilise a subset of telecommunications known as data communications. Data communications refers to the electronic collection, processing and distribution of data over networks.

The basic model of communication above can be modified for data communications:

- A *sender unit* transmits some signal to a...
- ...*telecommunication device*, which is a piece of hardware that performs a number of functions on the signal and then transmits the signal along a...
- ...*communication channel* to another...
- ...*telecommunication device*, which reverses the process performed by the sending telecommunications device and passes the signal on to a...
- ...*receiving unit*, which interprets the signal.

In general, a data communication system will therefore be made up of the following components:

- *Input and output devices* such as keyboards and monitors for the sending and receiving of data.
- *Computing devices* for the processing of data.
- *Communication channels* along which the data is transmitted.
- *Telecommunication devices* such as modems and multiplexers which support data transmission and reception functions.
- *Communication software* that controls input and output activities and other functions of the communication system.

11.3 COMMUNICATION CHANNEL

For communication to occur a signal must be sent along some communication channel. We may describe a communication channel in various ways. Some relevant properties are the capacity of the channel, the synchronisation, the modulation and the direction of the channel.

- *Modulation*. Generally speaking there are two types of signal: digital and analogue. A digital signal has a small number of possible values, two for a binary digital signal. An analogue signal has values drawn from a continuous range. The value of the signal varies over this range.
- *Capacity*. Generally speaking this refers to the amount of data that can be transmitted along the channel in some given period of time. The bandwidth of a channel refers to the minimum and maximum frequencies allowed along a channel. Bandwidth is related to baud rate, which is a measure of the amount of data that can be transmitted along a channel in a unit of time. In a digital channel baud rate corresponds to bit rate: the number of bits we can transfer per second between sender and receiver.
- *Direction*. This refers to the data flow between sender and receiver. In a simplex channel the flow is in one direction only. In a duplex channel data may flow in both directions simultaneously. In a half duplex channel flow can occur in both directions, but not at the same time.
- *Synchronisation*. This refers to whether the messages between sender and receiver are synchronised. In an asynchronous channel the sender and receiver are not synchronised. Hence a message may be sent at any time. In a synchronous channel the receiver has to wait to receive the message from the sender before it can respond with its message.

We can compare a number of different communication channels against some of these properties (Table 11.1).

Table 11.1 Properties of various media.

	Modulation	Direction	Synchronisation
Human voice	analogue	half duplex	synchronous
Radio	analogue	half duplex	synchronous
Optical fibre	digital	half duplex	asynchronous

11.4 TYPES OF TELECOMMUNICATION MEDIA

Various telecommunication media can be employed for the transmission of data in communication networks:

- *Twisted pair cable*. This consists of pairs of twisted wires, usually of copper, and offers a cheap communication solution but with low transmission rates.

- *Coaxial cable*. This consists of an inner conductor wire surrounded by insulation called the dielectric. The dielectric is in turn surrounded by a conductive shield usually made of a layer of foil or metal braiding. The conductive shield is in turn covered by a layer of non-conductive insulation known as the jacket. This form of media is more expensive than twisted pair cable but subject to fewer problems of transmission.

- *Fibre-optic cable*. This consists of many thin strands of glass or plastic bound together in a sheath. Signals are transmitted using high-intensity light beams generated by lasers. Fibre-optic cable is capable of very high transmission rates in the range 2.5 Gbps (billion bits per second).

- *Microwave transmission*. This is a form of 'wireless' medium. It involves high-frequency radio signals sent through the air. For it to work effectively, microwave transmitting and receiving stations have to be in line of sight.

- *Communication satellites*. These are basically microwave stations placed in low Earth orbit. The satellite receives a signal from Earth and re-broadcasts it either to some other satellite or to some Earth-bound microwave station. Thus it can be used to transmit signals over large geographic areas.

- *Cellular transmission*. This form of medium involves a local area being divided up into a number of cells. As some cellular device such as a mobile phone moves between cells the cellular system passes the connection from one cell to another. The signals from the cells are transmitted to a receiver and integrated into the regular phone system. This is the fundamental technology underlying the recent growth in mobile communication.

- *Infrared transmission*. This involves sending signals through the air using light waves. It requires line of sight transmission and short distances to be effective.

11.5 ◎ TYPES OF TELECOMMUNICATION DEVICE

A telecommunication device is a piece of hardware that allows electronic communication to occur. Various types of telecommunication device are used in communication networks. These include:

- *Modems*. These are modulation/demodulation devices. They translate analogue signals used by many telephone networks into digital signals used by computer machinery. Many telephone networks are moving over to digital transmission. Hence, over time, the need for modems will decrease.

- *Multiplexers*. This device allows several telecommunications signals to be transmitted over a single communications medium at the same time. The multiplexer may divide a high-speed channel into multiple channels of a slower speed or may continuously assign each channel small amounts of time for using the high-speed channel.

- *Front-end processors*. These are computers tasked with managing the interface, usually to larger computing machines, from thousands of communications lines. They poll communications devices periodically to see if they have any messages to send, keep logs of activity, determine the priority of messages and select optimal paths along the network to transmit messages.

11.6 ◎ TELECOMMUNICATION CARRIERS AND SERVICES

Telecommunication carriers and services provide the telecommunication infrastructure used to transmit data from one site to another. Carriers normally supply a range of services. Common carriers are the long-distance telephone companies. They provide the standard telephone network using switched lines – a special circuit that directs messages along specific paths in a telecommunications system by using switching equipment. Value-added carriers are companies that offer the use of their private telecommunications systems for a fee. Value-added carriers may offer dedicated lines to customers. Dedicated lines, sometimes called leased lines, provide a constant connection between two points.

In terms of telecommunications services the Internet Service Provider (ISP) is probably the most commonplace example currently. An ISP is a company supplying a permanent connection to the Internet (see below) and sells on temporary connections to the Internet for a fee. ISPs will also provide areas for subscribers to place information which is then accessible by other users of the Internet.

11.7 ◎ NETWORKS

A network is any set of computer systems joined by some communications technology. Networks can be described in terms of their topology and coverage.

In terms of coverage we may distinguish between the following types of network:

- *Local area network (LAN).* A type of network in which the various nodes are situated relatively close together, usually in one building or buildings in close proximity. The most common use of LANs are to link a group of personal computers together sharing peripheral devices such as printers.

- *Wide area network (WAN).* A type of network in which the nodes are geographically remote. WANs may consist of a mix of dedicated and non-dedicated communication lines as well as microwave and satellite communications.

- *Value added network (VAN).* A type of network in which a third-party organisation sets up and maintains a network and sells the use of the network on to other organisations.

Example ||||➤ Figure 11.1 illustrates the components of a typical LAN. The personal computers and the printer are linked to the cable forming the network by interface cards. These are pieces of firmware (a combination of hardware and software) which specify the data transmission rate, the size of message packets, the addressing information attached to each packet and the network topology. The cabling is likely to consist of coaxial or fibre optic cable. The server is likely to be a powerful PC which acts as a resource for programs and data used by other PCs in the network. The server will also run the network operating system that operates the server facilities and manages communication on the network. The gateway connects the LAN to other networks and consists of a processor that translates between the communication protocols of different networks.

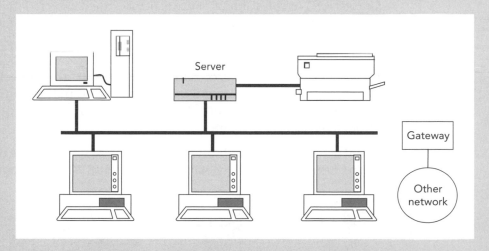

Figure 11.1 An example LAN.

There are generally three main types of topology for a communication network (Figure 11.2):

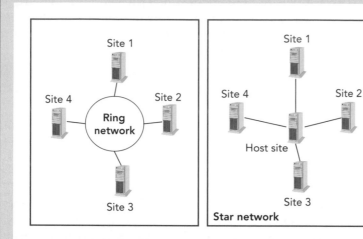
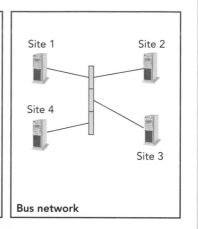

Figure 11.2 Network topologies.

- *Bus network*. In this form of network devices are connected to a main communication line called a bus, along which messages are sent. Messages can be broadcast to the entire network through a single circuit and messages may travel in both directions along the bus.

- *Ring network*. In this form of network devices are connected in a loop. Messages are transmitted from computer to computer flowing around a closed loop in a single direction. Since each computer operates independently, if one fails the network is able to continue uninterrupted.

- *Star network*. In this form of network devices are all connected to a central computer. The central computer acts as a form of traffic controller for all the other devices on the network. All communication between devices must pass through the central computer.

Practical networks will be hybrids of these topologies. Parts of the network may, for instance, have a star topology, while other parts utilise a ring topology.

11.8 ⦿ INTERNET

The most prevalent current example of the application of communications technology is the Internet. The Internet – short for inter-network – began as a WAN in the USA funded by its Department of Defense to link scientists and researchers around the world. It was initially designed primarily as a medium to exchange research data.

Currently the Internet is a set of interconnected computer networks distributed around the globe. The Internet can be considered on a number of levels. The

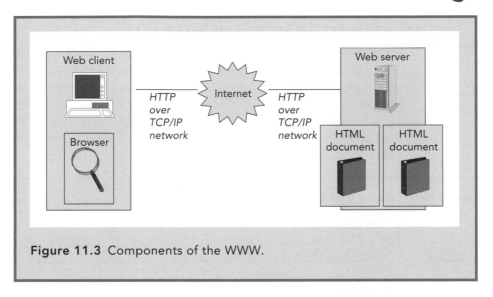

Figure 11.3 Components of the WWW.

simplest level of connection is that defined by electronic mail (e-mail) which allows diverse users to communicate by distributing electronic messages to each other. A step up from this includes electronic data interchange (EDI), a set of standards for transmitting electronic documentation between organisations. However, in this section we particularly concentrate on the technology of the World-Wide Web (WWW) as it appears to be the one most readily associated with the concept of the Internet at the current time.

The World-Wide Web (referred to colloquially as 'the Web') began as a project in 1992 at the European Centre for Nuclear Research (CERN) based in Geneva. Figure 11.3 illustrates the primary components of the Web.

11.8.1 HYPERTEXT TRANSFER PROTOCOL (HTTP)

HTTP is an object-oriented protocol that defines how information can be transmitted between clients and servers. An HTTP transaction consists of the following phases:

- *Connection*. The client establishes a connection with a Web server.
- *Request*. The client sends a request message to a Web server.
- *Response*. The Web server sends a response to the client.
- *Close*. The connection is closed by the Web server.

HTTP is said to be a stateless protocol. This means that when a server provides a response and the connection is closed, the server has no memory of any previous transactions. This has the advantage of simplicity in that clients and servers can run with simple logic and there is little need for extra memory. However, this stateless property makes it difficult to support the database concept of a session, essential to the idea of database processing (Chapter 10).

11.8.2 HYPERTEXT MARKUP LANGUAGE (HTML)

The WWW can be thought of as a collection of documents residing on thousands of servers or Web sites around the world. Each such document is written in the hypertext markup language (HTML). HTML is a standard for marking up or tagging documents that can be published on the Web, and can be made up of text, graphics, images, audio clips and video clips. Documents also include links to other documents stored either on the local HTML server or on remote HTML servers.

Example ⏵ Below we include a very simple document expressed in HTML:

```
<HTML>
<TITLE>Information Systems</TITLE>
<H1>Information Systems</H1>
<H2>Paul Beynon-Davies</H2>
</HTML>
```

The text between angled brackets constitutes tags. The HTML tags indicate the start and end of the document. The forward slash precedes an end-tag. TITLE provides a name for the page, and H1 and H2 indicate that 1st level and 2nd level headings should be displayed respectively.

11.8.3 UNIVERSAL RESOURCE LOCATORS

HTML documents are identified by Universal Resource Locators (URL): a unique address for each document on the Web. Links between documents are activated by 'hotspots' in the document: a word, phrase or image used to reference a link to another document. The syntax of a URL consists of three parts: the protocol used for the connection (such as HTTP), the host name, and the path name on the host from which the document can be located:

```
<protocol>://<host>[<:port>]/<path>[? arguments]
```

Example ⏵ As an example, the URL below represents a reference to the author's academic institution:

```
HTTP://www.swan.ac.uk/ebms
```

11.8.4 DOMAIN NAMES

The swan in the URL in the previous example is short for 'Swansea', the ac for academic and the uk for United Kingdom. This constitutes a so-called domain name, an agreed string of characters that may be used to provide some greater semantics to a URL. In practice, a domain name identifies and locates a host computer or service on the Internet. It often relates to the name of a business, organisation or service and must be registered in the same way as a company name.

A domain name is actually made up of three parts:

- *Subdomain*. This constitutes a provider of an Internet service. In this case it is University of Wales, Swansea.
- *Domain type*. This suggests the type of provider. In this case it is ac – indicating an academic institution based in the UK. The string edu (short for education) is used more generally for an educational institution.
- *Country code*. Every country has its own specific code. For instance, au is the code for Australia. If no country code is specified then the organisation is more than likely based in the USA.

11.8.5   BROWSERS

To access the WWW one needs a browser: programs that let the user read Web documents, view any in-built images or activate other media and hotspots. Browsers can also be used to link to FTP servers, gophers and WAIS:

- *File transfer protocol (FTP) servers* contain large collections of files that can be transferred over computer networks using e-mail and/or browser software.
- *Gopher* is the name given to a way of finding one's way around the Internet using menu-driven interfaces. The name is taken partly from the idea of its human counterpart 'going for things' and partly because a gopher is the mascot of the University of Minnesota, where the idea was developed. A gopher has two parts: one part, resident on the client, is used to specify the information required; the other part, stored on the server, contains an index of terms that the user can navigate.
- *Wide area information servers (WAIS)* are facilities which allow free-text retrieval searches against vast quantities of textual material.

11.9 INTRANET AND EXTRANET

Internet technology such as the WWW has become particularly popular because of the way it has established readily available 'open' standards for electronic communication. It is therefore not surprising that many organisations are beginning to use Internet technology for communications applications internal to the organisation. An intranet involves using Internet technology within the context of a single organisation. At its most basic it involves setting up a Web service for internal communications and coordination. At its most sophisticated, it involves using Web interfaces to core corporate applications such as corporate-wide database systems. Typically an intranet is connected to the wider Internet through a so-called firewall. The firewall consists of hardware and software placed between an organisation's internal network and an external network such as the Internet. The firewall is programmed to intercept each message packet passing between the external and internal networks, examine its properties, and reject any unauthorised messages. Hence the firewall constrains the types of information that can be passed into and out from an organisation's intranet.

Whereas an intranet is only accessible to the members of an organisation, an extranet provides a certain level of access to an organisation's Web-based information to outsiders. Extranets are becoming particularly popular as a way of enabling electronic connections to be made to an organisation's established customers and suppliers. The organisation will utilise firewalls to ensure that outside access is secure.

Intranets and extranets are discussed in more detail in Part 9.

11.10 SUMMARY

- Communications technology can be considered under the semiotics discipline as a concern of empirics.
- A communication channel can be described in terms of such features as modulation, capacity, direction and synchronisation.
- Various types of telecommunication media can be used to transmit data including twisted pair cable, fibre-optic cable and infrared transmission.
- Networks can be distinguished in terms of coverage and topology.
- The Internet is a set of interconnected computer networks distributed around the globe.
- An intranet involves using Internet technology within the context of a single organisation.
- An extranet provides a certain level of access to an organisation's information to outsiders.

11.11 QUESTIONS

(i) Describe the relationship between communications technology and the semiotic area of empirics.

(ii) List the component elements of any communication.

(iii) Describe four main characteristics of a communication channel.

(iv) List the range of communication media.

(v) List some communications devices.

(vi) Distinguish between a wide area network and a local area network.

(vii) Describe some of the component elements that make the Internet possible.

(viii) Explain the relevance of domain names to activity on the Internet.

(ix) Distinguish between the Internet, an intranet and an extranet.

11.12 EXERCISES

(i) Analyse some common form of communication known to you in terms of a sender–medium–receiver model.

(ii) Describe some chosen communication channel in terms of features such as bandwidth and modulation.

(iii) Consider some computer network known to you. Identify the types of communication media used to connect the network.

(iv) Determine the topology and coverage of some computer network known to you.

(v) Determine some organisation's use of the Internet. Does it have an intranet and extranet?

11.13 PROJECTS

(i) Investigate the limitations of bandwidth in supporting the information super-highway. Predict the needed growth of bandwidth.

(ii) What consequences does communication technology have for globalisation?

(iii) Develop a history of the Internet and assess its likely impact on communications technology in the medium term future.

(iv) Investigate the idea of mobile computing and its relevance for organisational informatics.

INFORMATION TECHNOLOGY SYSTEM

You've got be careful about getting locked into open systems.

Computer salesman

LEARNING OUTCOMES

After reading this chapter, you will be able to:

- Distinguish between an information system and an information technology system
- Describe the levels of an information technology system
- Outline how an IT system may be distributed over a computer network
- Relate some mega-package solutions to IT systems
- Describe the concepts of pervasive and mobile computing

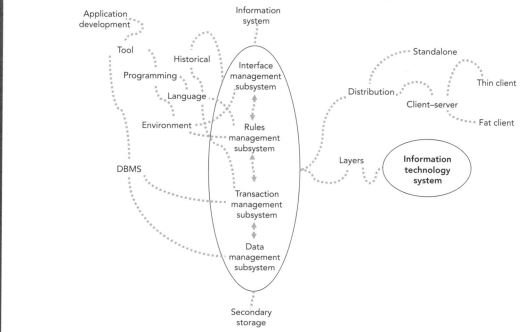

12.1 INTRODUCTION

In this chapter we review the distinction between an information system and an information technology system. We consider the makeup of an IT system in terms of a layered model. Elements of the model may be distributed over a computer network. In Chapter 5 we considered elements of a typical horizontal IS architecture for a commercial organisation. In this chapter we consider the vertical dimension of distributing processing power and data. We also consider the rise of the mega-package as one approach to providing an IT infrastructure (Chapter 21) for an organisation.

12.2 INFORMATION SYSTEMS AND INFORMATION TECHNOLOGY SYSTEMS

An information system is a system of communication between a group of people. An information system involves the flow of information in support of the human activity of the group. Information systems are distinct from information technology (IT) systems. IT systems are component elements of modern IS.

The systems concept has been applied both to technology and to human activity. An information technology system has data as input, manipulates such data as a process and outputs manipulated data (Figure 12.1). Information technology provides the means to construct aspects of information systems. Information technology (IT) includes computer software, hardware, data storage and communication technology. It is important to recognise that information systems have existed in organisations prior to the invention of IT, and hence IS do not need modern IT to exist. However, in the modern, complex organisational world, most IS rely on IT to a greater or lesser degree. Therefore within this book whenever we have referred to an IS we normally mean some system with elements of an

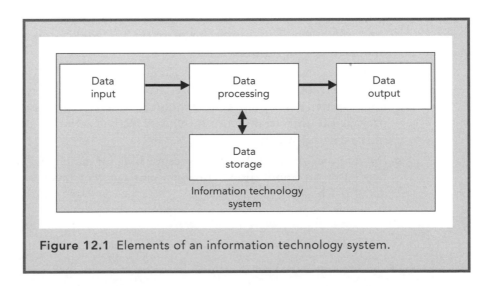

Figure 12.1 Elements of an information technology system.

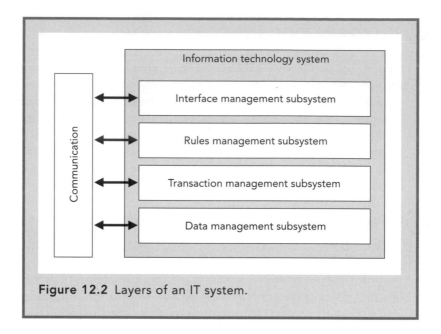

Figure 12.2 Layers of an IT system.

information technology system. An information technology system comprises software, hardware, communications and data designed to support some information system.

12.3 LAYERS OF AN INFORMATION TECHNOLOGY SYSTEM

In terms of software it is useful to consider an information technology system as being made up of a number of subsystems or horizontal layers (Figure 12.2):

- *Interface subsystem*. This subsystem is responsible for managing interaction with the end-user. This subsystem is generally referred to as the user interface.
- *Rules subsystem*. This subsystem manages the application logic in terms of a defined model of business rules.
- *Transaction subsystem*. This subsystem acts as the link between the data subsystem and the rules and interface subsystems. Querying, insertion and update activity is triggered at the interface, validated by the rules subsystem and packaged as units (transactions) that will initiate actions (responses or changes) in the data subsystem.
- *Data subsystem*. This subsystem is responsible for managing the underlying data needed by an application. This data management layer is discussed in more detail in Chapter 10.

Example Take the example of an IT system for storing research publications in a university:

- One part of the interface will be a data entry form to enter details of a journal publication.

- One of the rules or constraints used to validate data may be that the date entered for the publication must be less than or equal to today's date.

- A key transaction will be that update function involved in the entry of new publication data into the system.

- Part of the data management layer will have data structures for the storage of publication data.

12.4 DISTRIBUTION

In the contemporary IT infrastructure each of these parts of an application may be distributed on different machines, perhaps at different sites. This means that each part usually needs to be stitched together in terms of some communications backbone. For consistency, we refer to this facility here as the communication subsystem (Figure 12.2).

In Figure 12.3 the diagram is divided vertically into client computers and server computers. Clients request services from server computers. The figure illustrates a number of different distribution patterns for IT systems.

12.4.1 TIME-SHARING

In the first phase of information technology systems, each of the component layers of such a system was located on one machine. Large mainframe systems ran the data management, transaction management, rules management and much of the interface management functions of an application. Connection to such systems was via so-called 'dumb' terminals. They were referred to as dumb because they contained very little inherent functionality and primarily enabled operators to control systems via character-based interfaces – interfaces demanding users to type in commands. Most of the processing on such systems was conducted in batch mode, i.e. the processing of vast amounts of transactions in sequence with very little direct user input. Specialist data entry staff conducted data entry. Retrieval of information was available through paper reports produced from the system.

12.4.2 FAT CLIENTS

Over time, more and more functionality has been placed on the clients. Technological developments enabled the user interface layer and some of the rules management layer to be located on so-called 'intelligent' terminals. They were referred to as 'intelligent' because they were able to take some of the processing off

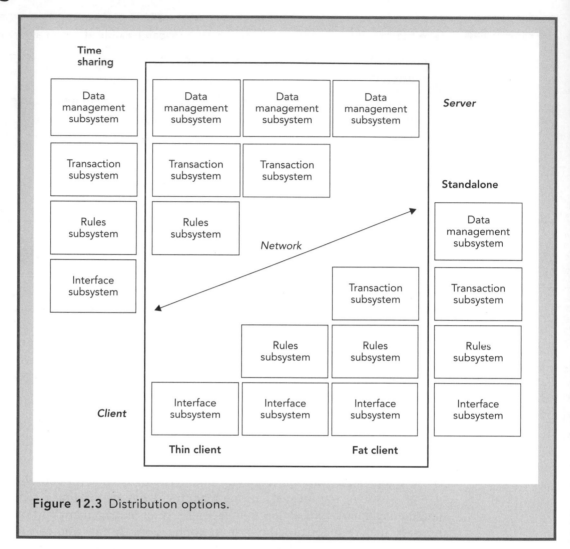

Figure 12.3 Distribution options.

of the centralised mainframe or minicomputer. This advance enabled the development of on-line systems. Such systems enabled users in the workplace to enter data directly into the information system and in certain respects to query the data in the system. The rise of on-line systems enabled the development of management information system (MIS) and decision support system (DSS) applications (Chapter 6).

With the rise of personal computers, much more of the functionality of the information technology system began to be placed on desktop machines. The sophistication of graphical user interfaces meant that more power needed to be available on the desktop to run such interfaces effectively. With the rise of software for the desktop, slices from the total functionality of an information technology system could be built using application development tools available for the desktop.

12.4.3 THREE TIER

Many current applications run on three-tier client–server architectures. The first tier runs the user interface layer, the second tier runs the application logic and the third layer runs the transaction and data management functions. In a Web-based approach the client will run a browser, the middle tier will comprise a Web server that will interact with a database server.

12.4.4 THIN CLIENTS

Some discussion has recently occurred within the computing fraternity over the way in which Internet technology may cause a profound change from 'fat' client to 'thin' clients. The corporate PC is currently a fat client. It requests information from a server and then processes and presents it at the client end using software resident on the PC. The network computer or NC is a thin client. In its extreme form, only a minimum of software (usually a Web browser) will be resident on the client. Applications will be resident on and accessed from the server. This means that each user will have a desktop system that looks like a PC but which has no secondary storage devices. Consequently, NCs, or so the argument goes, are likely to be considerably less expensive than a PC. Also, the network administrator will only need to buy and maintain one copy of each software application on the server.

Example ➤ Consider an ATM (automatic telling machine) run by a consortium of high-street banks. The client end comprises the ATM itself. The ATM is effectively a specialised computer system running a number of screens with associated dialogue and controlling the operation of a cash dispenser and other devices. At the server end there is likely to be a series of large banking databases storing data about customers and accounts. The mediating application layer is likely to consist of a business rules layer containing rules such as a customer should not be able to go overdrawn to a degree greater than his or her overdraft limit. It will also contain a transaction layer implementing transaction types such as: *check an entered customer identifier against a recorded identifier for the customer in the customer database and update the account balance of a customer by crediting or debiting a given account.*

12.5 INTEGRATING IT SYSTEMS

Integration and distribution of IT systems can be considered in a vertical sense as above. Generally such integration can be described as cooperative and distributed processing. Integration and distribution can also be considered in a horizontal sense. The aim of many information technology strategies (Chapter 35) is to integrate IT systems across the organisation. Generally speaking such integration is focused around issues of integrated and distributed data. This is illustrated in Figure 12.4.

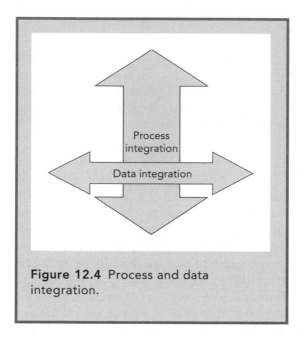

Figure 12.4 Process and data integration.

The importance of both horizontal and vertical integration of IT systems becomes evident when we consider the opposite scenario – that of piecemeal IT systems.

12.5.1 PIECEMEAL IT SYSTEMS

When organisations first began to use computers they naturally adopted a piecemeal approach to information systems development. One manual system at a time was analysed, redesigned and transferred onto the computer with little thought to its position within the organisation as a whole. This piecemeal approach was necessitated by the difficulties experienced in using a new and more powerful organisational tool. This situation is illustrated in Figure 12.5 in relation to some probable IT systems in a university setting.

This approach by definition produces a number of separate information technology systems, each with its own program suite, its own files, and its own inputs and outputs. As a result of this:

- The systems, being self-contained, do not represent the way in which the organisation works, i.e. as a complex set of interacting and interdependent systems.
- Systems built in this manner often communicate outside the computer. Reports are produced by one system, which then have to be transcribed into a form suitable for another system. These so-called 'workarounds' proliferate inputs and outputs, and create delays.
- Information obtained from a series of separate files is less valuable to personnel because it does not provide a complete picture of the activity of an organisation.

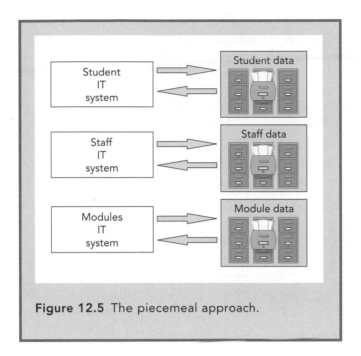

Figure 12.5 The piecemeal approach.

For example, a sales manager reviewing outstanding orders may not get all the information he needs from the sales system. He may need to collate information about stocks from another file used by the company's stock control system.

- Data may be duplicated in the numerous files used by different information technology systems in the organisation. Hence personnel may maintain data similar to that held by payroll. This creates unnecessary maintenance overheads and increases the risk of inconsistency.

Note that, although we have implicitly presented the piecemeal scenario described above as a historical one, in practice, many so-called 'legacy' IT systems in organisations adhere to many of the characteristics of piecemeal development. Legacy IT systems are those applications which have been produced some time in the past to support some form of organisational activity, but which are still critically important to the organisation.

Example ‖‖➡ Let us contrast the piecemeal approach with an integrated IT system scenario. Suppose we consider the data used in running a supermarket store – part of a larger national chain of supermarkets.

In each supermarket a number of checkouts operate electronic point of sale (EPOS) equipment. This equipment allows checkout staff to record sales by simply scanning bar-codes on products. Details of each sale are transmitted electronically to the store's database.

The sales data automatically updates data held on the current shelf levels of products. If the shelf level of a particular product falls below a certain amount a report is generated for store staff to replenish the shelves from the supermarket's available stock. In replenishing stock on the shelves staff update the database. If the stock level of a product held at the store falls below a limit an order is generated automatically and sent electronically to the central supplies division.

Data held within the database about sales, shelf and stock levels is also used by store management to decide on marketing strategies – which goods to promote, how to site products on shelves etc.

In this example, at least three effective uses are being made of the same integrated collection of data: the collection of customer transaction data, the management of stock and the marketing of goods.

12.6 ⊙ MEGA-PACKAGES

Traditionally, integration has been achieved by effective planning and management of IT systems built internally within organisations. More recently, many organisations have chosen to buy in large suites of software with in-built integration. This is the enterprise resource planning (ERP) package or mega-package (Davenport, 1998).

Recently the packaged software market has experienced an upturn with the increasing market penetration of such ERP systems. ERP systems integrate a number of different organisational functions under the umbrella of one system. Figure 12.6 illustrates the typical suite available in a mega-package. They promise the seamless flow of information through an organisation – financial and accounting information, human resource information, supply chain information and customer information.

Figure 12.6 represents a packaged approach to the horizontal IS architecture considered in Chapter 5.

Example ⫸ Leading vendors in this segment of the software industry are SAP, BAAN, Peoplesoft, JDEdwards and Oracle. There is evidence of significant acquisitions of such packages amongst organisations in Europe and the USA. To illustrate the state of the mega-package market-place, consider the case of SAP, the market leader.

SAP was founded in 1972 in Germany by a number of ex-IBM employees. It is now the fourth largest software supplier in world and the fastest growing software supplier. In 1992 its annual sales were $500 million. In 1997 its annual sales stood at $3.3 billion. SAP's main product is SAP/R3 an integrated suite of modules – sales, distribution, production, accounting, human resources – which runs on a client–server architecture. SAP/R3 includes a programming language – ABAP4 – and the company has a method specifically for SAP development known as ASAP.

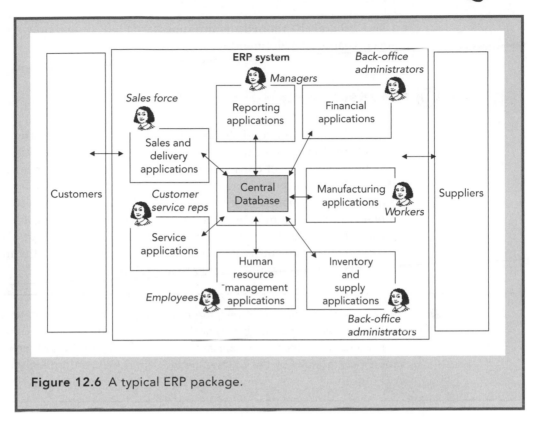

Figure 12.6 A typical ERP package.

12.6.1 MEGA-PACKAGE SUCCESS AND HORROR STORIES

The literature abounds with significant examples of organisations achieving key benefit from the implementation of ERP systems. For example:

- *Autodesk* reduced its customer delivery time from two weeks to 24 hours.
- *IBM Storage Systems Division* reduced the time required to re-price all of its products from 5 days to 5 minutes, the time to ship a replacement part from 22 days to 3 days and the time to complete a credit check from 20 minutes to 3 seconds.
- *Fujitsu Micro-electronics* reduced the cycle time for filling orders from 18 days to 1½ days and cut the time to close its financial books from 8 days to 4 days.

Equally, there are significant examples of companies having problems with their ERP implementations:

- *Fox-Meyer Drug* claim that a major SAP implementation drove it into bankruptcy.
- *Mobil Europe* abandoned a mega-package implementation (at a loss of hundreds of millions of pounds) because of a major merger.
- *Dell Computer* found that its intended ERP system would not fit with the decentralised business model of the company (millions lost).
- *Applied Materials* abandoned its ERP system when it found itself overwhelmed with the scale of the organisational changes involved (millions lost).

- *Dow Chemical* abandoned a mainframe-based ERP system on which it had spent seven years of development effort (billions lost).

12.7 PERVASIVE AND MOBILE COMPUTING

Recently a much-publicised slogan has been used to describe the changes to the architecture of IT systems that have occurred over the last decade – the *network is the computer*. As a direct consequence of the increasingly distributed nature of IT systems, the important element of the computing equation for organisations, groups and individuals is how to connect to the information network.

Advances in communication technology have made it possible to connect to networks from anywhere and at any time. Individuals are able to connect to networks while on the move through mobile phones and other hand-held devices. This whole area is generally referred to as mobile computing.

Example ▓▶ Utilities companies in the UK take meter readings through hand-held devices. The hand-held device can immediately update the corporate customer database. Maintenance engineers in such organisations also use hand-held devices to gain information on the state of the utilities network and help on appropriate operating procedures.

Pervasive computing is a related concept. Most electronic and electro-mechanical devices now utilise digital technology to a greater or lesser extent. Hence it becomes possible for various machines to communicate together and coordinate their processing. This is part of digital convergence, a topic discussed in Chapter 23.

Example ▓▶ Early prototypes of housing systems have been produced in which all the devices in a household – heater, cookers, washing machines, televisions, stereos – are controlled from a single computer. Some of the main practical benefits of such centralised control lies in the area of energy savings. Devices can also communicate faults and problems to vendor organisations to enable them to schedule appropriate maintenance.

12.8 SUMMARY

- Information technology systems are component elements of information systems
- An IT system can be considered to have five major layers or subsystems: interface subsystem, rules subsystem, transaction subsystem, data management subsystem and communications subsystem.

- The subsystems of an IT system may be distributed in various ways across a computer network.
- Integration of IT systems is a significant objective and problem for most organisations.
- Enterprise resource planning systems are now being used to integrate the IT in many organisations.
- Mobile computing and pervasive computing are likely to become commonplace aspects of corporate IT systems.

12.9 QUESTIONS

(i) Distinguish between an information system and an information technology system.

(ii) Describe the four levels of an information technology system.

(iii) Explain what is meant by piecemeal development.

(iv) Explain how the four layers of an IT system may be distributed.

(v) Distinguish between process and data integration.

(vi) Describe what is meant by a mega-package.

(vii) List some of the problems of using mega-packages.

12.10 EXERCISES

(i) Find some information technology system. Analyse the IT system in terms of the four-layer model described in this chapter.

(ii) Is the IT system distributed in any way? Which model of distribution best approximates the architecture of the system?

(iii) Consider some organisation's IT infrastructure. How closely integrated are the systems? How much distributed processing and/or data is present in the infrastructure?

(iv) Find some organisation that has adopted a mega-package. Why did the organisation decide to implement the package? What experience have they had of using the mega-package for their infrastructure?

12.11 PROJECTS

(i) Gather data on a limited range of information technology systems. Analyse their functionality in terms of the layered model discussed in this chapter.

(ii) Investigate the prevalence of mega-packages within a particular industrial sector.

(iii) Build a detailed description of the functionality of some mega-package. How much of an information systems infrastructure does it provide for organisations?

(iv) Investigate the problems and pitfalls of ERP implementation.

12.12 REFERENCE

Davenport, T. H. (1998). Putting the enterprise into the enterprise system. *Harvard Business Review*, July/Aug, 121–131.

PART **3**

USE AND IMPACT

A life spent making mistakes is not only more honorable, but more useful than a life spent doing nothing

George Bernard Shaw (1856–1950)

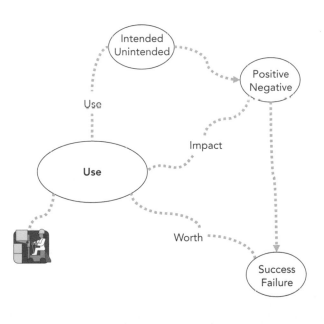

Information technology systems are designed to be used in the context of some information system. We argue that there are many examples of fully functioning information systems that never get used or the use of which causes significant problems for organisations. Therefore, in this part we examine more closely this context of use.

- We consider a number of issues situated around the general feature of the usability of information systems. Usability will be a key factor influencing satisfaction with information systems by system stakeholders (Chapter 13).

- We examine the issue of the impact of information systems upon individuals, groups and organisations. The impact upon organisations is primarily considered in terms of the utility or efficacy of information systems (Chapter 14).

- Usability and utility are key assessments of the worth of IS. In Chapter 15 we extend our discussion of worth to consider elements of the success and failure of information systems. We devote a chapter to examining the phenomenon of information systems failure with the intention of identifying elements of successful strategies for information systems planning, management and development.

Informatics is a dialectical discipline. A dialectical argument is one which has three parts: a thesis, an antithesis and a synthesis. The thesis and antithesis are two opposing but equally valid propositions about some real-world phenomenon. The synthesis is a proposition which serves to encapsulate the validity of both the earlier propositions

Dialectical argument and description permit a sophisticated description of many real-world phenomena, particularly those from the social world of which organisations are a part. Many dialectical descriptions inherently refer to cyclical processes. In a number of chapters in the book we use a dialectical form of presentation to illustrate how the relationships between IT and organisations are rarely simple and straightforward.

The relationships between information systems, their use and the impact they have on organisations are inherently dialectical in nature.

- *Thesis*. Organisations construct information systems to support organisational activity. In this sense information systems can be viewed as an inherently conservative force in organisations in that their use tends to emulate existing ways of working.

- *Antithesis*. Information systems may stimulate changes in organisational activity. The impact of information systems may cause organisations to change their forms of working. In this sense, information systems can be seen as an important revolutionary force in organisations.

- *Synthesis*. Information systems are both a product of organisations and an important force in organisational change. Information systems both impact upon organisations and are impacted upon by organisations.

THE USE OF INFORMATION SYSTEMS

Just because something doesn't do what you planned it to do doesn't mean it's useless.

Thomas A. Edison (1847–1931)

LEARNING OUTCOMES

After reading this chapter, you will be able to:

- Discuss the differences between the use and impact of IS
- Identify the importance of stakeholders to definitions of successful use
- Describe the issues of stakeholder involvement and stakeholder resistance

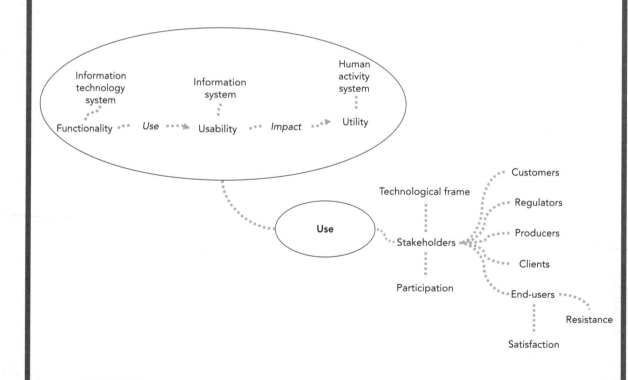

13.1   INTRODUCTION

After an information system is introduced into an organisation, the system begins to have effects on that organisation. We may distinguish between first-order effects and second-order effects. First-order effects concern issues of use. Second-order effects concern the impact of the system on individuals, groups and the organisation as a whole. The issue of use is the topic of the current chapter. The issue of impact is the topic of Chapter 14. Both use and impact are critical to the assessment of the success or failure of some information system (Chapter 15).

13.2   SYSTEM, USE AND IMPACT

DeLone and McLean (1992) performed a systematic review of the available published material immediately bearing on the question of the success of information systems. To organise this material and to establish a future research agenda they produced a model of the factors influencing information systems success, which is illustrated in Figure 13.1. Although this model has been much criticized since its publication, it is still useful as a means of highlighting some of the key variables that affect the success of information systems, and it is for this reason that we use the model to structure the discussion of this chapter.

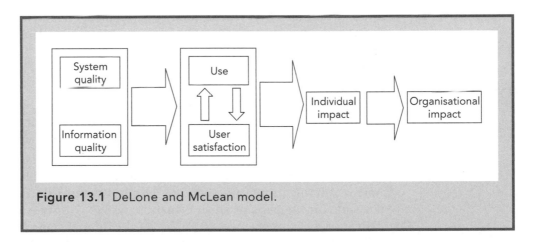

Figure 13.1 DeLone and McLean model.

To the left of the figure we have two issues of technical quality: the quality of the information system itself and the quality of the information it produces. The quality of the system and of the information are likely to influence the use of the system and perceptions of user satisfaction with the information system. In turn, the use of the system will have an impact on the individual within the organisation, which in turn will have an impact on the organisation as a whole.

The elements of this model can be overlaid on the far simpler scheme of functionality, usability and utility (Figure 13.2) which we introduced in Chapter 1.

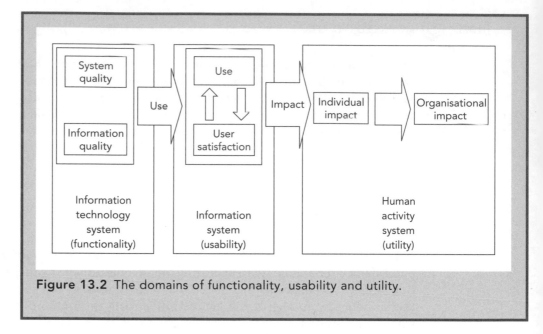

Figure 13.2 The domains of functionality, usability and utility.

Each of these dimensions forms a distinct context for the assessment or evaluation of information systems (Chapter 41):

- *Functionality*. Issues of system quality and information quality are primarily issues of functionality. Functionality is established in the context of information systems development (Part 6) and lies within the domain of the information technology system (Chapter 12).

- *Usability*. Issues of use and user satisfaction are primarily issues of usability. Usability is established in the context of use and lies within the domain of the information system (Chapter 4). Information systems are socio-technical systems and consist of an information technology system and its associated activity system of use. This is the concern of the current chapter

- *Utility*. Issues of impact at a number of levels are primarily issues of the utility of some information system within some human activity system or organisational process. A human activity system is a set of activities performed by some group of people on the basis of an information system. Utility is established in the context of the consequences or impact of the information system upon aspects of the human activity system. This is the topic of Chapter 19.

The worth of some information system will be determined in these three contexts. Hence judgements as to the success or failure of some information system will be determined in the interaction between each of these three areas:

- An information system may be deemed to lack certain functionality and hence to have failed.

- An information system may be regarded as adequately functioning but unusable and hence to have failed.

- An information system may be judged adequate in terms of both functionality and usability but having failed to deliver key organisational benefit. Hence it is judged to have failed in terms of utility.

The issue of the success or failure of information systems is the topic of Chapter 15.

13.3 THE CONTEXT OF USE

The context of use of some information system is defined by a number of key issues:

- *Usability*. Traditional conceptions of use are packaged in terms of the usability of IT systems. The usability of an information technology system is how easy an IT system is to use for the purpose for which it has been constructed. The definition of usability is critically set by the context of the human activity system which it is meant to serve.

- *Stakeholders and stakeholder involvement*. Evidence suggests that for successful use human activity systems must be designed in parallel with the design of information technology systems. The identification and involvement of key system stakeholders is therefore essential for the successful development and use of information technology systems.

- *Stakeholder satisfaction*. One of the key reasons for involving stakeholders in the development of information systems is that such involvement appears to increase levels of user satisfaction with information systems. Systems that are not accepted and do not have the commitment of system stakeholders are likely to be subject to stakeholder resistance.

- These issues are neatly summarised in a series of propositions concerning IT systems design (Chapter 29) expressed by Eason (1988):

  ...IT technical design is not enough because benefit can only come if these systems are effectively harnessed and exploited by their users. The achievement of this involves the creation of compatible social and technical systems to serve some important organisational purpose. This in turn means the design of a social system to serve this purpose and the creation of a technical system which will support the users in the social system. The design process by which this is achieved requires a process of planned change which not only creates the appropriate system but creates in the users a motivational and knowledge state where they are able and willing to exploit the technical capabilities. This involves the participation of the stakeholders in the design process and individual and collective learning processes.

Example ⫸ Somerville *et al.* (1994) discuss the characteristics of the human activity system of *en route* air traffic control (as distinct from take-off and landing control) in the UK. Consider this example and see if you can separate out elements of the human activity system from the information system and its use.

UK airspace is divided into a number of sectors with each sector having a team of five air traffic controllers responsible for it. Controllers work at a control suite consisting of radar screens and facilities for communications between aircraft and other control suites. The radar screens provide a real-time representation of the sector's airspace, consisting of aircraft positions and other features such as sector boundaries, coastlines and airports. Each control suite provides a working area for two teams of controllers.

The radar screens display what is happening currently but not what might be happening in the near future. Hence controllers supplement the radar data with information carried on flight progress strips. These strips contain information about expected and current flights being controlled as well as a record of the controller's instructions to aircraft.

Flight strips are printed forty minutes before an aircraft enters a controlled sector and are replicated across different control suites. Flight strips are organised on a flight progress board. The strips are organised on this board in a rack according to the reporting points over which a flight will pass. This board therefore provides an instantaneously recognisable representation of the flow of traffic through a controllers' sector.

Controllers use the information provided by the radar and strips to maintain separation levels between aircraft, and to direct course changes, airspeed and ascents and descents. When a controller updates data on a flight strip, he or she must inform controllers in other teams as aircraft move between sectors.

Flight progress boards are therefore not only a form of 'information technology' used to support individual activity, they are an essential element in supporting the coordination of activity between groups of people.

13.4 ⊚ THE USER INTERFACE

Every technology has an interface and information technology is no different. Every information technology system has an interface which is commonly called the user interface or sometimes the human–computer interface. The user interface is where, of course, use happens. Members of some organisation use the interface to input data into the system and to receive output from the system. The use activities of the IT system form part of the larger human activity system. Decisions are made on the basis of information interpreted from the information system and action is taken (Figure 13.3).

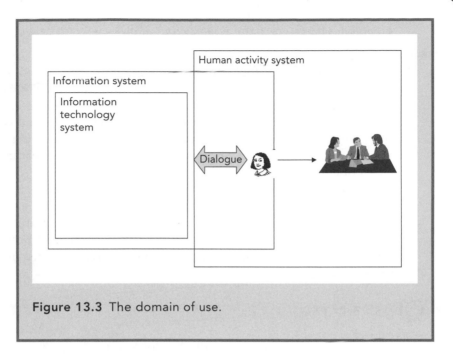

Figure 13.3 The domain of use.

Example ▌▌▌➡ A customer phones through an order for a certain quantity of an organisation's products to an order clerk. The order clerk inputs details of the order into the order-processing IT system through an order-entry screen. In the act of doing this the IT system may be able to automatically output details of an existing customer such that on the basis of previous orders the clerk may be able to make the decision to offer a discount on the purchase to the customer.

In this example, the human activity system might be described as the process of customer ordering. The IT system comprises the order-processing system and the interface is the order entry screen. To use this interface the clerk has to enter data using the keyboard and mouse and receives feedback of the entry on the computer monitor. The data output by the IT system is interpreted by the clerk as existing customer details and previous orders. The IT system plus this context of use therefore forms the information system in support of customer ordering.

A user interface can be seen as a collection of dialogues between the user and the IT system. Each dialogue is made up of a series of messages between the user and the IT system. It is useful to distinguish between three major aspects of such a dialogue:

- *Content*. This refers to the actual messages travelling between the user and the system.
- *Control*. This refers to the way in which the user moves between aspects of one dialogue or from one dialogue to another.

- *Format*. This refers to the actual layout of messages and data on input and output devices.

We can think of dialogues in terms of the four areas of semiotics described in Chapter 2: pragmatics, semantics, syntactics, and empirics. Format and control are largely aspects of the syntax and empirics of signs: the way in which signs are stored, transmitted and represented on the devices of some computer system. Some aspects of control, and certainly the matter of content, impinge on the pragmatics and semantics of signs: how signs are given meaning within various layers of context.

An essential function of most information technology systems is therefore to interact with users. Even a batch process system has to have some mechanism for the user to launch a process and complete a process. No matter how well built an information system is, its effectiveness is largely affected by its user interface. Hence the utility of an information system is heavily affected by its usability.

13.5 USABILITY

The usability of an information technology system is how easy an IT system is to use for the purpose for which it has been constructed. Nielsen (1993) considers five facets of usability:

- *Learnability*. An IT system should be easy to learn how to use.
- *Rememberability*. Having learned how to use a system the user should be able to remember how to use it easily.
- *Efficiency of use*. The system should be efficient to use. For instance, input operations should not be subject to delay.
- *Reliability in use*. The IT system should promote reliable human performance in the sense that it should lead the user to make fewer errors.
- *User satisfaction*. The interface should satisfy the users in the sense that it leaves them subjectively pleased with using the interface.

Since the interface is now an increasingly large part of the structure of most IT systems, design of this interface has now become an established part of information systems design. There is also an increasing emphasis on assessing, evaluating and testing the usability of systems. The discipline devoted to the design and evaluation of the user interface is now frequently known as usability engineering.

Usability is normally established in terms of two elements: a defined user group and a defined set of tasks. Hence the design of user interfaces must consider the roles of designed users of the proposed interface and what those roles represent in terms of a defined set of tasks that the role will wish to perform with the IT system through the interface.

13.6 STAKEHOLDERS

The concept of use implies the related concept of a user. However, the term *user* is a somewhat confusing one in that it is frequently used to refer to all those persons within the organisation who are not information technology personnel. The term is frequently used as a catch-all by developers to include all those who fall outside the boundaries of development work. Different job categories are frequently included in the user label – top-level managers, middle managers and operational staff. In many ways this term appears to be used as a boundary label to delineate developers from non-developers.

We prefer to use the term *stakeholder group* rather than *user*, in that it allows us to include various social groups within and without the organisation that potentially may influence the successful use and impact of some information system. We may distinguish between the following major types of stakeholders:

- *Producers*. Producers are the project organisation or the development team (Chapter 38).
- *Clients*. Clients sponsor and provide resources for the continuation of an IS project. Clients normally equate to managerial groups within organisations.
- *End-users*. In terms of users, managers are rarely the *end*-users of information systems. Most IS are produced for use by other levels within the organisation.
- *Customers*. Information systems normally impact upon the customers of organisations.
- *Suppliers*. Information systems are increasingly impacting upon the suppliers of some organisation.
- *Regulators*. These are groups or agencies that set environmental constraints for an IS.
- *Competitors*. Competitors will be impacted upon by information systems, particularly by that group of systems known as strategic information systems, and may quickly attempt to emulate an organisation's information systems in this area.

The concept of a stakeholder is clearly a political concept in that it is related to issues of power and its exercise. Stakeholder groups are social groups that have a 'stake' in and potentially a degree of influence over the development of some information system. An organisational group can also be defined in terms of a set of meanings shared in common – a subculture (Chapter 18). Each stakeholder group potentially may form a distinct subculture in some organisation. For our purposes, the set of assumptions, expectations and knowledge which a group may use to frame technological change is of primary interest.

13.6.1 TECHNOLOGICAL FRAMES

One important facet which serves to distinguish between modern organisational subcultures is the way in which members approach or 'frame' information technology. Orlikowski and Gash (1994) propose that people in organisations approach technology on the basis of their technological frame. A technological frame is a collection of underlying assumptions, expectations and knowledge that people have about technology and its use. They propose that the idea of a techno-logical frame is central to understanding the process of development, use and change of technology, and that key stakeholder groups in organisations, such as managers, technologists and users, hold significantly different technological frames.

Example ▐▐▐▐▶ Orlikowski and Gash (1994) illustrate the usefulness of this concept in an examina-tion of a project which attempted to introduce Lotus Notes – an information tech-nology package – into a consulting organisation. Technologists and users displayed different perceptions of this technology on a number of dimensions:

- *Nature of technology*. Technologists had an understanding of Notes that defined it in terms of an information-sharing and groupwork tool. Users, in contrast, framed it more as an individual productivity tool

- *Technology strategy*. Technologists expected the package to leverage the work of the firm. Users tended to see Notes merely as a substitute for existing informa-tion technologies such as fax and telephone.

- *Technology in use*. Technologists assumed that Notes was an end-user tool and hence needed little support from the informatics department. Users, however, lacked detailed knowledge of the functionality of the tool and hence felt that the technologists should demonstrate how it might be used.

13.7 STAKEHOLDER INVOLVEMENT AND SATISFACTION

A number of critical principles affecting use arise from the concept of stakeholder groups:

- It is important to identify stakeholder groups that are likely to influence the development process as part of the planning for an information system.
- It is important to involve representatives of various stakeholder groups in the development process.
- It is important to identify differences in meanings assigned to technology between stakeholders.

Stakeholder involvement in the development of information systems is seen to improve system acceptance and the satisfaction with systems (Newman and Sabherwal, 1996). Stakeholder satisfaction refers to a subjective assessment of the success of some IS. Determining the levels of such satisfaction is an important part of the assessment of the worth of some information system. Clearly satisfaction can be assessed at a number of levels:

- *Satisfaction with the interface*. This may serve as one measure of usability.

- *Satisfaction with the IT system.* This may serve as one measure of functionality.
- *Satisfaction with the information system.* This may serve as one measure of utility.

Since the interface is the major focus of the topic of use, we concentrate on user interface satisfaction here, although it is somewhat difficult to separate out issues of functionality from this assessment. Some user satisfaction criteria with systems include:

- Output assessments, such as accuracy, quality, completeness and relevance of output
- Process assessments, such as availability of service, mean time between failure, down-time and number of security breaches
- Input assessments such as ease of use and response time

The assessment of the satisfaction with interfaces is frequently assessed via questionnaires consisting of a series of attitude questions. One popular approach is QUIS (Chin *et al.*, 1988) – Questionnaire for User Interface Satisfaction – consisting of 27 items using a nine-point Likert scale.

Example ▐▐▐➡ The following is an example of a question from a user interface satisfaction questionnaire.

Please mark the positions that best reflect your impressions of the system:

Pleasing	_ _ _ _ _ _	Irritating
Complete	_ _ _ _ _ _	Incomplete
Cooperative	_ _ _ _ _ _	Uncooperative
Simple	_ _ _ _ _ _	Complicated
Fast to use	_ _ _ _ _ _	Slow to use
Safe	_ _ _ _ _ _	Unsafe

13.8 STAKEHOLDER RESISTANCE

After delivery, an information system is subject to use and maintenance (Chapter 32). The further development and maintenance of a given information system we can describe as the post-implementation trajectory of the IS.

One of the key ways in which organisational politics may affect the post-implementation trajectory of an IS is through user or stakeholder resistance. Hirschheim and Newman (1988), for instance, provide a case study that illustrates how user resistance differed in departments with differing rates of stakeholder involvement in implementation. Keen (1981) details a number of counter-implementation strategies that users may take to impede the development of the system or its implementation:

- *Lie low.* If you do not want a system to succeed, then the more you keep out of the way and do not give help and encouragement, the more likelihood there is of failure.
- *Rely on inertia.* If you can be too busy when asked then the implementation process may come to a halt.
- *Keep the project complex, hard to coordinate and vaguely defined.* If the goals are ambiguous or too ambitious there is every chance of failure as energy is dissipated in many different directions.
- *Minimise the implementers' legitimacy and influence.* If the designers are kept as outsiders, other users will probably not allow them to work effectively.
- *Exploit their lack of inside knowledge.* The design team probably know very little about the detailed nature of the work and if they are denied this knowledge, the system will probably prove to be inadequate when it is implemented.

13.9 SUMMARY

- After information systems are introduced into an organisation they have immediate effects in terms of the context of use.
- The context of use is largely determined by the human activity system into which the information system is placed.
- Information systems may be closely aligned with their human activity system, through design or accident. Information systems may be misaligned with their human activity systems.
- Successful use is predicated upon close alignment. Alignment is facilitated by the identification of stakeholders, an understanding of differences in the technological frames of stakeholders and involvement of representatives of stakeholder groups within the development process.
- Misaligned IS are likely to be subject to user resistance. User resistance can take numerous forms.

13.10 QUESTIONS

- **(i)** Describe the main elements of DeLone and McLean's model of IS success.
- **(ii)** Describe some of the key principles that characterise the area of use of information systems.
- **(iii)** What is meant by a system's usability?
- **(iv)** Define the concept of a stakeholder.
- **(v)** List the various types of stakeholder one might expect to find in an organisation.
- **(vi)** What is meant by a technological frame and why is it important?

(vii) Stakeholder or user resistance is a major problem for information systems development. Why?

(viii) Why is it important to involve stakeholders in the information systems development process?

13.11 EXERCISES

(i) In terms of some information system known to you, try to identify the major stakeholders that affected the project trajectory. Use the taxonomy of producers, clients, end-users, customers and regulators.

(ii) Investigate usability engineering as an approach to assessing the quality of user interfaces.

(iii) Were representatives of any stakeholder groups involved in the project? In what ways were they involved? Is it possible to assess the effect such involvement had on the success of the project?

13.12 PROJECTS

(i) Identify the stakeholders relevant to some information system and generate an analysis of the negative and positive effects of the information system upon each stakeholder group.

(ii) Investigate usability as a property of some information system and determine appropriate ways of assessing the usability of some information system.

(iii) Investigate the levels and forms of user resistance to information technology in a particular industrial sector.

13.13 REFERENCES

DeLone, W. H. and McLean, E. R. (1992). Information systems success: the quest for the dependent variable. *Information Systems Research*, 3(1), 60–95.

Chin, J. P., Diehl, V. A. and Norman, K. L. (1988). Development of an instrument for measuring user satisfaction of the human–computer interface. *CHI'88 Conference on Human Factors in Computing Systems*. New York, ACM, pp. 213–218.

Eason, K. D. (1988). *Information Technology and Organisational Change*. Taylor & Francis, London.

Hirschheim, R. and Newman, M. (1988). Information systems and user resistance: theory and practice. *Computer Journal*, **31**(5), 398–408.

Keen, P. (1981). Information systems and organisational change. *Communications of the ACM*, **24**(1), 24–33.

Keen, P. and Gerson, E. M. (1977). The politics of software systems design. *Datamation*, November.

Kling, R. and Iacono, S. (1984). The control of IS developments after implementation. *Communications of the ACM*, **27**(12), 1218–1226.

Landauer, T. K. (1995). *The Trouble with Computers: Usefulness, Usability and Productivity*. MIT Press, Cambridge, MA.

Newman, M. and Sabherwal, R. (1996). Determinants of commitment to information systems development: a longitudinal investigation. *MIS Quarterly*, 23–54.

Nielsen, J. (1993). *Usability Engineering*. Academic Press, Boston, MA.

Orlikowski, W. T. and Gash, T. C. (1994). Technological frames: making sense of information technology in organisations. *ACM Trans. on Information Systems*, **12**(2), 174–207.

Salabert, D. and Newman, M. (1995). Regaining control: the case of the Spanish air traffic control system – SACTA. *European Conference on Information Systems* (ed. G. Doukidis), Athens, Greece, pp. 1171–1179.

Sommerville, I., Bentley, R., Rodden, T. and Sawyer, P. (1994). Cooperative systems design. *The Computer Journal*, **37**(5).

CHAPTER 14

THE IMPACT OF INFORMATION SYSTEMS

Computers are useless. They can only give you answers.

Pablo Picasso (1881–1973)

LEARNING OUTCOMES

After reading this chapter, you will be able to:

- Distinguish intended from unintended effects, positive from negative impact and the importance of alignment of IS

- Consider the impact of information systems for organisations in terms of efficiency and effectiveness

- Address the impact of information systems on groups and individuals within organisations

- Understand the importance of summative evaluation of IS

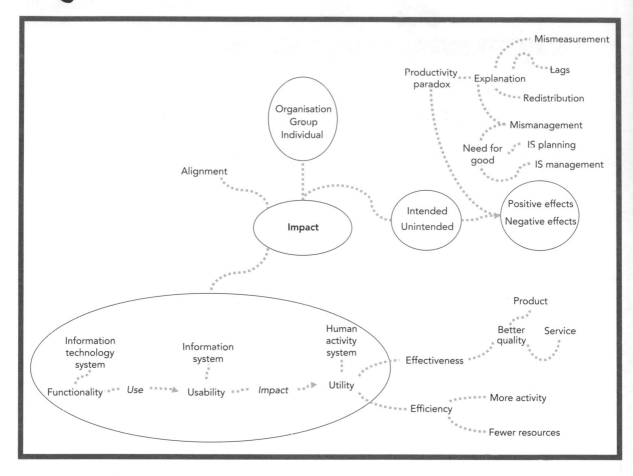

14.1 INTRODUCTION

After information systems are introduced into an organisation they have immediate effects in terms of the context of use (Chapter 13). The context of use is largely determined by the human activity system into which the information system is placed. Information systems may be closely aligned with their human activity system, through design or accident. Information systems may also be misaligned with their human activity systems.

Second-order effects, or what we have called impact on the informatics model (Chapter 1), may be distinguished in terms of impact on the individual, on groups and on the organisation as a whole. Impact may also be either positive or negative. At the level of groups and individuals, decisions about the positive or negative nature of impact will be relative to organisational position. In terms of impact on individuals and groups, one may cite the shifts in power and influence that may arise after the introduction of some information system. In terms of impact on the organisation as a whole, the relationship between information systems and productivity is one of the most hotly debated.

14.2 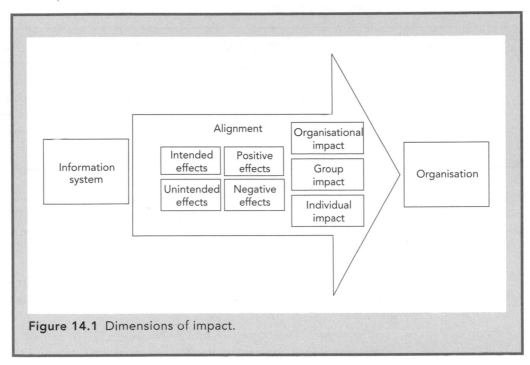 IMPACT

The issue of IS impact can be considered in terms of the following issues (Figure 14.1).

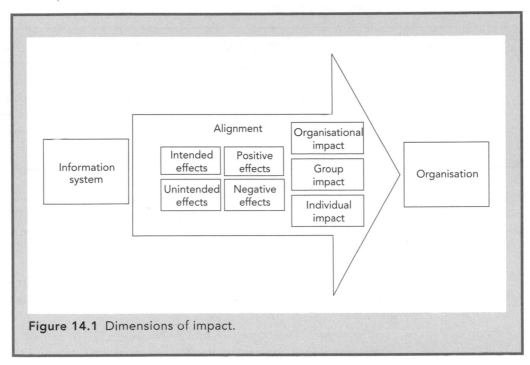

Figure 14.1 Dimensions of impact.

- *Intended and unintended effects.* The introduction of an information system into an organisation is an innovation that has the potential to perturb the organisation. This perturbation generates both intended and unintended effects. Some of the impact will have been predicted and designed for. However, much of the impact of information systems may be unintended.

Example ▶ In a study of the introduction of Lotus Notes into a company selling marketing software, Orlikowski (1996) observed the way in which this technology changed planned ways of working. Initially, the idea was to acquire and introduce this technology as a way of managing a large increase in telephone calls received by software support staff at local offices. The system was designed to enable the electronic entry and documentation of calls so as to enable individual call-handlers to more effectively track and respond to calls. However, after implementation, Orlikowski observed people starting to use the system to proactively respond to other people's calls for which they had a ready solution during down-time periods in their work. This change was so successful that managers began to assess support specialists in terms of their ability to collaborate proactively with their colleagues. Eventually, the system began to be used as a way of training new support staff in 'appropriate' ways of performing support work.

- *Positive and negative impact.* Such effects may be both positive and negative. Certain aspects of the human activity system may be deleteriously affected by the introduction of some information system. In contrast, a human activity system may also experience significant gain in efficiency and/or effectiveness with the introduction of an IS.

Example ▮▮▮➤ Button and Harper (1993) describe the introduction of a computerised order-processing system into a foam manufacturing company which clearly upset existing work practices to such a degree that the IS actually interfered with effective fulfilment of orders – 'It slowed things down'. Likewise, Sachs (1995) demonstrates how the introduction of a centralised work-scheduling system into a telephone engineering organisation disrupted the effective 'troubleshooting' work of maintenance engineers

- *Alignment.* The literature usually casts desirable impact in terms of the alignment of information systems with human activity systems. Effective information systems are those which are aligned with the human activity systems they support. The major premise is that the closer that the information system corresponds to or is aligned with the human activity system then the more successful the information system is likely to be. If the human activity system is not aligned with the human activity system then failure (Chapter 15) is a likely consequence.
- *Level of impact.* The impact of an information system can be considered on a number of levels: the organisation as a whole, stakeholder groups within the organisation and even at the level of individuals.

Example ▮▮▮➤ Landauer (1995) compiles an impressive case of evidence against the current usefulness and usability of computer systems. He maintains that the poor record of current computer systems on these two counts means that there is little evidence that computer systems actually contribute to organisational effectiveness, particularly to increases in productivity. There are examples of effective use of computer technology to improve business performance such as in the area of computer-aided telephony, but these are in the minority.

He makes the critical distinction between phase one and phase two computer applications. Phase one applications constitute those areas in which computers have been used to automate functions that have either traditionally been performed by humans or doing tasks that no human would be capable of. Both these areas exploit the power of numerical calculation performed by the computer. Examples are missile control and accounting systems. Landauer argues that there are fewer and fewer areas for the penetration of phase one applications available for computers. Phase two applications are about augmentation, encompassing that range of tasks that people do that cannot be taken over entirely by numerical calculations.

Phase one applications, because of their inherent deterministic and limited context, have proven relatively successful applications. It is, however, in the growing range of phase two applications that it is unclear precisely to what degree such computer systems are making a contribution to organisations.

Landauer does, however, believe that computer systems can be used to improve performance. At the moment, though, they have been introduced with little formative or summative evaluation of their usability and usefulness.

14.3 IMPACT UPON THE ORGANISATION

Information systems are normally introduced with the aim of making a positive contribution to organisational performance. However, information systems may have very little effect on organisational performance or alternatively a detrimental effect.

14.3.1 POSITIVE IMPACT

Business organisations overtly invest in information systems for one of two reasons:

- To be more efficient
- To be more effective

Information technology cannot deliver either efficiency or effectiveness gains by itself. Information technology can enable changes in information systems and human activity systems which in turn lead to changes in the efficiency and/or effectiveness of organisations. Such gains are the positive effects of technology innovations within organisations. Assessment of impact on the organisation or what we have called the utility or efficacy of an IS is a necessary activity at the phase of systems conception (Chapter 27) when a business case is built for the IS. It is also a key focus within summative evaluation when business objectives for an IS are revisited (Chapter 41).

Efficiency gains
Efficiency gains can be achieved in a human activity system through doing more with the same resources or the same with fewer resources. Hence efficiency gains can be measured in terms of comparing inputs against outputs using a systems model of the organisation (Figure 14.2).

In the traditional open systems model of organisations, capital and labour are the two inputs that the organisation takes from its environment. A micro-economic model of the firm permits capital to be freely substituted for labour to

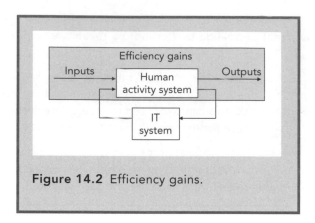

Figure 14.2 Efficiency gains.

produce similar levels of output or production. Such models predict that information technology can be freely substituted for labour, thereby introducing cost savings.

Another type of economic model of the firm is based around the idea of transaction costs. Transaction costs are those costs incurred by the organisation when it buys in the market-place. Firms seek to reduce transaction costs, particularly by reducing the costs associated with using markets, such as locating and communicating with suppliers, maintaining contracts and obtaining information on products. Information technology can help firms reduce the costs associated with such activity.

Example IIII➡ Take the case of teaching within a university. Efficiency gains would be evident in terms of some teaching process if more students are taught with the same resources of staff, buildings etc. Other forms of efficiency gains may be evident in the cost charged to students for undertaking higher education. Hence charging less for a particular education module may be an example of an efficiency gain.

Effectiveness gains

Effectiveness gains normally involve delivering greater value to the customer of some organisation. Hence effectiveness is primarily focused on the outputs from some organisation (Figure 14.3). Effectiveness gains can be measured in terms of improvements in the quality of the service or product.

Example IIII➡ Again using teaching as an example, the effectiveness of the teaching process may be measured in terms of the number of students achieving degree awards as compared to those starting a degree or in terms of the profile of students exiting from a particular university. For instance, a measure of effectiveness may be based on the number of students achieving first-class awards at undergraduate level.

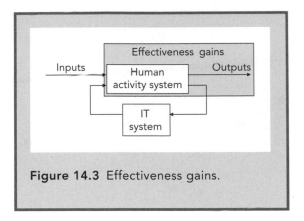

Figure 14.3 Effectiveness gains.

As far as commercial organisations are concerned, both efficiency and effectiveness are strategies to make more money, i.e. to increase profitability. Efficiency and effectiveness gains will lead to more customers and will improve the competitive position of the company.

14.3.2 NEGATIVE IMPACT

But does the introduction of an information system always have a positive impact? Evidence suggests that there are some inherent paradoxes/contradictions involved with the introduction of IS into organisations. One of the most significant is known as the productivity paradox.

Productivity paradox

One key reason why organisations use IS is the expectation that employing such systems will raise the productivity of the workforce. However, over a number of years, this link between IS usage and productivity has been questioned. This has become known as the productivity paradox, and is illustrated by the graphs produced by Brynjolfson (1993) in Figure 14.4.

Brynjolfson's paper examines the literature on the relationship between productivity and the application of information technology. The available evidence seems to suggest that whereas delivered computing power has increased by two orders of magnitude since the 1970s, productivity, particularly in the service sector (the heaviest users of IT), has stagnated. Hence in the graphs in Figure 14.4, although the spending on computers has gradually increased amongst office-based (white collar) organisations in the USA since the 1950s, productivity amongst office workers has remained relatively stable over the same period.

Brynjolfson considers four main explanations for the productivity paradox:

- *Mismeasurement of inputs and outputs.* A proper indicator of IT impact has yet to be formulated and analysed. Traditional measures, such as the number of service transactions multiplied by their unit value, tend to ignore non-traditional sources of value, such as increased quality and speed of customer service.

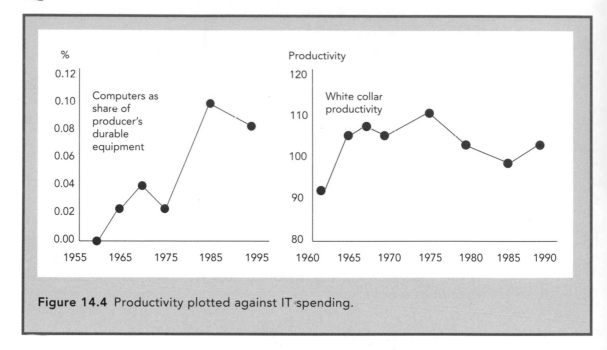

Figure 14.4 Productivity plotted against IT spending.

- *Lags due to learning and adjustment.* The long-term lag between cost and benefit may be due to the extensive learning required on the part of the individual, groups and the organisation to fully exploit IT.

- *Redistribution and dissipation of profits.* This explanation proposes that those investing in technology benefit at the expense of others in a particular industry, Hence there is no aggregate benefit to an industrial sector such as financial services.

- *Mismanagement of IT.* This is the basic informatics argument. It proposes that companies have systematically mismanaged and have not planned systematically for the introduction of IT. This explains the lack of piecemeal benefit from the introduction of IS/IT.

14.4 IMPACT UPON GROUPS AND INDIVIDUALS

At a more micro level, as well as having an impact upon organisations, information systems have an impact upon groups and individuals. Again, the impact may be positive or negative. The assessment of the value of such impact depends on the position of the stakeholder group within the organisation. Some potential consequences for groups and individuals from the introduction of IT systems are listed below:

- *Increased monitoring of work.* IT systems may increase levels of monitoring of work and create greater control of work by managerial groups. IT systems may enable large amounts of transactional information to be captured about the day-to-day activities of the workforce. Such information may be used, for instance, to decide upon redundancy strategies.

- *Job enrichment.* IT systems can be used to enrich jobs and provide greater degrees of worker empowerment. IT systems may be used to remove many burdensome administrative activities, freeing up workers to devote more time to issues such as customer service. One key way in which customer service may be improved is by letting customer service personnel make instantaneous decisions about actions to take in relation to customers with the aid of IT systems.

- *Collaboration and coordination.* IT systems may cause changes in forms of collaboration and coordination between groups. For instance, electronic mail (e-mail) systems have caused substantial changes to the way in which people collaborate and coordinate work activities. E-mail is now extensively used in organisations as a means of scheduling meetings, for instance. This may have a consequential impact on degrees of face-to-face contact in organisations.

- *Shifts in power and influence.* IT systems may cause changes in forms of power and influence within and between groups. For example, substantial shifts of this nature were experienced in relation to the position of office workers such as secretaries when information systems were first introduced to replace typical secretarial skills, such as typing.

- *Visibility of work.* Zuboff (1988) has argued that IT makes work more visible. This has the potential for workers to establish more clearly what is happening in their organisation, identify problems with work processes and suggest alternative ways of doing things. Hence IT systems have significant potential as vehicles for learning in organisations.

The design of information systems (Chapter 29) is not a value-neutral activity. Decisions made particularly about the shape of a human activity system to be used in association with some information system can affect the following dimensions of work in a positive or negative way:

- *Upskilling/deskilling.* Information systems can increase the levels of skills (upskilling) required in a particular work setting or decrease the level of skill (deskilling) required.

- *Task variety.* Information systems can increase the variety of tasks required of the worker or decrease the variety of tasks.

- *Task scope.* Information systems can be used to increase the size of the task relative to the overall purpose of the organisation. Alternatively, tasks can be reduced in size.

- *Autonomy.* Information systems can be designed to increase the autonomy of workers in the sense that they are given responsibility for planning and controlling their own work. Alternatively, information systems can be designed to control, sometimes in minute detail, the everyday work of personnel.

- *Social interaction.* Information systems can be designed to encourage social interaction between workers or to decrease levels of social interaction.

14.5 SUMMATIVE EVALUATION

It is important for organisations to study closely the impact of their information systems, to learn from this experience and on this basis to better plan for the development and introduction of future IT systems. This process is what we call summative evaluation of information systems (Chapter 41). Summative evaluation traditionally revisits the issues of costs and benefits associated with information systems. However, it should also consider the important interaction between such information systems and the human activity systems they support.

14.6 SUMMARY

- Impact on the interaction model may be distinguished in terms of impact on the individual, on groups and on the organisation as a whole.
- The impact of introducing information technology systems may be either positive or negative.
- Judgements about the positive or negative nature of IT impact are necessarily dependent on who is judging the situation.
- Most common assessments of information technology are concerned with assessing the effects IT has on organisational efficiency and/or effectiveness.
- IT does not deliver efficiency or effectiveness gains in and of itself. IT can contribute to changes in human activity systems which in turn can affect the efficiency and effectiveness of organisations.
- It is important for organisations to summatively evaluate their IT systems and the effect these technology systems have on human activity systems.

14.7 QUESTIONS

(i) Distinguish between the intended and unintended effects of information systems and describe some of the intended and unintended effects of information systems.

(ii) Describe the main forms in which information systems may positively impact upon the organisation.

(iii) What is meant by alignment in terms of information systems?

(iv) How does the micro-economic model of the firm and the idea of transaction costs help us understand the efficiency gains that information technology can offer organisations?

(v) Distinguish between efficiency gains and effectiveness gains in terms of the organisation.

(vi) Describe the productivity paradox of information technology.

(vii) List some of the major explanations for the productivity paradox.

(viii) Describe some of the ways in which information technology impacts upon individuals and groups within organisations.

(ix) The design of information systems is not a value-neutral activity. Discuss some of the reasons why this might be the case.

(x) Why is summative evaluation important for assessing the impact of information systems?

14.8 EXERCISES

(i) Consider an organisation or part of an organisation known to you. In what ways has an information system been used to improve either the efficiency or the effectiveness of some human activity system within the organisation?

(ii) How can you measure the improvements in efficiency and effectiveness?

14.9 PROJECTS

(i) Conduct an impact analysis of the effect information systems innovations have had in a company. Determine both positive and negative impact.

(ii) Investigate whether the productivity paradox holds in another sector, such as manufacturing or government.

14.10 REFERENCES

Brynjolfson, E. (1993). The productivity paradox of information technology. *Communications of the ACM*, **36**(12), 67–77.

Button, G. and Harper, R. H. R. (1993). Taking the organisation into accounts. In *Technology in Working Order: studies of work, interaction and technology* (ed. G. Button). Routledge, London.

Landauer, T. K. (1995). *The Trouble with Computers: Usefulness, Usability and Productivity*. MIT Press, Cambridge, MA.

Orlikowski, W. J. (1996). Realising the potential of new technologies: an improvisation model of change management. *Business Information Technology*. Manchester Metropolitan University.

Sachs, P. (1995). Transforming work: collaboration, learning and design. *Communications of the ACM*, **38**(9), 36–45.

Zuboff, S. (1988). *In the Age of the Smart Machine: the Future of Work and Power*. Heinemann, London.

CHAPTER 15

THE SUCCESS AND FAILURE OF INFORMATION SYSTEMS

Haste in every business brings failures.

Herodotus (485–425 BC)

LEARNING OUTCOMES

After reading this chapter, you will be able to:

● Describe the major dimensions of IS failure

● Relate some of the material studying IS failure and success

● Outline a number of lessons from this literature

● Highlight a number of strategies for avoiding IS failure and achieving IS success

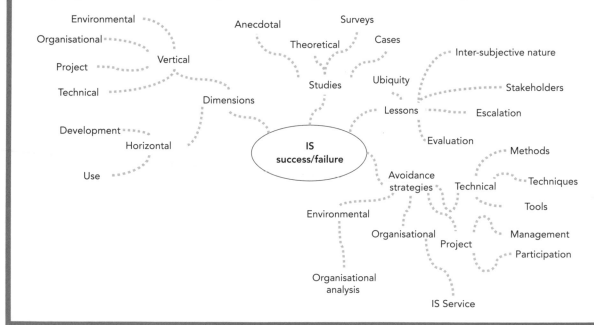

15.1 INTRODUCTION

The two issues of the use of information systems and the impact of such use are inherently associated with assessments of the worth of an IS. In very broad terms, assessments of worth focus on considerations of the success and failure of IS.

In many ways the success/failure of information systems can be seen to be the key dependent variable for the discipline of informatics (Chapter 48). In this chapter we primarily consider the issue of IS failure, using the assumption that learning from IS failures will provide us with important lessons for formulating successful strategies for the planning, management and development of information systems.

15.2 DIMENSIONS OF FAILURE

Information systems failure can be considered in terms of both the horizontal and vertical dimensions of the informatics model discussed in Chapter 1. The horizontal dimension is expressed in terms of the difference between development failure and use failure. The vertical dimension is expressed in terms of failure at the level of IT systems, IS projects, or organisations, or at the level of the external environment. These two axes are illustrated in Figure 15.1.

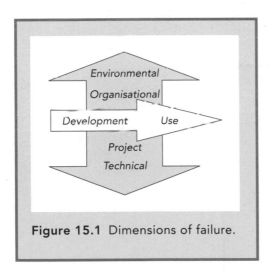

Figure 15.1 Dimensions of failure.

Information systems failure can be addressed on a number of levels in terms of the vertical dimension: technical, project, organisational and environmental (social/economic/political). In very general terms these levels form a hierarchy of complexity in terms of information systems problems.

- *Technical failure.* Failure of hardware, software and communications, such as system crashes.

- *Project failure*. Failures in project management and control, such as cost or time overruns.
- *Organisational failure*. Failures of a system to deliver organisational benefits, such as decreases in efficiency or effectiveness.
- *Environmental failure*. Failure caused by changes in environmental factors such as changes in regulation and labour relations.

We might argue that there are two important phases in the way human beings approach problems: problem-setting and problem-solving. For certain areas of human activity problems are relatively easy to set; for other areas there is vast disagreement as to how to define key problems.

Technical problems tend, by their very nature to be relatively tractable. At this level we can usually identify quite precisely what constitutes a problem, and in terms of this definition identify suitable solutions. Such problems are hence best described as being 'hard'. We might argue that in this area, problem-setting is uncontentious, whereas problem-solving is the activity to which most effort is devoted.

At the opposite end of the scale lie organisational and environmental problems. Problems in this area are frequently difficult to identify, if only because different stakeholder groups will have different definitions as to what the problems are. Such problems are hence best described as being 'soft'. We might argue that these problems (sometimes referred to as 'wicked' problems) are characterised by a focus on issues of problem-setting rather than problem-solving. This distinction is illustrated in Figure 15.2.

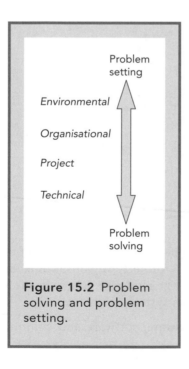

Figure 15.2 Problem solving and problem setting.

Problems at the project level tend to lie between the poles of 'hard' and 'soft'. By their very nature, certain problems, such as forming project teams, are relatively tractable. Other aspects of project management are less clearly definable. A good example here are the difficulties frequently experienced in terms of estimating the scale of an IS project and the resources necessary to complete it (Chapter 38).

We may also distinguish between failure during development and failure in use. Development failure occurs when the whole or part of a system is abandoned prior to implementation. Use failure occurs during the post-implementation trajectory of some IS. Use failure may be evident if a system is abandoned after a period of use or if a system is subject to large amounts of adaptive maintenance (Chapter 32). This distinction is illustrated in Figure 15.3.

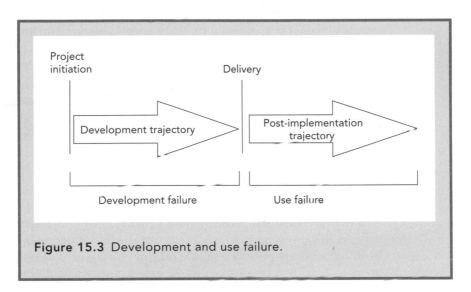

Figure 15.3 Development and use failure.

15.3 STUDIES OF FAILURE

Studies of IS failure fall into four categories: anecdotal evidence, theory building, case studies and survey research.

15.3.1 ANECDOTAL EVIDENCE

For a number of years a collection of anecdotal descriptions of IS failures has been accumulating in the ACM's *Software Engineering Notes*. McKenzie (1994) has analysed this material and found that of computer-related accidents (examples mainly of use failures) reported, 92% involved failures in what McKenzie calls human–computer interaction: 'More computer-related accidental deaths seem to be caused by interactions of technical and cognitive/organisational factors than by technical factors alone'.

15.3.2   THEORY BUILDING

Lyytinen and Hirschheim (1987), in conducting a survey of the literature on IS failure, identify four major theoretical categories of such phenomena:

- *Correspondence failure.* This is the most common form of IS failure discussed in the literature and typically reflects a management perspective on failure. It is based on the idea that design objectives are first specified in detail. An evaluation is conducted of the information system in terms of these objectives. If there is a lack of correspondence between objectives and evaluation the IS is regarded as a failure.

- *Process failure.* This type of failure is characterised by unsatisfactory development performance. It usually refers to one of two types of failure: first, when the IS development process cannot produce a workable system; and second, when the development process produces an IS but the project runs over budget in terms of cost, time etc.

- *Interaction failure.* Here, the emphasis shifts from a mismatch of requirements and system or poor development performance to a consideration of usage of a system. The argument is that if a system is heavily used it constitutes a success; if it is hardly ever used, or there are major problems involved in using a system, then it constitutes a failure. Lucas (1975) clearly adheres to this idea of failure.

- *Expectation failure.* Lyytinen and Hirschheim describe this as a superset of the three other types of failure. They also describe their idea of expectation failure to be a more encompassing, politically and pluralistically informed view of IS failure than the other forms. This is because they characterise correspondence, process and interaction failure as having one major theme in common: the three notions of failure portray a highly rational image of IS development; each views an IS as mainly a neutral technical artefact (Klein and Hirschheim, 1987). In contrast, they define expectation failure as the inability of an IS to meet a specific stakeholder group's expectations. IS failures signify a gap between some existing situation and a desired situation for members of a particular stakeholder group.

Sauer (1993) has criticised the model proposed by Lyytinen and Hirschheim for its plurality. Sauer's model posits a more conservative definition of information systems failure. According to his account, an information system should only be deemed a failure when development or operation ceases, leaving supporters dissatisfied with the extent to which the system has served their interests. This means that a system should not be considered a failure until all interest in progressing an IS project has ceased. This definition of *termination failure* is hence stricter than Lyytinen and Hirschheim's concept of *expectation failure*.

Sauer develops a model of IS failure based on exchange relations. He portrays the development of information systems as an innovation process based on three components: the project organisation, the information system, and its supporters (see Figure 15.4). Each of these components is arranged in a triangle of dependencies. The information system depends on the project organisation, the project

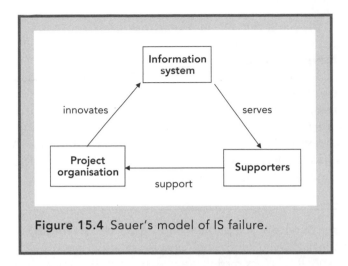

Figure 15.4 Sauer's model of IS failure.

organisation depends on its supporters, and the supporters depend on the information system. The information system requires the efforts and expertise of the project organisation to sustain it; the project organisation is heavily dependent on the provision of support in the form of material resources and help in coping with contingencies; and supporters require benefits from the information system.

One of the key ways in which Sauer distinguishes termination failure from expectation failure is in terms of the concept of a flaw. Information systems are the product of a process which is open to flaws. Every information system is flawed in some way. However, flaws are different from failures. Flaws may be corrected within any innovation process at a cost, or accepted at a cost. Flaws describe the perception of stakeholders that they face undesired situations that constitute problems to be solved. Examples of flaws are program bugs, hardware performance, organisational changes etc. Unless there is support available to deal with flaws they will have the effect of reducing the capacity of an information system to serve its supporters and may result in introducing further flaws into the innovation process. At some stage, the volume of flaws may trigger a decision to remove support and hence to terminate a project.

15.3.3 CASE STUDIES

Benbasat *et al.* (1987) describe case research as being particularly important for those types of problems where research and theory are still at their early, formative stages. They see a key use of case studies in the generation of theory from practice. The topic of IS failure has been seen to be a particularly formative research area and therefore one particularly amenable to the case study approach.

The London Ambulance Computer Aided Despatch System project has been one of the most frequently quoted UK examples of information systems failure in recent times. Beynon-Davies (1995) makes the case that the prominence of this particular example is probably due more to the 'safety-critical' nature of this system and the claim that 20–30 people may have lost their lives as a result of this failure, than the scale of the project. Indeed, LASCAD (£1.1–1.5 million) is dwarfed by other British IS 'failures', such as the Wessex Regional Health Authority's RISP project (£63 million) (Public Accounts Committee, 1993) and the UK Stock Exchange's TAURUS settlement system (£75–300 million) (Flowers, 1996).

IS failure is, of course, not specifically a British malaise. For instance, Oz (1994) takes a similar documentary approach to describing the important case of the CONFIRM reservation system in the USA ($125 million). Also, Sauer (1993) comprehensively describes a large Australian government IS project – Mandata (A$30 million) – that was abandoned during the 1970s.

Example: London Ambulance Service's Computer Aided Despatch System ‖‖▶

On 27 October 1992 an information system made the lead story on the BBC's *Nine O'Clock News*. It was reported that a new computerised system established at the headquarters of the London Ambulance Service (LAS) (The London Ambulance Service's Computer Aided Despatch System – hereafter referred to as the LASCAD system) failed, and that as a direct result of this failure the lives of 20–30 people may have been lost.

The major objective of the LASCAD system was to automate many of the human-intensive processes characteristic of ambulance despatch systems. The essential functionality of the proposed system is described below (see Figure 15.5):

- BT operators route all 999 calls concerning medical emergencies as a matter of routine to LAS headquarters (HQ) in Waterloo.

- The 18 HQ 'receivers' were then expected to record on the system the name, telephone number and address of the caller, and the name, destination address and brief details of the patient.

- This information was then transmitted over a local area network to an 'allocator'. The system would pinpoint the patient's location on a map display of areas of London.

- The system was expected to continuously monitor the location of every ambulance via radio messages transmitted by each vehicle every 13 seconds. The system would then determine the nearest ambulances to the patient.

- Experienced ambulance despatchers were organised into teams based on three zones (south, north-east and north-west). Ambulance despatchers would be offered details by the system of the three nearest ambulances and the estimated time each would need to reach the scene.

- The despatcher would choose an ambulance and send patient details to a small terminal screen located on the dashboard of the ambulance. The crew would then be expected to confirm that they were on their way.

- If the selected ambulance was in an ambulance depot then the despatch message would be received on the station printer.

- The ambulance crew would always be expected to acknowledge a message. The system would automatically alert the HQ of any ambulance where no acknowledgement was made. A follow-up message would then be sent from HQ.

- The system would detect from each vehicle's location messages whether any ambulance was heading in the wrong direction. The system would then alert controllers.

- Further messages would tell HQ when the ambulance crew had arrived, when it was on its way to a hospital and when it was free again.

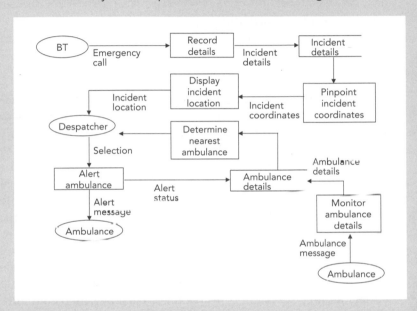

Figure 15.5 The LASCAD system.

According to the public inquiry, the system 'failure' was attributable not to the system crashing but to poor performance. Basically, problems caused particularly by the communications system, such as ambulance crews pressing wrong buttons or ambulances being in radio blackspots, caused a build-up of the amount of incorrect vehicle information recorded by the system. This had a knock-on effect in that the system made incorrect allocations on the basis of the information it had. For example, multiple vehicles were sent to the same incident, or the closest vehicle was not chosen for despatch. As a consequence, the system had fewer ambulance resources to allocate. The system also placed calls that had not gone through the appropriate protocol on a waiting list and generated exception messages for those incidents for which it had received incorrect status information. Indeed, the number of exception messages appear to have increased to such an extent that staff were not able to clear the queue. It became increasingly difficult for staff to attend to messages that had scrolled off the screen. The increasing size of the queue slowed the system. All this meant that, with fewer resources to allocate, and the problems of dealing with the waiting and exception queues, it took longer to allocate resources to incidents. Eventually, a decision was made to switch off the system and return to a manual mode of operation.

The LAS chief John Wilby resigned within a couple of the days of the events described above, quoting as his reason the evident lack of confidence in the LAS. Under pressure from a number of sources, the Health Secretary, Virginia Bottomley, announced a Public Inquiry into the system headed by South Yorkshire ambulance chief Don Page. The findings of the inquiry were eventually published in an 80-page report in February 1993, which immediately became news in the computing and national press.

15.3.4   SURVEY RESEARCH

Lucas (1975) describes a series of quantitative investigations used to verify a number of general hypotheses on IS failure. Unfortunately, the data collected does little to illuminate the complex reality of organisational IS, and indeed the factors contributing to IS failure.

Lyytinen (1988) describes an exploratory study looking at systems analysts' perceptions of information systems failure. Systems analysts are discussed in terms of being a major stakeholder group in systems development projects. Their view of IS and IS failure differs from users or management views. Interestingly, Lyytinen found that systems analysts believed that only 20% of projects are likely to turn out to be failures. They also preferred to explain failures in highly procedural and rationalistic terms. Reasons mentioned for failure include inexact development goals and specifications, inadequate understanding of user's work and inadequate understanding of system contingencies. This, Lyytinen concludes, is concomitant with a set of professional expectations of the IS development process which conceives of it as an overtly rational act involving high technical and professional competence.

Ewusi-Mensah and Przasnyski (1994) distinguish between what they call IS project abandonment and IS failure. IS failure in their terms deals with the failure of usage and/or operations of the IS, whereas IS project abandonment is concerned with the process of IS development. This is similar to Lytinnen's distinction between development and use failure. In Ewusi-Mensah and Przasnyski (1995) they distinguish between:

- *Total abandonment.* Complete termination of all activities on a project prior to full implementation.

- *Substantial abandonment.* Major truncation or simplification of the project to make it radically different from the original specification prior to full implementation.

- *Partial abandonment.* Reduction of the original scope of the project without entailing significant changes to the IS's original specification, prior to full implementation.

They suggest that, from their small survey study, total abandonment is the most common type of development failure experienced in the USA. They also found that organisational factors, particularly the amount of senior management involvement and the degree of end-user participation in the project development, were the most widespread and dominant factors contributing to IS success/failure.

15.4 LESSONS FROM THE EVIDENCE ON IS FAILURE

We may glean a number of lessons from the available material on IS failure.

15.4.1 IS FAILURE IS COMMONPLACE

A survey conducted by the US Government's Accounting Agency in 1979 (US, 1985) found that less than 3% of the software that the US Government had paid for was actually used as delivered. More than half of the software was never used at all. Gladden (1982) reports in a similar survey that 75% of all system development undertaken is either never completed or the resulting systems are not used. In an international survey conducted by Coopers and Lybrand (Coopers, 1996), 60% of organisations internationally and 67% of organisations in the UK had suffered at least one systems project that had failed to deliver planned business benefits or had experienced cost and time overruns.

15.4.2 THE INTER-SUBJECTIVE NATURE OF IS FAILURE

It is important to understand that failure is not an objective concept. The definition of failure depends on the position and perspective of the definer – it is an inter-subjective concept. Hence Lyytinnen and Hirschheim's (1987) concept of expectation failure is critical.

15.4.3 THE IMPORTANCE OF STAKEHOLDERS

The identification of stakeholders and their likely impact on the trajectory of an IS project is important. Expectation failure is defined as the inability of an IS to meet a specific stakeholder group's expectations. IS failures signify a gap between some existing situation and a desired situation for members of a particular stakeholder group.

15.4.4 PROJECT TRAJECTORY

The trajectory of a project is defined as the historical shaping of an information system both before and after delivery. Frequently, the shape of an information system is determined by the power-play between different stakeholder groups (Hirschheim and Newman, 1988; Keen, 1981). It should be recognised that an IS, and hence an IS project, is a significant power resource in organisations. Failure can occur prior to the delivery of an information system. This is the notion of project abandonment or what Lyytinen and Hirschheim (1987) call development failure. Sauer's conception of termination failure (Sauer, 1993) corresponds to the idea of total abandonment of a project. However, projects may be substantially or partially abandoned. In this case, the goals of the information system may be reduced or reconfigured. Failure may also occur after an IS has been delivered to its user community. This is the idea of use failure (Lyytinen, 1988). Use failure normally occurs because the end-user stakeholders feel that the information system does not match their expectations (Kling and Iacono, 1984).

15.4.5 PROJECT ESCALATION

IS projects are frequently the subject of escalation in decision-making. Drummond (1994) defines escalation as 'the predicament where decision-makers find themselves trapped in a losing course of action as a result of previous decisions. Costs are incurred; there is an opportunity to withdraw or persist; and the consequences of withdrawal or persistence are uncertain. Typically the response to such dilemmas is irrational persistence'. The important point about the escalation concept is that support for an IS project can continue even in the face of major system flaws. Major stakeholders in a project may be reluctant to withdraw support because of the heavy investment in personnel and other resources devoted to a project (Newman and Sabherwal, 1996).

15.4.6 IMPORTANCE OF EVALUATION

Evaluation is the process of assessing the worth of something. The notion of worth is inherently associated with definitions of success or failure. IS evaluation is therefore critical to identifying success or failure of IS. In terms of IS we can distinguish between the worth of the product (the information system) and the worth of the process (the activities involved in producing the information system).

In practice, it is clearly difficult to separate the two. The worth of the IS development process is normally evaluated in terms of some assessment of the worth of the product:

- *Functionality*. Does the information system do what is required? Assessing the degree to which a system is functionally complete and consistent is a classic concern of systems development.
- *Usability*. Is the information system usable by its intended population?. Assessing the usability of systems has become important with the continuing progress and use of graphical user interfaces and multimedia interfaces.
- *Utility*. Does the information system produce benefit for the organisation? The main problem with assessing utility is that this can only be done in terms of changes to the human activity system which the information system supports.

15.5 AVOIDANCE STRATEGIES

Since the success of information systems is a key dependent variable for the discipline of informatics, strategies for ensuring success or avoiding failure assume an important significance. In this section we shall examine briefly a number of conventional and extended strategies for preventing failure and ensuring success and place pointers to relevant material discussed elsewhere in the book. Clearly, solutions or avoidance strategies to the problem of failure tend to become more tractable the lower level one is in the hierarchy of failures.

15.5.1 TECHNICAL

At the level of information technology systems the appropriate selection and use of tools can significantly reduce the risk of failure. Appropriate use of IS development methods (Chapter 26) and analysis and design techniques (Chapters 28 and 29) will also have a critical bearing on reducing the risk of failure.

15.5.2 PROJECT

At the level of projects, good and effective management and control of IS personnel (Chapter 38) and their activities can significantly reduce the occurrence of failure. Participation by the business community in development projects has also been shown to increase the likelihood of IS success.

15.5.3 ORGANISATION

At the organisational level, effective planning of the IS development portfolio and the structure and activities of the informatics service can affect risk of failure. Proper management of the informatics services function (Chapter 40) is also crucial to the long-term health of organisations.

15.5.4 ENVIRONMENT

At the environmental level, effective alignment of information systems strategy with business strategy is critical to the performance of the information systems function and the IS under their development and control. Effective organisational analysis (Chapter 33) needs to be conducted to guide such alignment.

In summary, ideally an organisation wishing to avoid IS failure would do well to engage in all of the suggested stages in the IS development process: organisational analysis; IS planning; IS management; project management; IS development; and IS maintenance. Many years of experience has been accumulated in the development of information systems and many lessons have been learned as to how to, for instance, manage IS projects. Yet IS failures are still commonplace.

This may be partly because, although frequently most medium to large-scale organisations engage in IS management, development and maintenance, few seem to take organisational analysis, IS planning and particularly IS evaluation seriously.

15.6 ⊚ SUMMARY

- IS failure can be analysed on a number of levels: technical, project, organisational and environmental. Technical problems tend to be 'hard' problems while environmental problems tend to be 'soft' problems.
- A distinction can be made between failures which occur during development and those which occur during use.
- The literature on IS failure is large and divides into anecdotal evidence, theory-building, case studies and survey work.
- From this literature a number of lessons can be gleaned.
- Such lessons direct attention at a number of strategies for avoiding failure and ensuring success.

15.7 ⊚ QUESTIONS

(i) Distinguish between technical, project, organisational and environmental failure.

(ii) What is the difference between problem-setting and problem-solving?

(iii) Distinguish between development failure and use failure.

(iv) Describe some of the main lessons from the literature on IS failure.

(v) Describe some conventional and extended strategies for avoiding IS failure.

15.8 ⊚ EXERCISES

(i) See if you can estimate the percentage of IS projects in an organisation known to you that are regarded as successes.

(ii) What percentage of projects in the organisation are regarded as failures?

(iii) In terms of the failures, what are seen as the major reasons for failure?

(iv) In terms of the successes, what are seen to be the major features of success?

15.9 ⊚ PROJECTS

(i) IS failure is frequently due to such systems not meeting expectations. Investigate why expectations are an important facet of the phenomenon of information systems failure.

(ii) Investigate a range of published case studies of failure and classify them in terms of development or use failure.

(iii) Develop a natural history of one or more IS development projects. Assess the degree to which they can be considered as a success or failure.

15.10 REFERENCES

Benbasat, I., Goldstein, D. K. and Mead, M. (1987). The case research strategy in studies of information systems. *MIS Quarterly*, September, pp. 368–386.

Beynon-Davies, P. (1995). Information systems 'failure': The case of the London Ambulance Service's Computer Aided Despatch System. *European Journal of Information Systems*, **4**, 171–184.

Coopers (1996). *Managing Information and Systems Risks: Results of an International Survey of Large Organisations*. Coopers and Lybrand.

Drummond, H. (1994). Escalation in organisational decision-making: a case of recruiting an incompetent employee. *Journal of Behavioural Decision-Making*, **7**, 43–55.

Ewusi-Mensah, K. and Przasnyski, Z. H. (1994). Factors contributing to the abandonment of information systems development projects. *Journal of Information Technology*, **9**, 185–201.

Ewusi-Mensah, K. and Przasnyski, Z. H. (1995). Learning from abandoned information system development projects. *Journal of Information Technology*, **10**, 3–14.

Flowers, S. (1996). *Software Failure, Management Failure: Amazing Stories and Cautionary Tales*. Chichester, John Wiley.

Gladden, G. R. (1982). Stop the lifecycle I want to get off. *Software Engineering Notes*, **7**(2), 35–39.

Hirschheim, R. and Newman, M. (1988). Information systems and user resistance: theory and practice. *Computer Journal*, **31**(5), 398–408.

Keen, P. (1981). Information systems and organisational change. *Communications of the ACM*, **24**(1), 24–33.

Klein, H. K. and Hirschheim, R. A. (1987). A comparative framework of data modelling paradigms and approaches. *The Computer Journal*, **30**(1), 8–14.

Kling, R. and Iacono, S. (1984). The control of IS developments after implementation. *Communications of the ACM*, **27**(12), 1218–1226.

Lucas, H. C. (1975). *Why Information Systems Fail*. Columbia University Press, New York.

Lyytinen, K. (1988). The expectation failure concept and systems analysts view of information systems failures: results of an exploratory study. *Information and Management*, **14**, 45–55.

Lyytinen, K. and Hirschheim, R. (1987). Information systems failures: a survey and classification of the empirical literature. *Oxford Surveys in Information Technology*, **4**, 257–309.

McKenzie, D. (1994). Computer-related accidental death: an empirical exploration. *Science and Public Policy*. **21**(4), 233–248.

Newman, M. and Sabherwal, R. (1996). Determinants of commitment to information systems development: a longitudinal investigation. *MIS Quarterly*, **20**(1), 23–54.

Oz, E. (1994). When Professional standards are lax: the confirm failure and its lessons. *Communications of the ACM*, **37**(10), 29–36.

Public Accounts Committee (1993). *Wessex Regional Health Authority Regional Information Systems Plan*, HMSO.

Sauer, C. (1993). *Why Information Systems Fail: A Case Study Approach*. Alfred Waller, Henley-On-Thames.

US (1979). US Government Accounting Office Report FGMSD-80-4. Reported in *ACM Sigsoft Software Engineering Notes*, **10**(5), October.

PART 4

ORGANISATION

We trained hard, but it seemed every time we were beginning to form up into teams, we would be reorganised. I was to learn later in life that we tend to meet any new situation by reorganising, and a wonderful method it can be for creating the illusion of progress while producing confusion, inefficiency and demoralisation.

From Petronii Arbitri Satyricon AD 66 (Attributed to Gaius Petronus, a Roman General who later committed suicide)

Information systems support human activity. Generally speaking, the discipline of organisational informatics is interested in human activity within organised groupings of individuals – organisations. This part examines the issue of what an organisation is and the relevance of information, information systems and information technology to organisations.

Organisations are social collectives, but not all social collectives are organisations. Organisations are social collectives in which formal procedures are used for coordinating the activities of members in the pursuit of joint objectives.

Generally speaking there are two major ways in which we may view an organisation (Chapter 16). We may examine organisations in a top-down way as units, systems or structures with their own particular characteristics and behaviour. This we call the institutional perspective on organisations. Alternatively, we may consider an organisation in a bottom-up fashion, as formed from the everyday actions of people engaged in the process of organising. This we call the action perspective on organisations.

These two perspectives form collections of a number of metaphors used in considering organisations. Each metaphor highlights a number of different ways in which information systems and information technology are relevant to organisations. From an institutional perspective we may view organisations as structures, closed and open systems and as information processing units. From an action perspective we may view an organisation as informal networks of people constructing action and accounting for such action in various ways.

The remaining chapters within Part 4 consider the elements of organisation described in the informatics model of information systems (Chapter 1). We consider the issue of organisational structure, organisational culture, organisational strategy and the informatics infrastructure of organisations. Each of these elements is considered both in terms of an institutional and action perspective.

- *Structure*. The structural metaphor (Chapter 17) is a dominant one and has clear links to the systems metaphor (Chapter 5). From an institutional perspective, organisational structure is interested in the way in which organisations are formed out of relationships between units. From an action perspective, organisational structure is a dynamic thing continually renegotiated within organisations.

- *Culture*. Culture (Chapter 18) is a much-used term in modern management thinking. There are clear links to the networks, productions and constructions metaphor on organisations. From an institutional perspective, organisational culture is a set of expectations imposed upon organisational members – the emphasis is on unitary culture. From an action perspective, organisational culture is a dynamic thing continually renegotiated between social groups. Separate subcultures may exist in the same organisation.

- *Strategy*. Organisation strategy (Chapter 19) is concerned with the future activities of some organisation. The environmental and information processing metaphors are particularly dominant in the area of strategy. From an institutional perspective, organisational strategy is derived in a formal top-down planning process. From an action perspective, organisational strategy is formed in a bottom-up way through bricolage.

- *Infrastructure*. Informatics infrastructure (Chapter 20) consists of the information, information systems and information technology architecture of some organisation. From an institutional perspective, an informatics infrastructure is a constraining force in organisations. From an action perspective, an informatics infrastructure is an enabling force.

CHAPTER 16

ORGANISATION THEORY

It is the theory that decides what we can observe.

Albert Einstein (1879–1955)

LEARNING OUTCOMES

After reading this chapter, you will be able to:

- Describe the institutional and action perspectives on organisation
- Relate the essential features of the process of structuration
- Distinguish between a number of different metaphors of organisation
- Describe the relevance of different metaphors for organisational informatics

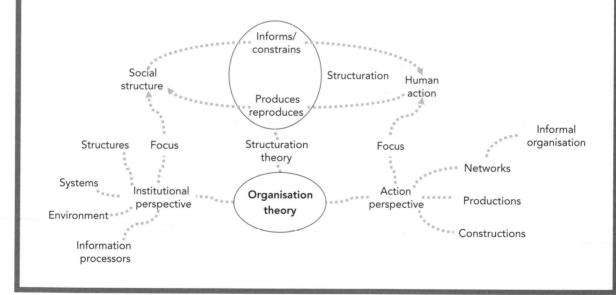

16.1 INTRODUCTION

Organisations form the immediate context for information systems. It has become something of a truism that the success of an organisation is dependent on its information systems. Information systems contribute by supporting efficient and effective human activity. The development of information systems may be an important part of the redesign of human activity within organisations. Modern societies and economies rely on effective information systems for effective functioning.

Hence an understanding of the crucial question of what is organisation is critical for any informatics professional. The proper place to start is with an examination of the theory of organisations. Unfortunately, there is not one coherent theory of what constitutes an organisation. There are a series of useful viewpoints on organisations that offer partial insights (Morgan, 1986).

Broadly speaking, these differing viewpoints can be classified as using one of two major perspectives. In this chapter we consider these two different perspectives on organisations. We use each perspective to organise a description of some foundation material from the area of organisation theory and also draw out from each perspective some of the consequences for information systems and information technology.

16.2 ACTION AND INSTITUTIONAL PERSPECTIVES

Organisations are social collectives. There are two alternative positions or viewpoints in relation to social collectives: what we might call the action and the institutional perspectives.

The action perspective is a bottom-up perspective on organisations. The action perspective (Silverman, 1982) maintains that social institutions are fundamentally constructed in action performed by human beings. Social institutions do not exist independently of the humans belonging to them. Consequently, organisational reality is subjective, i.e. different for each individual. Hence the only valid way of studying organisational reality is through the interpretation of human action (Chapter 49).

In a sense the action perspective focuses on the process of organising. The critical interest is in how humans generate structures of coordination and cooperation in work.

The institutional perspective is a top-down perspective on organisations. The institutional perspective (Durkheim, 1936) maintains that organisations are structures which exist independently of the humans belonging to them. Human actions are directed or constrained by such larger social structures. Institutions have a life over and above the life of their members. In this sense they are objective structures and can be studied in terms of patterns or features representative of these institutions.

In a sense, the institutional perspective focuses on the unit of organisation. The institutional perspective is interested in the features of organisations as wholes.

For much of its history organisation theory has tended to portray these two positions as mutually exclusive. Whole schools of social science have become established which take as their orienting principles one or other of these positions (see Chapter 49). In practice, of course, each is a legitimate and valid position. We all act and interact with fellow human beings within organisations and appreciate the fluidity of organisational life. We all also experience the monolithic nature of organisations and the constraints imposed on us by these institutional structures. Recently, there has been an attempt to recognise the validity of both these positions and integrate them in a proposal known as structuration theory.

16.3 🌀 STRUCTURATION THEORY

Structuration theory was created by the sociologist Anthony Giddens (Walsham and Han, 1991) as an attempt to reconcile the action and institutional perspectives. Structuration theory speaks of the 'duality of structure'. On the one hand, the structure of social institutions is created by human action and is only evident in human action. Through human interaction, structures are reproduced, but may also change. On the other hand, human action is constrained by the way in which humans utilise institutional structure as a resource in interpreting their own and other people's actions. Giddens calls this cyclical process the process of structuration.

Figure 16.1 illustrates the process of structuration. Social structure both informs and constrains human action. In turn, human action both produces and reproduces social structure.

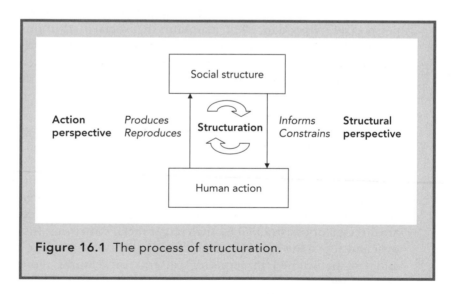

Figure 16.1 The process of structuration.

Example ||||➡ The example of human natural languages illustrates the importance of this duality. Human languages such as English can be seen as having many of the features of a social institution. A language common to a group of persons is a necessary pre-condition for speech acts (actions of speech). A language can be seen as a social structure in that it can be described and studied somewhat independently of given speech acts. In this sense it can be seen to have an existence independent of the humans using it. However, spoken language is only really evident in actual speech acts. People use language as a resource for communication. Language is produced and re-produced through speech acts. Over time speech acts may change the structure of a language. New vocabulary, grammar and syntax may evolve.

Much of organisation theory has taken one or other of the action or institutional perspectives as their foundation. In the next section we briefly review some of the work in this area under these two perspectives. We also consider the influence that each of these perspectives have had on informatics work.

16.4 INSTITUTIONAL PERSPECTIVE

In terms of the institutional perspective, organisations have been considered as structures, as closed and open systems, and as information processing units.

16.4.1 ORGANISATIONS AS STRUCTURES

The most pervasive model of organisations sees them as structures that are divided into parts or functional departments. Each department is characterised by a pattern of precisely defined jobs. Jobs are organised in a clear hierarchical fashion with designated lines of authority from superior to subordinate. This hierarchical structure is so well formalised that it can be captured in an 'organisational chart'.

This classical account of organisations is related to the ideas underlying the 'scientific management' movement popularised by Frederick Taylor in the USA in the early years of the twentieth century (Taylor, 1911). Scientific management focuses on three principles:

- *Management*. Managers should be given total responsibility for the organisation of work; workers should concentrate on manual tasks. A 'thinking' department of managers should be set up responsible for task planning and design.
- *Tasks*. All tasks should be examined and if necessary redesigned to improve efficiency. By studying the approach adopted, the tools utilised and the fatigue generated for any task, an optimum procedure for the task can be generated.
- *Efficient methods*. Methods should be adopted for the selection, training and monitoring of labour to ensure that work is done efficiently.

Example ▐▐▐▶ Taylor was particularly interested in analysing the performance of manual tasks such as shifting coal from a railway truck into a factory coal store. By experimenting with different numbers of men and different ways of conducting this manual task, Taylor was able to determine the optimal form of task organisation in terms of such criteria as the amount of labour expended and the time taken to complete each task.

The underlying assumption of this approach is that the actions of people within organisations can be rationalised and closely defined or designed. This model is clearly associated with that type of organisation known as a bureaucracy (Weber, 1946) (see Chapter 17). In a bureaucracy, jobs are precisely defined, tasks are explicitly documented and control is exercised in a strict hierarchical fashion.

The structural model of organisations has been a particularly dominant model of organisations for informatics work. Information systems are generally built to support the existing structure within organisations. Systems analysis (Chapter 28) is normally conducted in terms of identifying the precise functions of particular units. Because of this, workers in informatics have been accused of building information systems which reinvent existing organisational divisions.

The approach of business process re-engineering has recently directed attention at utilising IS and IT to breakdown existing structural divisions and design new forms of organisational work. The idea of process design, considered in Chapter 33, can be seen to align itself with the ethos of Taylorism. Indeed, Taylor's work can be seen to be an early form of business process re-engineering.

16.4.2   ORGANISATIONS AS SYSTEMS

The system concept discussed in Chapter 3 is clearly a dominant one within the domain of informatics. The product of the domain, an information system, is clearly conceived of in system terms. The human activities reliant on such information systems are also generally seen as human activity systems. An organisation can be considered on the macro level as a system. On the micro level, a business organisation can be considered to be made up of a number of subsystems or functional areas.

Organisations are treated as open systems (Chapter 3). An organisation is conceived of as a unit which takes resources from its environment and processes them to produce products or services which it supplies back to its environment. Capital and labour are the two types of the resources provided by the environment. The environment consumes the products/services produced by the organisation and supplies additional capital and labour to the organisation.

The idea of an information system and a human activity system have been inextricably inter-linked by Checkland (Checkland 1987). Every organisation can be considered as a human activity system or as a series of human activity systems. This means that every organisation will have a number of information systems of some form. This has resonance with the focus of BPR on so-called business processes (Chapter 19).

The systems model of organisations has also particularly affected the way in which many informatics workers traditionally conceive of appropriate ways for constructing information technology systems. A longstanding problem in information systems development is to identify the functions that an information technology system should perform. One solution is to analyse organisational work in terms of tasks and specify the functions of an information system in terms of these tasks. Such task analysis may also later be used as a basis for deciding on an appropriate division of labour between computerised systems and the users of such systems.

16.4.3 ORGANISATIONS AS ENVIRONMENTS

The organisation can be seen as an open system in an environment. The environment of the organisation is likely to influence the form of organisation. Pioneering work by Burns and Stalker (1961) established a link between the stability of the external environment and the shape of an organisation. Generally speaking, they found that those organisations that were positioned in an environment subject to rapid rates of change were more likely to be what they called organic organisations. In contrast, in external environments that were relatively stable for extended periods of time the organisational form was most likely to be what they called mechanistic.

The mechanistic organisation has many similarities with the bureaucratic form of organisation discussed above. In organic organisations jobs are less formally defined and there are flatter organisational hierarchies. Burns and Stalker were proposing an evolutionary model of organisational change. Organisations were seen as adapting in form to the changes in their environment.

The influence of the environment on organisations is an important strand in strategic thinking. The importance of knowing about your environment and reacting to this environmental information underpins so-called strategic thinking and planning within organisations (Chapter 20).

More recently, strategic thinking has influenced the whole area of informatics planning, particularly the need to consider strategic uses for information systems. The aim of informatics planning is to identify clear ways in which informatics strategy can be aligned with business strategy (Chapter 34).

16.4.4 ORGANISATIONS AS INFORMATION PROCESSORS

The metaphor of the organisation as an information processor arose primarily during and immediately after the Second World War with the invention of the electronic computer. During the late 1940s and 1950s much popular discussion arose around the computer being an electronic brain. It was a short step from the analogy between brain and computer to that between organisation and computer.

A key figure in the work of both computer science and management science is the person of Herbert Simon. Simon originally worked for the RAND corporation in the US. RAND was influential in establishing systems analysis as a valid method for analysing organisational problems (Chapter 28).

Simon's work was particularly directed at the study of decision-making within organisations (Simon, 1976) (Chapter 6). Effective decision-making by managerial groups is clearly critical to organisational success. However, Simon argued that human decision-making was not rational; it was satisficing. For a rational decision to be made, two conditions must be satisfied: a human needs all the information relevant to a problem and a human needs to be able to process all of this information. Simon argued that in most practical organisational situations these conditions could not be satisfied. All the information relevant to a problem is not normally available, and even if it were the average human being is only able to consider a limited amount of information at any one time. Hence managers normally make satisficing decisions. They consider enough information to make a satisfactory decision for a particular problem.

Besides the obvious re-emphasis of the importance of decision-making to organisations, Simon's work on satisficing directed attention at the importance of 'good' information to effective decision-making. This influenced the idea of information being the life-blood of organisations and the consequent importance of building information systems to supply this need. Good information can be defined in a number of ways. One particular criterion is relevance to the task at hand. Consequently, there were a number of attempts to identify levels of decision-making, the most popular having three levels of operational, tactical and strategic decisions.

The emphasis on managerial decision-making also generated interest is constructing specialised information systems for managers. Hence the whole domain of MIS/DSS/EIS was created as described in Chapter 6.

16.5 ACTION PERSPECTIVE

Under the action perspective, organisations have been seen as informal networks of people constructing action and accounting for their action to other people in various ways.

16.5.1 ORGANISATIONS AS NETWORKS

During the 1930s in the USA, partly as a reaction to Taylorism, a number of social psychologists began conducting experimental research at the Hawthorne Electric company. Hence these studies became known as the Hawthorne experiments. Initially the interest was in what later became known as *ergonomics* – the effect of the work environment upon worker performance. Not surprisingly, the experimenters found that when they made changes to such things as lighting conditions or decor within the factory this had a positive effect on worker productivity (Mayo, 1933). However, when the researchers studied why this was occurring in more detail they found that informal networks of interaction in the workplace mediated between environmental changes and productivity increases. Informal networks between people in work were shown to be important to people in supplying support and context for the work of members.

This research led to a number of changes to managerial practice which are still reflected in many modern organisations. One of the most significant was the emphasis on team working in such situations as manufacturing plants. The work also influenced the movement in socio-technical design – the idea that the design of technical systems should occur in parallel with the design of social systems. Within informatics socio-technical projects emphasise the importance of user participation in design and designing work in parallel with designing IS (Chapter 29).

16.5.2   ORGANISATIONS AS PRODUCTIONS

During the 1970s, studies of organisations shifted from the macro level to the micro level. Researchers became interested in the question of how people in work produce organisational life. Some of the most significant work in this area was conducted by Erving Goffman (1990) in his studies of institutional life. His work particularly focused on the importance of work to an individual's self and identity. He also studied the importance of particular ideologies to the organisation of work.

This focus on the process of organising emphasises the ways in which actors in social situations account for their behaviour to others. So-called 'accounting' devices are essential in organisational work to enable organisational actors to effectively coordinate their activity. Information systems have an important role to play in this accounting process, since information systems have the potential to make work more visible (Zuboff, 1988). Zuboff considers the difference between the monitoring potential of systems versus the informating potential of systems. This is a key issue for design within informatics.

16.5.3   ORGANISATION AS CONSTRUCTIONS

The work of Garfinkel has influenced recent work in information systems, particularly in the area of systems analysis and design. Garfinkel is interested in the low-level study of human interaction. The focus is on the 'methods' individuals use in achieving their work and also on the way in which they reason practically about such activity.

Garfinkel's *ethnomethodology* is particularly useful as a way of emphasising the richness of organisational work and the importance of tacit knowledge to work (Chapter 39). Tacit knowledge is the name given by Michael Polanyi (1962) to the ability of human beings to perform skills without being able to articulate how they do them. In this context, tacit knowledge seems to be used mainly to mean the unexplicated knowledge involved in enabling individuals to orient their own work to those of others in a particular work setting. If much of organisational work is reliant on tacit knowledge, then conventional means of sudying such work for information systems projects are limited. This has led to calls for new forms of requirements analysis and representation – particularly the use of ethnographic approaches (Chapter 28).

16.6 🌀 SUMMARY

- Organisations are social institutions
- There are two major perspectives on organisational life – the institutional perspective and the action perspective.
- The action perspective considers that organisations arise out of human interaction.
- The institutional perspective considers organisations as units which constrain or structure people's behaviour.
- The institutional perspective emphasises features of the organisation such as relationships of control, systems of activity, processes of information flow or interactions with some environment.
- The action perspective emphasises informal networks of organisational members producing behaviour and using established methods for accounting for this behaviour.
- Each perspective on organisations implies a distinct role for IS and IT.

16.7 🌀 QUESTIONS

(i) Distinguish between the structural and action viewpoints of organisations.

(ii) What is meant by the term structuration?

(iii) List the major structural perspectives on organisations.

(iv) What consequences do the structural perspectives have for informatics practice?

(v) List the major action perspectives on organisations

(vi) What consequences have the action perspectives for informatics practice?

16.8 🌀 EXERCISES

(i) Provide an example of the process of structuration and discuss its importance.

(ii) Consider an organisation known to you. Use one or more of the perspectives from organisation theory to characterise the organisation. For instance, would you class it as a bureaucratic (mechanistic) or an organic organisation?

(iii) Which are the dominant perspectives employed by information systems people within the chosen organisation?

(iv) In what way are information systems characterised in the organisation: e.g. as support systems, as decision-making tools, as coordination systems or as strategic weapons?

16.9 PROJECTS

(i) Research the information systems literature and determine which of the models of organisation discussed in this chapter is the most prevalent.

(ii) Investigate the limitations of a structural perspective on organisations to re-engineering the IS development process.

(iii) Investigate the limitations of an action perspective on organisations to re-engineering the IS development process.

(iv) Investigate the relevance of structuration theory to IS development.

16.10 REFERENCES

Burns, T. and Stalker, G. M. (1961). *The Management of Innovation*. Tavistock, London.

Checkland, P. (1987). *Systems Thinking, Systems Practice*. John Wiley, Chichester.

Durkheim, E. (1936). *The Rules of Sociological Method*. The Free Press, Glencoe.

Goffman, E. (1990). *Stigma: Notes on the Management of Spoiled Identity*. Penguin, Harmondsworth, Middlesex.

Mayo, E. M. (1933). *The Human Problems of an Industrial Civilisation*. Macmillan, New York.

Morgan, G. (1986). *Images of Organisation*. Sage, London.

Polanyi, M. (1962). *Personal Knowledge*. Anchor Day Books, New York.

Silverman, D. (1982). *The Theory of Organisations*. Macmillan, London.

Simon, H. A. (1976). *Administrative Behavior: a Study of Decision-Making Processes in Administration*, 3rd edn. Free Press, New York.

Taylor, F. W. (1911). *Principles of Scientific Management*. Harper & Row, New York.

Walsham, G. and Han, C.-K. (1991). Structuration theory and information systems research. *Journal of Applied Systems Analysis*, **17**, 17–85.

Weber, M. (1946). *Essays in Sociology*. Oxford University Press, Oxford.

Zuboff, S. (1988). *In the Age of the Smart Machine: the Future of Work and Power*. Heinemann, London.

CHAPTER 17

ORGANISATION STRUCTURE

Bureaucracy defends the status quo long past the time when the quo has lost its status.

Laurence J. Peter

LEARNING OUTCOMES

After reading this chapter, you will be able to:

- Define organisational structure
- Discuss the impact of organisational structure on IS/IT
- Outline examples of the impact of IS/IT on organisational structure

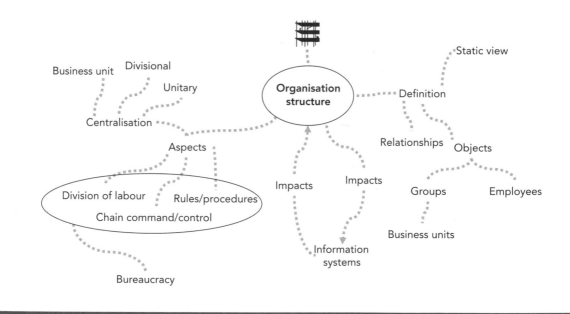

17.1 INTRODUCTION

A structural view implies a static view. At a fundamental level a structural representation of a phenomenon implies a set of objects and a set of relationships between such objects. Objects of interest in organisational terms are employees, customers, suppliers, products and services. Generally, a structural model of an organisation is normally described in terms of some map of the relationships between its employees. Of particular interest are relationships of power and authority. Such relationships are classically expressed in an organisation chart.

In this chapter we consider the mutually enhancing relationship between information systems and organisational structure. An organisation's structure may influence the design of information systems as well as the success of these IS. Conversely, an organisation's IS may contribute to changes in structure.

17.2 STRUCTURE

The term *organisational structure* generally refers to the formal aspects of an organisation's functioning. Three aspects of formal structure are important to most organisations:

- *Division of labour.* This is the way in which tasks and responsibilities are assigned to members of the organisation.
- *Chain of command and control.* This refers to the relationships of power and authority (Chapter 16) established in the organisation between its members.
- *Specifications of rules and procedures.* Most medium- to large scale organisations will have explicit rules and procedures which detail expected ways of working.

These three aspects of organisational structure are present in their most extreme form in that type of organisation known as a bureaucracy. Bureaucracies have rigid formal structures of clearly defined roles, clearly defined procedures for action and clearly delineated chains of command and control. Such aspects are frequently given expression in some form of organisation chart, such as the one illustrated in Figure 17.1.

One critical characteristic of the chain of command in an organisation is the span of control. This refers to the number of subordinates a superior can successfully supervise. Research suggests that the span of control for most organisations varies between four and twelve subordinates. The size of the span of control clearly influences the shape of the organisational hierarchy in terms of the number of levels in the hierarchy. An increased span of control traditionally leads to communication problems within organisations.

Large organisations have historically maintained unitary structures in which there is direct chain of command and centralised control of operations. Such organisations constitute rigid hierarchies in which decisions flow down the hierarchy and information flows up the hierarchy.

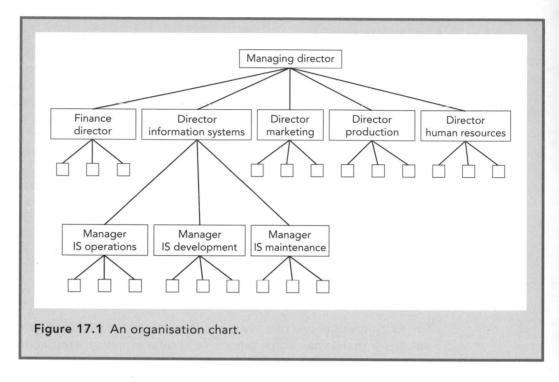

Figure 17.1 An organisation chart.

More recently, large organisations have changed over to multi-divisional structures with each division running as a semi-autonomous operation. This form of structure has particularly been characteristic of so-called multinational organisations – organisations which operate on a global scale. Divisional distinctions in such organisations frequently occur on national lines.

Modern organisations have decentralised even further. The trend has been to introduce so-called business units within divisions which act as semi-autonomous profit centres. Such units are frequently structured either around functions, such as marketing and finance, or products and services, such as different manufacturing plants producing different automobile models.

These forms of organisational structure are illustrated in Figure 17.2.

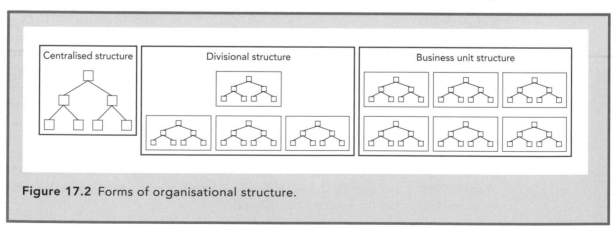

Figure 17.2 Forms of organisational structure.

Given rapid changes occurring in the environment (Part 5) of modern organisations, such institutions frequently need to restructure rapidly. Restructuring is frequently rationalised in terms of needed responses to the external environment of the organisation. For commercial organisations it is usually important to restructure to maintain competitive position.

There is clearly an interplay between organisational structure and culture (Chapter 18). Organisational structure may foster the development of distinct subcultures. This reflects the recent attempt in the management science area to use corporate culture as a unifying force within decentralised organisations.

17.3 ORGANISATIONAL STRUCTURE AND ITS IMPACT UPON IS

The structural model of organisations has been a particularly dominant model of organisations for informatics work. A business organisation can be considered to consist of a number of functional areas such as:

- *Marketing*. That area concerned with advertising, selling, pricing and distribution.
- *Accounting and finance*. That area concerned with generating and investing money and its accounting.
- *Production*. That area concerned with puchasing raw materials, inventory control and manufacture.
- *Research and development*. That area concerned with developing new products and improving existing products.

Clearly a number of structural issues have a direct bearing on the design, as well as the introduction and use, of an IS.

The traditional approach to information systems development is to build on existing organisational structure. Hence the marketing department will have its marketing information system and the production department will have its production information system. This is perhaps not surprising when one considers that information systems derive their purpose from supporting organisational work. Hence an organisation's informatics architecture (Chapter 21) must in some way model or reflect such human activity.

Example IIII➤   A heavily centralised organisation is likely to develop quite different information systems from a decentralised one. Also, divisional, functional, matrix or network structures for organising people can all influence the likely portfolio of IS.

For instance, the introduction of enterprise resource planning systems – large software packages that offer integration of organisational data – has led to a greater centralisation of decision-making in many organisations.

However, the argument has been made that taking existing organisational structure as a base-line from which to build new information systems can guarantee only incremental improvements in organisational performance (Chapter 33). In this scenario information technology is likely to improve the efficiency of existing ways of doing things, but is unlikely to offer radical improvements in organisational performance. For such radical improvement information technology needs to be used as a vehicle to support organisational re-structuring. The problem is that implementation of any information technology system is a risky process. Adding substantial organisational change to this process can make it even riskier.

Organisational structure can be impacted upon in ways which include:

- *Span of control*. A classic example of the effect of IT on organisational structure is in terms of span of control. IT has been used for reducing middle management layers, effectively increasing the span of control of top-level managers.

- *Empowerment*. Alternatively, IS/IT can push decision-making down the organisation closer to the workforce. For instance, workers can be encouraged to make decisions quickly with the aid of customer relationship systems, thus improving customer satisfaction.

- *Newer organisational forms*. IS/IT can also facilitate newer forms of organisation, such as virtual or network organisations. A virtual organisation is one in which the members of the organisation communicate and collaborate using information technology. Work is organised in terms of loose projects which workers join and leave in a flexible way. Such a structure means that the traditional resources of the organisation such as office space can be much reduced. Workers are encouraged to 'hot desk' – to share office facilities on a booking basis.

Examples |||▶ Information systems are vehicles for improving communication flow in organisations. Management information systems were introduced with the express purpose of improving managerial information and consequent decision-making. Middle managers have traditionally been involved in filtering information and decisions for strategic management. Information systems have largely automated many of these functions in organisations. Hence there is less of a need for middle management.

17.5 ⊙ SUMMARY

- Structure refers to the formal aspects of an organisation's functioning such as division of labour, hierarchical authority and job descriptions.

- Organisational restructuring frequently occurs in the modern world, often as a needed response to changes in the external environment of the organisation. It is important to restructure to maintain competitive position. IS and IT can be key enablers of organisational restructuring.

- The traditional approach to IT construction is to build on existing organisational structure. The argument is that such an assumption can guarantee only incremental improvements in IT performance. IT needs to be used as a vehicle to support restructuring. However, the problem is that IT implementation is risky. Adding organisational change to this can be even riskier.
- A classic example of the effect of IT on organisational structure is in terms of span of control. IT has been blamed for reducing middle management layers, effectively increasing the span of control of top-level managers.

17.6 QUESTIONS

(i) Define the term *organisational structure*.

(ii) In what way is an organisation chart a representation of organisational structure?

(iii) List some of the major structural divisions in organisations.

(iv) Describe some of the ways in which organisational structure affects information systems.

(v) Describe some of the ways in which information systems may impact upon organisational structure.

17.7 EXERCISES

(i) Consider an organisation known to you. Draw an organisation chart for the organisation.

(ii) Detail the division of labour of some organisation.

(iii) Detail the chain of command and control of some organisation.

(iv) Detail some examples of organisational rules and procedures.

(v) Consider an organisation known to you. Does the organisational structure reflect its information systems and vice versa?

17.8 PROJECTS

(i) Determine the degree to which chains of command and control are exercised through information systems.

(ii) Determine the degree to which the division of labour in an organisation is reflected in its information systems.

(iii) Information systems implement organisational rules and procedures. Collect data pertaining to this proposition and investigate its importance for both information systems and organisational design.

(iv) Investigate the role that information technology plays in organisational restructuring in an industrial sector.

(v) Investigate the concept of the virtual organisation.

CHAPTER 18

ORGANISATION CULTURE

I do not want my house to be walled in on all sides and my windows to be stuffed. I want the cultures of all the lands to be blown about my house as freely as possible. But I refuse to be blown off my feet by any.

Mahatma Gandhi (1869–1948)

LEARNING OUTCOMES

After reading this chapter, you will be able to:

- Define organisational culture
- Describe some examples of the impact of organisational culture on IS/IT
- Relate some examples of the impact of IS/IT on organisational culture
- Outline the idea of an information system as a sign-system

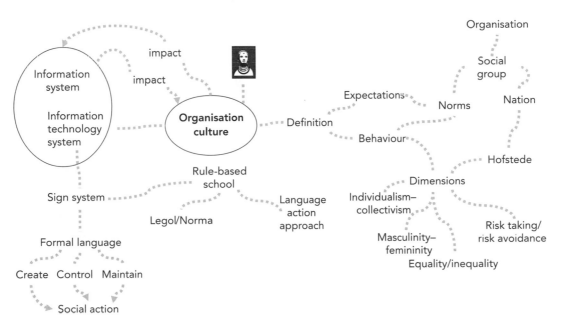

18.1 INTRODUCTION

The culture of a social group consists of the set of expectations of behaviour associated with the group. Culture is generally applied at the level of societies. More recently it has become popular to speak of organisation culture. An organisation's culture may influence the design of information systems as well as the success of these IS. An organisation's IS may also contribute to changes in organisation culture.

18.2 CULTURE

A culture is the set of behaviours expected in a social group. It is a truism that any long-standing social group develops its own expected set of behaviours or norms. A norm is an expectation that people will behave in a certain way in a certain social situation. If a person infringes the norms of some social situation, then frequently sanctions will be exercised against that person by members of the social group. Norms will frequently depend on roles and context. Members of social groups take on roles, and for each role different expectations are involved. Also, different social situations demand different behaviours. Hence context is important to determining the appropriateness of behaviour.

In terms of semiotics (Chapter 2) the cultural dimension is embodied in the study of the pragmatics of communication. Pragmatics supplies the common understandings which provide context for any communication.

18.3 ORGANISATIONAL CULTURE

Organisations are frequently seen as coherent social groupings, and hence it makes sense to speak of an organisational culture that exists within a larger societal culture. Nowadays, top managers are called upon to create 'strong' cultures within their organisations. In making this call, management writers make three assumptions about organisational culture:

- It is open to manipulation and can be designed by business leaders.
- It is a unifying force.
- It is linked to organisational effectiveness/performance via employee motivation.

Each of these assumptions is open to question. Sociologists would argue that groups develop strong cultures if they have stable and homogeneous membership and stay together for long periods. Culture forms and changes slowly, if only because it takes time for new members to be socialised into the culture. Organisation culture may also be a major conservative force within organisations, preventing improvements in work practices and the adoption of information technology.

18.3.1 SUBCULTURES

Unfortunately, particularly in relation to some of the management science literature, the cultural metaphor has been used by many authors as a monolithic concept in the sense of implying an organisation-wide culture. In practice, medium- to large-scale organisations are likely to be made up of a number of interacting subcultures. The term *subculture* is used to refer to a subgroup, within a broader social unit such as an organisation, who share sets of meanings which perpetuate their distinctive character within the unit as a whole. Subcultures may form around distinct structural units such as departments within organisations or in terms of distinct stakeholder groups within organisations.

Example ||||➤ In a utility company with which the author was involved, two distinct groups of workers displayed quite different subcultures. This is particularly interesting in that the work both groups conducted was very close. Also, both groups were sited very close together in the headquarters of the utility company.

One group of workers had responsibility for maintaining and servicing a network of utility lines over a large geographical area. Both groups of people were 'lines-people', that is, workers with responsibility for inspecting, maintaining and repairing parts of the utility network. However, one group of lines-people serviced low-power electricity lines while the other group serviced high-power electricity lines.

The low-power lines people worked as a group with decisions about which lines to service and what maintenance to be conducted made at the centre. In contrast, the high-power lines-people worked very much as individuals with maintenance decisions very much delegated to the lines-people themselves. Part of the rationale provided for such differences in behaviour was the dangerous nature of the high-power line maintenance and the consequent need for delegation of authority.

18.4 DIMENSIONS OF CULTURE

Culture may be directly experienced in differences in expectations between organisations. A convenient framework for analysing differences between cultures is to consider a number of dimensions of culture (Hofstede, 1991). Some possible cultural dimensions are listed below:

● *Individualism/collectivism*. In certain organisations there may be a general expectation that people will work and be rewarded as individuals. In contrast, in other organisations there may be a general expectation that people should work and be rewarded in teams.

● *Risk taking/risk aversion*. In some organisations there may be a general expectation that people should take risks. In other organisations people are expected to not take risks.

- *Masculinity/feminity*. Masculinity refers to a set of values including the importance of assertiveness in personal relations, acquisitiveness of money and things and a lack of care in interpersonal relationships. Femininity refers to a set of values focused around people and the importance of nurturing interpersonal relationships.

- *Equality/inequality*. In some organisations inequalities in the distribution of power amongst individuals and groups is accepted. In other organisations power is expected to be distributed more equitably amongst organisational members.

18.5 ◎ IMPACT OF CULTURE UPON INFORMATION SYSTEMS

Organisational cultures and subcultures can influence the development, adoption and use of information systems in various ways. For example:

- *Different organisations may value information technology differently*. For instance, Japanese companies seem to adopt significantly lower amounts of IT than Western companies. This appears to have something to do with distinct cultures in Japanese companies which values face-to-face communication as opposed to communication at a distance.

- *Cultural differences may influence the implementation of IT systems*. For example, information technology systems designed to improve groupwork may find difficulty in being introduced into an organisation where individuality is valued rather than teamwork.

- *Different subcultures may frame the purpose of technology differently*. One important facet which serves to distinguish between modern organisational subcultures is the way in which members approach or 'frame' information technology. Orlikowski and Gash (1994) propose that people in organisations approach technology on the basis of their technological frame. A technological frame is a collection of underlying assumptions, expectations and knowledge that people have about technology and its use. They propose that the idea of a technological frame is central to understanding the process of development, use and change of technology, and that key groups in organisations such as managers, technologists and users hold significantly different technological frames.

- *Organisational subculture of the informatics service*. Examples of the cultural metaphor used in the context of information systems development are Robey and Markus's (1984) argument that elements of the systems design process can be interpreted as rituals, and Hirschheim and Newman's (1991) exploration of the role of symbolism in IS development.

- *Differences in national cultures impact upon the success of global information systems*. For information systems that have to operate effectively on the global scale, differences amongst cultures in different national units of the organisation may impact upon the effectiveness of the IS. For instance, an information system designed around individualistic and masculine values may experience significant degrees of user resistance in cultures that display a collectivist and feminine value orientation.

Example ▐▐▐➡ In the utility company described above, an attempt was made to build a single information system to service the work of both groups of lines-people. A major part of this system was the intended use of hand-held computing devices to capture data by lines-people while out in the field. Whereas the low-power lines-people were happy to accept this new technology, it was heavily resisted by the high-power lines-people. Part of the explanation for this lies in the fact that the low-power lines-people were well-used to collecting and disseminating information amongst themselves. However, the individualistic culture of work characteristic of the high-power lines-people meant that little information was recorded and exchanged. Hence these lines-people saw very little justification for the new data capture technology.

18.6 ⊚ IMPACT OF INFORMATION SYSTEMS UPON ORGANISATION CULTURE

Information systems may impact on organisational culture in various ways:

- *IS as agents of cultural change.* Information systems are frequently used as ways of introducing attempted changes to organisation culture by managerial groups. For instance, information systems may be introduced with the aim of encouraging group working rather than individual working.
- *IS as ideological systems.* Particular stakeholder groups with distinct subcultures may use information systems as ways of promulgating particular ideologies. Different stakeholder groups may promote their own ideas as to appropriate ways of doing things through the design of a particular information system.
- *IS as systems of commitments.* Information systems can be seen as systems for making commitments between individuals and groups. The design of the information system incorporates the types of commitments recorded and acted upon. It is this aspect of culture that we focus on in the next section.

18.7 ⊚ INFORMATION SYSTEMS AS SIGN-SYSTEMS

Information systems are systems of signs in the sense that they act as a linguistic communication medium between different groups of people. Linguistic communication is an essential component of culture. Hence the design of these artefacts can be seen as a cultural act. A number of researchers have contributed to what might be called a language action approach to information systems design including Stamper's work on LEGOL/NORMA (Stamper and Liu, 1991) and a number of researchers contributing to work within an approach known as SAMPO (Auramaki *et al.*, 1992). These approaches can be seen to fall within an action approach to organisations (Chapter 16).

At the semiotic level of pragmatics, information systems are formal languages that are used to create, control and maintain social action. An information system is tied to action. Language action approaches are interested not only in language which makes statements, but also in that which gives orders, makes promises, classifies things etc. An information system consists of different groups of people communicating in a formal language which is stored, manipulated and transmitted via information technology.

In this view information systems are a significant cultural force in that they serve to frame human action. The language of some information includes formal messages that create, set up, control and maintain social interactions in an organisational context. Correspondingly, the IS should include messages with a correct syntactic structure, a meaningful semantic context and a significant pragmatic use (Chapter 2).

An information system is an institution in itself, surrounded with expectations and social rules. Information systems development is an activity by which a communication institution is created and maintained. An information system is purposely developed, but also developing and changing. IS development is a process of changing the languages of user communities and formalising them through agreement. It also involves the assumption that meanings change over time, and that changes in rules are to be expected, but must involve collective agreement amongst all interested parties.

Most of the language action literature is notationally complex. We therefore only provide a brief overview of one of the language action approaches as evident in the SAMPO approach here.

In the language action approach an information systems specification is framed in terms of speech acts and conversations, both concepts being taken from speech act theory (Chapter 2), a branch of linguistics. Speech act theory is the study of the way people do things with words. The main idea is that uttering a sentence is the performance of an act, a speech act. However, although they are called speech acts, such things are not restricted to spoken language. The term *speech act* would also be taken to cover written texts and the use of other signs such as gestures and flags. Speech acts are therefore seen as the basic unit of human communication and have been categorised into numerous different types. The most important type of speech act for information systems work is the illocutionary speech act.

An illocutionary act is performed whenever a speaker utters a sentence, or a set of sentences, in an appropriate context with certain intentions, e.g. 'I promise to write a letter' or 'I refuse to pay a bill'. The structure of any illocutionary act consists of three parts: content, context and illocutionary force:

- *Content* refers to the propositional content of the message. The content of illocutionary acts above are 'to write a letter' and 'to pay a bill'.
- *Context* is defined in terms of the speaker, hearer, time, place and the 'world' within which the act takes place. Hence the context defines a message from a speaker to a hearer at time *T* and in place *P*. *World* is used to collect together a

range of other features of context which are important for understanding the meaning of a message, such as channel (speech, writing etc.), code (language style) and message-form (chat, debate, sermon etc.)

- *Illocutionary force* is used to represent the kind of commitment a speaker makes when he or she says something and the direction of fit between the world and the propositional content of the speech act (the word). For instance, a business order has a word-to-world direction of fit, as it is intended to change the world (precipitate some action), and the speaker is committed to the future action of paying an invoice in return for receiving some goods or services.

Illocutionary acts normally occur in ordered sequences. These sequences are referred to as 'conversations'. The major feature of conversations is their game-like character. A particular speech act creates the possibility of usually a limited range of speech acts as response.

In the language action view, then, information systems are seen as communication networks which create, maintain and fulfil commitments. The role of the systems analyst is to analyse existing 'conversations' and from such analysis to develop a more coherent, complete and relevant specification of communication which can be used to design an information system.

Example ▐▐▐▶ Consider, for example, a simple case in which a conference secretary is tasked by members of a conference committee to contact a range of selected lecturers and to see if they would agree to speak at the conference. The secretary also has to arrange flights for the accepting speakers. In this situation, some of the commitments made through illocutionary acts are as follows:

- The conference committee member makes a promise to the lecturers to pay for their flights.

- The conference committee member makes a promise to the lecturers to arrange the flight reservation.

- The lecturer tells the conference committee member how s(he) wants the arrangements to be made.

- The conference committee member requests the secretary to arrange the flights in accordance with the wishes of the lecturer.

- The secretary requests the travel agency to make the flight reservations.

- The secretary promises the travel agency to pay for the flights of lecturers.

- The travel agency confirms the reservation made by the secretary by sending the ticket.

Each of these acts can only occur at particular points in conversations between conference committee members, the secretary and the travel agency. Each speech act also calls into play a limited number of other speech acts in response. This means that a graph can be produced in SAMPO to document the discourse.

18.8 SUMMARY

- Culture refers to the set of shared expectations held by some social group.
- Shared expectations are evident in social roles and social norms.
- Organisations are likely to have subcultures associated with particular groups.
- Certain dimensions of culture can be identified.
- Culture impacts on the development, adoption and use of information systems.
- Information systems are used as ways of supporting organisational culture or causing changes to organisational culture.
- Information systems are sign-systems and therefore can be seen to be the embodiment of organisational culture.

18.9 QUESTIONS

- **(i)** Define the term *culture*.
- **(ii)** In what way is it sensible to describe an organisation as having a culture?
- **(iii)** Describe the major dimensions of organisation culture.
- **(iv)** In what ways may organisation culture impact upon its information systems?
- **(v)** In what ways may information systems impact upon organisational culture?
- **(vi)** Describe the key features of the language action approach to information systems.
- **(vii)** What is an illocutionary act?

18.10 EXERCISES

- **(i)** Consider some organisation in terms of the dimensions of culture discussed in this chapter. How would you classify your chosen organisation on these dimensions?
- **(ii)** Identify two distinct subcultures in some organisation known to you.
- **(iii)** Identify any differences in technological frames between different subcultural groups.

(iv) Consider a university – investigate in what ways organisation culture may differ between higher education institutions and hence may impact upon their information systems.

(v) Detail three examples of illocutionary acts.

18.11 PROJECTS

(i) Examine the issue of culture and globalisation as far as information systems are concerned.

(ii) Determine the importance of organisational culture to the successful implementation of information systems – the issue of subculture is likely to be important.

(iii) Does the culture of the informatics service need to change to improve its relationship with the rest of the organisation?

(iv) Have information systems had any impact upon culture within the higher education sector? Investigate.

(v) Investigate the SAMPO approach and use it to describe the network of commitments in some area of organisational life.

18.12 REFERENCES

Auramaki, E., Hirschheim, R. and Lyytinen, K. (1992). Modelling offices through discourse analysis: the SAMPO approach. *The Computer Journal*, **35**(4), 342–352.

Hirschheim, R. and Newman, M. (1991). Symbolism and IS development: myth, metaphor and magic. *IS Research*, **2**(1), 29–62.

Hofstede, G. (1991). *Cultures and Organisations*. McGraw-Hill, New York.

Orlikowski, W. T. and Gash, T. C. (1994). Technological frames: making sense of information technology in organisations. *ACM Trans. on Information Systems*. **12**(2), 174–207.

Robey, D. and Markus, M. L. (1984). Rituals in information systems design. *MIS Quarterly*, **8**, March, 5–15.

Stamper, R. and Liu, K. (1991). From database to normbase. *International Journal of Information Management*, **11**, 67–84.

CHAPTER 19

ORGANISATION PROCESSES

If you can't describe what you are doing as a process, you don't know what you're doing.

W. Edwards Deming

LEARNING OUTCOMES

After reading this chapter, you will be able to:

- Define the concept of an organisation process
- Introduce the idea of business process re-engineering
- Discuss the value chain model of organisation processes
- Relate the idea of modelling organisational processes

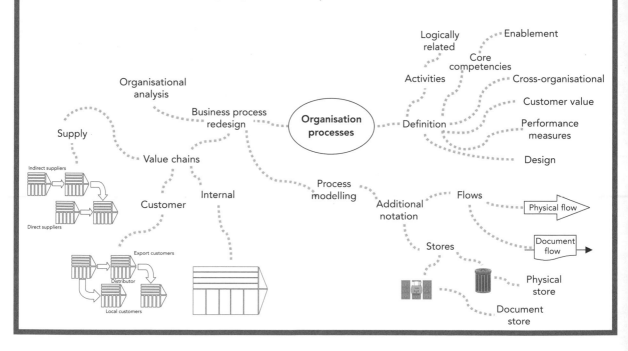

19.1 INTRODUCTION

Organisations can be viewed in structural or dynamic terms. Systemic models must necessarily take both positions, but particularly emphasise the way in which wholes are made up of dynamically interacting components or subsystems. The concept of a process is fundamental to systems theory (see Chapter 3).

In this chapter we look in more detail at the application of the process concept to organisations (Davenport, 1993). We particularly focus on the use of this concept in a movement popular in the early 1990s known as business process re-engineering. We describe a generic internal value chain model of organisational processes and describe the importance of two external value chains: the customer chain and the supply chain.

19.2 BUSINESS PROCESS REDESIGN

A branch of management science arose during the 1990s which concerned itself with the design of so-called business processes. This became known as business process re-engineering or business process redesign – BPR for short (Hammer and Champy, 1993). Some of the major premises of BPR are as follows:

- Information technology in and of itself delivers little value for most organisations.
- Information technology delivers value in terms of enabling changes to human activity within organisations.
- Changes to human activity have the potential to deliver increases in organisational performance.

These premises have a number of consequences for the way in which organisations approach information systems development (Chapter 25).

- *IT systems should initiate organisational change.* Many of the problems of traditional IT arise from the tendency of the IS industry to 'pave over the cowpaths'. In other words, IT has been used conventionally to automate existing processes. People like Davenport, Hammer and Champy have argued that when business processes are automated without first improving them, organisations will not continue to achieve significant benefits from their large investments in IT. There are clearly links to the productivity paradox in this assumption (Chapter 14).
- *Human activity systems have to be designed in parallel with information technology systems.* This is really an established principle within the socio-technical design movement.
- *Radical redesign of major business processes is likely to generate the greatest benefit.* The major premise here is that when automation is confined to small pieces of a business process (such as that which falls within the domain of a particular functional unit) then the large process may become degraded. IS cannot work in

isolation. The most effective use of IT frequently involves redesigning entire business processes.

Business process redesign is an established approach to organisational analysis and will be discussed in more detail in Chapter 33.

19.3 ⊚ BUSINESS PROCESSES

An organisation can be seen as being made up of a limited number of human activity systems or business processes. A business process is a set of activities cutting across the major functional boundaries of organisations by which organisations accomplish their missions, particularly the key one of delivering value to the customer.

> Example ⫸ Order fulfilment is a business process. It takes an order as its input and results in the delivery of ordered goods to a customer. The delivery of goods into a customer's hands is the value that this process creates.

There are a number of key characteristics of any business process:

- *Business or organisational processes are processes*. As such we should be able to define the inputs to the process, outputs from the process and the transformation undertaken by the process.

- *Business processes support core organisational competencies*. There are a limited number of business processes which underlie the key mission of an organisation (Chapter 20).

- *Business processes frequently cut across structural and functional organisational boundaries*. Business processes are cross-organisational. A process view of the organisation emphasises organisational dynamics rather than organisational structures.

- *Business processes have external customers*. Being cross-organisational, the value of the business process is determined in terms of the value it delivers to customers of the organisation.

- *Business processes have definable measures of performance*. Objectives must be set for a business process and clear criteria established for measuring the performance of the process.

- *Business processes can be designed*. This assumption can be seen to be a direct consequence of an institutional position on the organisation (see Chapter 16). BPR takes a rational stance on the organisation in assuming that work can be designed to optimise performance.

- *Information technology can be used to enable aspects of the design of a business process*. IT is not the only enabler of process re-engineering. However, it is a significant force in modern process design.

Example ▐▐▐➡ Consider the case of a university. The university can be considered as having three main business processes: teaching, research and consultancy. These are clearly the three core competencies of a higher education institution. Teaching is a business process because it has a defined customer – the student – with identifiable value. The process of teaching cuts across academic faculties, schools and departments within a university. We can define measurable units of performance for the teaching process, such as the number of students taught or the exit qualifications of students. Information technology is being used to enable significant savings in the teaching process amongst universities in the UK and elsewhere.

19.4 PORTER'S VALUE CHAIN

Porter (1985) offers a template for considering an organisation's key processes. This is a generic model of organisational processes known as the value chain. In this view organisations are seen as social institutions that deliver value to customers through defined activities.

An organisation's value chain is a series of interdependent activities that delivers a product or service to a customer. It is described as a value chain because it provides value to a customer. Such activities are of two types: primary and secondary activities. Primary activities constitute the core competencies of the organisation. Secondary activities are important to the successful operation of primary activities. This is illustrated in Figure 19.1.

Primary activities in the value chain consist of the following:

- *Inbound logistics*. Materials receiving, storing and distribution to manufacturing premises
- *Operations*. Transferring inputs into finished products
- *Outbound logistics*. Storing and distributing products
- *Marketing and sales*. Promotions and sales force
- *After sales service*. Services that maintain or enhance product value

Secondary activities consist of the following:

- *Corporate infrastructure*. Support activities for the entire value chain, such as general management, planning, finance, accounting, legal services and quality management
- *Human resource management*. Recruiting, hiring, training and development of human resources
- *Technology development*. Improving the product and manufacturing process
- *Procurement*. Function or purchasing input

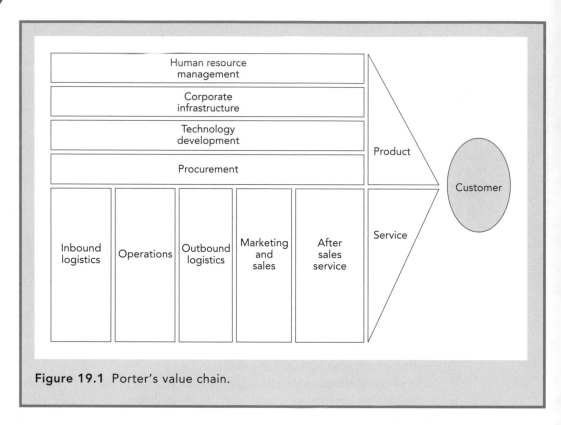

Figure 19.1 Porter's value chain.

Example ▐▐▐➡ Consider the case of teaching in a university. We can map the activities from Porter's value chain onto the process of teaching. As far as primary activities are concerned:

- Inbound logistics involve the processes of enquiries, applications, admissions and enrolment.

- Operations involve the processes of delivering teaching, assessing students and grading students.

- Outbound logistics involve the process of graduating students.

- Marketing and sales are processes involved in the attempted recruitment of students.

- After sales service involves processes such as maintaining a register of alumni.

19.5 SUPPLY CHAIN AND CUSTOMER CHAIN

An organisation exists within a competitive environment. Porter's notion of the value chain focuses on the internal processes of an organisation. Two other chains of value critical to the competitive environment assume significance for most

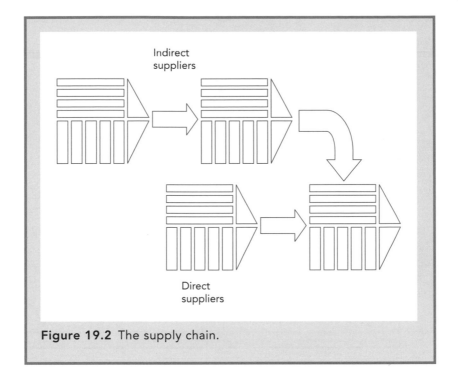

Indirect
suppliers

Direct
suppliers

Figure 19.2 The supply chain.

organisations: the supply chain and the customer chain. They are both chains in the sense that both customers and suppliers will usually be other organisations. Hence an economic system (Chapter 22) will be composed of a complex network of such chains.

The supply chain is illustrated in Figure 19.2. The broad arrows on the diagram indicate the flow of goods and services between organisations. On the diagram we distinguish between direct suppliers one step removed in the supply chain and indirect suppliers more than two steps removed in the supply chain. Indirect suppliers are sometimes referred to as channel organisations or intermediaries.

Figure 19.3 illustrates the customer chain of a particular organisation. We may distinguish between local customers in the immediate market-place of some organisation and export customers in some form of global market-place. For both forms of customers, but particularly in the global market-place, some form of distribution organisation (channel or intermediary) may mediate between an organisation and its customers.

Example ▐▐▐➡ Consider the case of a university. The supply chain of a university includes organisations such as schools and colleges which supply people wishing to take up higher education courses at a university. It also includes suppliers of office, IT and educational materials, such as publishers. The customer chain of a university includes not only individual students but also industrial, commercial and government organisations which may employ the services of a university in the areas of research and consultancy.

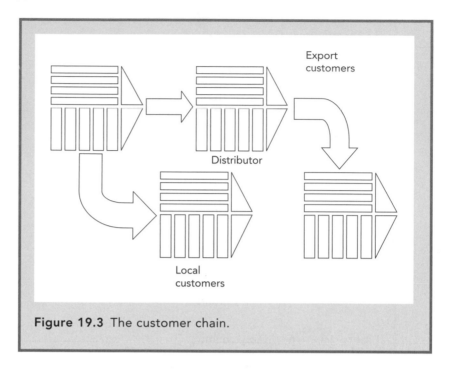

Figure 19.3 The customer chain.

Clearly the value chain will vary depending upon the type of business an organisation is in. In Figure 19.4 we illustrate three value chains:

- In automobile manufacturing components are produced both by subsidiaries of the major car manufacturers and by external component suppliers. Such components are used to assemble cars which are passed on to the dealer network which sells cars to consumers.

- In food retailing, foodstuffs are supplied to supermarkets from warehouses and foodstuff suppliers and are sold on to the consumer.

- In insurance there is little in the way of a supply chain. Insurance products are sold on to consumers via agents and brokers.

19.6 ⦿ MODELLING ORGANISATIONAL PROCESSES

The concept of a process is a systems concept. Hence processes can be decomposed in a hierarchical fashion. At the highest possible level an entire organisation can be considered as a human activity system. The value chain model identifies some of the main processes of a typical human activity system of this nature. Each process can be subdivided into a number of activities and each activity can be subdivided into a number of tasks.

The notation described in Chapter 7 can be used to describe major elements of processes and activities underlying information systems. However, we need

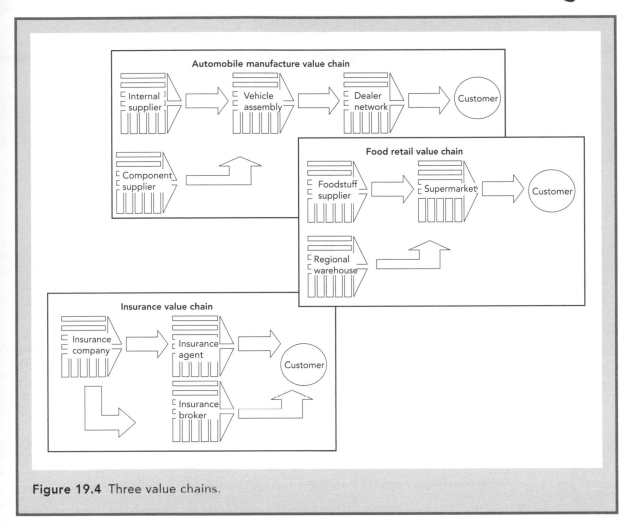

Figure 19.4 Three value chains.

extensions to the notation to handle organisational processes. Four additional constructs in the areas of flow and storage are needed as a minimum (Figure 19.5):

- *Physical flow*. This represents the flow of tangible or physical goods and services such as foodstuffs and automobiles.
- *Document flow*. This represents the flow of physical (normally paper-based) documentation such as invoices, orders and contracts.
- *Physical stores*. This represents a place where collections of physical artefacts accumulate, such as warehouses.
- *Document stores*. This represents a place where physical documentation accumulates, such as a filing cabinet.

Figure 19.5 illustrates a graphical notation for each of these constructs. We apply some of these additional constructs in the description of process redesign (Chapter 33).

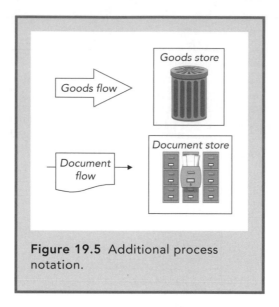

Figure 19.5 Additional process notation.

Tom Malone (Malone *et al.*, 1999) and his group at the Centre for Coordination Science at MIT's Sloan School of Business have initiated a project that they call the process handbook. The process handbook is a tool for sharing and managing knowledge about organisational processes and is intended to help people:

- Redesign existing organisational processes
- Invent new organisational processes, particularly ones that take advantage of information technology
- Learn about organisations by sharing 'best practice' business processes
- Automatically generate software to support organisational processes

The handbook essentially offers a method for specifying organisational processes and a repository of existing organisational processes expressed in the notation of the method. Hence somebody may be able to reuse aspects of an existing organisational process in the redesign of a process for his chosen organisation.

19.7 🌀 SUMMARY

- Organisations can be viewed as systems of human activity. Critical to the concept of system is that of a process.
- An organisation can be seen as being made up of a limited number of human activity systems or business processes.
- A business process is a set of activities cutting across the major functional boundaries of organisations by which organisations accomplish their missions, particularly the key one of delivering value to the customer.

- Business processes or more generally organisation processes are collections of interrelated activities that have the following characteristics: involved in delivering value to customers; have quantifiable measures of performance; frequently cut across functional organisational boundaries.

- Porter's value chain model offers us a generic template for understanding organisation processes. It consists of a number of high-level primary and secondary processes.

- Porter's model addresses the internal value chain. There are two forms of external value chain: the customer chain and the supply chain.

- Human activity systems are made up of processes. Processes consist of activities and activities consist of tasks.

- Four additional constructs are needed for modelling organisational processes as a minimum: physical flow, document flow, physical stores, document stores.

19.8 QUESTIONS

(i) Define what is meant by a process.

(ii) Describe the key elements of an organisation process.

(iii) Describe the key principles of business process redesign.

(iv) In what way is Porter's value chain useful for business process redesign?

(v) Define the key elements of the value chain.

(vi) What is the supply chain?

(vii) What is the customer chain?

(viii) What constructs do we need for modelling organisational processes?

19.9 EXERCISES

(i) Describe why research or consultancy may be regarded as business processes within a university setting.

(ii) In terms of Porter's value chain, describe the processes in a university which map to secondary activities on the model.

(iii) Draw a process map for an organisation known to you.

(iv) Consider a business in terms of Porter's value chain – how useful is Porter's model in describing the key activities of the business?

(v) List the major elements of the supply chain of some organisation known to you.

(vi) List the major elements of the customer chain of some organisation known to you.

19.10 PROJECTS

(i) Develop process maps amongst organisations in the same industrial sector. Investigate the similarity amongst maps.

(ii) Apply process re-engineering in an organisation known to you. Consider the importance of IT to re-engineering this process.

(iii) Investigate two distinct notations for specifying organisational processes, develop some criteria of comparison and analyse each approach in terms of the set criteria.

(iv) Investigate the Malone notation for describing organisational processes. Assess its efficacy in specifying two organisational processes.

(v) Determine to what degree it is possible for organisations to reuse existing generic process models.

(vi) Study closely the supply or customer chain of some organisation and determine the degree to which ICT may enable the process to be re-engineered.

19.11 REFERENCES

Davenport, T. H. (1993). *Process Innovation: Re-engineering Work Through IT*. Harvard Business School Press, Cambridge, MA.

Hammer, M. and Champy, J. (1993). *Reengineering the Corporation: a Manifesto for Business Revolution*. Nicholas Brearley, London.

Malone, T. W., Crowston, K. G., Lee, J. and Pentland, B. (1999). Tools for inventing organisations: toward a handbook of organisational processes. *Management Science*, **45**(3), 425–443.

Porter, M. E. (1985). *Competitive Advantage: Creating and Sustaining Superior Performance*. Free Press, New York.

CHAPTER 20

ORGANISATION STRATEGY

To conquer the enemy without resorting to war is the most desirable. The highest form of general-ship is to conquer the enemy by strategy.

Sun Tzu: *The Art of War*

LEARNING OUTCOMES

After reading this chapter, you will be able to:

- Define what is meant by an organisation strategy
- Explain the links between organisation strategy and organisation planning
- Relate the relationship between organisation strategy and informatics strategy

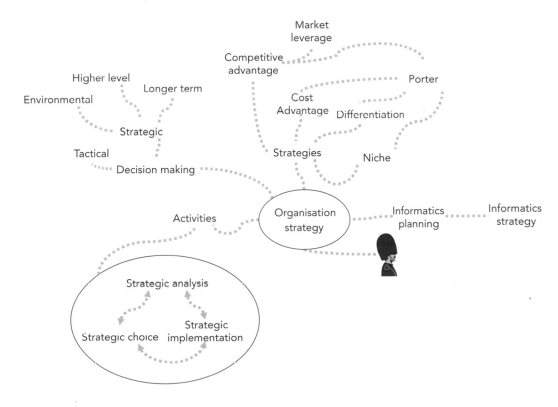

20.1 ⊚ INTRODUCTION

In 1991 a key report was published which documented the results of a major investigation into management issues during the last decade of the twentieth century. Called the 'Management in the 90s' programme, a key emphasis of this report was on how informatics strategy needed to align itself with organisation strategy (Scott-Morton, 1991). By organisation strategy we mean the general direction or mission of an organisation.

In this chapter we consider the distinction between strategy and tactics. This leads to a discussion of how organisation strategy is formed in the planning process and how an informatics strategy needs to align itself with an organisation strategy.

20.2 ⊚ STRATEGY AND TACTICS

The term *strategy* has historical roots in military operations. According to the *Oxford English Dictionary*, strategy is the art of a commander-in-chief; the art of projecting and directing the larger military movements and operations in a campaign. Strategy is seen to differ materially from tactics. Tactics belongs only to the mechanical movement of bodies set in motion by strategy. The term *strategy* is now very much used in the same sense in which it is used in the military, but directed towards organisational and particularly business activities.

Ansoff (1965) defines strategic decisions as being primarily concerned with external rather than internal problems of the firm and specifically with selection of the product mix which the firm will produce and the market to which it will sell. Strategic decisions are concerned with establishing an 'impedance match' between the firm and its environment, or, in more usual terms, it is the problem of deciding what business the firm is in and what kinds of business it will seek to enter.

Over the last twenty to thirty years managers within organisations have become very much concerned with developing explicit organisation strategy and with initiating effective ways of planning and implementing strategy. Much recent organisational informatics literature has followed this trend and concerns itself with how strategies for information, information systems and information technology can be developed which aligns itself with organisation strategy.

Examples ⊪⇒ Some examples of strategic informatics decisions include:

- How much are we going to invest in information systems and information technology (Chapter 27)?

- How much development, maintenance and support are we going to source internally or outside (Chapter 40)?

- How are we going to organise and resource the informatics service (Chapter 40)?

- How much software are we going to build ourselves and how much will we buy in (Chapter 25)?

- What information technology standards are we going to employ (Chapter 35)?

20.3 ORGANISATION STRATEGY

The notion of alignment suggests clearly that business strategy formulation should come ideally before informatics strategy formulation, as is illustrated in Figure 20.1. Organisation planning is the process of formulating an organisation strategy. Informatics planning is the process of formulating an informatics strategy. An organisation strategy will critically affect the direction of an informatics strategy.

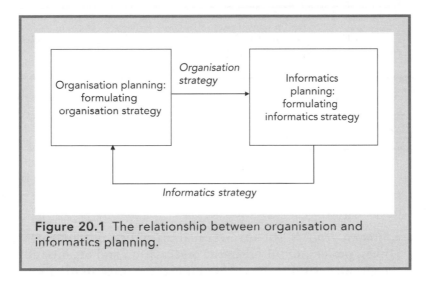

Figure 20.1 The relationship between organisation and informatics planning.

The results of an informatics strategy are likely to critically affect the formulation of future business strategy.

Example ▍▍▍➡ Part of an organisation's informatics strategy might be to develop an electronic commerce strategy which would indicate how, perhaps, the company's products or services will be delivered on-line in the future (Part 9). The relative success of this strategy in terms of increasing sales or opening up new customers will influence future business decisions about organisational strategy.

The success of an Italian motor-cycle manufacturer's e-commerce strategy led it to review the role of its physical dealerships. In Japan it decided to remove the sales function of its dealership operation entirely, leaving it only with the marketing and after-sales service.

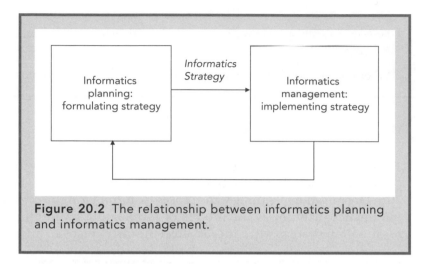

Figure 20.2 The relationship between informatics planning and informatics management.

Informatics management is the process of implementing and evaluating an informatics strategy (Figure 20.2).

Example ▐▐▐▶ An electronic commerce strategy clearly needs to be managed in terms of activities such as the development of customer interfaces and the integration of such front-end systems with the existing informatics infrastructure.

According to Johnson and Scholes (2000), the formulation of business strategy involves three interdependent activities. Figure 20.3 lays out these activities in a linear sequence.

- *Strategic analysis*. This involves analysis of the environment, expectations, objectives, power and culture in the organisation and organisational resources. Strategic analysis involves determining the organisation's mission and goals. Strategic analysis involves answering the questions what should we be doing and where are we going?

- *Strategic choice*. This involves generating strategic options, evaluation of such options and the selection of a suitable strategy to achieve the selected option. Strategic choice involves answering the question what routes have we selected?

- *Strategic implementation*. This involves organising resources, restructuring elements of the organisation, and providing suitable people and systems. Strategic implementation comprises determining policies, making decisions and taking action. Strategic implementation involves answering the questions of how do we guide our collective decisions to get there, what choices do we have and how shall we do it?

Strategic tinking is normally documented in terms of an organisation's mission statement. An organisation's mission statement will have a limited number of statements of future intention. In terms of each statement of intention a number

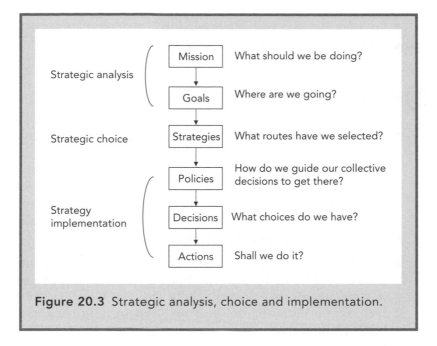

Figure 20.3 Strategic analysis, choice and implementation.

of goals may be formulated. For each such goal a number of strategies or routes forward may be planned. Each strategy has to be made operational in a series of plans. Plans, in turn, are collections of decisions which involve a series of actions. Hence strategic planning involves constructing a hierarchy of goals, strategies, policies, decisions and actions.

Example ||||➡

Mission: to be the industry cost leader

Goal: achieve staff productivity gain of 5% within 3 years

Strategy: reduce time lost due to ill health

Policy: maintain a healthy workplace

Decision: ban smoking

Action: inform staff, put up the signs and police the decision

An organisation's mission statement at various levels of the hierarchy consists of a limited number of objectives stipulated as a guide to future intention. Such objectives should be SMART objectives:

- *Specific*. Each objective should be clear and focused.
- *Measurable*. The objective should clearly include means by which achievement will be measured.
- *Achievable*. The objective should be achievable with organisational resources.

- *Realistic*. The objective should be realistic in terms of organisational constraints.
- *Timely*. The objective should contain details of the duration of achievement.

20.4 ⊚ ORGANISATIONAL STRATEGIES

In commercial environments an organisation takes up a particular position in relation to its competitors. This we might define as the competitive position of the organisation. The development of organisational strategy in terms of the business has normally its prime objective as being the improvement of this competitive position. This is normally expressed as the attempt to gain competitive advantage.

According to Porter (1985), competitive advantage can be gained by engaging in one or more of three generic organisational strategies:

- *Cost advantage strategy*. This essentially aims to establish the organisation as a low-cost leader in the market. The organisation aims to sell its products or services cheaper than its competitors. This may be achieved in a number of ways, such as concentrating on areas involved in improving overall efficiency via better planning.
- *Differentiation strategy*. The organisation undertaking this strategy aims to differentiate its product or service from its competitors. The aim is probably to establish amongst customers in the market-place the perception that the organisation's product or service is better in some way than its competitors. This may be through improving quality and reliability relative to price, better market understanding, image promotion etc.
- *Location strategy*. A location strategy involves the organisation attempting to find a niche market to service. A niche market is one where no other organisation currently has an established presence. This may be achieved in a number of ways: by producing innovations in products or services or by placing distribution, marketing and information outlets in areas not utilised currently.

These three generic strategies have to be implemented in terms of organisational changes. Hence lower-level organisational strategies have to be put in place to achieve cost advantage, differentiation and/or location improvements. Modern organisations may be subject to a number of such lower-level organisational strategies:

- *Low-cost production*. This is an efficiency strategy generally directed at cost advantage.
- *Focus on quality and service*. This is an effectiveness strategy directed at differentiation.
- *Globalisation*. Developing a global focus for your products and/or services. In different ways organisations may utilise globalisation strategies for cost advantage in terms of their supply chains and for differentiation or location advantage in terms of their customer chains.

- *Right-sizing*. Finding appropriate organisational structures for particular changes in environments. This is primarily a cost advantage strategy but also possibly a differentiation or location strategy.
- *Customer intimacy*. Building better relationships with customers. A clear differentiation strategy.
- *Supplier intimacy*. Building better relationships with suppliers. A possible cost advantage strategy.
- *Just-in-time manufacturing*. Keeping inventory levels at a minimum through efficient supply chains. This is primarily a cost advantage strategy.

20.5 INFORMATICS STRATEGY

Many IS projects are closely linked to organisational strategy, many are not. In ideal terms, business or organisational strategy should be a key driver of informatics strategy. In Chapter 34 we consider informatics planning as being the process of generating informatics strategy from organisation strategy. Ideally, informatics strategy should be closely aligned to organisation strategy.

An informatics strategy can be subdivided into three critical elements:

- An information strategy. This details what information is required to support the organisation's mission.
- An information systems strategy. This details what information systems are essential to deliver information.
- An information technology strategy. This details the information technology systems essential to support the information systems.

Example ▐▐▐▶ **Mission**: to be the industry cost leader

Goal: achieve staff productivity gain of 5% within 3 years

Strategy: reduce the time to process a customer transaction

Policy: improve systems integration

Decision: introduce a corporate-wide ERP system

Action: Set up and resource an implementation project

A number of frameworks have been suggested for analysing the informatics/organisational strategy relationship, such as Porter's five forces model and value chain analysis (Chapter 35). The key emphasis of the literature in this area is on the development of so-called strategic information systems (Chapter 36).

20.6 SUMMARY

- Strategic decision-making is focused on the future and the environment of the organisation.
- Organisation strategy is a detailed plan for future action.
- Planning is the process of formulating strategy; management is the process of implementing strategy.
- Business strategy should drive informatics s.trategy
- Informatics strategy is a detailed plan for future informatics activities.
- Organisation strategy should determine what information is relevant.
- Information strategy should determine what information systems are important.
- Information systems strategy should determine which information technology is relevant.

20.7 QUESTIONS

(i) Define the differences between strategy and tactics.

(ii) Define the key elements of a strategic decision.

(iii) How does the development of organisational strategy relate to the development of informatics strategy?

(iv) List the three interdependent activities of strategy formulation.

(v) What is meant by an organisation mission statement?

(vi) List the properties of a SMART objective.

(vii) Distinguish between cost advantage, differentiation and location strategies.

20.8 EXERCISES

(i) Find two examples of a strategic decision made by some organisation.

(ii) Find two examples of a tactical decision made by some organisation.

(iii) In terms of the goal expressed in the example in this chapter, what other strategies, policies, decisions and actions might we have in terms of this goal?

(iv) Are there any information strategies that might contribute to this goal?

(v) In terms of an organisational goal such as improving worker productivity, what other strategies, policies, decisions and actions might we have in terms of this goal?

(vi) Are there any information strategies that might contribute to this goal?

(vii) List two SMART informatics objectives.

20.9 PROJECTS

(i) Study strategic and tactical decision-making in some organisation and determine the types of information systems needed to support each type of decision-making.

(ii) Study one organisation and identify how closely organisation strategy and informatics strategy are linked.

(iii) Collect a number of organisation mission statements. Compare and contrast them. Consider how effective they are as strategic planning tools.

(iv) Take one part of an informatics strategy of some organisation and trace the activities of strategic analysis, choice and implementation in relation to the element.

(v) Analyse elements of some organisation strategy in terms of cost advantage, differentiation and location.

20.10 REFERENCES

Ansoff, H. I. (1965). *Corporate Strategy*. McGraw-Hill, New York.

Johnson, G. and Scholes, K. (2000). *Exploring Corporate Strategy: Text and Cases*, 2nd edn. Prentice Hall, Englewood Cliffs, NJ.

Porter, M. E. (1985). *Competitive Advantage: Creating and Sustaining Superior Performance*. The Free Press, New York.

Scott-Morton, M. S. (ed.) (1991). *The Corporation of the 1990s: Information Technology and Organisational Transformation*. Oxford University Press, New York.

CHAPTER 21

THE INFORMATICS INFRASTRUCTURE

Men of sense often learn from their enemies. It is from their foes, not their friends, that cities learn the lesson of building high walls and ships of war...

Aristophanes

LEARNING OUTCOMES

After reading this chapter, you will be able to:

- Define what is meant by an organisation's informatics infrastructure
- Distinguish between information, information systems and information technology architectures
- Discuss the relationship between informatics planning and the informatics architecture

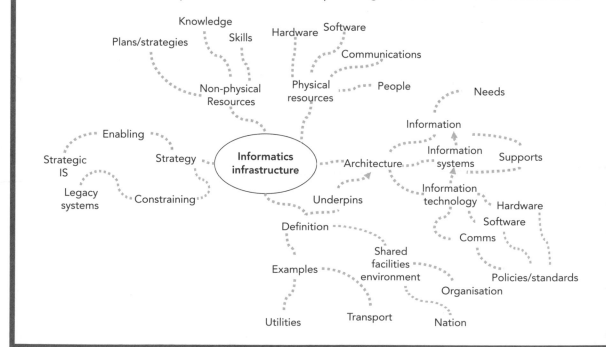

21.1 INTRODUCTION

In this chapter we consider the informatics infrastructure (sometimes called the informatics architecture) of an organisation. We consider a three-layer model of the informatics infrastructure encompassing information, information systems and information technology. We discuss how the architecture may be implicit or explicit and how it is both an enabling and disabling force in organisations. Finally, we consider the importance of an informatics architecture to differing types of organisations.

21.2 INFORMATICS INFRASTRUCTURE

The term *informatics infrastructure* is best considered in terms of an analogy with a transport infrastructure. Consider Figure 21.1, which illustrates part of a road infrastructure. A road infrastructure is a supporting technological infrastructure for travel. A road infrastructure enables traffic to get from point A to point B using motorways, carriageways and major or minor roads.

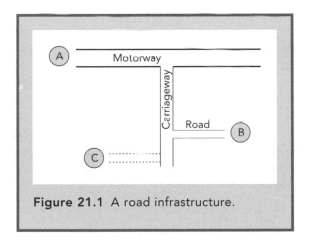

Figure 21.1 A road infrastructure.

The existing road infrastructure facilitates the development of new roads. For instance, Figure 21.1 illustrates that a new route to point C may be developed off the existing road infrastructure. However, the existence of a road infrastructure may disable certain strategic alternatives in terms of transport planning. It may, for instance, disable or constrain development of alternative transport infrastructures, such as railways.

The informatics infrastructure of an organisation consists of the technological infrastructure supporting communication in the organisation. As such, the informatics architecture supports current forms of human activity in the organisation to a greater of lesser extent.

An informatics infrastructure consists of the sum total of information, information systems and information technology resources available to the organisation at any one time. The informatics infrastructure consists not only of physical resources such as hardware, software, communications technology and people, but also of non-physical resources such as knowledge, plans and skills.

The informatics architecture is the foundation on which the organisation may plan and implement the development of new IT systems. The informatics infrastructure also constrains what new systems are feasible and desirable.

The informatics architecture may be implicit or explicit, either in whole or in part. If the architecture is explicit it is documented. If it is implicit it may be part of the informal and even tacit knowledge (Chapter 39) of organisational members.

Informatics planning is the process devoted to formulating plans for the future development of the informatics architecture. Informatics management is the process of implementing such plans and maintaining this architecture.

21.2.1 ORGANISATION STRUCTURE AND THE INFORMATICS INFRASTRUCTURE

The informatics infrastructure of an organisation normally reflects organisational structure. If changes are made to organisation structure then consequent changes have to be made to the informatics infrastructure.

Example ▐▐▶ Goodhue *et al.* (1992) demonstrate a clear linkage between organisation structure and the need for data integration. Data integration is the standardisation of data definitions and structures throughout an organisation. Data integration is implicitly assumed to always result in net benefits to the organisation. The authors question this view by using organisational information processing theory to construct a model of the costs as well as the benefits of data integration. This model is based on the central importance of mechanisms for handling uncertainty to organisations. Data integration is clearly one such mechanism for reducing uncertainty. However, a distinction is made between three major types of uncertainty:

● uncertainty generated by complex or non-routine subunit tasks

● uncertainty generated by unstable subunit task environments

● uncertainty generated by interdependence amongst subunits

Goodhue *et al.* argue that data integration can only satisfactorily address the last type of uncertainty. Hence one would expect that organisations in which there is heavy interdependence between subunits would have strong data integration as part of their informatics infrastructure.

21.3 🌀 LEVELS OF THE INFORMATICS INFRASTRUCTURE

The informatics infrastructure of an organisation can be considered as consisting of three mutually interdependent layers or levels:

- *Information architecture.* This consists of definitions of information need and activities involved in the collection, storage, dissemination and use of information within the organisation.

- *Information systems architecture.* This consists of the information systems needed to support organisational activity in the areas of collection, storage, dissemination and use.

- *Information technology architecture.* This consists of the hardware, software, data and communication facilities as well as the IT knowledge and skills available to the organisation.

Figure 21.2, discussed in Chapter 5, can be considered as a high-level map of the information systems likely to be found in a typical commercial organisation. The IS currently directly emulate some standard human activity systems such as sales, accounting, stock control and procurement. From such a map it is possible to infer some of the information needs of the typical organisation. For example, most

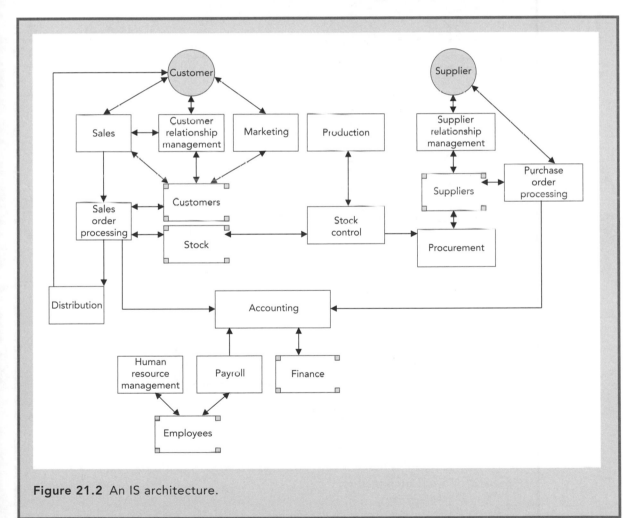

Figure 21.2 An IS architecture.

organisations need to store data about their employees, customers, suppliers, stock and finance.

An IT architecture will consist of the IT systems that support information systems. It is likely that the organisation may adopt significant standardisation in the areas of hardware, software data and communications technology to facilitate integration of IT systems.

A possible map of an IT architecture corresponding to the IS architecture illustrated in Figure 21.2 is given in Figure 21.3. Note that the data stores of the information systems architecture have been replaced by a number of database systems (Chapter 10). Hence the Customers data store has been replaced by a Customers database. Also, the information systems in Figure 21.2 have been replaced by a number of information technology systems. However, not all the IT systems

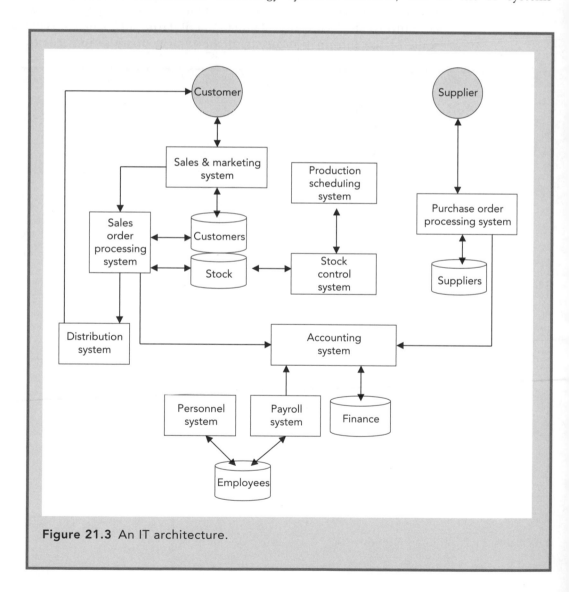

Figure 21.3 An IT architecture.

correspond directly to the information systems. More than one IS may be supported by one IT system. Hence the purchase order processing IT system in Figure 21.3 combines the functions of the procurement, supplier relationship management and purchase order processing information systems in Figure 21.2.

We made the point in Chapter 4 that not all information systems may utilise modern information technology. Some information systems within organisations may rely on traditional 'paper-based' information technologies such as filing systems. Hence it is perfectly possible for an information systems architecture to document some information systems which have not been computerised to any significant extent. Such anomalies between either the information technology and information systems architecture or the information systems architecture and the information architecture may indicate significant areas for consideration in informatics planning (Chapter 34).

The strategy of purchasing enterprise resource planning (ERP) systems can be seen as an attempt to buy in a complete information technology architecture. An ERP system consists of a series of packaged software modules feeding off a central database of organisational data.

Example   In a university an informatics architecture would contain:

- *Information architecture.* A university needs to collect and store data pertaining to teaching, research and consultancy. Information is essential to the effective performance of these three organisational processes. For instance data about students and their progression is essential to the teaching process. ·

- *Information systems architecture.* On a very broad level a university needs information systems to support the teaching, research and consultancy processes. In terms of teaching, for instance, a university needs to record data about its student population, the courses and modules students are currently taking and the grades that students have achieved. Hence some form of integrated student management information system is an essential part of the organisation's information systems architecture.

- *Information technology architecture.* A university needs an integrated communications infrastructure enabling technology such as email and the Internet. It also needs standards established in terms of hardware and software for both administrative and teaching purposes. Most universities will also maintain some form of informatics service.

21.4 EXPLICIT AND IMPLICIT INFORMATICS ARCHITECTURES

Many organisations, both large and small, have implicit informatics architectures. They have information needs, information systems for fulfilling these needs and technological systems to facilitate information dissemination and use, but:

- They have not explicitly documented the data they collect, disseminate and use on a day-to-day basis. They also have little idea of which organisational activities use which data.
- There is no clear map of what information systems there are in the organisation and how they relate together.
- The organisation does not have an inventory of their information technology systems, software, hardware, data and communications technology.

Most medium- to large-scale organisations will have a mix of explicit and implicit architectures. This situation frequently arises because the organisation has not engaged in any systematic planning process. Systems have been built in a piecemeal manner and with little thought to how they interrelate to the rest of the business.

There are a number of advantages to having a more explicit information systems architecture. The key is that integration and interoperability of systems becomes more feasible. Many benefits such as these are discussed in the chapter on informatics planning (Chapter 34).

21.5 INFRASTRUCTURE AS ENABLING AND CONSTRAINING

It must be recognised that an informatics infrastructure is both an enabling and a constraining force within organisations.

Any application of informatics can leverage or extend the existing informatics infrastructure. A given IS leverages the infrastructure when it draws upon the resources the existing infrastructure offers. An IS extends the infrastructure by contributing physical or non-physical resources that can be drawn upon by other applications. Strategic information systems (SIS) (Chapter 36) are one example of the way in which the informatics infrastructure can be enabling. SIS are those IS that improve the competitive position of the organisation.

Example |||▶ A key example of infrastructure as an enabling force is the way in which the Republic of Singapore's extreme reliance on foreign trade led it to develop an IS (Tradenet) that significantly reduced the time required for shippers to clear customs. The objective was to give Singapore a competitive advantage over other ports in the Far East. Tradenet leveraged existing governmental transaction processing systems by linking traders in. The process of implementing Tradenet also extended Singapore's stock of IS related skills.

However, an IT infrastructure may also be a constraining influence. For instance, legacy systems (large and ageing corporate support systems) generally constrain the organisation in the sense that they determine the way in which much corporate data must be collected, manipulated and distributed.

Example ||||➡ The so-called 'millenium bug' is one important example of the constraining influence of the existing informatics infrastructure. This bug represented the way in which many systems were found to be deficient in their ability to handle 21st century dates. The presence of this bug forced many organisations on an international scale to divert vast development resources to solving the problem and consequently placed a brake on new information system developments.

21.6 ⊚ THE IMPORTANCE OF INFORMATICS INFRASTRUCTURE

In Chapter 16 we described a number of models of organisation that have a crucial bearing on the way in which we approach informatics in organisations. Another way of looking at organisations is in terms of the relative importance of an informatics infrastructure to the activity of the organisation. Cash *et al.* (1992) provide a useful way of conceptualising organisations in terms of:

● The importance of existing IS to the strategy of organisations

● The importance of future IS to the strategy of organisations

Considering these as two dimensions, four organisational possibilities are illustrated in Figure 21.4.

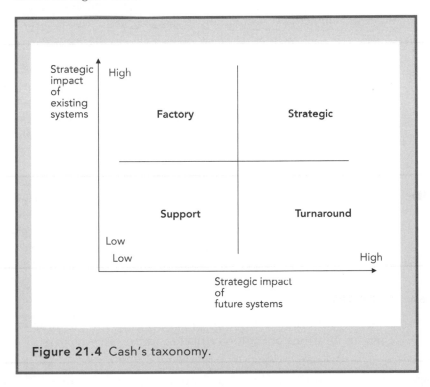

Figure 21.4 Cash's taxonomy.

21.6.1 STRATEGIC

Strategic organisations are those in which smooth functioning of existing IS activity is critical to their daily operation. Also, applications under development are critical to the organisation's future competitive success.

Example ‖‖▶ Many organisations in the financial industry are clearly in this sector. IT is at the heart of modern banking, for instance. Future developments in the area of Internet banking are likely to be critical to the industry.

21.6.2 TURNAROUND

Turnaround organisations require considerable amounts of IS support, but the organisation's activities are not absolutely dependent on the uninterrupted, cost-effective functioning of IS support to achieve its short-term or long-term objectives. Applications under development, however, are absolutely vital to the long-term health of the organisation.

Example ‖‖▶ Many organisations in the retail industry have traditionally been in this camp. However, for the large supermarket chains IS and the development of applications have become critical to competitive success.

21.6.3 FACTORY

For smooth operation, the organisation is heavily dependent on cost-effective, reliable IS. The IS development portfolio however is heavily dominated by maintenance work, and the applications under development, though important, are not fundamental to the ability of the organisation to compete.

Example ‖‖▶ The manufacturing sector has implemented many systems, such as just-in-time manufacturing systems, that are heavily reliant on IS. However, it is currently unclear in many organisations how IS can stimulate further improvements in manufacturing processes in the future.

21.6.4 SUPPORT

Some organisations are not dependent on the smooth functioning of IT, nor are their applications portfolios critical to future effectiveness.

Example ‖‖▶ Organisations in agriculture have historically not been heavy investors in IT and are also unlikely to be large investors in this technology in the future.

One should emphasise that this taxonomy is probably equally relevant to parts of organisations as well as the whole organisation. Different divisions and departments may be in different quadrants of the innovation matrix at different times. For instance, manufacturing operations may be in factory or support, whereas the marketing division may be in the strategic or turnaround quadrant. Also, organisations may move around the quadrants over time, starting in the support quadrant, then moving through turnaround and strategic quadrants into the factory quadrant.

21.7 SUMMARY

- The informatics infrastructure of an organisation equals the set of organisational resources that give the organisation the capacity to generate new IT systems. An informatics infrastructure includes not only physical resources such as existing hardware, software, and communications, but also non-physical resources such as knowledge, plans, people and skills.

- The informatics infrastructure can be considered on three levels: information architecture, information systems architecture and information technology architecture.

- An information architecture consists of activities involved in the collection, storage, dissemination and use of information within the organisation.

- An information systems architecture consists of the information systems needed to support organisational activity in the areas of collection, storage, dissemination and use of information.

- An information technology architecture consists of the hardware, software, communication facilities and IT knowledge and skills available to the organisation.

- The informatics infrastructure of an organisation may be implicit or explicit.

- An organisation has an explicit informatics infrastructure if all three elements are documented.

- An organisation has an implicit informatics architecture if the three elements remain undocumented. It remains an architecture but the inventory of organisational activities and resources has not taken place.

- Most large- to medium-scale organisations will have some aspects of their architecture which are explicit and many aspects of their architecture which are implicit.

- An infrastructure is both an enabling and a constraining force for change in organisations.

21.8 QUESTIONS

(i) Define the term *informatics infrastructure/architecture*.

(ii) List the three layers of an informatics infrastructure/architecture.

(iii) In what ways may an informatics architecture be implicit?

(iv) Describe how an informatics architecture may enable an informatics strategy.

(v) Describe how an informatics architecture may constrain an informatics strategy.

(vi) Distinguish between a strategic company and a turnaround company.

21.9 EXERCISES

(i) Apply the concept of infrastructure to higher education. What would make up the higher education infrastructure of some nation?

(ii) Consider some organisation known to you. Does it have an informatics architecture?

(iii) If the preceding answer is 'no', attempt to describe in overview its informatics infrastructure. Describe its information, information systems and information technology architectures.

(iv) Classify the organisation in terms of Cash et al.'s framework.

21.10 PROJECTS

(i) Develop a case study of the informatics infrastructure of some organisation. Determine the degree to which the informatics infrastructure reflects organisational structure.

(ii) Collect a number of organisation informatics strategies. Compare and contrast. Consider how effective they are as tools for planning IS and IT.

(iii) Survey a range of organisations in a particular sector and determine the degree to which their informatics strategies are implicit or explicit.

(iv) Survey a range of organisations in a particular sector and determine the degree to which their informatics strategies are enabling and constraining.

(v) How frequently do organisations distinguish between information, information systems and information technology architectures?

(vi) Use the Cash framework to determine the relevant quadrant for organisations in a particular sector.

21.11 REFERENCES

Cash, J. I., McFarlan, F. W. and McKenney, J. L. (1992). *Corporate Information Systems Management*, 3rd edn. Richard Irwin, Homewood, IL.

Goodhue, D. L., Wybo, M. D. and Kirsch, L. J. (1992). The impact of data integration on the costs and benefits of information systems. *MIS Quarterly*, **16**(3), 293–311.

PART 5

ENVIRONMENT

We do not know, in most cases, how far social failure and success are due to heredity, and how far to environment. But environment is the easier of the two to improve.

J. B. S. Haldane

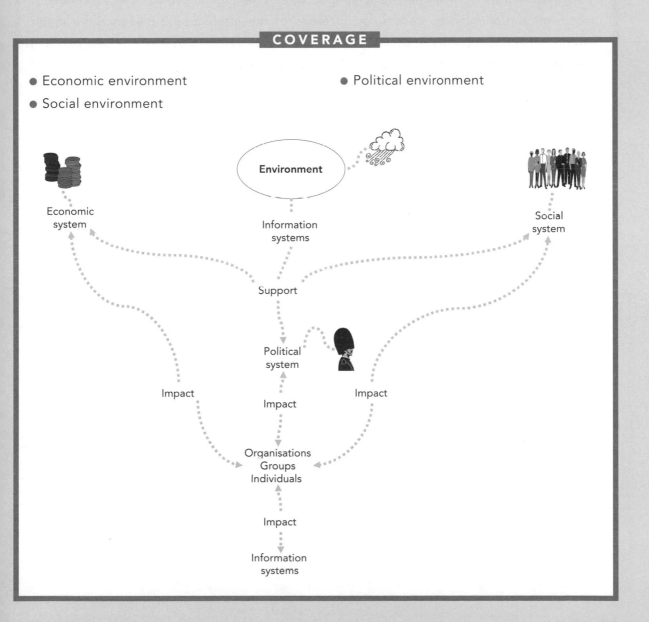

An organisation is a human activity system (or more accurately a collection of human activity systems) that is affected by forces found within its environment. Organisations are not isolated entities, they are open systems. The success of any organisation will depend on how well it integrates with aspects of its environment. An organisation is an open system that builds information systems to cope with environmental forces. The shape of its information systems will also be shaped by environmental constraints.

By environment we normally mean anything outside of the organisation. The environment of most organisations can be considered in terms of the interaction between three major systems: an economic system, social system and political system (Figure P5.1). The external environment can be seen to be made up of a network of activities and relationships in each of these systems between the organisation and other agencies.

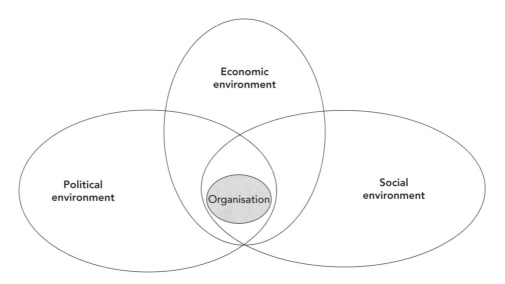

Figure P5.1 The external environment of organisations.

The external environment in each of these systems will exert an impact on the information systems activities of an organisation, group or individual. Likewise, the information systems activities of individuals, groups and organisations are likely to impact on social, economic and political systems. Also, information technology and information systems will have a significant impact on the shape of economic, social and political systems.

An economic system is the way in which a group of humans arrange their material provisioning. It essentially involves the coordination of activities concerned with such provisioning. An organisation's economic environment is defined by activities and relationships between economic actors and the organisation (Chapter 22). The economic environment is particularly concerned with the performance of national and international commerce and trade and is influenced by such factors as levels of taxation, inflation rates and economic growth. Information systems are key to organisational performance within economic markets. Recently, growth has been experienced in specialised markets focused around the use of electronic networks. Electronic business and electronic commerce have become significant strategies for modern organisations.

The social environment of an organisation concerns its position in the cultural life of some grouping such a nation state. The social system can be seen to be made up of a series of cultural activities and relationships (Chapter 23). The social system concerns ways in which people relate to organisational activity. It concerns issues of fashion, taste and ethical and moral considerations. Organisational culture has multiple influences on its information systems. In turn, an organisation's information systems will impact upon organisational culture. This equally applies to the larger social environment of societies.

The political environment or system concerns issues of power. Political systems are made up of sets of activities and relationships concerned with power and its exercise (Chapter 24). The political environment is particularly concerned with government and legal frameworks within nation states and is a major constraining force on organisational behaviour. The political environment of Western countries has been much subject to the influence of information technology in the areas of electronic government and tele-democracy in recent times.

THE ECONOMIC ENVIRONMENT

Business is a good game – lots of competition and a minimum of rules. You keep score with money.

Atari founder Nolan Bushnell

LEARNING OUTCOMES

After reading this chapter, you will be able to:

- Define the concept of an economy or economic system
- Consider the issue of markets as competitive environments
- Outline the effect of the economic environment on an organisation's information systems
- Describe the place of information systems in improving the competitive position of the firm
- Relate the importance of information systems and information technology to the information economy

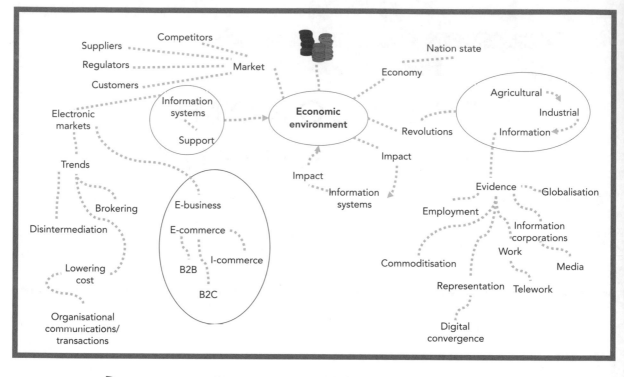

22.1 ⊚ INTRODUCTION

For commercial organisations the economic environment of the organisation is probably the most important. An organisation exists within some economic system. At the level of the nation state we speak of such an economic system as being an economy. Each economy will be made up of a number of markets. A market is fundamentally a medium of exchange between buyers and sellers. A market, or for larger companies a series of markets, forms the immediate environment of a company. It forms the competitive environment of the organisation.

The state of an economic environment and an organisation's position in it influences various issues such as the state of informatics planning, management and development. The state of an organisation's informatics planning, management and development is likely to affect the competitive position of the organisation in its economic environment. Economic systems are also heavily reliant in themselves on effective information systems. Modern economies are information economies.

22.2 ⊚ ECONOMIC SYSTEMS

The economic environment of an organisation can be considered as a system. An economic system is the way in which a group of humans arrange their material provisioning. It essentially involves the coordination of activities concerned with such provisioning.

Two major sets of such activities are relevant to economic systems: production and distribution. Production is that set of activities concerned with the production of goods for human existence. Production is undertaken by producers. Distribution is the associated process of collecting, storing and moving goods into the hands of consumers.

An economy is an economic system based usually within some notion of a nation state (a political construct). Power normally depends on economic wealth and hence there is a clear relationship between economic and political systems.

One can argue that historically three major forms of economic system have been invented by humankind for coordinating the production and distribution of goods:

- *Tradition-based economic system*. Historically speaking this form of economic system has been the most prevalent. In it, the production of goods and the distribution of goods to consumers is based on well-established traditions. Most feudal economies ran on such lines.

- *Command-based economic system*. In this form of economic system the planning and management of production and distribution are centralised in a political authority. Key examples of command-based economies were those of Communist states such as the Soviet Union.

- *Market-based economic system*. In a market-based economy production and distribution are subject to the free interplay of buyers and sellers. Capitalist economies are all examples of market-based economic systems and currently dominate the modern Western world.

22.3 MARKETS

A market is a medium for exchanges between buyers and sellers. An organisation's economic environment is defined by activities and relationships between four main types of economic actors and the organisation (Figure 22.1). These activities and relationships define a particular market.

- *Competitors*. Other organisations in the same fundamental area of business

- *Suppliers*. Those organisations supplying resources to the organisation

- *Customers*. Those individuals, groups or organisations purchasing products or services from the organisation

- *Regulators*. Groups or organisations which set policy for appropriate activities in a particular market

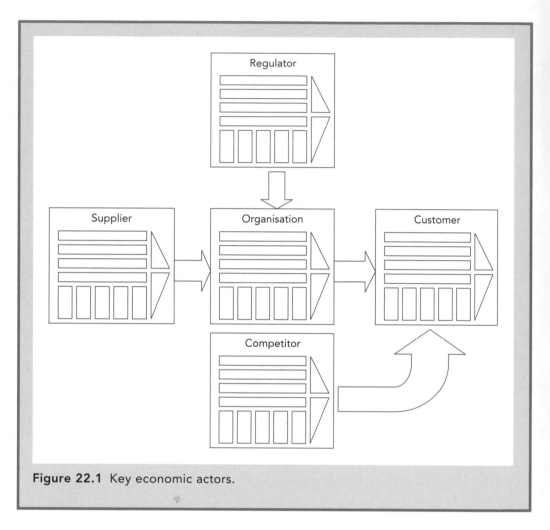

Figure 22.1 Key economic actors.

Example ▐▐▐▶ Take the case of an organisation such as a supermarket chain. The economic environment of this organisation could be described as food retail. In the UK this economic environment is characterised by the dominance of four major competitors: Tesco, Asda, Sainsbury and Safeway. Each supermarket chain has many suppliers, ranging from farms providing fresh foodstuffs to factories providing processed foods and other products. The customers of the supermarkets are the general public. Food retail is heavily regulated by bodies such as the Food Standards Agency within the UK.

Michael Porter (Porter and Millar, 1985) defines an economic environment in terms of the following factors that involve interaction between the four main types of economic actors described above:

- *Competitive structure of the industry.* This really defines the relative power of competitors to determine things like the pricing policy in the economic environment.
- *Relative power of buyers and sellers.* This highlights the important position that customers and suppliers play in markets.
- *Basis of competition.* This means describing the main products or services sold and the main ways in which organisations compete in the economic environment.
- *State of regulation in the economic environment.*
- *State of technological deployment in the environment.*
- *Whether the industry is growing, shrinking or stable.* This is a reflection of the state of regulation, competition and demand in a particular market.

Example ||||➡ In food retail in the UK the dominance of four big supermarkets means that they have enormous power in determining pricing levels for key foodstuffs from their suppliers. However, the food retail industry is subject to quite heavy degrees of regulation in such areas as environmental health legislation. The food retail sector is still growing in the UK. In recent years the major supermarkets have increased their levels of technological deployment quite dramatically and have utilised their information systems in new areas such as financial services. The basis of competition has traditionally been on matters of pricing, although other bases, such as the quality of foodstuffs (particularly in relation to organic foodstuffs), have recently come into play.

22.3.1 COMPETITIVE POSITION

An organisation takes up a particular position in a market defined by its activities and relationships with its competitors, suppliers, customers and regulators. The strategy of a business is normally developed with the objective of at least maintaining and more usually improving the competitive or market position of the company. Informatics strategy is developed to fulfil some aspects of business strategy. Strategic information systems (Chapter 36) are attempts to influence an organisation's position and relationships through its relative technological capability.

Example ||||➡ Information systems, such as customer databases for marketing and sales, can have a strategic impact on an organisation's competitive position by:

- Changing the basis of competition; for example, winning customers from competition by using large customer databases

- Strengthening customer relationships, such as the use of market research databases to target customer 'need'

- Overcoming supplier problems, such as the use of telemarketing and direct mailing to improve sales

- Building barriers against new entrants; for example, the cost of setting up and maintaining an accurate customer database as a barrier to entry

- Generating new products; electronic shopping as a new product

22.4 ⊚ THE EFFECT OF THE ECONOMIC ENVIRONMENT UPON IS

The state of an economic environment and a firm's position in it influences, amongst other things:

- which information systems the firm chooses to maintain
- which information systems the firm chooses to strategically develop
- the design of any information system
- the adaptations an organisation makes to its internal information systems
- whether an organisation chooses to develop an information system in-house or outsource its development to an external supplier
- whether an organisation chooses to control the informatics service internally or outsource the informatics service either in whole or part

Examples ▐▐▐➡ An organisation needs information systems of at least a comparable level to its competitors to perform effectively in its market-place. Hence there is a certain amount of maintaining an equivalent informatics infrastructure to ones competitors. The informatics infrastructure of customers and suppliers of some organisation may also influence the development of key information systems. A good example here is the way in which suppliers of large organisations frequently have to build links into the informatics infrastructure of their major customer.

Regulatory changes frequently impact on the logic of an organisation's transaction processing and reporting systems. A classic example here is the way in which changes in tax regulations or the calculation of value added tax (VAT) cause changes to be made to accounting, payroll and financial information systems within organisations. Also, European Monetary Union has forced a level of standardisation amongst financial information systems in the European Union.

Many organisations do not see IS as one of their core competencies. Hence decisions may be made to outsource either the whole or part of the organisation's informatics infrastructure to an external supplier. Frequently organisations in the same market may all decide to outsource their IS/IT in the same way. Alternatively, organisations in the same market-place may choose to implement the same software package for core information systems functions.

22.5 THE EFFECT OF INFORMATION SYSTEMS UPON THE COMPETITIVE POSITION OF THE FIRM

The state of an organisation's information systems may influence:

- what activities an organisation undertakes
- the efficiency and/or the effectiveness of an organisation's activities
- relationships with suppliers
- relationships with customers
- relationships with competitors
- relationships with regulators

Examples ▐▐▐➡ The state of an organisation's informatics infrastructure will determine whether or not it is able to perform its activities, such as order processing. Its information systems will also have a crucial bearing on the efficiency with which it does things and the effectiveness of the service or products it provides to customers.

Information systems are increasingly being used to manage and control customer and supply chains. For instance orders are being taken via the Internet and extranets are being used to allow suppliers to inspect inventory levels within organisations.

Reporting from an organisation's information systems may be an essential requirement of a regulatory authority. For instance, a utility company may need to supply details of how many of its customers it has had to disconnect from the gas or electricity supply to national watchdogs.

22.6 THE INFORMATION ECONOMY

In the 1970s Daniel Bell, a US sociologist, wrote an influential book entitled *The Coming of Post-Industrial Society* (Bell, 1972). In this work, Bell made a series of predictions about the state of Western societies. His major premise is now generally accepted: that Western societies are becoming information economies. He maintained that whereas the revolution of the latter part of the 19th century was an industrial revolution, the revolution of the latter part of the 20th century was an information revolution.

Since the publication of Bell's seminal work a great deal of debate has ensued over the question of whether modern economies are information rather than industrial economies. A number of indicators may be used to provide evidence for the information economy.

22.6.1   ECONOMIC TRENDS

Over the last half-century significant change has occurred in the structure of Western economies. These economies have changed from goods-producing economies to service economies. Many more people are now employed in service industries than in agricultural, tertiary and manufacturing industries. Information and information technology is particularly important to the service industries.

22.6.2   GLOBALISATION

The structural forms which emerged in Western economic markets have now diffused throughout the world. There is significant evidence that many commercial organisations work or must work within global rather than local markets. This process has been referred to as globalisation (Currie, 2000). Information is essential to the management of organisations in global markets.

22.6.3   INFORMATION CORPORATIONS

Many organisations in economic systems now devote most of their activities to information-related activities. They are information corporations.

Examples ||||➤   The trend of information becoming a major commodity for organisations is evident, for instance, in the work of the advertising industry. Advertisements for particular products will be placed within television programmes that are watched by a significant proportion of people who are likely to buy such products. The advertising company makes decisions about which adverts to place where on the basis of information from market researchers who conduct detailed surveys of viewing behaviour. In this context, information has become a currency that determines the cost of particular advertisements. Adverts placed within programmes watched by peak viewing populations clearly become more costly to place than those embedded within less watched programmes.

The news agency Reuters is another example of an organisation where information is its life-blood. Reuters prepares and sells news reports to broadcasting companies, newspapers and other news outlets around the world. In this sense, information is Reuter's product or commodity.

22.6.4   CHANGES TO WORK (TELE-WORK)

Information and communications technology have caused changes to the way in which work is conducted. One significant phenomenon is the degree to which individuals now work from home and utilise information technology and communications technology to maintain connection to an organisational hub.

22.6.5 INFORMATION COMMODITISATION AND REPRESENTATION

Much discussion has been made of the commoditisation of information. In information economies information is seen to be a commodity itself.

However, Bell (1972) believes that information is not a commodity in the sense of industrial commodities. Industrial commodities are produced in discrete, identifiable units, and are exchanged and sold to be consumed. Classic industrial commodities are loaves of bread and automobiles. Some have called these tangible commodities. Such commodities are characterised by the fact that one buys the product from a seller and thereby take physical possession of it. The exchange is also governed by legal rules of contract.

Information is an intangible commodity. The problem with information is that even when it is sold, it remains with the producer. Bell sees it as a collective commodity in that when it is created it is by its very nature available to all. For information to be a commodity, information must have value, but not all information may be valuable or useful. What determines the value or utility of information is clearly dependent on the particular perspective of some individual or group. The idea of determining the use-value of information is one approach to attempt to commoditise information.

For commercial organisations there is a key use-value in the transactional data they can collect on their customers.

22.6.6 TRANSACTIONAL INFORMATION

Companies collect significant amounts of transactional data about their activities, suppliers and customers (Burnham, 1983). Transactional data is data that records events taking place between individuals, groups and organisations. Transactional data is essential to the effective running of most organisations and markets.

Example ▌▌▌▶ One of the major UK supermarket chains maintains a large database of retail transactional data produced from its point-of-sale machines in each supermarket. This information is used not only to automatically determine stock reordering, but also to determine the major purchasing strategy for the chain as well as the siting of new stores.

22.6.7 E-BUSINESS AND E-COMMERCE

Business can be considered either as an entity or as the set of activities associated with a commercial organisation. Commerce constitutes the exchange of products and services between businesses, groups and individuals. Commerce can hence be seen as one of the essential activities of any business. We have argued throughout this work that considerable transformation in both business and commerce has been affected by information and communication technology (ICT). Recently the labels electronic business (e-business) and electronic commerce (e-commerce) have been attached to features of this transformation (Part 9).

Despite the recent obsession, we would argue that e-business and e-commerce are not new phenomena. The current interest in e-business and e-commerce is merely indicative of the level to which modern economies are e-economies. Since the use of ICT to transform internal and external business processes has been ongoing for at least three decades, one might argue that much of the discussion surrounding e-business and e-commerce is an acknowledgement of the centrality of information systems to the effective performance of the internal processes of modern business and the external processes of trading.

22.7 SUMMARY

- An organisation exists within an economic system. An economic system defined on some geographical area such as the nation state can be considered an economy.
- Each economy will be made up of a number of markets. A market defines the immediate environment of the commercial organisation.
- Markets are made up of four major stakeholder groups: customers, suppliers, competitors and regulators.
- The state of an economic environment and a firm's position in it influences the organisation's information systems.
- The state of an organisation's information systems affect the competitive position of the organisation.
- Many economic markets are now heavily reliant on the effective utilisation of information technology. Modern Western economies are information economies.

22.8 QUESTIONS

(i) In what ways may an economy be considered as a system?

(ii) Define the concept of a market.

(iii) What major stakeholder groups interact in a market?

(iv) List Michael Porter's characteristics of a market.

(v) What is meant by an organisation's competitive position?

(vi) Describe some of the ways in which an organisation's economic environment may affect its information systems.

(vii) Describe some of the ways in which information systems may affect the competitive position of the firm.

(viii) In what way is it appropriate to describe modern Western economies as information economies?

22.9 EXERCISES

(i) Choose some part of the economic market-place. Conduct an environmental analysis to determine the competitors, suppliers, customers and regulators in the market.

(ii) Find a relevant economic market and develop an analysis of the market in terms of Porter's features.

(iii) Consider some nation and in terms of the defined indicators in this chapter assess the level to which you believe it is an information economy.

(iv) Find some examples of transactional data collected by organisations such as universities.

(v) Find some examples of information commodities.

22.10 PROJECTS

(i) Select one industrial sector and detail the changes caused within the sector over the last twenty years through the application of information technology.

(ii) Investigate the feasibility of the concept of a virtual university.

(iii) Conduct a SWOT (Strengths, Weaknesses, Opportunities, Threats) analysis on the appropriateness of introducing tele-working for some company.

(iv) In terms of some company develop a case study of the effects of the economic environment on the company's information systems.

(v) Develop a case study of the way in which a particular company has used IS and IT to improve its competitive position.

(vi) Investigate the degree to which music constitutes an information commodity and the consequences that this has for the music industry.

22.11 REFERENCES

Bell, D. (1972). *The Coming of the Post-industrial Society*. Addison-Wesley, Reading, MA.

Burnham, D. (1983). *The Rise of the Computer State*. Random House, New York.

Currie, W. (2000). *The Global Information Society*. John Wiley, Chichester.

Porter, M. E. and Millar, V. E. (1985). How information gives you competitive advantage. *Harvard Business Review*, **63**(4), 149–160.

CHAPTER 23

THE SOCIAL ENVIRONMENT

Man seeketh in society comfort, use and protection.

Francis Bacon (1561–1626)

After reading this chapter, you will be able to:

- Define the social environment of some organisation
- Discuss the effect of the social environment on information systems
- Describe the effect of information technology and information systems on the social environment

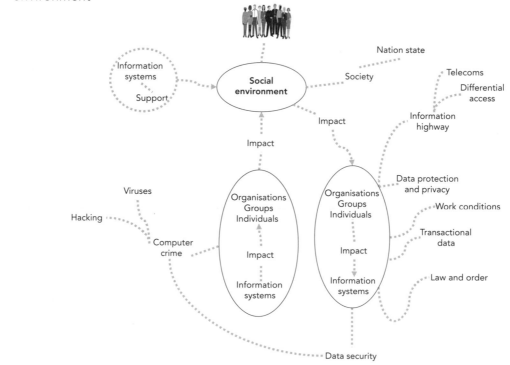

23.1 ◎ INTRODUCTION

Individuals, groups and organisations exist within a social system. A social system is made up of a set of cultural activities and relationships. Culture equals expectations of behaviour (Chapter 18). At the level of the nation state we speak of such a social system as being a society. In recent times it has become popular to speak of the information society, thus identifying the important impact of information, information systems and information technology upon modern social systems.

The relationship between social systems and information technologies is a dialectical one. Information technologies cause changes in behaviour within social systems. Likewise, changes in a social system will impact upon the application of information technology.

The impact of information technology upon society is considered here in terms of four major forces: digital convergence, transactional data, IT-related crime and the effect of IT upon work. Each of these forces has stimulated a reaction within the social system to the potentialities of IT. IT crime has stimulated the growth in IT security, the rise of transactional data has stimulated legislation in the area of data protection, the increasing use of computers within work has stimulated concerns over the misuse of IT and the increasing convergence of technologies around the digital standard has raised reactions to the globalisation of the media. These dialectical relationships are illustrated in Figure 23.1.

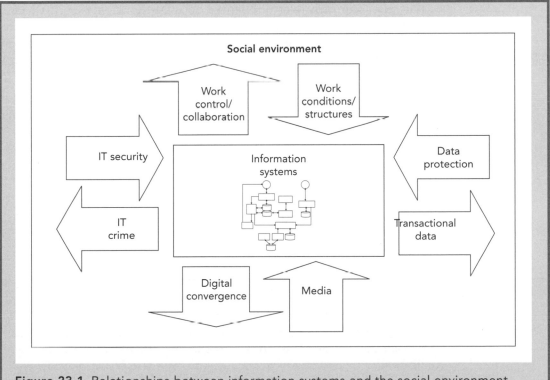

Figure 23.1 Relationships between information systems and the social environment.

The use of information technology by individuals, groups and organisations can impact on the shape of social systems. For instance:

- *Digital convergence.* Most information technologies are now converging around the digital standard, allowing interoperability of such technologies on the global scale. Digital convergence, it is argued, is a significant force in the globalisation of Western attitudes, beliefs and values.

- *Transactional data.* Concerns exist over the use of information technology to infringe human rights in a number of ways. For instance, transactional data is data that records events taking place between individuals, groups and organisations. Transactional data is essential to the effective running of most organisations and markets. However, the increase in transactional data has potentially insidious consequences for increased monitoring and control by organisations and government agencies.

- *Changes to work.* The pervasive nature of information technology and communication networks has stimulated social changes in the way in which individuals and groups behave. A simple example of this is the way in which electronic mail has replaced many aspects of face-to-face interaction in organisations.

- *Differential access.* The centrality of information technology within social life has raised concern over differential access to elements of this technology by various groups in society. Concern has been raised that disparities in access to information technology and networks may engender or be representative of other differences in society. A growing gulf may emerge between those who have access to information technology and those who do not.

- *Global protest.* Pressure groups and terrorist organisations are beginning to use information technology and global networks as a vehicle both to organise their activities and to exert pressure on national governments and organisations. For instance, many anarchist organisations are now using computer hacking as a weapon in their attempt to bring down global capitalism and its manifestations.

- *IT crime.* As IT systems become more and more a part of everyday economic, social and political activity, one would expect that the volume of deviant behaviour experienced in relation to such systems is likely to increase. One would also expect that various reactions will be made in the area of information security to counter this increase in information technology-related crime.

Example ▐▐▐➤ During 2000 the UK economy experienced two weeks of chaos when a loose collection of interest groups protesting against the high levels of taxation levelled on petroleum in the UK blockaded oil terminals and conducted go-slow convoys on the major motorways. This protest was apparently organised using information technologies to coordinate political action. The two-week long protest brought many organisations (such as the National Health Service) close to collapse.

23.2.1 DIGITAL CONVERGENCE

Digital convergence is the capture, storage and dissemination of media of various types in a digital format. Traditional forms of content provision such as radio and television are now all moving over to digital transmission. This allows a convergence with various media utilised by information technology systems.

Example ||||➡ The British Broadcasting Corporation (BBC) has initiated a considerable re-investment of its strategy into offering its material as digital media. Its conventional television and radio programmes are now offered digitally as well as a number of specialist channels, particularly its 24-hour news channel. Each conventional channel is supported by a parallel Internet presence.

23.2.2 TRANSACTIONAL DATA

Transactional data is data that records events taking place between individuals, groups and organisations. Transactional data is essential to the effective running of most organisations and markets. However, the increase in transactional data has potentially insidious consequences. Burnham (1983) particularly illustrates the way in which transactional information can be used to record the daily lives of almost every person in the USA. This information can be combined with more traditional kinds of information, such as people's age and place of birth, to permit organisations to make decisions about the planning of their work.

Example ||||➡ Within the UK the Driver and Vehicle Licensing Agency (DVLA) collects details of car ownership within the country. The UK supermarket chain Safeway pays the DVLA for address details of persons illegally parked at their stores. It uses such information to collect parking fines.

23.2.3 INFORMATION TECHNOLOGY CRIME

With the increasing penetration and permeation of information technology into modern society such societies have experienced a consequent increase in the levels of crime associated with such technology. We may categorise information technology crime in a number of ways, such as:

- Illegal access and use of IT systems.
- Alteration and destruction of data in IT systems.
- Data and hardware theft.
- Software piracy – infringing software copyright rights, particularly copying programs.
- Password sniffers may be hidden in a network or system that records user names and passwords.

- IT system-related scams such as sites which take money from people, promising returns which do not materialise – e.g. bogus investment details.
- Creation and dissemination of computer viruses. A computer virus is a program which 'infects' application systems, operating systems or file systems making them inoperable.
- Use of established IT systems for criminal purposes, typically on an international scale – e.g. use of global international banking networks and various forms of computer terrorism.

Example ▶ During 2000 a computer virus originating in the Far East paralysed computer networks around the world. The virus was transmitted via an email with the simple title *I Love You*. The email contained a program which when activated sent an email message to all persons on the address lists of the person receiving the email.

23.3 THE EFFECT OF THE SOCIAL ENVIRONMENT UPON INFORMATION SYSTEMS

The state of a social system may constrain organisational activities in a number of ways. For instance, a society may exercise prohibition in terms of using information technology in certain ways:

- *Data protection and privacy*. The social system may exert expectations of sustaining data protection and privacy. Some have argued that issues of privacy and freedom assume greater significance in the information age.
- *Work conditions*. Organisations are expected to behave in certain ways towards their employees. The most prevalent set of expectations are those in the area of providing suitable work conditions in the sense of providing a healthy and safe workplace.
- *Media*. Information is a critical component of modern societies. This is nowhere more evident than in the 'media' – the news and entertainment industry. It has been argued that the media are a significant social force in influencing attitudes, beliefs and even values amongst society. Castells (1996) argues that the media control information flow on the global scale and therefore exert considerable influence in the political arena worldwide.
- *Law and order*. Information technology has stimulated a new type of criminal behaviour. In response to this organisations have to had to plan for and maintain appropriate levels of security in relation to their information systems.

23.3.1 DATA PROTECTION AND PRIVACY

The rise of transactional information has brought to the fore the issue of ensuring the privacy of data held about an individual. In the UK, the Data Protection Act of

1984, laid down a number of principles that enforce good practice in the management of personal data by organisations. In 2000, the UK Government implemented new legislation to bring the Act in line with the Data Protection Directive of the European Union.

According to the Act, anyone processing personal data must comply with eight enforceable principles of good practice. Data must be:

- *Fairly and lawfully processed.* Individuals must be informed who will process their details.

- *Processed for limited purposes.* Individuals must be informed of the precise purposes to which the data will be put.

- *Adequate, relevant and not excessive.*

- *Accurate.* Individuals have the right to access any data held about them to check its accuracy.

- *Not kept longer than necessary.* Individuals can require businesses to stop direct marketing activities which involve them.

- *Processed in accordance with the data subject's rights.*

- *Secure.*

- *Not transferred to countries without adequate data protection.* Before sending data outside the EU, the organisation must ensure it is permitted to do so.

Personal data covers both facts and opinions about the individual. Processing incorporates the concepts of collecting, storing and disseminating data about individuals. Both manual data and computerised data are covered by the act.

Within the UK, all organisations that maintain personal data must register the data held with the Data Protection Register and are obliged to ensure that their use of such data conforms to the principles above. Many other European countries, such as those in Scandinavia, also have data protection legislation in place.

23.3.2   THE WORK ENVIRONMENT

Besides data protection and privacy, societies normally impose regulation of the work environment surrounding the use of information systems and information technology. This is generally done to establish appropriate levels of health and safety in organisations.

The design of the physical work environment is known as ergonomics. Ergonomics emphasises the importance of good design of office work-spaces to worker health. Good office design and establishing good work practices can much reduce problems such as repetitive motion disorders. These are health problems caused by working with computer keyboards and other equipment. One of the most commonplace of such disorders is repetitive strain injury. This is caused by repeated and incorrect use of keyboards and mice and can cause such problems as tendinitis: the inability to hold objects and sharp pain in the fingers. Some key ergonomic principles for computer use include:

- The use of a standard keyboard and monitor.
- Good lighting should be supplied, but should be placed so as to reduce glare on the screen.
- Wrists should be supported and should never be angled downwards; this can be achieved by angling keyboards suitably and employing wrist wrests.
- Back and other related problems can be reduced through correct alignment of chairs and desks. For instance, adjustable chairs should be supplied that support the lower back. Computer monitors should be placed one arm's length away from the operator
- Staff should be trained in the importance of good posture and other techniques, such as stretching at periodic intervals.

23.3.3 THE MEDIA

The media is a term used to encapsulate the news and entertainment industries. The modern media consist of multinational companies that offer news and entertainment services across the world. Generally we may distinguish between two types of company in this industry: content producers and content providers.

- Content producers create media content such as newspapers, news programmes, films and cartoons.
- Content providers distribute media content to customers.

Over the last decade or so, information and communications technologies have effected significant change in both content production and content provision. In terms of content production and provision there have been a number of significant changes, such as:

- *Broadcasting to narrowcasting.* The traditional model of content provision has been to broadcast the content to mass populations allowing the members of such populations to tune into areas of interest amongst the continuous stream of content. Over the last decade there has been a significant move from broadcasting to narrowcasting in the industry, with technological changes founded in the idea of digital convergence. The Internet offers a different paradigm for content provision based on digital convergence, but focused on narrow markets in terms of the consuming population.
- *Consolidation of content producers and providers.* Digital convergence has stimulated the consolidation of companies in this area. For instance, the merger of the US entertainment giant Time Warner with the large Internet service provider America Online (AOL) integrates a major content producer with a major content provider.

23.3.4 IT SECURITY

With the rise in IT-related crime, organisations have begun to invest in ways of preventing it. Such strategies include:

- Improving organisational security, perhaps by setting up an IT security function.
- Use of encryption to make data transmission secure.
- Use of biometrics (measurements associated with the body) to identify staff and authorise access to IT systems.
- Use of anti-virus software to prevent the dissemination of viruses.
- Increased levels of monitoring and control in an attempt to detect fraudulent uses of IT.

23.4 SUMMARY

- Individuals, groups and organisations exist within a social system. At the level of the nation state we speak of such a social system as being a society. A social system is made up of a set of cultural activities and relationships. Culture equals expectations of behaviour.
- The use of information technology by individuals, groups and organisations can also impact on the shape of social systems: digital convergence, transactional data, IT-related crime and the effect of IT upon work.
- The state of a social system may constrain organisational activities in a number of ways. IT crime has stimulated the growth in IT security; the rise of transactional data has stimulated data protection; the increasing use of computers within work has stimulated concerns over the misuse of IT; and the increasing convergence of technologies around the digital standard has raised reactions to the globalisation of the media.

23.5 QUESTIONS

(i) List the four major forces within the social environment upon information systems.

(ii) Define what is meant by digital convergence.

(iii) Why is the increasing capture of transactional data a problem for individuals?

(iv) Describe what is meant by data protection.

(v) List some of the major forms of information technology crime.

(vi) Explain the importance of information security as a problem for organisations.

23.6 EXERCISES

(i) How seriously is data protection treated as an issue in some organisation known to you?

(ii) Investigate what steps are taken in some organisation to create a safe and healthy workplace for computer users.

(iii) Organisations such as the BBC are offering digital services. Investigate the reasons why organisations such as the BBC are taking this route.

(iv) Investigate the level of IT-related crime impacting upon some organisation known to you.

(v) What security measures is the organisation taking to combat IT-related crime?

23.7 PROJECTS

(i) Collect evidence of a number of countries' data protection legislation. Compare and contrast them.

(ii) Investigate the ethics of using information technology to closely monitor people's work in organisations.

(iii) Police forces are now able to identify people using genetic fingerprinting. Suggestions have been made that a DNA database should be compiled of all the citizens in a country. Examine the ethical and privacy concerns of such an innovation.

(iv) Build a case study of one organisation's use of transactional data about its customers to develop strategy.

23.8 REFERENCES

Burnham, D. (1983). *The Rise of the Computer State*. Random House, New York.
Castells, M. (1996). *The Rise of the Network Society*. Blackwell, Malden, MA.

CHAPTER 24

THE POLITICAL ENVIRONMENT

Man is by nature a political animal.

Aristotle (384–322 BC)

LEARNING OUTCOMES

After reading this chapter, you will be able to:

- Define the component elements of the political environment
- Consider the impact of the political environment on an organisation's information systems
- Relate the impact of information technology and information systems on the political environment in terms of electronic government and tele-democracy

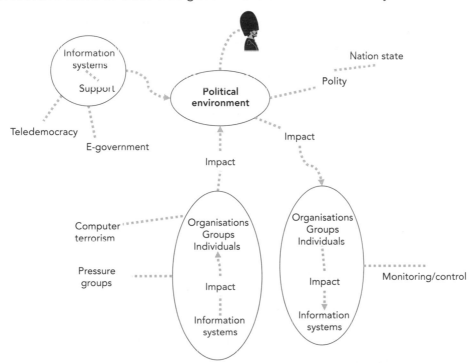

24.1 INTRODUCTION

The political environment or system concerns issues of power relationships. Political systems are made up of sets of activities and relationships concerned with power and its exercise. A polity is a political system centred on some geographical area. The central idea of a polity is a political system centred on the nation state.

The relationship between information systems, organisations and political systems is a dialectical one. Political systems influence what information systems are developed, the design of such systems and their use within organisations. Information systems may also be important to the coordination and collaboration of political interest groups in a polity and hence may help shape aspects of a political system.

24.2 SHAPE OF A POLITY

The shape of a polity will clearly be different depending on the country to which it refers. Some polities such as the European Union may be supra-national polities in the sense that they impose a certain level of communality amongst the political systems of the member states of the union.

Generally speaking, a polity will consist of a governmental structure of various forms taken from one of three main forms of governmental structure:

- *Dictatorship*. This is a form of governmental structure founded in rule by one person, or more realistically a small group or party of individuals. Nazi Germany was a dictatorship. Adolf Hitler and his National Socialist party gained power in the 1930s and intended that their Third Reich should last for a thousand years.

- *Oligarchy*. This is a form of governmental structure founded in rule by the few, or more realistically representatives of some ruling 'elite'. Republican Rome was an oligarchic polity in which senators were chosen from members of the patrician class.

- *Democracy*. This is a form of governmental structure founded in rule by the many, or more realistically representatives of the people. The term *democracy* derives from the Greek words *demos*, 'the people', and *kratein*, 'to rule'. So-called direct democracies are rare in the modern world. Direct democracy involves the members of some political grouping, such as a nation state, having direct involvement in the governmental process. Most modern democracies are representative democracies in which members of a political grouping nominate representatives to govern. Representative democracy generally takes the form of some form of parliamentary democracy in the Western world.

In many Western European countries representative democracy may be exercised at three interdependent levels: national, regional and local. Members of the nation state will normally be elected to represent the populace in policy-forming and legislative bodies such as parliaments, assemblies and councils. The legislation produced from such bodies will be enacted and administered by various government agencies.

24.3 POLITICAL SYSTEMS IMPACT UPON INFORMATION SYSTEMS

Political systems can exert significant pressure on the development and use of information systems in organisations. This normally occurs through the requirements of particular aspects of legislation. Most polities require that commercial organisations behave in certain ways. Legislation is enacted to ensure this, and an organisation's information systems are normally critically shaped by such legislation. For instance:

- *Company Legislation.* The Companies Act in the UK defines various forms of business organisation and prescribes the various forms of documentation that must be produced in the form of a trading statement, profit and loss statement and balance sheet. Since such legislation details the precise format in which companies must prepare accounts, it clearly affects the design of financial information systems run by companies.

- *Contract legislation.* Contract law defines the use and nature of contracts between individuals and business organisations. A contract is an agreement between parties which is enforceable in law. Such legislation defines valid business activity between customers, suppliers and organisations. Hence the design of trading systems between customers, suppliers and organisations will be heavily affected by contractual regulation.

- *Employment legislation.* Employment law is concerned with protecting employees in their relationships with their organisations. This form of legislation defines valid employment practice particularly in relation to issues such as health and safety. Clearly any human resource information system must be built with reference to such employment law.

- *Intelligence gathering.* Many Western governments are concerned at the use of the Internet by extreme political groupings in their attempt to undermine existing political orders. To combat such deviant use of an information highway, many governments have put in place legislation enabling intelligence organisations to tap into Internet traffic.

24.4 INFORMATION SYSTEMS AFFECT POLITICAL SYSTEMS

The use of information systems affects both the smooth operation and shape of modern polities. Information systems support political systems in the sense that they are relevant to the operation of the political system itself. Information is essential to the relationship between the citizen of a nation state and the government of that nation state.

- *Democratic representation.* The process of democratic representation relies on information for effective functioning. For instance, governmental representatives have to be voted into power at various times. Referenda, which are effectively large-scale surveys of opinion from a national population, may be held on various issues at various times. Also, government representatives will wish to communicate information to their constituents at various times.

- *Tax collection*. Government demands financial support from the citizen and from the business organisation in the form of taxation. The assessment of levels of taxation and the effective collection of fiscal revenue relies heavily on large and complex information systems.

- *Benefit payment*. Payments of monies and other forms of support are made to citizens by government agencies as part of welfare programmes. The effective identification of people in need and the timely payment of benefits to such people is heavily reliant on effective information systems.

- *Pressure groups*. Pressure groups in democracies maintain information systems for effective operation. They may also use information systems to help organise forms of protest. Terrorist organisations also use media like the Internet to publicise their activities and organise terrorist action.

- *Social control*. The use-value of some types of information as a commodity for social control has caused concern amongst civil liberties groups in many countries. Modern information technology permits organisations to collate information from various sources to form profiles of people and their behaviour. Such information may be used to detect and punish any behaviour seen to be deviant.

24.5 ⊙ ELECTRONIC GOVERNMENT AND TELE-DEMOCRACY

Information technology and information systems are being used to re-engineer aspects of governmental processes and the relationship between government and the citizen (Chapter 19). The interface between government and citizen in terms of services such as tax collection and benefit payment and the associated use of IT systems to deliver these services via government agencies is sometimes referred to as electronic government. The term tele-democracy may be restricted to the use of IT in the service of democratic representation between government and citizen and the associated use of IT within democratic processes in government. This is illustrated in Figure 24.1.

24.6 ⊙ TELE-DEMOCRACY

Tele-democracy can be defined in broad or narrow terms. In narrow terms, tele-democracy can be used to refer solely to the enablement of democratic processes between members of some political grouping and their governmental representatives. This we call *external* tele-democracy. In a sense, external tele-democracy can be seen to be an attempt to introduce elements of direct democracy into situations of representative democracy. On the other hand, tele-democracy can refer to the way in which information and communications technology (ICT) can be used to

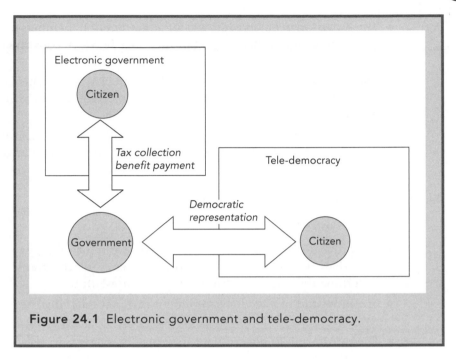

Figure 24.1 Electronic government and tele-democracy.

improve internal democratic processes within government. This we call *internal tele-democracy*. These distinctions are illustrated in Figure 24.2.

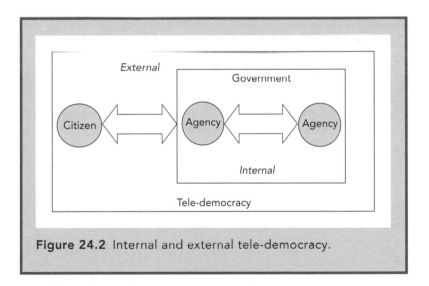

Figure 24.2 Internal and external tele-democracy.

24.6.1 EXTERNAL TELE-DEMOCRACY

External tele-democratic initiatives include:

- The provision of Web sites for governmental units, allowing the publication of debates and the schedule of governmental proceedings.

- The provision of email addresses for governmental members to improve the efficiency and effectiveness of communications between constituents and representatives.
- The running of the electoral process through IT systems which can capture votes and process results in a fraction of the time required by conventional paper-based ballot approaches.
- The provision of conferencing facilities which enable citizens to contribute directly to the formation of legislative policy in particular areas.

24.6.2 INTERNAL TELE-DEMOCRACY

Internal tele-democratic initiatives include:

- The provision of computer and communication technology to democratic representatives in order to improve the efficiency of the transfer and storage of governmental documentation between representatives.
- The provision of a secure government intranet enabling the efficient and effective transfer of government information between departments.
- The integration of government information systems to provide effective up-to-date statistics on the population of a nation state, essential to the effective formulation of legislative policy.

24.7 SUMMARY

- Political systems are made up of sets of activities and relationships concerned with power and its exercise. A polity is a political system centred on some geographical area such as the nation state.
- Generally speaking a polity will consist of a governmental structure which is either a dictatorship, an oligarchy or a democracy.
- Representative democracy is the most commonplace form of polity in the Western world.
- Political systems influence what information systems are developed, the design of such systems and their use within organisations.
- Information technology and information systems are essential to the effective performance of a modern polity.
- Information technology is an important enabler in initiatives to re-engineer key governmental processes and to improve forms of democratic representation.

24.8 QUESTIONS

(i) Define the concept of a polity.

(ii) List the major forms of political system.

(iii) Describe some of the effects a political environment may have on an organisation's information systems.

(iv) Describe some of the effects an information systems infrastructure may have on an organisation's political environment.

(v) Define the term *tele-democracy*.

(vi) Distinguish between internal and external tele-democracy.

24.9 EXERCISES

(i) Find out whether electronic government is an issue in your nation state.

(ii) Find out whether tele-democracy is an issue in some nation known to you.

(iii) Describe one area of government besides tax collection and benefits management where electronic government is important.

(iv) Describe one example of internal tele-democracy.

(v) Describe one example of external tele-democracy.

24.10 PROJECTS

(i) Study the effect of the legislative environment upon one organisation's information systems.

(ii) Collect evidence of a number of countries' initiatives in the areas of teledemocracy or electronic government. Compare and contrast them.

(iii) Study one tele-democracy initiative in close detail. Determine to what extent it improves democratic processes.

(iv) Study one electronic government initiative in close detail. Determine to what extent it improves government processes.

(v) Investigate the degree to which increasing electronic government is likely to initiate greater social control.

PART **6**

DEVELOPMENT

All growth depends upon activity. There is no development physically or intellectually without effort, and effort means work.

Calvin Coolidge (1872–1933)

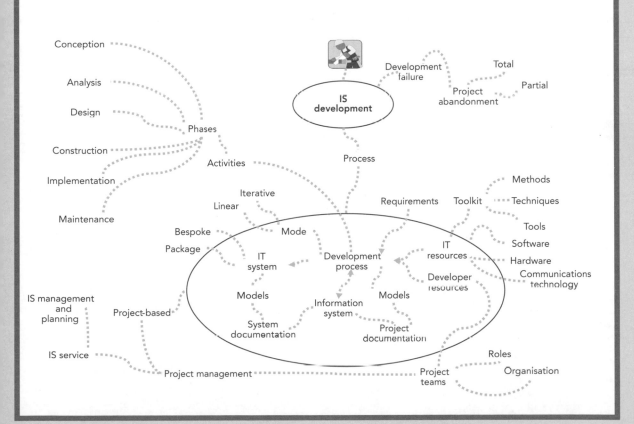

309

In this part we consider information systems development as one of the key organisational processes for many organisations (Chapter 25).

Since it is a process it can be considered as a system in itself. The key inputs into the process are information technology resources and developer resources. A critical part of developer resources is the toolkit of methods, techniques and tools available to the developer (Chapter 26).

The key outputs are an information system and some associated human activity system. A number of key activities are involved in the development process: systems conception, analysis, systems design, systems construction, systems implementation and systems maintenance (Chapters 27–32).

The development process needs an information system itself. A development information system is essential to ensure the effective and efficient operation of the human activity system which is the development process. Such an information system consists of both systems documentation and project documentation.

CHAPTER 25

THE INFORMATION SYSTEMS DEVELOPMENT PROCESS

I must create a system, or be enslaved by another man's

I will not reason and compare: my business is to create.

William Blake: *Jerusalem* (1815), Chapter 1

LEARNING OUTCOMES

After reading this chapter, you will be able to:

● Describe key elements of the IS development process

● Outline key phases of the IS life cycle

● Relate the differences between bespoke and package development and iterative and linear development

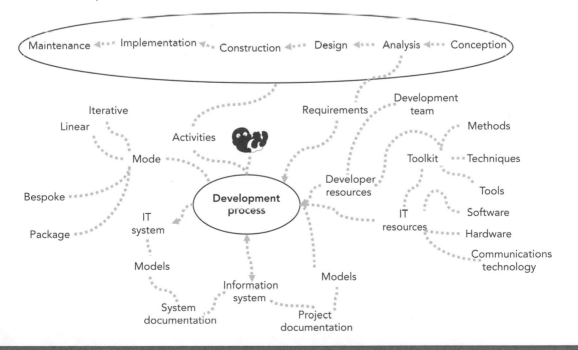

Information systems development is the science and art of designing and making, with economy and elegance, information systems that support the activity of particular organisations. In modern organisations the development of information systems is a key organisational process. In this chapter we describe some of the key activities of this process, and its key outputs and inputs. We also consider a number of major approaches to conducting this process.

Information systems development is a key organisational process for many organisations. Since it is a process it can be considered as a system in itself (Figure 25.1). The key inputs into the process are information and communications technology resources and developer resources. Information and communications technology resources may comprise systems construction tools or software packages. Developer resources include not only people but a toolkit which includes methods, techniques and tools available to the developer. This toolkit is the topic of Chapter 26.

The key outputs are an information system and some associated human activity system. Information systems in themselves are socio-technical systems. They include both an information technology system and a system of use. Ideally, the

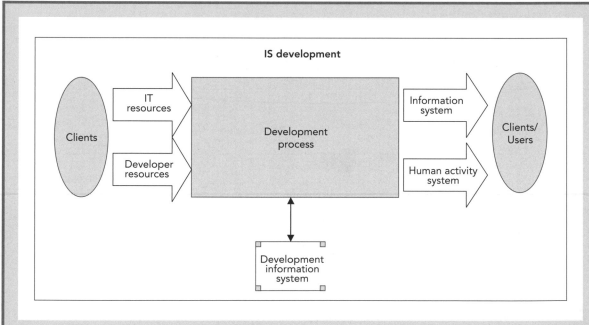

Figure 25.1 The IS development process.

human activity system and the information system should be designed in parallel. The IT system produced may be a bespoke system or a configured/tailored software package.

A number of key activities are involved in the development process, sometimes referred to collectively as the information systems development life cycle. Such activities include systems conception, systems analysis, systems design, systems construction, systems implementation and systems maintenance.

A development information system is essential to ensure the effective and efficient operation of the human activity system which is the development process. Any reasonable-sized development project will need a consequent information system to support communication between teams of developers, to feed into a project management and an informatics management process and to communicate with other stakeholder groups such as users and business managers. Such an information system consists of both system documentation and project documentation. System documentation acts as a model of the developing system; project documentation acts as a model of the development process. The key point here is that all information systems in a sense model elements of other systems. Such elements may be artefacts or organisational activities.

The development process is normally organised in terms of projects (Chapter 38) – organised units of activity consisting of teams with a defined goal and a finite duration. It is also normally undertaken by a sub-organisation: the informatics service (Chapter 40).

25.3 DEVELOPMENT TEAM

Prior to the initiation of the development process a development team is assembled. A number of development roles will be critical to particular phases of the development process:

- *Business analyst*. This role undertakes organisational analysis and systems conception activities such as cost–benefit analyses and risk analysis.
- *Systems analyst*. This role undertakes feasibility study, analysis and design activities.
- *Project manager*. This role is concerned with managing the development process as a unit.
- *Programmer*. This role undertakes construction and maintenance activities.
- *Change manager*. This role undertakes implementation activities.

Various representatives of other stakeholder groups, particularly clients and end-users, are also likely to form part of the development team, either throughout the development process or at key points in the life of the IS.

A process is a set of logically related activities. The development process is normally portrayed in terms of a life cycle made up of a number of key phases of activity. Different development approaches highlight different phases. Here we have created a high-level model of the life cycle which does not attach itself to any one approach and is applicable to the four major modes of development: bespoke/ package development and linear/iterative development.

Figure 25.2 illustrates the six major activities of the development process. Each of these phases will write data to a development information system and read data from such a system within the process of development. The last three phases – construction, implementation and maintenance – involve the transfer of an information system through various phases of its life within an organisation.

Key stakeholders will affect various stages of the development process. Clients will determine the initial parameters for the information system and hence input into the process of systems conception. Representatives of end-users are likely to be involved in the analysis of the requirements for the system as well as feeding into the process of systems design. The end-user community receive the IS from the process of implementation and are also likely to suggest corrections, amendments and changes to systems for the maintenance process.

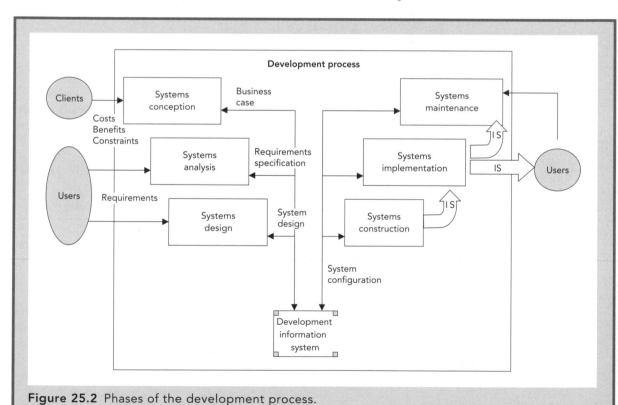

Figure 25.2 Phases of the development process.

25.4.1 CONCEPTION

Conception (Chapter 27) is the phase in which we develop the key business case for an information system. Clients are the major stakeholder group (Chapter 13) that will determine the parameters of the business case for such a system. In such a business case the IS is evaluated strategically in terms of its contribution to organisational performance. An assessment is also made of its feasibility, particularly in terms of organisational resources and constraints. The informatics service, in association with organisational clients, also attempts to estimate the degree of risk associated with a project to construct the proposed information system. All this data will be written to the development information system.

25.4.2 ANALYSIS

Analysis (Chapter 28) is the phase concerned with documenting the workings of existing systems and/or establishing requirements for a new system. Analysis involves the two interrelated activities of requirements elicitation and requirements specification. Ideally, systems analysis will be undertaken with the participation of representatives of intended users of the information system. The requirements specification for some application will be a key input into the development information system.

25.4.3 DESIGN

Design (Chapter 29) is the process of planning the shape of some new information system, and ideally its associated human activity system. Design is also ideally undertaken in association with the participation of user representatives. A systems design will be entered into the development information system.

25.4.4 CONSTRUCTION

This phase involves the actual construction of the information system. This may either be conducted by a team internal to the organisation or undertaken by an outside contractor (a form of IS construction known as outsourcing (Chapter 30)). Many information systems are now also bought in as a package and tailored to organisational requirements. Whatever the form of development, descriptions of the configuration of the developing system will be input into the development information system. The information system application itself will be passed on to implementation.

25.4.5 IMPLEMENTATION

Implementation involves first testing the system in terms of its specification, then the delivery of the system into its context of use. Test plans and delivery plans will be entered into the development information system. Users are normally required to formally accept the system into its context of use.

25.4.6   MAINTENANCE

This is the feedback process which involves changes to information systems and to elements of the organisation. It must be acknowledged that information systems rarely remain in their original form. Information systems may change for a number of reasons:

- In the process of using an information system errors may be found or changes may be proposed. Hence requests for corrections from the user and client community may be fed into the maintenance process.
- At some point in time a system may be abandoned or need to be re-engineered to fit new organisational circumstances.
- Changes also occur over time in terms of adjustments made to the way both the IS and its context of use works.
- How the system is used, and its perceived consequences for performance and people, will affect the organisational context over time.

25.5 🌀 APPROACHES TO INFORMATION SYSTEMS DEVELOPMENT

There are a number of distinct approaches to information systems development. Here we consider alternatives in terms of two major dimensions: type of information systems product and form of sequencing of activities (Figure 25.3).

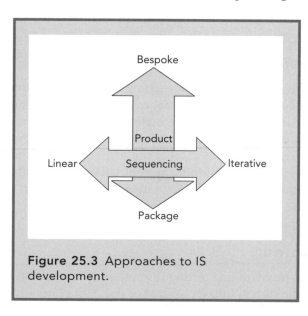

Figure 25.3 Approaches to IS development.

25.5.1 TYPE OF INFORMATION SYSTEMS PRODUCT

In terms of information systems product we may distinguish two main types of development activity: bespoke development and package development.

In bespoke development an organisation builds an information system to directly match the requirements of the organisation. This may involve programming the entire system, or the organisation may build a system out of pre-established components. Bespoke development normally offers the organisation the opportunity to closely match some information system to organisational requirements. The main disadvantage is that the organisation must make a considerable investment in developing the information system, particularly in terms of maintaining a suitably skilled internal informatics service.

In package development an organisation purchases a piece of software from a vendor organisation and tailors the package to a greater or lesser extent to the demands of a particular organisation. A software package is a software application designed to encapsulate the functionality necessary to support activity in some generic business area and may be customisable to a specific organisation's needs.

Packaged software has been built and used since the 1960s in UK industry and commerce. A recent survey plots the rise of packaged software in the UK: in 1991 respondents indicated an average of 31% of their corporate software as being of the packaged variety. In 1995 this figure had risen to 51%, and a figure of 64% adoption in the year 2000 was predicted.

There are a number of reasons why an organisation may select package implementation rather than bespoke development:

- A package may be seen as the embodiment of best industry practice in some domain.
- A package may offer greater compatibility with customers' and suppliers' software.
- A package may be perceived as being reliable and tested software.
- A package implementation may be undertaken to avoid costly software development and maintenance.

Component-based development lies between these two traditions. It consists of the process by which an IT system is assembled from pre-established software components.

25.5.2 FORM OF SEQUENCING

By sequencing we mean the way in which the various phases of the development process are organised. We may distinguish between two broad forms of sequencing: linear and iterative.

The linear model of the development process is indicated in Figure 25.4. Here the phases discussed above are strung out in a linear sequence with outputs from each phase triggering the start of the next phase. In the first three phases the key

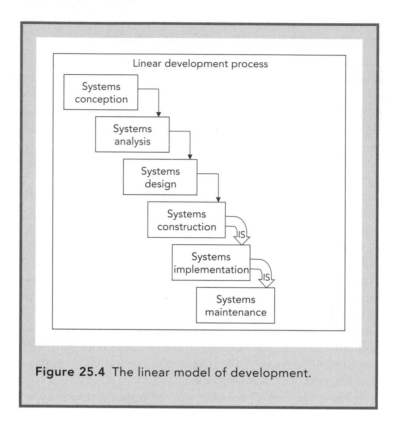

Figure 25.4 The linear model of development.

outputs are forms of system documentation. In the last three phases the outputs are elements of some information system.

The linear model has been particularly popular as a framework for large-scale development projects. This is mainly because a clear linear sequence makes for easier project planning and control (Chapter 38). The major disadvantages of the approach lie in the difficulties associated with changing early analysis and design decisions late in a project.

The iterative model of the development process is illustrated in Figure 25.5. In this model systems conception triggers an iterative cycle in which various versions of a system (prototypes) are analysed, designed constructed and possibly implemented.

The iterative model has been particularly popular in small- to medium-scale projects. Iteration – the construction of prototypes (prototyping) and significant amounts of user involvement – seems to reduce the risk associated with IT innovations and generates stronger commitment from system stakeholders. However, because it is frequently uncertain in an iterative approach how much resource will need to be devoted to the project, iterative approaches generally appear to suffer from more difficult project planning and management.

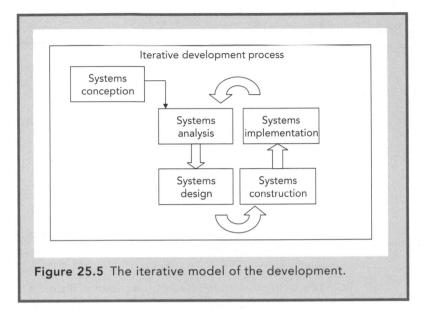

Figure 25.5 The iterative model of the development.

25.6 SUMMARY

- Information systems development is the science and art of designing and making, with economy and elegance, information technology systems that support the activity of particular organisations.

- The development process can be seen as a human activity system. It has key inputs and outputs and relies on an information system for effective performance.

- The development process consists of a number of key phases. They are conceived, analysed, designed, constructed, implemented and maintained.

- These phases may either be expressed as a linear sequence or as some form of cycle.

- Information systems are built either as bespoke products or tailored from software packages.

25.7 QUESTIONS

(i) List the key inputs into the development process.

(ii) List the key outputs from the development process.

(iii) Why is an information system essential to supporting the development process?

(iv) Describe some of the standard activities of the development process.

(v) Distinguish between the linear and iterative models of the development life cycle.

(vi) Distinguish between bespoke development and package development.

25.8 🌀 EXERCISES

    (i) See if you can find a completed information systems development project and describe the elements contained in the information system supporting the project.

    (ii) Look through job advertisements in IS and IT and see if you can develop precise job descriptions for the roles listed in this chapter.

    (iii) Consider an organisation known to you. Investigate what percentages of development are bespoke and package.

    (iv) Investigate whether development primarily occurs in a sequential or iterative manner in some organisation known to you.

    (v) Find some past information systems development project. Determine how closely the project undertook activities similar to the phases described in the life cycle.

    (vi) Take one of the three case studies described in Fitzgerald (2000) and analyse them in terms of the lessons from the development chapters.

25.9 🌀 PROJECTS

    (i) Investigate the common elements of the project information system amongst a range of development projects.

    (ii) Survey the structure of development teams across a range of projects.

    (iii) In a limited range of organisations investigate how many new systems have been developed in a bespoke manner and how many systems have been package development projects.

    (iv) Investigate the degree to which organisations utilise a linear or iterative development process.

    (v) Determine the precise functionality of the information system needed to support the development process.

25.10 🌀 REFERENCE

Fitzgerald, G. (2000). Adaptability and flexibility in IS development. In *Business Information Technology Management: Alternative and Adaptive Futures* (eds. R. Hackney and D. Dunn). Macmillan, London, pp. 13–24.

CHAPTER 26

DEVELOPMENT TOOLKIT

If the only tool you have is a hammer, you tend to see every problem as a nail.

Abraham Maslow

LEARNING OUTCOMES

After reading this chapter, you will be able to:

- Describe components of the information systems developers toolkit
- Discuss the elements of an information systems development method
- Outline available options in terms of development techniques
- Define some possible tools for IS development

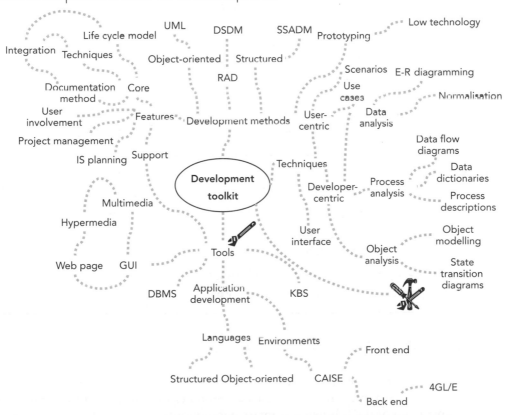

26.1 INTRODUCTION

Humans are *Homo Habilis* – man the toolmaker. We make tools in order to aid in the construction of artefacts and to extend our physical and mental grasp. Therefore, to undertake any development effort the information systems developer needs a toolkit. Such a toolkit will consist of methods, techniques and tools for supporting the activities of the development process – conception, analysis, design, implementation and maintenance. In this chapter we consider some of the primary elements of the developer's toolkit.

26.2 METHODS, TECHNIQUES AND TOOLS

Methods, techniques and tools are what we might call supporting 'technology' for information systems development. The term technology is used here in its broadest sense to refer to any form of device that aids the work of some person or group of persons.

- *Methods*. These constitute frameworks which prescribe, sometimes in great detail, the tasks to be undertaken in a given development process. Methods are used to guide the whole or a major part of the development process.
- *Techniques*. These form the component parts of methods in that they constitute particular ways of undertaking given parts of process. Techniques are normally used to guide activity within one phase of the development process.
- *Tools*. By tools we primarily mean here available hardware, software, data and communication technology for engaging in some part of the information systems development process or its set of associated external activities. Tools are frequently used to support the application of particular techniques.

Examples ▶ Structured Systems Analysis and Design Method (SSADM) constitutes a method for the analysis and design of information systems, while PRojects IN Controlled Environment (PRINCE) comprises a method for project management.

Entity-relationship diagramming is an established analysis technique while PERT is an established project management technique.

Microsoft Access is an established tool for systems construction, while Microsoft Project is an established tool to aid project managers.

26.3 DEVELOPMENT METHODS

Development methods comprise frameworks which prescribe development activity. An information systems development method might be defined as being made up of the following primary components:

- A model of the information systems development process (Chapter 25).
- A set of techniques.
- A documentation method associated with these techniques. This consists of a notation for representing constructs and some principles for relating representations of different techniques.
- Some indication of how the techniques chosen along with the documentation method fit into the model of the development process.

Generally we may identify three major types of development methods:

- *Structured methods*. Structured methods developed during the 1980s and initially used a linear model of the development process. Clear phases are identified with clear inputs and outputs from each phase. Techniques in areas such as data modelling and process modelling developed within structured frameworks. Structured methods propose a standard notation for data and process modelling.
- *Rapid application development (RAD) methods*. These methods (Stapleton, 1997) use an iterative model of the development process and generally specify high-level phases based around some form of prototyping. RAD methods are generally contingent in that they do not prescribe in detail the techniques to be used. A variety of techniques can be adapted to the needs of a particular project.
- *Object-oriented (OO) methods*. Most such approaches utilise a contingent model – sometimes a linear model, sometimes an iterative model. OO methods tend to use an object modelling focus as discussed in Chapter 7.

The three types above focus on the development of information technology systems. A number of methods focus more on the development of human activity systems such as those in the area of participatory design (Chapter 29).

Examples ||||➡ Structured Systems Analysis and Design Method is a structured development method which was developed initially in the early 1980s as a public domain standard development method. It has been extensively used in both the public and private sectors and has undergone a number of substantial revisions during its lifetime.

Dynamic Systems Development Method (DSDM) is a non-proprietary RAD method. It is produced by the DSDM consortium: a non-profit-making organisation of vendors, users and individual associates of RAD (Stapleton, 1997). Its intention is to become the UK and international standard for RAD work.

Unified Modeling Language (UML) and the Rational Development Process is a popular OO development method. UML is a standard notation for object modelling developed as a hybrid of earlier OO specification methods. Rational development process is a method which specifies how UML may be used within a model of the development process based in OO development.

26.4 DEVELOPMENT TECHNIQUES

Techniques guide activity within one phase of the development process. They constitute particular approaches to supporting the processes of systems analysis, systems design and systems construction. The modelling approaches discussed in Chapter 7 are all examples of techniques primarily for supporting the process of analysis. A given technique consists of the three elements discussed in Chapter 7: a set of constructs, a notation for representing constructs and principles of constructing models in the chosen technique.

We may distinguish between developer-centric techniques and user-centric techniques. Developer-centric techniques are designed particularly for enabling developers to understand, document and communicate IS problems to other developers. Hence most such techniques are primarily directed at specification and constitute major forms of input into the development information system. Such techniques include:

- *Data analysis techniques* directed at specifying the structure of some information system
- *Process analysis techniques* directed at specifying the behaviour of some information system
- *Object analysis techniques* directed at specifying the object-space of some information system

---

Examples ▌▌▌▶ Examples of data analysis techniques include entity-relationship diagrams (Chapter 7) and normalisation.

Examples of process analysis techniques include data flow diagrams (Chapter 7), data dictionaries and process descriptions.

Examples of object analysis techniques include object modelling (Chapter 7) and state transition diagrams.

User-centric techniques are those directed at supporting the development of understanding of some work environment and the potentialities of information technology in such settings. Hence user-centric techniques are primarily directed at elicitation and negotiation. User-centric techniques include:

- *Prototyping*. Building various representations or early versions of some information system to show to clients and end-users to obtain feedback (Chapter 25).
- *Scenarios*. Informal descriptions of the use of information technology systems within some situation.
- *Use cases*. Representations of the major actors and interactions with some information system (Chapter 29).

26.5 DEVELOPMENT TOOLS

Development tools comprise hardware, software, data storage and communications technology used to construct information systems and to support the development process. A useful way of considering the variety of such tools in this area is in terms of the layered model of an information technology system discussed in Chapter 12.

Historically, the four parts of a conventional IT application were constructed using one tool, the high-level or third generation programming language (3GL). A language such as COBOL was used to declare appropriate file structures (data subsystem), encode the necessary operations on files (transaction subsystem), validate data processed (rules subsystem) and manage the terminal screen for data entry and retrieval (interface subsystem). However, over the last couple of decades there has been a tendency to use a different, specialised tool for one or more of these layers. For instance:

- Graphical user interface tools have developed as a means of constructing sophisticated user interfaces.
- Fourth generation languages have developed as a means of coding business rules and application logic.
- Transaction processing systems have developed to enable high throughput of transactions.
- Database management systems have developed as sophisticated tools for managing multi-user access to data.
- Communications are enabled by a vast array of software supporting local area and wide area communications.

26.6 COMPUTERISATION OF THE DEVELOPMENT PROCESS

Information systems development is a human activity system. Most human activity systems need information systems to support them and the development process is no different. Also, information technology has been used to help automate aspects of the development process. This area is frequently known as Computer-Aided Software Engineering (CASE) or Computer-Aided Information Systems Engineering (CAISE). CAISE is a logical consequence of a recursive or incestuous view of information systems development. It has stimulated the view that information systems development, considered as a human activity system with its associated information system, should be subject to and benefit from the same sorts of automation that characterise everyday information systems.

CAISE is therefore based upon a particular model of the information systems development process. In this model, the development process is seen as a set of activities operating on objects to produce other objects. The objects manipulated by such activities will frequently be documents, diagrams, file structures or even programs. Similarly, the activities involved may be relatively formal (e.g. compile a program) or informal (e.g. obtain user's requirements). It is not surprising therefore that the linear model of information systems development and the associated adoption of development methods is particularly suited to the application of CAISE. In recent times many existing CAISE tools have adapted themselves to handling object-oriented methods. Many such tools have been marketed specifically at the area of object-oriented analysis and design.

A distinction is normally made between back-end CAISE tools, front-end CAISE tools and integrated CAISE tools:

- *Front-end CAISE tools* are generally directed at the analysis and design stages of information systems development.
- *Back-end CAISE tools* are directed at the construction, implementation, testing and maintenance stages of information systems development.
- *Integrated CAISE tools* offer assistance at all the stages of information systems development, and normally work in association with an integrated data repository which models the developing information system at various stages of development.

Example ||||➡ Select is an integrated and relatively inexpensive CAISE tool. It offers a number of specific versions tailored for specific methodologies such as SSADM. The facilities offered by this package fall mainly into the front-end category, although there are some facilities for things such as database generation that fall into the back-end category.

26.7 @ SUMMARY

- A developer's toolkit consists of methods, techniques and tools.
- Methods constitute frameworks which prescribe, sometimes in great detail, the tasks to be undertaken in a given development process.
- Techniques are particular approaches to supporting the processes of systems analysis, systems design and systems construction.
- Development tools comprise hardware, software, data storage and communication technology used to construct information systems and to support the development process.
- The development process has been subject to automation through the use of CAISE tools.

26.8 @ QUESTIONS

(i) Distinguish between an IS development method, technique and tool.

(ii) Define the concept of an IS development method.

(iii) Define the concept of an IS development technique.

(iv) Define the concept of an IS development tool.

(v) Explain the degree to which the information systems development process has been automated.

(vi) Distinguish between front-end CAISE and back-end CAISE.

26.9 EXERCISES

(i) Choose some method such as SSADM and list its features under the headings used in this chapter.

(ii) In what way are the modelling approaches described in Chapter 7 techniques?

(iii) Find out what normalisation or state transition diagrams are as techniques.

(iv) In terms of some informatics service known to you, determine what methods, techniques and tools they use.

(v) Find one example of a front-end CAISE tool.

(vi) Find one example of a back-end CAISE tool.

26.10 PROJECTS

(i) Compare two information systems development methods in terms of the dimensions described in this chapter.

(ii) Investigate which analysis and design techniques are most used in industrial practice.

(iii) Conduct a survey of tools used amongst a range of organisations.

(iv) Survey the use of front-end, back-end and integrated CAISE in contemporary organisations.

(v) To what extent are packages tools?

26.11 REFERENCE

Stapleton, J. (1997). *DSDM – Dynamic Systems Development Method: the Method in Practice*. Addison-Wesley, Harlow.

SYSTEMS CONCEPTION

In life, the first thing you must do is decide what you really want. Weigh the costs and the results. Are the results worthy of the costs? Then make up your mind completely and go after your goal with all your might.

Alfred A. Montapert

LEARNING OUTCOMES

After reading this chapter, you will be able to:

- Produce a business case for an information system
- Distinguish between IS costs and IS benefits
- Use a number of techniques for conducting a cost–benefit analysis
- Define the process of risk analysis and the conduct of a feasibility study

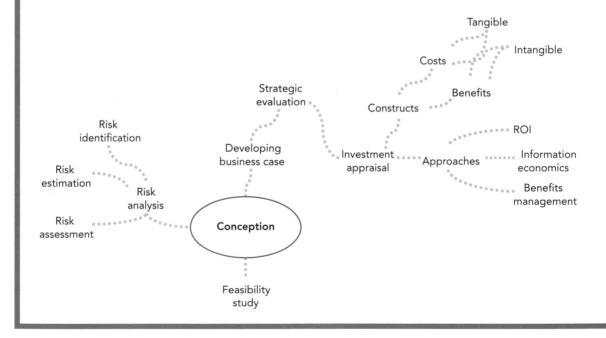

27.1 INTRODUCTION

Conception is the first phase in the development process and will follow on from IS planning. Conception is the phase in which the information development team produce the key business case for an information system. This is a form of evaluation of the system in strategic terms. We also attempt to estimate the degree of risk associated with a project to construct the proposed information technology system. Finally, we consider the feasibility of the IS project in terms of organisational resources. A project which succeeds the strategic evaluation, risk analysis and feasibility exercise will pass on to a process of systems analysis. The process of system conception is illustrated in Figure 27.1.

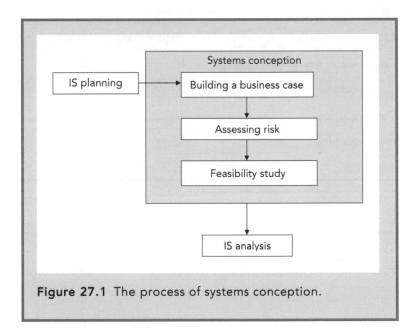

Figure 27.1 The process of systems conception.

27.2 DEVELOPING A BUSINESS CASE

Developing a business case for a proposed information system is a part of strategic evaluation (Chapter 41). Strategic Evaluation involves assessing or appraising an IS investment in terms of its potential for delivering benefit against estimated costs. As part of a business case an organisation would also need to conduct an assessment of risk.

IS projects which do not satisfactorily meet an appropriate level of benefits and a satisfactory level of risk would be rejected. Those projects that have a reasonably substantial business case may then be subject to some form of feasibility study. This involves conducting some preliminary analysis of the ability of the organisation to resource and complete the development project.

27.2.1 IS COSTS

It is useful to make the distinction between two types of costs associated with IS projects: tangible or visible costs and intangible or invisible costs. Tangible costs are frequently referred to as visible costs because they are reasonably straightforward to measure. Intangible costs are frequently referred to as invisible costs because most organisations experience difficulty in assigning actual measurable quantities to such costs. Keen (1981) in his study of a number of large-scale IS projects illustrates the way in which tangible and intangible costs are distributed in relation to typical phases in a bespoke as compared to a packaged software development effort (Tables 27.1 and 27.2).

Table 27.1 In-house software development project.

Phase	Visible (%)	Hidden (%)
Conception, analysis and design	40	0
Construction	10	0
Testing	10	20
Implementation	10	10
Total	70	30

Table 27.2 Purchased software package.

Phase	Visible (%)	Hidden (%)
Conception, analysis and design	0	40
Construction	25	0
Testing	5	10
Implementation	0	20
Total	30	70

The interesting point here is that far more of the costs are likely to be intangible in a packaged development project than in a bespoke development project.

A typical list of cost types associated with IS projects is given below:

- *Hardware costs*: computers, printers, storage, accessories etc.
- *Software costs*: off-the-shelf packages, bespoke software, development tools etc.
- *Installation costs*: data entry, data conversion etc.
- *Environmental costs*: wiring, furniture, air-conditioning etc.
- *Running costs*: electricity, communication costs etc.

- *Maintenance costs*: on hardware and software
- *Security costs*: risk management and disaster recovery mechanisms
- *Networking costs*: network hardware, software and maintenance
- *Training costs*: frequently underestimated
- *Wider organisational costs*: new salary structures, management etc.

The important point to make in relation to this list is that the costs of an IS must be taken into account over its entire life, not solely in terms of its development cost. Frequently organisations forget that the initiation of an IS means a permanent commitment to costs in terms of continuing resources being committed to the running and maintenance of the IS.

27.2.2   IS BENEFITS

IS benefits concern the value that the organisation gains from having an IS. Again we may distinguish between tangible and intangible benefits. IS have frequently been initiated with the objective of gaining tangible benefits such as reducing staff count or increasing productivity. Intangible benefits are more generally associated with issues of organisational efficiency. More recently people have started to argue that intangible benefits such as increasing customer satisfaction or building better links with suppliers have equal relevance in investment decisions. Intangible benefits are more generally concerned with organisational effectiveness. Below we list some of the classic benefits associated with information systems:

- *Accuracy*: increased accuracy of information
- *Quality*: better quality information
- *Usability*: more useful information
- *Flexibility*: ability to use information more flexibly
- *User satisfaction*: increased work satisfaction
- *Functionality*: more effective working
- *Reliability*: more reliable service
- *Utilisation*: more information used
- *Relevance*: more focused information
- *Productivity*: increased levels of working
- *Security*: more secure information
- *Profitability*: more money
- *Speed*: getting information quicker
- *Volume*: more information

Example ▐▐▐▶ A university has identified an information system to support research administration as part of its informatics strategy. It sees such a system as important to its future organisation strategy because research is one of the key business processes for the university. Whereas information systems are currently in place for support of teaching and consultancy there are no information systems in place to support research activity.

The pragmatic objective for the system is to gather data needed to produce a research assessment submission for the university to central UK government agencies. The system needs to collect store and analyse data on key research outputs. Key research outputs are publications (journal and conference), grant income, research students and completions of postgraduate degrees.

Research outputs have been historically collected in academic departments by research coordinators. Currently there are difficulties of collecting information for such a submission, and there are numerous errors introduced in the manual process.

The longer-term aim is to utilise such an information system to support the long-term research strategy of the university. The university has introduced the idea of research units and research centres to manage research. Research units are collections of research active staff working in the same area. Research centres are collections of research units.

A number of constraints exist:

- Needs to be built in six months max. in order to be able to perform a mini-research assessment

- To be initially built in registry and used by 6+ staff there

- Eventually to be used by research coordinators/administrators, possibly by active researchers in departments

- One programmer and one analyst/project manager available for the project

- One development machine available

27.3 TECHNIQUES FOR COST–BENEFIT ANALYSIS

Cost–benefit analysis is critical to assessing whether or not the process of developing an IS is a worthwhile investment. Investment in IS can be justified in terms of:

- Efficiency gains such as cost savings
- Effectiveness gains such as better customer relations
- Strategic advantage such as business growth

Most of the established techniques for evaluating information system investments focus on tangible costs and benefits and thus are directed primarily at assessments of efficiency gain. Two of the most popular are return on investment and payback period. It must be said that most practitioners still seem to rely mainly on one or other of these 'hard' evaluation techniques.

In recent years, a number of techniques have been suggested for focusing on intangible as well as tangible benefits and hence are directed at including assessment of effectiveness and strategic advantage. One of the most popular of such approaches is that known as information economics.

27.3.1   RETURN ON INVESTMENT

The return on investment (RoI) associated with an IS project is calculated using the following equation:

RoI = average (annual net income/annual investment amount)

Hence to calculate an RoI one must be able to estimate the income accruing from the introduction of an IS and the cost associated with an IS for a period into the future. The average of this ratio of annual costs to benefits is then taken to indicate the value of the IS to the organisation.

Example ▐▐▐▶ Assume, for instance, that we need to calculate the RoI for a new information system at a university. The table below contains estimates as to the amount of extra income generated by the introduction of the system plotted against the costs associated with the development and maintenance of the system. We have assumed here that the system will take two years to complete and that the development costs will be of the order of £300,000. We also assume that the life of the project will be ten years.

Year	Income	Investment	Income/investment
1	£0	£200,000	0
2	£0	£100,000	0
3	£50,000	£10,000	5
4	£300,000	£10,000	30
5	£500,000	£10,000	50
6	£600,000	£11,000	55
7	£600,000	£11,000	55
8	£600,000	£12,000	50
9	£600,000	£12,000	50
10	£500,000	£13,000	38
11	£400,000	£13,000	31
12	£300,000	£14,000	21

RoI = average (annual net income/annual investment amount) = 32

27.3.2 PAYBACK PERIOD

Payback period still assumes that one is able to estimate the benefit of the introduction of an IS to the organisation for a number of years ahead. Benefit is measured in terms of the amount of cash inflow resulting from the IS. Payback is then calculated on the basis of:

Payback = Investment – cumulative benefit (cash inflow)

The payback period is equal to the number of months or years for this payback figure to reach zero. Clearly the assumption here is that those systems that accrue financial benefits the quickest are the most successful. In terms of the example above, if we assume that the cumulative benefit is the same as the income generated (which may not always be the case), then the payback period is four years.

27.3.3 INFORMATION ECONOMICS

Information economics (Parker *et al.*, 1988) attempts to include the evaluation of intangible as well as tangible benefits into the process of IS evaluation. It does this by assessing feasibility in the business domain and viability in the technological domain. Information economics uses an extended form of RoI:

Traditional + Value + Value + Value + Innovation
cost–benefit linking accelerating restructuring valuation
analysis

Value linking and accelerating are attempts to estimate the ripple effect of technology change on the organisation. Value restructuring is an attempt to assess the increases in productivity that arise from the introduction of IS/IT systems.

At a practical level, information economics involves completing a scorecard for each IS and computing the weighted score as an indication of the value of the system to the organisation:

Evaluator	Business domain						Technology domain				
	RoI (+)	SM (+)	CA (+)	MI (+)	CR (+)	OR (–)	SA (+)	DU (–)	TU (–)	IR (–)	
Business domain											
Technology domain											Weighted score
Weighted value											

Each of the columns on the scorecard stands for the following:

- RoI = return on investment

- SM = strategic match, i.e. the degree to which the system matches the strategy of the organisation
- CA = competitive advantage, i.e. the degree to which the system will afford competitive advantage
- MI = management information support
- CR = competitive response, i.e. the degree to which the system will enable the organisation to react quickly to its environment
- OR = organisational risk
- SA = strategic IS architecture, i.e. the degree to which it matches the architecture for IS in the organisation
- DU = definitional uncertainty, i.e. the degree to which requirements for the system remain uncertain
- TU = technical uncertainty, i.e. the number of technical imponderables in the project
- IR = IS infrastructure risk, i.e. the degree to which the system can adversely affect the IS infrastructure

Note that some of the columns are labelled as '+', in which case they are taken as positively contributing to value and hence should be added to the score. Other columns are labelled '−', in which case they are seen as negatively contributing to value and hence should be subtracted from the score. Note also that each of the factors on the scorecard can be weighted. This allows the evaluator to indicate the importance of each factor to the particular project under consideration. Hence, in one project, strategic match may be a critically important factor and hence weighted as 10. In terms of another project, perhaps to produce a more operationally based or support system this factor may be rated as of low importance and perhaps weighted as 4.

27.4 RISK ANALYSIS

Perhaps because of the apparent ubiquity of IS failure (Chapter 15), the area of risk and risk assessment has become particularly prominent in the software engineering and IS development literature in recent times (Boehm, 1989). Risk is clearly involved in all IS projects.

Risk might be defined as a negative outcome that has a known or estimated probability of occurring based on some experience or theory. The idea of IS failure is clearly the negative outcome most prominent in most people's minds. However, emphasising the relationship between stakeholders and risk, Wilcocks and Margetts (1994) note that:

> Risk of a negative outcome only becomes a salient problem when the outcome is relevant to stakeholder concerns and interests. Different settings and stakeholders will see different outcomes as salient

A number of distinct activities are associated with risk analysis:

- *Risk identification*. This involves generating a checklist of risks for a particular project.
- *Risk estimation*. This involves assessing the likelihood or probability of a risk occurring and determining the likely impact of each risk.
- *Risk assessment*. This involves prioritising risks and planning activities for avoiding or monitoring risks.

Risk assessment is the process involved in estimating the degree of risk associated with a given project. A number of frameworks have been generated which suggest characteristics indicative of risky IS projects. For instance, Cash *et al.* (1992) suggest that there are at least three important dimensions that influence the risk of a project:

- *Project size*. In general, the smaller the IS project the less risk associated with the project. Project size can be defined in a number of ways such as the level of investment needed to be made. Of equal importance is some assessment as to the number of stakeholder groups affected by an IS project.
- *Experience with the technology*. In general, the more experienced the organisation is with the technology in question the less risk. This clearly applies to the skills developers have in systems construction in the chosen tool-set. It also applies to the prior experience of various stakeholder groups in using or being aware of particular technologies.
- *Project structure*. In general the more highly structured the project the less risk is likely to be associated with it. If the project has clearly established and uncontroversial goals then the project is likely to succeed. If the goals are a matter of difference between stakeholder groups then failure is likely to happen.

27.5 FEASIBILITY STUDY

A feasibility study can be considered as part of systems conception or the first activity within the systems analysis process. A feasibility study is an attempt to determine whether an information system is achievable given organisational resources and constraints. To assess feasibility, some initial idea of the functionality, usability and utility of the proposed information system needs to be established. An initial scope for the IS is then compared against the existing informatics infrastructure. Feasibility should assess whether available hardware, software, data storage and communications are sufficient for the proposed system. It should also assess the likely shape of a project organisation for the project and the feasibility of assigning such resources. Ideally, the feasibility study will assess a number of alternative solutions to the systems problem.

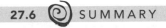

27.6 SUMMARY

- Conception will follow on from IS planning. Conception is the phase in which we develop the key business case, analyse risk and assess the feasibility of an information system.
- Any business case or strategic evaluation of an information system should consider IS costs and IS benefits.
- It is useful to make the distinction between two types of costs/benefits: tangible or visible costs/benefits and intangible or invisible costs/benefits.
- Investment in IS can be justified in terms of efficiency and effectiveness such as better customer relations and strategic advantage.
- Appraisal techniques such as payback period primarily assess efficiency gain.
- Appraisal techniques such as information economics are directed at assessing effectiveness and strategic advantage.
- Risk analysis is the process of identifying risks, estimating the likelihood of risks and planning for avoiding risks.
- A feasibility study is an attempt to determine whether an information system is achievable given organisational resources and constraints.

27.7 QUESTIONS

(i) Define the term *systems conception*.
(ii) Distinguish between IS costs and IS benefits.
(iii) List some typical IS costs and benefits.
(iv) Define the concept of investment appraisal.
(v) Describe how you would determine return on investment.
(vi) Describe how you would determine payback period.
(vii) Define the process of risk analysis.
(viii) Explain the importance of a feasibility study.

27.8 EXERCISES

(i) Try to come up with some other benefits and/or costs associated with information systems.
(ii) Categorise the costs and benefits in terms of tangible costs/benefits and intangible costs/benefits.
(iii) Choose an intended information system. Try to assess its utility using one of the standard techniques such as RoI.

(iv) In terms of some known information system, apply the information economics scorecard to the project.

(v) Apply the three risk factors identified in this chapter to some project known to you.

27.9 ⊙ PROJECTS

(i) Build a business case for some small-scale information system.

(ii) Establish empirically by collecting data on a number of IS projects the breakdown of tangible and intangible costs on bespoke projects.

(iii) Establish empirically by collecting data on a number of IS projects the breakdown of tangible and intangible costs on package projects.

(iv) Investigate the range of approaches that include ways of assessing intangible benefits. How often are they used in organisations?

(v) Develop a more complete range of risk factors associated with IS projects.

27.10 ⊙ REFERENCES

Boehm, B. W. (ed.) (1989). *Software Risk Management*. IEEE Computer Society Press, Washington.

Cash, J. I., McFarlan, F. W. and McKenney, J. L. (1992). *Corporate Information Systems Management*, 3rd edn. Richard Irwin, Homewood, IL.

Keen, P. (1981). Information systems and organisational change. *Communications of the ACM*, **24**(1), 24–33.

Parker, M., Benson, R. and Trainor, H. (1988). *Information Economics: Linking Business Performance to Information Technology*. Prentice Hall, Englewood Cliffs, NJ.

Wilcocks, L. and Margetts, H. (1994). Risk assessment and information systems. *European Journal of Information Systems*, **3**(2), 127–138.

CHAPTER 28

SYSTEMS ANALYSIS

Do not believe in anything simply because you have heard it. Do not believe in anything simply because it is spoken and rumoured by many. Do not believe in anything simply because it is found written in your religious books. Do not believe in anything merely on the authority of your teachers and elders. Do not believe in traditions because they have been handed down for many generations. But after observation and analysis, when you find that anything agrees with reason and is conducive to the good and benefit of one and all, then accept it and live up to it.

The Buddha

LEARNING OUTCOMES

After reading this chapter, you will be able to:

- Explain the key activities of systems analysis
- Describe the process of requirements elicitation
- Relate a number of requirements elicitation techniques
- Outline the process of requirements specification
- Define the available requirements specification techniques

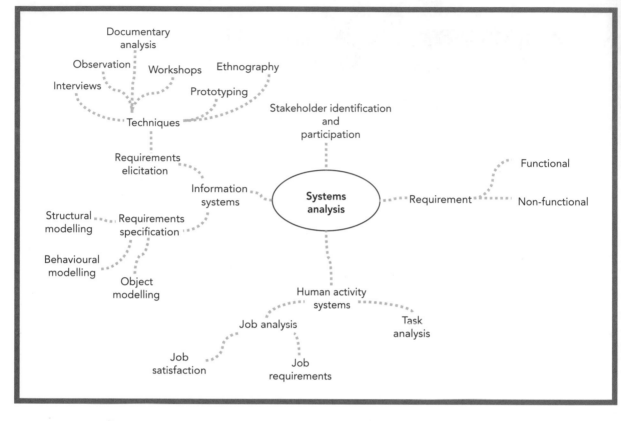

28.1 INTRODUCTION

Analysis can be conducted on any system. Here we use the term *systems analysis* to cover analysis of two types of systems: information systems and human activity systems. The analysis of such systems must occur in parallel. Systems analysis as far as information systems development is concerned is a form of socio-technical analysis and is normally conducted by specialists known as systems analysts.

Analysis may begin in terms of documenting current information systems and current human activity systems. It is more likely that systems analysis will also involve the analysis of requirements for new information systems and new human activity systems.

The analysis of human activity systems will receive inputs from the process of organisational analysis (Chapter 33). Organisational analysis can be seen to be a variant of systems analysis focusing on social systems. The analysis of information systems will receive inputs from the process of systems conception and outputs to the process of systems design. This process is illustrated in Figure 28.1.

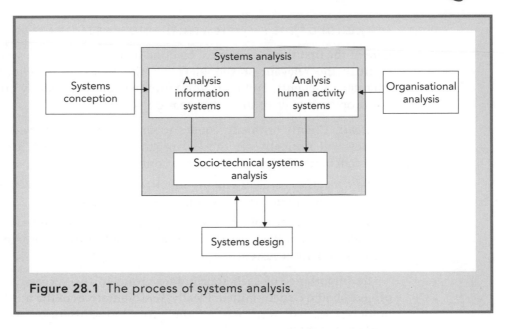

Figure 28.1 The process of systems analysis.

28.2 INFORMATION SYSTEMS ANALYSIS

Information systems analysis involves two primary and interrelated activities – requirements elicitation and requirements specification. Both sets of activities demand different techniques. Requirements elicitation demands approaches for identifying requirements. Requirements specification demands techniques for representing requirements. Systems analysis benefits from forms of stakeholder participation, particularly in the elicitation phase. This is illustrated in Figure 28.2.

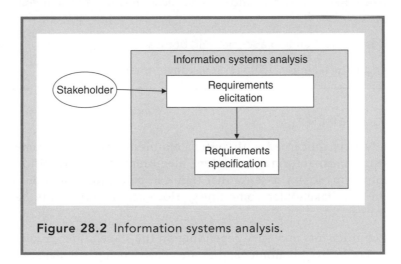

Figure 28.2 Information systems analysis.

28.2.1   STAKEHOLDER IDENTIFICATION AND PARTICIPATION

One of the first things that must be done in any information systems project is to identify the relevant stakeholders. Of the types of stakeholder identified in Chapter 13, clients, end-users and customers are particularly critical to defining the proposed shape of some information system.

- *Clients*. Clients normally equate to managerial groups within organisations. They will normally set the key organisation objectives for the information system particularly in terms of the concept of utility.

- *End-users*. Users are particularly important for setting the key functionality and usability requirements for an information system.

- *Customers*. The customers of some organisation may also be an important stakeholder group in the sense that they assess the worth of the activity supported by the information system.

The importance of each stakeholder group to the successful trajectory of the project should be determined. Ideally, representatives of the most important stakeholder types will form part of the project organisation and will particularly contribute to the systems analysis process.

Example ▶ In terms of the research management information system we might identify the following stakeholder groups:

- Producers. A team of two programmers and one analyst

- Clients. Management layers in the university – vice-chancellor, pro-vice chancellors, deans of faculty and heads of school

- Users. Research coordinators in each academic school and members in academic registry

- Customers. Funding agencies and bodies

- Regulators. National and regional government

28.2.2   REQUIREMENT

Analysis is concerned with system requirements. A requirement is any desired feature of an information system. Requirements are traditionally portrayed as unproblematic in the sense that they can be captured without to much problem from the stakeholder community. However, requirements have the following features:

- Requirements may vary depending on the stakeholder group. Requirements are not objective phenomena, they are relative to a particular stakeholder's perspective.

- Requirements may be in conflict. Analysis involves attempting to achieve some inter-subjective agreement amongst stakeholder groups about requirements.

- Requirements must be frozen at some point in order to construct an information technology system – an artefact. However, requirements are likely to change over time. Part of the reason for the maintenance (Chapter 32) of systems is because requirements change.

Example ▐▐▐▶ In terms of a system to manage research information for some university, the following may be a list of proposed requirements for the system:

- The system must have the ability to capture information about all journal research papers produced by members of staff at the university.

- The system must have the ability to capture information about research student completions.

- The system must have the ability to capture information about all research grants submitted to external research bodies.

- The system must have the ability to provide information on research active staff in the university.

- The system should enable management in the university to monitor the research performance of academic departments.

- The system must have the ability to capture information about research income achieved by the university.

- The system should enable academic departments to monitor their research activity.

- The system must have the ability to capture information about all research papers given by members of staff of the university at conferences.

- The system should be able to generate information for use in reports provided for external agencies: prospectuses, research reports, brochures etc.

- The system must have the ability to capture information about research student supervision.

- The system must have the ability to capture information about all books or chapters in books produced by members of staff at the university.

- The system should enable academic research coordinators to maintain records of research students, publications, grants etc.

- The system must have the ability to capture information about research student progression.

In the classic software engineering literature a distinction is made between so-called functional and non-functional requirements. Functional requirements are the expected features of an information system. The set of requirements for the research database system above are functional requirements. Non-functional requirements are constraints set on the systems development project. The set of functional and non-functional requirements establishes the scope of the information system.

Example ▐▐▐▶ A set of non-functional requirements for this research information system might be:

- Needs to be built in six months max. in order to be able to perform an internal research assessment exercise

- To be initially built in registry and used by 6+ staff there

- Eventually to be used by research coordinators/administrators, possibly by active researchers in departments

- One programmer and one analyst/project manager available for the project

- One development machine available

28.2.3 REQUIREMENTS ELICITATION

Requirements elicitation is that process devoted to the identification of requirements. Unfortunately, this process is sometimes referred to as requirements capture, thus implying that requirements are objective constructs that can be collected and represented in an unproblematic way. The features of requirements described above clearly indicate that requirements cannot be captured. They are inter-subjective constructs. Hence requirements elicitation necessarily involves a process of negotiation between various stakeholder groups in organisations. The differences between these two models of the requirements elicitation process are illustrated in Figure 28.3.

A number of techniques exist for requirements elicitation. Many such techniques are used in common with those for information systems research (Chapter 49). Requirements elicitation techniques include the following (see Figure 28.4):

- *Interviews*. Interviews are certainly the most commonplace requirements elicitation technique. Interviews constitute either formal or informal discussions with representatives of key stakeholder groups. Formal interviews are structured conversations in which the questions are determined before hand. Informal interviews are a form of discussion in which the questions are formulated within the flow of the interview itself.

- *Observation*. Frequently what people describe in interviews only partly reveals the reality of human activity systems and information systems. Hence interviews will often be used with other elicitation techniques such as observation.

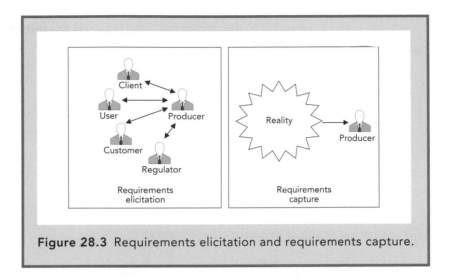

Figure 28.3 Requirements elicitation and requirements capture.

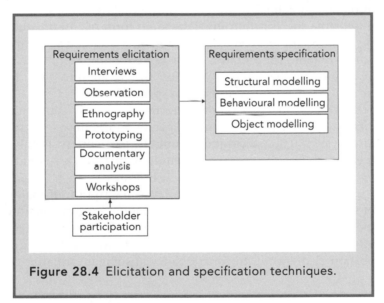

Figure 28.4 Elicitation and specification techniques.

Observation usually involves being present in work settings recording the detailed work behaviour of people.

- *Documentary analysis.* Documents are a valuable resource in most organisations. They are particularly important in indicating the data that needs to be stored within some information system and the type of reports that need to be generated from the information system.

- *Workshops.* Workshops constitute sessions in which developers and representatives of stakeholder groups get together in a structured situation to formulate requirements for systems. Workshops are controlled environments for the negotiation of requirements.

- *Prototyping*. Frequently stakeholder groups may not be able to formulate what they require until they see some representation of a proposed innovation. Prototyping involves building early versions of particular parts of a system to demonstrate to stakeholder representatives in order to obtain their feedback.

- *Ethnography*. Ethnography does not constitute one technique but a set of techniques for requirements elicitation. Ethnography frequently involves observers participating in some work setting and attempting to empathise with stakeholders to gain an in-depth appreciation of both explicit and tacit work processes. Ethnography has only comparatively recently been used to gather rich representations of work situations as a precursor to systems design.

28.3 REQUIREMENTS SPECIFICATION

Requirements specification is that process concerned with the representation of requirements established in the requirements elicitation process. Traditionally requirements specification involves some form of intermediate representation – some notation for representing requirements over and above its structure in terms of some system. The notation used is frequently graphical, sometimes textual, occasionally mathematical. Most of the modelling techniques described in Chapter 7 have been used for system specification.

Here we describe two user-centric requirements techniques – use cases and scenarios – particularly relevant to specifying the high-level scope of some information system. These techniques would be particularly useful within some development workshop for negotiating requirements which would then be specified in more detail using developer-centric techniques.

A use case model provides a high-level description of major user interactions with some information system. Such a model uses two constructs: actors and use cases. An actor is any person, organisation or system that interacts with some information system. A use case is a delimited set of activities that we can specify as being important elements of the functionality of some information system.

Example ▐▐▶ Figure 28.5 represents a simple use case model for an automatic teller machine (ATM) system. Three main actors are defined: bank customers, ATM operators and back-end banking systems. Four main use cases are defined:

- withdrawing cash from the ATM
- transferring funds between bank accounts
- depositing funds in bank accounts
- administering the ATM

The first three use cases constitute generic interaction between customers and banking systems. The last use case is a specialised function provided for technicians of the machine.

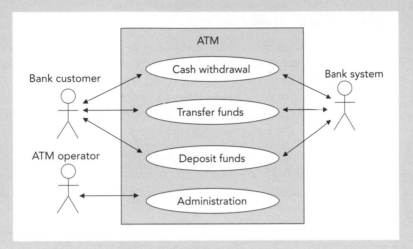

Figure 28.5 A use case model.

Each use case in a use case model can be specified in more detail as a scenario. Scenarios are described by Carroll (1995) as, '...a narrative description of what people do and experience as they try to make use of computer systems and applications'. Although discussed in a number of different ways in the literature, the concept of a scenario seems to have a number of characteristics in common:

- *Key episodes*. Scenarios normally constitute key situations or episodes in the activity of people working with computers.
- *Concreteness*. The emphasis in a scenario is on concrete representation of use rather than abstraction of use. The focus is on specific instances of use located within a work context.
- *Groundedness*. Scenarios should be grounded in the existing or potential work activities of users of computer systems.
- *Informality*. Scenarios tend to be open-ended, fragmentary, informal and rough. They are particularly directed at enhancing communication and envisionment rather than displaying the representational characteristics of consistency, rigour and completeness.
- *Middle-level abstractions*. Scenarios are a middle-level abstraction between the formality of a systems specification and the informality of everyday discussions between developers and users. Consequently a scenario tends to be more of a user-centric rather than a developer-centric design representation.
- *Multiple media*. Although usually expressed in narrative form, scenarios may also

comprise storyboards of annotated cartoon panels, video mock-ups, scripted prototypes, or physical situations contrived to support certain activities.

Example The details of a short scenario describing the use of a company database for marketing purposes are given below:

An advert is placed in the local newspaper for short courses. A person phones up with an enquiry but is not in the company database. Operator needs to record the person's details while on the phone. Enter company details including interests as tags. Company details copied across to contact form. Enter contact details. Tag with interest in courses on personal computing. Place memo against contact – posting a letter. Back to to-do list. Removing items from to-do list.

This short scenario describes key elements of interaction with the company data screens of this company's information system.

28.4 HUMAN ACTIVITY SYSTEMS ANALYSIS

In a sense, any information system consists of a human activity system and an information technology system. The use case technique described in the previous section is one that can be used to specify aspects of the human activity system of the use of the ATM – an information technology system.

In many information systems projects it is also important to analyse the larger context of human activity surrounding some information technology system. At the macro level this may involve some form of organisational analysis (Chapter 33). At the micro-level the analysis of human activity systems will focus on issues such as task analysis and job analysis.

28.4.1 TASK ANALYSIS

A human activity system or organisational process may be decomposed into a set of activities. Each activity, in turn, may be decomposed into a set of tasks and sub-tasks. Hence a hierarchy of processes, activities and tasks can be specified for a given human activity system.

Example Consider the very simple example of an ATM again. The use of the ATM can be conceived of as a major element of some human activity system of a high street bank. The process of using an ATM can be considered as a set of activities or use cases as indicated above. Each activity can in turn be decomposed into a series of constituent tasks. Hence the activity of cash withdrawal will involve the following tasks:

- Inserting a cash card
- Entering a personal identifier number (PIN)

- Selecting/entering an amount
- Selecting a withdrawal slip
- Receiving the cash
- Receiving the returned card
- Receiving the withdrawal slip

Workflow

A variant of task analysis is the analysis of workflow. This involves determining ways in which IT can be used to support more effective collaborative work. A key feature of this activity is mapping existing workflow. This has many similarities with the constructs of process redesign as considered in Chapter 19.

28.4.2 JOB ANALYSIS

Job analysis involves the analysis of the content and relationships of current jobs in terms of both organisational and individual objectives. Organisations will generally have objectives such as improving the efficiency and/or effectiveness of work. Individuals will generally have objectives such as increasing levels of self-fulfilment and job-satisfaction.

Traditional approaches to analysing human activity systems undertake the breakdown of such systems in terms of various levels of tasks. Such tasks are then closely studied in terms of tangible performance measures. Increasing specialisation and the segmentation of tasks are seen as the primary ways of achieving organisational objectives. Unfortunately, such approaches have an equal tendency to conflict with individual objectives. The heavy specialisation of work can lead to substantial deskilling of the workforce leading to high levels of demotivation and a decreasing level of flexibility in work.

Ideally, requirements will be generated for new work systems as well as new technical systems. The aim is to achieve an optimal balance between both social and technical objectives.

Job satisfaction

A large literature exists on determining the satisfaction experienced in defined roles in organisations. Generally the following features seem to be characteristic of jobs that supply satisfaction for workers:

- *Skills*. Jobs which allow ample opportunity for the exercise of skills and the extension of skills through learning.
- *Meaning*. Jobs in which it is easy to understand how the work fits into the organisation and the work is explicitly valued.
- *Autonomy*. The greater the level to which the worker can control his or her own work, the higher the levels of satisfaction.

- *Social relations*. Jobs which include collaboration and communication with others.
- *Demands*. Jobs which include a mix of routine and new demands; also, that the worker has control over which new demands to accept.
- *Outside life*. Jobs which do not interfere with the person's ability to participate in family and community life.

Job requirements

Requirements for new jobs are taken from a two-dimensional space in which the horizontal dimension is defined in terms of the specialisation of tasks and the vertical dimension is defined in terms of the specialisation of decision-making (Figure 28.6). A number of strategies may be employed to increase levels of job satisfaction:

- *Job rotation*. This involves rotating people on the horizontal plane. Job rotation increases variety and learning opportunities for the workforce. It also has substantial benefits in terms of improving levels of organisational flexibility. However, there is little evidence that it increases motivation levels amongst the workforce.
- *Job enlargement*. This involves combining a number of tasks on the horizontal plane. It offers the potential of creating more complete and hence more meaningful jobs. Clearly, it reduces the levels of specialisation in an organisation.
- *Job enrichment*. This involves increasing the scope of a job on the vertical plane. Job enrichment consists of giving workers more responsibility for making deci-

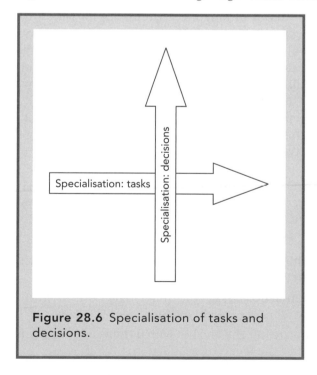

Figure 28.6 Specialisation of tasks and decisions.

sions about their own work. The key aim is to improve the motivational aspect of work.

- *Group working.* This consists of an extension both on the horizontal and on the vertical dimension but in terms of a group of workers. The group acts as an important source of support, encouragement and security for the individual worker.

28.5 SUMMARY

- Systems analysis involves two primary and interrelated activities – requirements elicitation and requirements representation.
- Requirements elicitation is that process devoted to the identification of requirements.
- Requirements specification is that process concerned with the representation of requirements.
- A requirement is any desired feature of an information technology system.
- Requirements may vary depending on the stakeholder group. Requirements are not objective phenomena. Requirements elicitation involves attempting to achieve some inter-subjective agreement amongst stakeholder groups about requirements.
- Requirements are likely to change over time. Part of the reason for adaptation of systems is because requirements change.
- Requirements must be frozen at some point in order to construct an information technology system – an artefact.
- Ideally, requirements will be generated for new work systems as well as new technical systems. The aim is to achieve an optimal balance between both social and technical objectives.

28.6 QUESTIONS

- (i) Define the term *systems analysis*.
- (ii) Discuss some of the characteristics of an information systems requirement.
- (iii) Why is *requirements capture* an inappropriate term?
- (iv) Distinguish between requirements elicitation and requirements specification.
- (v) Why is identification of stakeholders important to analysis?
- (vi) List the major elicitation techniques.
- (vii) Describe some techniques for requirements specification.
- (viii) Define the process of job analysis.

28.7 EXERCISES

(i) Identify actual clients, end-users and customers for some project known to you.

(ii) What requirements elicitation techniques are most readily used in an organisation known to you and why?

(iii) List two actual requirements from some IS project.

(iv) Perform a small use-case analysis of some information system known to you.

(v) Develop one scenario of use for a system.

(vi) Consider some information system. Assess the degree to which the surrounding human activity system encourages job satisfaction.

28.8 PROJECTS

(i) If requirements elicitation is a process of inter-subjective negotiation, investigate the key skills needed by successful analysts.

(ii) Conduct a systems analysis for some small-scale information system.

(iii) Determine which are the most commonly used of the requirements elicitation techniques.

(iv) Build a detailed analysis of the strengths and weaknesses of the range of requirements elicitation techniques.

(v) Gather some actual requirements specification documents. Investigate how long it took to produce them and how closely the resulting information systems matched them.

(vi) Determine which are the most commonly used requirements specification approaches.

(vii) In terms of IS projects, determine the degree to which job considerations enter the analysis activities.

28.9 REFERENCE

Carroll, J. M. (ed.) (1995). *Scenario-Based Design: Envisioning Work and Technology in Systems Development*. John Wiley, New York.

CHAPTER 29

SYSTEMS DESIGN

A common mistake that people make when trying to design something completely foolproof is to underestimate the ingenuity of complete fools.

Douglas Adams

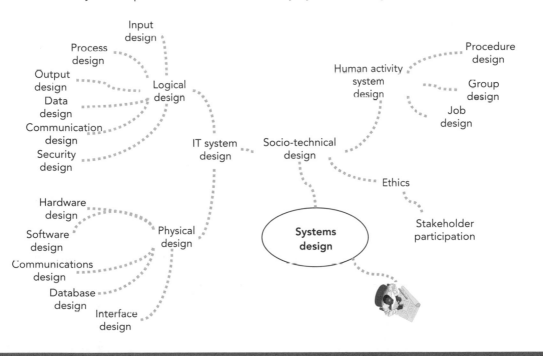

Design can be conducted on any system. Here we use the term systems design to cover design of two types of systems: information systems and human activity systems. The design of such systems must occur in parallel. Systems design is hence a form of socio-technical design.

Systems analysis provides the major input into systems design. Design is planning a technical artefact to meet requirements established by analysis. Design involves a reflective conversation with the situation – the consideration of requirements and constraints and the selection amongst design alternatives. Design benefits from the participation of system stakeholders.

Systems design produces a system specification that is the major input into systems construction. This system specification acts as a blueprint for construction work. This is illustrated in Figure 29.1.

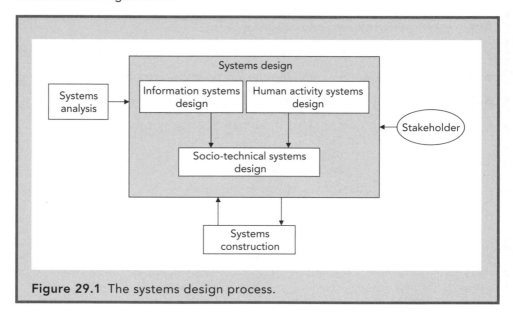

Figure 29.1 The systems design process.

29.2 ◎ HUMAN ACTIVITY SYSTEMS AND INFORMATION SYSTEMS

The design of information systems and the work or human activity systems within which they take place are related together in a cyclical way (Figure 29.2).

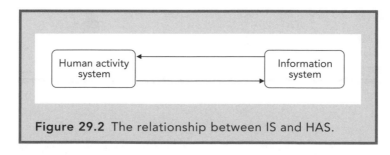

Figure 29.2 The relationship between IS and HAS.

Building and implementing an information system increases the levels of uncertainty in an organisation:

- *Reflection*. Information systems are normally built as a reflection of organisational work. Designing an information system involves investigating and defining organisational work. This is a critical activity of systems analysis.

- *Change*. Introducing and using an information system may cause changes to organisational work. Implementing an information system involves changes in organisational work.

- *Improvement*. The introduction of information technology is normally an attempt to improve organisational work. There is some evidence that the introduction of information technology actually decreases organisational effectiveness.

Example ⦀➡ The interdependence of human activity systems and IS can be demonstrated by considering an example from the domain of nursing in general hospitals. There are three basic models of human activity systems appropriate for organising nursing on a hospital ward:

- *Round nursing*. This is very much task oriented. Each nurse has responsibility for one task on the ward. For example, one nurse is responsible for giving all patients their prescribed medicines.

- *Primary care*. This is patient oriented. One nurse has the responsibility for carrying out all the tasks associated with one patient. Usually the nurses are responsible for a small group of patients. In primary care, for instance, one nurse is likely to be responsible for giving all medicines to her group of patients.

- *Group nursing*. This is a mixture of the above. A group of nurses have the responsibility for carrying out several tasks, but only tasks related to one group of patients. In group nursing one nurse may be given the responsibility for distributing regular medicines while all nurses give out additional medicines according to patient's needs

Each of these human activity systems demands a substantially different information system. To illustrate this three different data (structural) models are presented in Figure 29.3.

- *Round nursing*. In round nursing there is need to exchange medical information such as which medicines have been given to which patients. There is little need for information to coordinate tasks between nurses.

- *Primary care*. In primary care there is very little exchange of medical information between nurses. There is a need for some coordination information with the hospital, such as which nurses care for which patients.

- *Group nursing*. In group nursing there is need both to exchange medical information and for much information necessary to the effective coordination of nursing tasks.

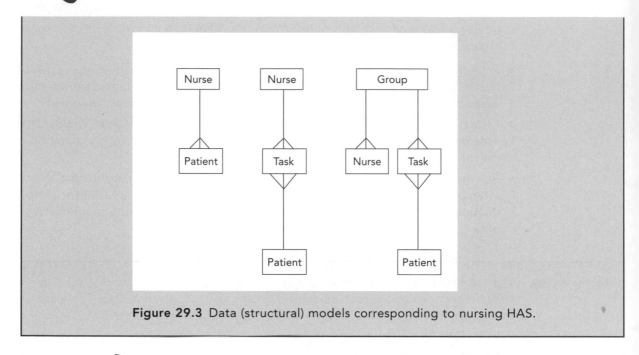

Figure 29.3 Data (structural) models corresponding to nursing HAS.

29.3 ⊚ SOCIO-TECHNICAL DESIGN

The work of Enid Mumford (1983) provides one of the most coherent accounts of how socio-techical design may be undertaken in an informatics context. She has developed a method for such design from her decades of work on the effective design of socio-technical systems called ETHICS (Effective Technical and Human Implementation of Computer Systems). The objective of ETHICS is to design a new form of work organisation with the dual objectives of improving job satisfaction (the social system) and work efficiency (technical system). The steps of the method are laid out below and illustrated in Figure 29.4:

- *Diagnosis of technical and human needs.* This is undertaken primarily by collecting and analysing questionnaire data. This data is used to determine the fit between the present work situation and a valued work situation in terms of a typology of needs. Both job satisfaction objectives (such as provide work variety, and performance incentives) and efficiency objectives (such as improve level of worker performance) are then constructed.

- *Set out a range of technical and social alternatives.* An assessment is then made of each alternative in terms of human advantages and disadvantages and technical advantages and disadvantages.

- *Rank each technical and human alternative.* This is done in terms of the ability of each alternative to meet both human and technical objectives. The designer chooses the highest ranking human and technical alternative that are compatible.

- *Develop detailed socio-technical design.*

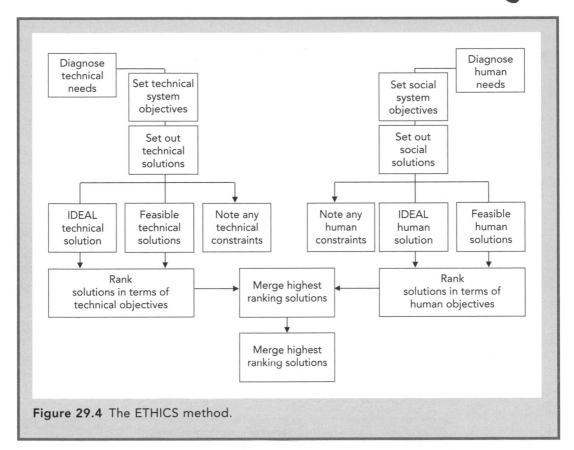

Figure 29.4 The ETHICS method.

Example ▐▐▐▶ Mumford provides a case study of a customer orders and accounts system which was analysed by the ETHICS approach, and from which a new social and technical system emerged. Although this was conducted in the 1980s, it illustrates the essential principles of the approach.

The basic technical system involved orders clerks filling out order forms, accounts clerks updating customer ledgers and any problems being resolved by lots of paper-passing. The social system represented a clear distinction between orders clerks and accounts clerks, each accounts clerk working across a number of different customer accounts, and problems being resolved by two senior clerks. This socio-technical system is illustrated in Figure 29.5.

The motivations for change were both technical and social. Examples of technical problems were orders incorrectly filled out, customer ledgers incorrectly updated and slow methods of resolving problems. Examples of social problems included high absenteeism, high staff turnover, and some 'industrial vandalism'.

Results from the job satisfaction questionnaire identified low job satisfaction in the present work situation as a result of piece-work, lack of overall picture, individual

Socio-technical system (*before*)

Information system Order clerks fill out order forms Accounts clerks update customer ledgers Problems resolved via paper-passing	*Human activity system* Orders clerks and accounts clerks Individual working across customer accounts Problems resolved by two senior clerks

Figure 29.5 The *before* socio-technical system.

isolation, low status and poor prospects for advancement. The valued work situation was characterised in terms of more responsibility, group working, more important work and better opportunities for advancement.

After the study was complete a new work and technical system was put into place. The technical system constituted terminal input of orders, batch update of a central database and regular reports output from the system. The social system was changed to small workgroups of five clerks, each workgroup handling orders and accounts for a group of customers. The group handled customer problems thrown up by printouts. This is illustrated in Figure 29.6.

Socio-technical system (*after*)

Information system Terminal input of orders Batch update of a central database Reports output from system	*Human activity system* Small workgroups Specialisation of work around customers Group resolution of problems

Figure 29.6 The *after* socio-technical system.

In the ETHICS approach the left-hand stream is an exercise in information systems design. The right-hand stream is an exercise in human activity system design.

29.4 ⊚ STAKEHOLDER PARTICIPATION

Systems design benefits from forms of stakeholder participation. End-users are probably the most significant stakeholder group to involve in a development project. Some benefits of participation include:

- A closer match between the information system and the requirements of stake-holders.
- A closer match between the information system and the human activity system.
- Greater commitment of stakeholders to a system.

Hirschheim (1983) maintains that participation is not the same as involvement. All IS projects have some degree of stakeholder involvement, if only in the implementation phase, but only some are participatively developed. The major differences between user involvement and user participation relate to decision-making power. In user involvement the users are normally given a degree of power over decisions relating to the shape of the information system. In user participation that power is extended to decisions about social and job considerations.

Types of participation can be distinguished in terms of the level of participation and form of participation. Mumford has distinguished between three different levels of user -participation:

- *Consultative participation.* Decision-making is still in the hands of systems analysts and systems designers, but there is a great deal of staff at every level consulted about such decision-making.
- *Representative participation.* A design group is formed made up of representatives of all grades of staff with systems analysts. The representatives, however, are selected by management.
- *Consensus participation.* A design group is formed as in representative participation, but representatives are elected by staff and given the responsibility to communicate group decisions back to staff.

The form of participation can vary between an intensive mode and a phased mode. In intensive mode representatives of stakeholders will be assigned on a continuous basis for the entire duration of the project. They will form a permanent part of the development team. In phased participation stakeholders are invited to review the development effort at regular intervals. Intensive participation tends to be used more frequently on iterative development projects whereas phased participation is characteristic of linear development projects (Chapter 25).

29.5 THE COMPONENTS OF SYSTEMS DESIGN

The major components of information systems design and human activity systems design are illustrated in Figure 29.7.

We may distinguish between two levels of information systems design:

- *Logical design.* This is an attempt to specify the design of a system independent of any requirements.
- *Physical design.* Physical design is the design of the implementation of a system – a blueprint for its development.

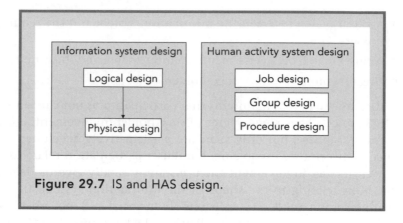

Figure 29.7 IS and HAS design.

29.5.1 LOGICAL DESIGN

Logical design involves the following activities (Figure 29.8):

- Input design – the design of key data inputs
- Output design – the design of key forms of input
- Processing design – the design of key system processes
- Data design – the design of key data structures
- Communications design – the design of the communications framework
- Controls and security design – the design of disaster and security management

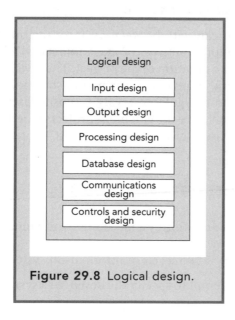

Figure 29.8 Logical design.

29.5.2 PHYSICAL DESIGN

Physical design involves the following interdependent activities (Figure 29.9):

- Hardware design – detailing hardware devices needed
- Software design – detailing the shape of programs
- Communications design – detailing the form of communications hardware and software
- Database design – designing database systems
- Interface design – designing the user interface

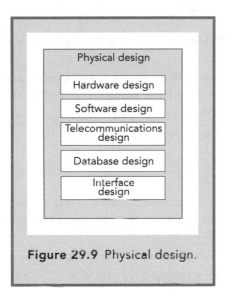

Figure 29.9 Physical design.

29.5.3 HUMAN ACTIVITY SYSTEMS DESIGN

Human activity systems consist of people and activities or procedures. Hence three interrelated activities are part of human activity systems design:

- *Job design*. Clearly the aim is to balance the needs of job satisfaction with work efficiency.
- *Team design*. The aim is to establish teams with clear structures of authority and control.
- *Procedure design*. This involves detailing established patterns of work.

In most commercial organisations, managerial groups usually determine the major shape of human activity systems. McGregor (1960) identified two distinct mind-sets or theories that influence the way in which managers think about workers. McGregor called these Theory X and Theory Y:

- *Theory X*. According to this theory the average human being is perceived as disliking work and hence avoiding it wherever possible. The average human being avoids responsibility and has little ambition.
- *Theory Y*. According to this theory physical and mental effort are important and natural human functions. If humans are committed to certain objectives they will exercise self-direction and self-control. The capacity to exercise imagination, ingenuity and creativity are widely distributed in the population.

These two theories have clear consequences for the way in which both human activity systems and information systems are designed:

- *Theory X*. HAS have to be designed with the clear intention of monitoring the workforce and controlling their behaviour through coercion. The objective of IS should be to provide sufficient information to management to exercise such close control
- *Theory Y*. HAS have to be designed to encourage ingenuity and creativity. Information systems are there to encourage cooperation and collaboration amongst the workforce in the achievement of objectives

29.6 SUMMARY

- Design is planning the shape of some technical artefact to meet the requirements established in systems analysis. It also involves designing the human activity system in which the IS will be placed.
- Information systems design is a form of socio-technical systems design.
- We may distinguish between two levels of information systems design – logical design and physical design.
- Information systems design benefits from forms of stakeholder participation.
- Information systems design outputs to systems implementation.

29.7 QUESTIONS

(i) Define the term *systems design*.

(ii) Describe how information systems and human activity systems design are a cyclical process.

(iii) List the major phases of the ETHICS approach to socio-technical information systems design.

(iv) Distinguish between consultative, representative and consensus participation.

(v) Describe the major benefits of stakeholder participation.

(vi) Distinguish between logical and physical design.

(vii) Describe the major activities of logical design.

(viii) Describe the major activities of physical design.

(ix) What are the major differences between a Theory X and Theory Y perspective on human behaviour?

29.8 EXERCISES

(i) Find one other example of the interdependence of information systems with human activity systems.

(ii) Assess the commercial feasibility of ETHICS as an approach for information systems design.

(iii) Assess the degree of stakeholder participation in some information systems project known to you.

(iv) Determine whether such participation is consultative, representative or consensus.

(v) Determine whether the participation is intensive or phased.

(vi) Follow through the consequences for project management of a Theory X and Theory Y model of human behaviour.

29.9 PROJECTS

(i) Develop a systems design for some small-scale information system.

(ii) Take one area of work and investigate alternative ways of organising this work. Then draw a data model for the information systems that would be needed to support each form of work.

(iii) Determine whether socio-technical considerations influence IS design in practice.

(iv) Investigate the degree to which ETHICS has been applied in organisations.

(v) Investigate the degree to which participatory design has been applied in the UK and the USA.

(vi) Investigate the forms of participation amongst a range of development projects.

(vii) Determine whether Theory X and Theory Y models impact on the design of information systems.

29.10 REFERENCES

Hirschheim, R. A. (1983). Assessing participatory systems design: some conclusions from an exploratory study. *Information and Management*, **6**, 317–327.

McGregor, D. (1960). *The Human Side of the Enterprise*. McGraw-Hill, New York.

Mumford, E. (1983). *Designing Participatively*. Manchester Business School Press, Manchester.

30

SYSTEMS CONSTRUCTION

Programming today is a race between software engineers striving to build bigger and better idiot-proof programs, and the universe trying to produce bigger and better idiots. So far, the universe is winning.

Anonymous

LEARNING OUTCOMES

After reading this chapter, you will be able to:

- Define the process of systems construction
- Describe the key ways in which information systems may be built
- Explain the key ways in which human activity systems may be formed

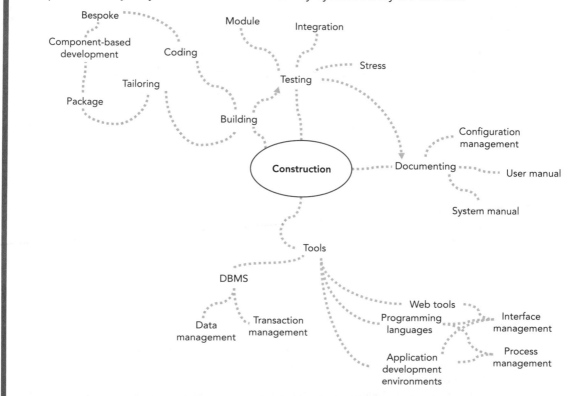

30.1 INTRODUCTION

Systems construction involves the actual process of building the information system. Systems construction follows on from systems design and is followed by systems implementation. This sequence is illustrated in Figure 30.1.

An information system is a socio-technical system. Hence two parallel construction activities must take place: constructing the IT system and constructing the human activity system.

Traditionally IT system construction involves the three related processes of programming, testing and documentation. These activities differ depending on whether the development is based around the purchase of packages or is a form of bespoke development.

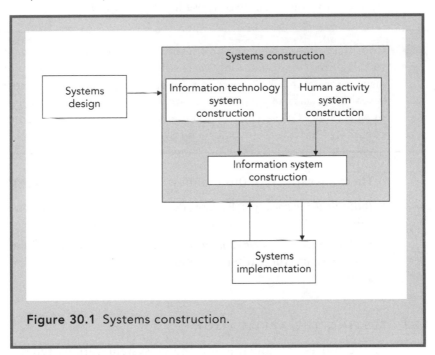

Figure 30.1 Systems construction.

30.2 INFORMATION TECHNOLOGY SYSTEM CONSTRUCTION

IT system construction involves three interrelated activities: building the application, testing the application and documenting the application.

30.2.1 BUILDING THE APPLICATION

The building of IT systems normally involves building the four layers of the IT systems model (see Chapter 12) and its associated communication facilities. Hence an IT system's build construction normally involve:

- *Building the user interface*: typically constructing data entry forms, menus and reports.
- *Building the business rules and application logic*: typically specifying integrity constraints and elements of processing.
- *Building the transaction layer*: typically specifying the major update functions for the system.
- *Building the data management layer*: typically creating the data structures for storing data.

Historically, the four parts of a conventional IT application were built using one tool, the high-level or third generation programming language (3GL). However, over the last couple of decades there has been a tendency to use a different, specialised tool for one or more of these layers (Chapter 12).

Example ||||▶ Consider a research information system constructed for a university. The interface to this system was built using Microsoft Access. Some of the rules and logic were also programmed in Access; some were programmed in Microsoft Visual Basic. Visual Basic was used to communicate with the application programming interface of Microsoft SQL Server to implement transaction. The data management layer constitutes a database managed by SQL Server.

There are variants of this tool-based approach to building IT systems:

- *Building using packages*. Package development involves the two interrelated activities of package selection and package tailoring.
- *Building using software components*. This involves using pre-built software components to construct either the whole or the part of some information technology system.

30.2.2 TESTING THE APPLICATION

In the process of constructing the IT system various types of tests have to be conducted to ensure that the system is working effectively. Effectiveness may be established in terms of the specified functional requirements and in terms of certain non-functional requirements such as performance. There are a number of distinct types of testing:

- *Unit testing*. Testing of individual programs or software modules.
- *System testing*. Testing of an entire system as a unit.
- *Volume testing*. Testing the application with large amounts of data and use.
- *Integration testing*. At some point the system has to be assembled as a complete unit and testing conducted of all related systems together.
- *Acceptance testing*. Conducting any tests required by the user to ensure that the user community is satisfied with the system.

Generally these are performed in sequence and some of the testing may pass over into the implementation phase (Chapter 31).

30.2.3 DOCUMENTING THE APPLICATION

An IT system needs to be documented to ensure that it can be used and that adequate information is provided to ensure effective maintenance (Chapter 32) of the system. Hence two major types of documentation are required:

- *User documentation.* A source of reference for users to turn to when puzzled about aspects of use.
- *System documentation.* This describes the structure and behaviour of the IT system for developers.

30.3 CONSTRUCTING THE HUMAN ACTIVITY SYSTEM

If the IT system is to be used in an existing HAS then this activity will restrict itself to forming the context of use. If socio-technical design has been used, then construction of the HAS will involve:

- Specifying jobs and roles
- Specifying the organisation of any teams
- Specifying procedures for work

30.4 PACKAGE CONSTRUCTION

Package construction involves a 'buy not build' strategy for systems construction. Hence there is a fading between the traditional boundaries of systems construction and systems implementation. Typically, package construction involves the implementation of standard software modules for core business processes usually combined with bespoke customisation for competitive differentiation. Package implementation normally involves the selection of software modules then deciding upon the profile of adoption throughout the company. At one end of the scale an organisation may choose to standardise modules across organisational functions. At the other end of the scale, the organisation may choose to implement variability in module adoption throughout the organisation. Customisation normally involves 'programming' configuration (tables) associated with each module.

Example ▐▐▐▶   SAP/R3 has some 3000 tables to enable customisation of this mega-package.

Mega-package construction is subtly different from traditional package construction. In terms of the traditional model, companies decide what they want in terms of functionality, usability and utility, choose a package to closely meet those needs and then rewrite large portions of the software to ensure that there is a close fit with organisational imperatives. The mega-package model of development involves a change of emphasis. The organisation selects the ERP system and then adapts the enterprise to fit the ERP system. Some degree of customisation is possible, but the complexity of the system makes major modifications impractical. In this sense, mega-package procurement can be considered as another form of outsourcing of IS development (Chapter 40).

30.4.1 ISSUES

An analysis of current experience indicates the following issues to be taken into consideration when considering the implementation of mega-packages:

- An ERP system implementation is not just technology change. It involves significant organisational change.
- Many ERP vendors propose their products as vehicles for BPR. However, some concern has been expressed over the way in which ERP-enabled BPR exercises are IT-driven rather than IT-enabled.
- Because ERP system implementation involves a degree of outsourcing, it normally involves a certain loss of control as far as IS/IT competency is concerned to the vendor.
- ERP systems are large, monolithic systems and therefore experience all the problems of support associated with such systems.
- There is no agreed, existing framework available to guide organisations in the process of mega-package selection, implementation and evaluation.
- There is a substantial amount of anecdotal evidence to suggest that ERP implementations can be slow, particularly because of difficulties experienced in the customisation process.
- Package implementation skills are in short supply. This normally puts a reliance on external package implementation skills by many organisations.
- If working practices differ significantly from those able to be supported by the ERP system, then there may be a need to adapt working practices to the package.
- Commentators have questioned whether the implementation of mega-packages will offer sustainable competitive advantage to companies. The significant industrial convergence in the use of generic packages poses a longer-term danger of differentiation between organisations, particularly in terms of service and cost.
- There have been a number of cases where the introduction of a package clashed with organisational structure and culture. Some companies have used ERP systems as a way of imposing uniform organisational structure and culture – as a means of imposing some form of 'discipline' on their companies. However,

differences in national and regional markets may demand differences in the ways in which different organisational units work. In such situations imposing standard business processes may prove difficult.

30.5 SUMMARY

- Systems construction involves the actual process of building the information system.
- Systems construction follows on from systems design and is followed by systems implementation.
- An information system is a socio-technical system. Hence two parallel construction activities must take place: constructing the IT system and constructing the human activity system.
- Traditionally IT system construction involves the three related processes of programming, testing and documentation.
- Package development involves customising a package for the particular requirements of an organisation.

30.6 QUESTIONS

(i) Define the term *systems construction*.

(II) List the three major activities of systems construction.

(iii) Describe the major forms of testing.

(iv) Distinguish between system and user documentation.

(v) Why are companies turning to package construction?

(vi) Discuss some of the major issues involved in package approaches to systems construction.

30.7 EXERCISES

(I) Find one example of each of the forms of testing described in this chapter.

(ii) Find some user documentation and describe its key elements.

(iii) Consider some IT system. How many tools were used in its construction and for what purpose?

(iv) Find three examples of a mega-package.

(i) Build a prototype for some small-scale information system.

(ii) Take one organisation known to you. Investigate how many information systems have been built in a bespoke manner and how many through package purchase.

(iii) Determine the degree to which user documentation is now offered on-line and consider some of the disadvantages and advantages of this.

(iv) Consider the main drivers for package implementation amongst organisations.

CHAPTER 31

SYSTEMS IMPLEMENTATION

A little tact and wise management may often evade resistance, and carry a point, where direct force might be in vain.

Anonymous

LEARNING OUTCOMES

After reading this chapter, you will be able to:

- Define the process of information systems implementation
- Distinguish between technical and social systems implementation
- Outline the activities of technical systems implementation
- Relate the activities of social systems implementation

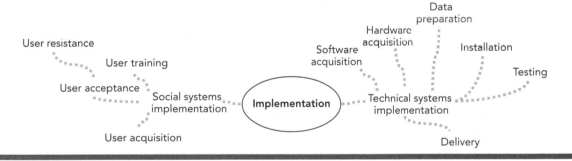

The process of systems implementation (sometimes called systems delivery) follows on from systems construction. Systems implementation involves delivering an information system into its context of use. Since an information system is a socio-technical system, implementation of such systems involves the parallel implementation of both an information system and some form of human activity system. Once a system is delivered into its context of use it will be subject to the process of operation and the process of systems maintenance (Chapter 32). This is illustrated in Figure 31.1.

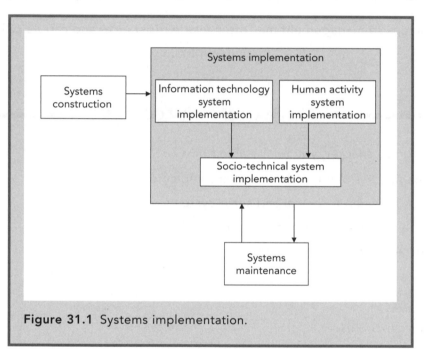

Figure 31.1 Systems implementation.

31.2 TYPES OF SYSTEMS IMPLEMENTATION

Systems implementation involves both technical and social systems implementation. Technical systems implementation involves ensuring that the appropriate hardware, communications, software and data are in place. Social systems implementation involves ensuring that the appropriate users are identified, trained and supported in the use of the technology.

Systems implementation can take place in three major ways:

- *Direct conversion*. This is sometimes called 'Big Bang' implementation and constitutes the confident approach to systems implementation. Using this approach, the new system directly replaces the old system. There is no temporal overlap between the implementation of the new system and the system it replaces.

- *Parallel implementation*. This is a form of implementation in which two systems, the old and the new system, run in parallel. It constitutes the cautious approach in that if problems are experienced with the new system the organisation may revert to running the old system until the problem is resolved. Eventually some stage is reached where the organisation is happy with the new system and consequently the old system is terminated.

- *Hybrid implementation*. This form of implementation phases in particular components as replacements or pilots major modules of the system. It is an evolutionary approach in the sense that the impact of implementation is distributed more evenly over time than in direct conversion.

31.3 TECHNICAL SYSTEMS IMPLEMENTATION

Technical systems implementation involves the following activities, generally in some form of sequence (see Figure 31.2):

- *Software acquisition*. Acquiring operating systems, DBMS, and possibly packaged software.

- *Hardware acquisition*. Purchasing computers, peripheral devices and communication networks.

- *Data preparation and conversion*. If a new system replaces an old system, then some form of data transfer between the systems must be undertaken. Data may have to be prepared for such transfer. For 'green field' systems certain data elements such as reference data will probably need to be prepared for entry into the system.

- *Installation*. Installing hardware, software and entering data into the system.

- *Testing*. Making sure that the system works effectively as a complete configuration. This issue was discussed in Chapter 30. Acceptance testing normally is completed in terms of some formal or informal signoff of the system. This indicates some level of acceptance with the levels of performance the system provides.

- *Introduction/delivery*. Going 'live' with the system in its context of use.

31.4 SOCIAL SYSTEMS IMPLEMENTATION

As a minimum social systems implementation involves (see Figure 31.2):

- *User group formation*. Forming the appropriate user groups for using the system.

- *User and operator training*. Training the users in work practices and procedures for use of the system. This can be done by the developers of the system or by a user representative who becomes expert in the use of the system and is then required to pass on this knowledge to other users.

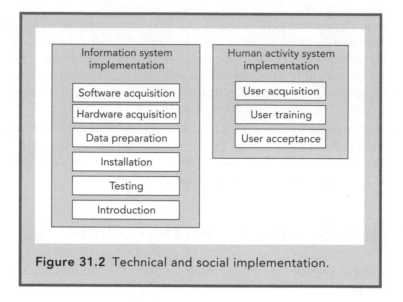

Figure 31.2 Technical and social implementation.

- *User acceptance.* Acceptance of the system by user groups. Part of this will be some acceptance testing.

As part of any implementation a user document or manual will normally be produced. This should act as a source of reference for the use of the system (Chapter 13). Support is also usually provided in terms of provision of some form of help desk or supporting service. This is a specialised service designed to answer any questions users may pose on the use of the system.

One should not suppose that users always inherently accept the implementation of some information technology system. A system is not always unconditionally accepted by its user community. There is a lot of evidence of systems being resisted by their user community (Chapter 13).

31.5 SUMMATIVE EVALUATION

After a period of operation a post-implementation audit or summative evaluation of the system should be conducted. Kumar (1990) reports on a US empirical study of the prevalence and form of evaluation of information systems after they have been implemented. Three major results are evident from his data:

- The major reason for performing post-implementation evaluation is the formalisation of the completion of the development project. Summative evaluation is thus a major tactic in a project disengagement strategy.
- Much of the evaluation is managed and performed by those who have designed the system being implemented.
- The most frequently evaluated criteria seem to be information quality criteria (accuracy, timeliness, adequacy and appropriateness) along with facilitating

criteria such as user satisfaction and attitudes. Socio-technical criteria such as the system's impact on the user and the organisation are evaluated much less frequently.

Effective conduct of summative evaluation of information systems may suggest various improvements to such information systems that may be incorporated into the systems maintenance process.

31.6 SUMMARY

- Systems implementation involves delivering an information system into its context of use.
- Systems implementation involves both technical and social systems implementation.
- Technical systems implementation involves software acquisition, hardware acquisition, data conversion, installation, testing and delivery.
- Social systems implementation involves user group formation, user training and user acceptance.
- After a period of operation a post-implementation audit or summative evaluation of the system should be conducted.

31.7 QUESTIONS

(i) Define the term *systems implementation*.
(ii) Describe the three major forms of implementation.
(iii) List the major phases of implementation.
(iv) List the major activities of technical systems implementation.
(v) List the major activities of social systems implementation.
(vi) Why is summative evaluation important?

31.8 EXERCISES

(i) Consider some information systems project. What approach to implementation was taken and why?
(ii) Determine a more complete analysis of the advantages and disadvantages of each form of implementation strategy.
(iii) Assess the relative importance of data preparation and conversion to two IT system projects known to you.

(iv) Investigate the prevalence of user resistance to information systems in an organisation known to you.

31.9 PROJECTS

(i) Construct an implementation plan for some small-scale information system.

(ii) Investigate which type of system implementation is the most popular amongst a group of organisations and why.

(iii) Investigate the activities of a help desk in two or more organisations.

(iv) Determine how much time and effort go into social systems implementation amongst a range of projects.

31.10 REFERENCE

Kumar, K. (1990). Post implementation evaluation of computer-based information systems: current practices. *Communications of the ACM*, **33**(2), 236–252.

CHAPTER 32

SYSTEMS MAINTENANCE

Adapt or perish, now as ever, is nature's inexorable imperative.

H. G. Wells (1866–1946)

LEARNING OUTCOMES

After reading this chapter, you will be able to:

- Define the term *systems maintenance*
- Explain some of the reasons for systems maintenance
- Describe some of the strategies for managing the process of systems maintenance

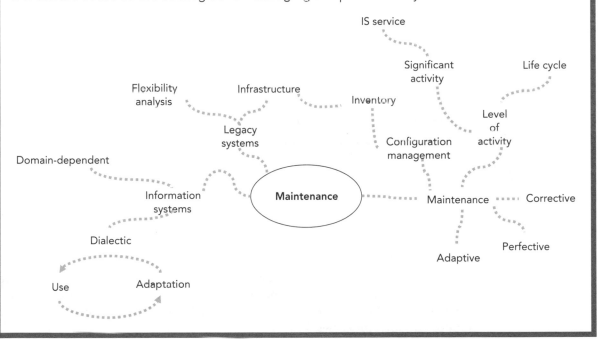

Systems maintenance follows on from systems implementation. Maintenance is the process of making needed changes to the structure of some information system. Maintenance activity may stimulate suggestions for new systems. Hence it may act as a key input into the process of systems conception and thus provide closure to the process of information systems development (Chapter 25). These relationships are illustrated in Figure 32.1.

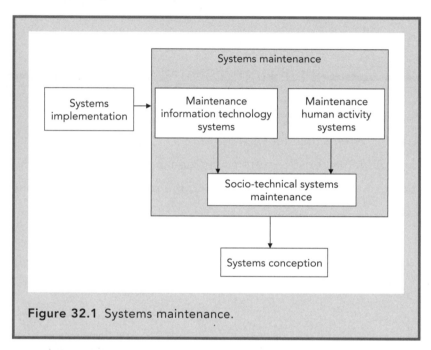

Figure 32.1 Systems maintenance.

32.2 REASONS FOR MAINTENANCE

There are a number of reasons that an organisation may decide to make changes to an information system:

- *Bugs in systems*. A bug is usually an error in a system which needs to be corrected.

- *Changes in processes*. An organisation rarely stays still. It continually needs to make changes to its organisational processes to compete in its environment. Changes are therefore likely to be required in the information systems supporting such processes.

- *New requests from organisational stakeholders*. The use of an information system by stakeholders is likely to generate a whole range of requests for changes in the way a system works.

- *Technical problems with hardware and software*. Hardware and software forming component elements of some IT system may be faulty or may fail to perform

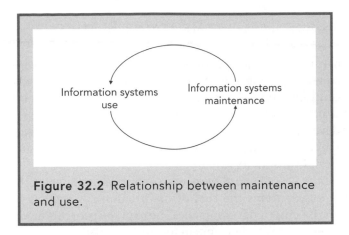

Figure 32.2 Relationship between maintenance and use.

effectively in terms of criteria such as response time. Such hardware and software may need to be upgraded.

- *Changes in the environment.* Environmental changes such as changes in government regulation may cause needed maintenance of a information system.

Maintenance activity is an inherent part of the work of most informatics departments in organisations. This is primarily because information systems are domain-dependent systems. Information systems are domain-dependent because there is a necessary interdependence between the system and its universe of discourse, typically the organisation which sponsors the development of the IS. Such systems are characterised by an intrinsic uncertainty about the universe of discourse. In particular, the use of the information system may change the nature of the universe of discourse and hence the nature of the problem being solved. Hence, in turn, the information system may need to be adapted to the changes in the universe of discourse. This is illustrated in Figure 32.2.

We may identify four major types of maintenance activity:

- *Perfective maintenance.* Changes made to the information system which make improvements but without affecting its functionality.
- *Adaptive maintenance.* Changes made to the information system to provide a closer fit between an information system and its environment, the human activity system.
- *Corrective maintenance.* Changes made to correct previously unidentified system errors.
- *Preventative maintenance.* Changes aimed at improving a system's maintainability, such as documentation or improving the flexibility of some information technology system.

Maintenance costs are traditionally a heavy component of the costs of supporting the informatics infrastructure. Over 50% of the activity of informatics departments can be taken up with maintenance activity. Hence an explicit plan for maintenance needs to be an inherent part of any informatics strategy.

Systems maintenance is a stage of both the bespoke and package development life cycle (Chapter 25). One might argue that tailoring a software package to the specific requirements of some organisation is a form of maintenance. Unfortunately in many organisations systems maintenance is not seen as a valued activity either by developers themselves or by the organisation at large. Therefore it is not surprising to find that there is an underdeveloped literature on the area of systems maintenance (Swanson, 1992).

Surveys of the cost of maintenance to organisations suggest that for old information technology systems the cost of maintenance can be as much as five times greater than the cost of development. The average programmer can spend as much as fifty per cent of his or her time maintaining existing systems.

Since maintenance is a significant activity for many organisations, this suggests that systems maintenance must be managed as a process. There are various ways in which this may be achieved. Some strategies are suggested below:

- *Maintenance teams*. Organisations may initiate specialist maintenance teams responsible for modifying, fixing and updating information technology systems. Reward structures can be created which reward good maintenance activity.

- *Flexibility analysis*. Systems can be designed with maintenance in mind. Systems can be designed to be as flexible as possible in terms of likely future changes. This is termed flexibility analysis (Fitzgerald, 2000).

- *Configuration management*. Effective configuration management is a necessary condition for effective maintenance. Every IT system configuration in the organisation must be documented as fully as possible.

- *Rejuvenation of ageing systems*. Planning for the upgrade of ageing systems onto new software, hardware and communication environments should be an essential part of any information technology strategy.

32.4 🌀 CONFIGURATION MANAGEMENT

Configuration management is an umbrella activity applied throughout the development process. Configuration management is a key activity of the informatics service and involves the following activities:

- Identifying changes to products of the development process
- Controlling the changes made to products
- Ensuring that the changes are properly made
- Reporting the changes to others

Products of the development process include programs, data structures and documentation. Each type of product may be subject to change at various points during the development process. For instance, in terms of changes to documentation, changes may be made to requirements specifications during analysis or test plans during construction. Such changes may hence be made to the development information system and to the developing information technology system. Both form elements of what we might call the project repository – an organised collection of all output from the development process.

Configuration management overlaps with systems maintenance but is also distinct from it. Systems maintenance occurs after the system is delivered to the customer. Configuration management is a set of monitoring and control activities that begins with the start of some development project and terminates only when the system is taken out of operation.

Configuration management is an important element of quality assurance. Quality assurance is a planned and systematic pattern of all the actions necessary to provide adequate confidence that some system conforms to established requirements. Quality assurance is a form of evaluation activity.

A configuration management process works with baselines established in the project repository. A baseline is a version of a development product that is formally reviewed and agreed upon. Any changes to a baseline involve formal change control procedures.

A simplified configuration management process is illustrated in Figure 32.3. Any person wishing to make a change to a baseline will access the product in the project repository. Control will be in place to ensure that only authorised persons are allowed access to certain development products. Once the changes have been made the modified product is subject to a formal review. This review will consider such issues as the impact of the change on other aspects of the repository and will review the suitability and validity of releasing the change into the project repository. If the change is sanctioned then the approved product is released into the project repository and forms the next baseline for development work.

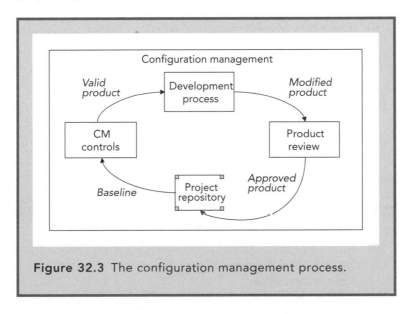

Figure 32.3 The configuration management process.

32.5 SUMMARY

- Maintenance is the process of making needed changes to the structure of some information system.
- We may distinguish between corrective, perfective, adaptive and preventative maintenance of information systems.
- Maintenance is a significant activity for most organisations.
- Maintenance should be planned for and managed by informatics services.
- Configuration management is an umbrella activity applied throughout the development process involving: identifying changes to products of the development process; controlling the changes made to products; ensuring that the changes are properly made; and reporting the changes to others.

32.6 QUESTIONS

(i) Define the term *systems maintenance*.

(ii) List some of the major reasons for systems maintenance.

(iii) Distinguish between corrective, adaptive and perfective maintenance.

(iv) Why would an organisation maintain explicit maintenance teams?

(v) Explain the importance of configuration management to effective maintenance.

32.7 EXERCISES

(i) How much of some organisation's informatics service activity is taken up in maintenance?

(ii) Break down the levels of maintenance into the categories of perfective, corrective and adaptive maintenance.

(iii) What strategies has an organisation taken to manage maintenance activity more effectively?

(iv) Develop a brief configuration management strategy for a small-scale development.

32.8 PROJECTS

(i) In terms of the reasons for maintenance described in this chapter, determine the relative occurrence of each reason amongst the maintenance portfolio of some organisation.

(ii) Investigate the area of Web site maintenance. What particular problems arise in this specialised area of software development?

(iii) In terms of one operational information system, attempt to determine the levels of perfective, corrective adaptive and preventative maintenance that have been applied to it.

(iv) Determine the degree to which organisations exercise effective configuration management strategies.

32.9 REFERENCES

Swanson, E. B. (1992). *Maintaining Information Systems in Organisations*. John Wiley, Chichester.

Fitzgerald, G. (2000). Adaptability and flexibility in IS development. In *Business Information Technology Management: Alternative and Adaptive Futures* (eds. R. Hackney and D. Dunn). Macmillan, London, pp. 13–24.

PART 7

PLANNING

When we are planning for posterity, we ought to remember that virtue is not hereditary.

Thomas Paine (1737–1809)

Because of the centrality of informatics to organisational activity, information, information systems and information technology have to planned for. This part describes a number of issues in the area of informatics planning:

- Organisational analysis is the process that ideally should be undertaken prior to informatics planning and subsequent to the formulation of organisation strategy (Chapter 20). It involves the identification of key organisational processes and implementing the redesign of such processes (Chapter 33).

- Informatics planning is the process of developing an informatics strategy (Chapter 34). It is the process devoted to planning closer alignment of information systems, better utilisation of informatics resources and more effective management of information, information systems and information technology within organisations.

- An informatics strategy is a plan for the application of information, information systems and information technology in support of organisational strategy (Chapter 35).

- Strategic information systems are particularly relevant to strategy and are considered in Chapter 36. Strategic IS are those systems which have a direct impact on the competitive position of the organisation.

CHAPTER 33

ORGANISATIONAL ANALYSIS

There is nothing more difficult to take in hand, more perilous to conduct, or more uncertain in its success than to take the lead in the introduction of a new order of things.

Niccolo Machiavelli (1469–1527)

LEARNING OUTCOMES

After reading this chapter, you will be able to:

- Define the process of organisational analysis
- Describe the approach of business process redesign to organisational analysis
- Discuss the approach of soft systems analysis to organisational analysis

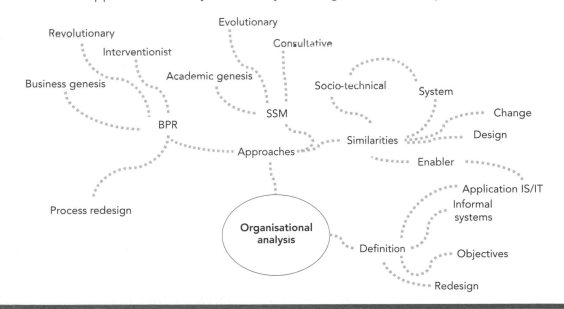

33.1 INTRODUCTION

In this chapter we consider the process of organisational analysis, sometimes called business analysis. A specialist role – the business or organisational analyst – has arisen to meet the need for such activity in organisations. We first define the process of organisational analysis. Then we consider two approaches to conducting organisational analysis: business process re-engineering and soft systems methodology.

Organisational analysis may be part of, or a parallel activity to, business planning, and may occur prior to, or in parallel with, informatics planning. The results of an organisational analysis are also likely to be a significant input into systems design (Chapter 29). Such interactions are illustrated in Figure 33.1.

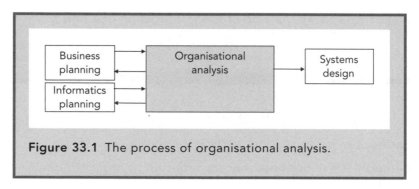

Figure 33.1 The process of organisational analysis.

33.2 ORGANISATIONAL ANALYSIS

The term *organisational analysis* is used in a number of different senses, some of which include:

- The analysis of the informal systems of organisations; that is, those systems of activity that are not formalised in the sense of being written down.
- Analysing the overall objectives and needs of an organisation and identifying the place of the organisation within its environment.
- Considering different ways in which an organisation or part of an organisation may work.
- Identifying the most fruitful place for information systems and information technology within some organisation.

It is the latter two connotations of the term that we focus upon in this chapter.

33.3 APPROACHES TO ORGANISATIONAL ANALYSIS

A number of different approaches exist to conducting organisational analysis. In this chapter we shall consider two distinct approaches: Business Process Re-engineering/Redesign (BPR) and Soft Systems Methodology (SSM).

BPR was originally promoted by Hammer and Champy in the early 1990s (Hammer, 1990; Hammer and Champy, 1993). The key focus of this approach is on business or organisational processes (see Chapter 19) (Hammer, 1996). There is unfortunately no one method for conducting BPR. Instead, there are a range of approaches and techniques.

SSM was originally created by Peter Checkland and his team at the University of Lancaster and focuses on the issue of soft systems (Checkland, 1987; Checkland and Scholes, 1990). This method has been refined in a number of industrial and public sector projects since the 1970s. Hence SSM constitutes a highly dynamic method for organisational analysis.

There are a number of inherent similarities between SSM and BPR:

- Both utilise a systems model of organisations, BPR implicitly and SSM explicitly.

- Both focus on the issue of business change.

- Both assume that organisations can be designed.

- IS and IT are seen as key enablers of business change in both approaches.

- Both maintain that the design of organisational work and the design of IT systems must be considered together. Hence they can both be seen as founded in the socio-technical tradition of organisational thinking (Chapter 16).

There are also some key differences between SSM and BPR:
- BPR had its genesis in the business arena, particularly the US business arena. SSM had its genesis in the academic arena.

- BPR in its original form focuses on radical business transformation, revolutionary change in organisations. SSM focuses on more evolutionary forms of business change.

- BPR is interventionist and top-down. It works with the premise that change should be initiated by managers planning and introducing change into organisations. SSM is consultative and bottom-up. It works with the assumption that representatives of various stakeholder groups should participate in the redesign of organisational activity

We first consider BPR, then briefly review SSM.

33.4 CLASSIC EXAMPLES OF PROCESS REDESIGN

Two classic examples from Hammer (1990) illustrate the essential features of process redesign – one conducted at the Ford motor company and one conducted for IBM.

Ford example |||▶

Hammer (1990) describes an accounts payable process at the Ford motor company that was re-engineered. The accounts payable department originally employed

500 employees. A competitor's accounts payable department had 5 people. Hence Ford set out to reduce the workforce by hundreds to match its competitors. To do this it re-engineered the invoicing process.

The old process is illustrated in Figure 33.2. The purchasing department wrote an order and sent a copy to accounts payable. Later, when the materials control department received goods, it sent a copy of the receiving document to accounts payable. Meanwhile the vendor sent an invoice to accounts payable.

The accounts payable department were hence involved in matching 14 data items between the receipt order, the purchase order and the invoice before it could issue payment to the vendor. In fact, this department spent most of its time trying to sort out mismatches between these three documents.

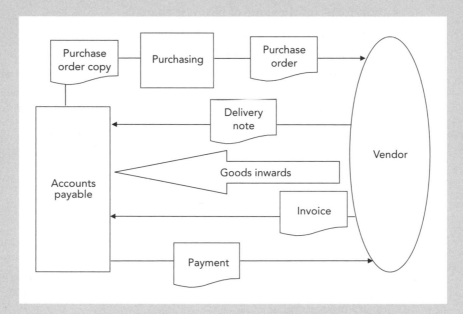

Figure 33.2 The old accounts payable process.

The new process was built using the principle of invoice-less processing (see Figure 33.3). In the new process, the purchasing department now entered order information into a database. No copy of this data was sent to anyone. When goods arrived at the receiving dock, a receiving clerk checked the material against the outstanding purchase record in the database. If they matched, he accepted the goods and payment was automatically sent to the vendor. If they did not match, the order was returned. Hence matching of only three data items was required – part number, unit of measure and supplier code – between a purchase order and a receipt order. Consequently, Ford achieved a 75% cut in head count.

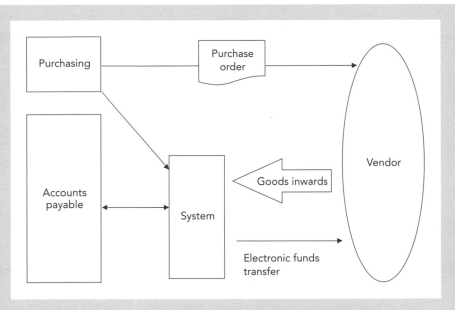

Figure 33.3 The new accounts payable process.

IBM example ▐▐▐▐➤

IBM Credit (Hammer and Champy, 1993) was an organisation devoted to the financing of customers' purchases of IBM hardware.

In the old process, a salesperson called in with a request for financing. One of 14 people logged the request on a paper form. The form was then carried to a department which entered details of the request into a computer system and determined the creditworthiness of the customer. Credit check details were written on to the form and the form was passed to the business practices department, which modified the standard form of loan to suit the customer. Any special terms were attached to the form and it was passed to a pricer who determined, with the help of a spreadsheet, the appropriate interest rate to charge the customer and then delivered this form to a clerical department which turned the information into a quote. The main problem was that the entire process consumed six days on average and valuable customers were lost in the intervening period.

The new process replaced specialists with generalists. One person called a deal structurer dealt with one straightforward order. A computer system was developed to support the deal structurer. This enabled a reduction in turnaround time from six days to four hours.

These two examples, and many others like them, demonstrate a number of key principles underlying process redesign:

- *Several jobs are combined into one*. Jobs evolve from narrow and task-oriented to multidimensional. A case manager provides a single point of contact for a customer.

- *Workers make decisions*. Work units change from functional departments to process teams. Processes cross traditional departmental boundaries.

- *The steps in a process are performed in a 'natural' order*. Work is performed where it makes the most sense, not to suit traditional boundaries or divisions.

- *Checks and controls are reduced*. People's roles change from controlled to empowered. The focus is on performance measures, but reward shifts from activity to results.

- *Information technology is a key enabler in process reengineering*. IT particularly enables traditionally fragmented activities to be stitched back together.

33.5 PHASES OF PROCESS RE-ENGINEERING

Process re-engineering will normally be conducted in terms of a project with an established organisation and resources to conduct the task. Personnel are likely to be seconded to the project from a number of organisational areas and external consultants may be employed on a regular basis.

Figure 33.4 illustrates the major phases of process redesign. The figure constitutes a synthesis of a number of published methods for business process redesign. Organisational analysis will be conducted in association with both business and

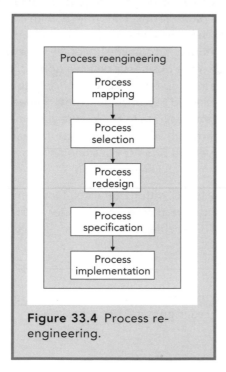

Figure 33.4 Process re-engineering.

informatics planning. The business strategy produced as part of business planning will clearly influence the selection of processes to redesign. Likewise, the redesign of processes will probably demand a substantial degree of IT support and hence will critically affect an organisation's informatics strategy (Chapter 35).

Five major phases are identified on the diagram. The first three stages constitute *unfreezing* activities in the sense that they involve studying current inadequacies in organisation activities and generating plans for new ways of doing things. The last two stages constitute *freezing* activities in the sense that they involve specifying a new process in some detail and implementing the new process within the organisation.

33.5.1 PROCESS MAPPING

This involves constructing a high-level map of organisational processes and indicating on such a map key process boundaries. Some form of systems modelling notation is normally used for this activity.

Example ▶ A high-level process map for the company Texas Instruments is illustrated in Figure 33.5.

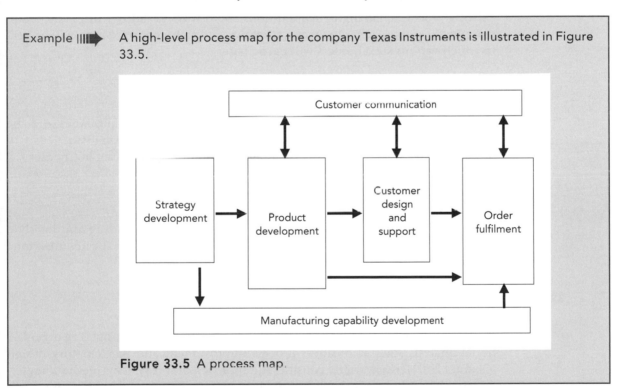

Figure 33.5 A process map.

33.5.2 PROCESS SELECTION

From the process map, particular processes or sub-processes need to be prioritised in terms of the importance of redesign to them. Three sets of criteria may be used to rank processes for redesign:

- *The 'health' of the process*. Clearly, dysfunctional processes need to be identified. The key question is, which processes are in the deepest trouble? Some key indicators of dysfunctional processes include extensive information exchange, redundancy of work and information and unnecessary iteration of tasks.
- *The criticality of the process*. Processes can be ranked on the basis of how important they are to the core competencies of the organisation. The key question here is which processes have the greatest impact on the organisation's performance? Here we are looking for those processes that offer the greatest potential for improving the efficiency and effectiveness of the organisation.
- *Feasibility of redesign*. Some processes are more feasible than others to redesign. This may involve questions of cost or issues such as whether redesign is politically and culturally feasible in the organisation.

33.5.3 PROCESS REDESIGN

This will involve the re-engineering team identifying the problems with the existing process, challenging assumptions about ways of doing things and brainstorming new approaches to organisational activity. Design workshops will be held in which various stakeholders will participate.

33.5.4 PROCESS SPECIFICATION

This phase generally involves the modelling of both existing processes and the design of new processes using some agreed representation formalism. This will usually involve some of the process modelling notation as discussed in Chapter 7.

33.5.5 PROCESS IMPLEMENTATION

This is probably the most difficult phase of process re-engineering and involves introducing new work practices and associated technologies into the organisation.

33.6 SOFT SYSTEMS METHODOLOGY

There are a number of other approaches that suggest ways of conducting organisational analysis such as business process improvement and participatory design (Chapter 29). Here we briefly consider the approach of soft systems methodology.

Figure 33.6 illustrates the essential elements of soft systems methodology. We first must have a situation in everyday life that is regarded by at least one person as being problematic. The situation, being part of human affairs, will be the product of a particular history. Facing up to the problem situation are some 'would-be-improvers' of it. These persons are the users of SSM. They are what we called stakeholders in Chapter 13.

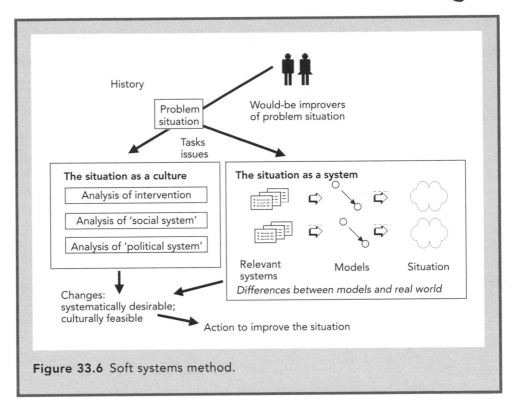

Figure 33.6 Soft systems method.

Soft systems methodology follows two interacting streams of enquiry: a stream of cultural enquiry, and a stream of logic-based enquiry. Both streams may be regarded as stemming from the perception of purposeful actions (tasks) in the problem situation and various things about which there are disagreements (issues).

On the right-hand side of Figure 33.6 is a stream of enquiry in which a number of models of human activity systems are used to illuminate the problem situation. This is accomplished by comparing the models with the perceptions of the real-world situation. These comparisons serve to structure a debate about change.

The left-hand side of Figure 33.6 consists of three examinations of the problem situation. The first examines the intervention itself, since this will inevitably effect some change in the problem situation. The second examines the situation as a 'social system', the third as a 'political system'. This is similar to considering the structure and culture of organisations as described in Part 4.

The logic-driven stream and the cultural stream interact. Which selected human activity systems are found relevant to people in the problem situation will be determined by the culture in which it is immersed.

SSM, like BPR, is interested in organisational change. Human activity systems (HAS) are a central concept for SSM and have much similarity with the organisational processes of BPR. SSM engages in a type of process mapping phase by modelling HAS using techniques such as root definitions. A root definition expresses the core purpose of a human activity system in terms of an input–process–output model (Chapter 3). Checkland has suggested that most useful root definitions be made out of six elements making up the acronym CATWOE:

- *Customers*. The victims or beneficiaries of the transformation
- *Actors*. Those who would do the transformation
- *Transformation*. The conversion of input to output
- *Weltanschauung*. The world view which makes the transformation meaningful
- *Owners*. Those that could stop the transformation
- *Environmental constraints*. Elements outside the system which it takes as given

The core of CATWOE is the pairing of transformation with the world view, which makes it meaningful. For any human activity system there will always be a number of different transformations by means of which it can be expressed, these deriving from different interpretations or world views of its purpose. The other elements of the mnemonic add the ideas that someone must undertake the purposeful activity, someone could stop it, someone will be its victim or beneficiary, and that the system will take some environmental constraints as a given.

Example ▐▐▐▶ Consider a university as an example. A number of stakeholders exist in this organisation, each with a different world view as to its purpose. For example, a student's world view might be characterised as follows:

- C – Myself

- A – Other students, lecturers and administrators

- T – The process of attending modules, achieving satisfactory assessments and getting a degree

- W – That higher education is a passage to better job prospects

- O – The lecturers and administrators

- E – The British higher education system

Root definitions provide the material for constructing conceptual models. These represent pictorial representations of key relationships between the minimum necessary activities needed to support the key transformation process. Such conceptual models have many elements of similarity with the system models presented in Chapter 3.

33.7 🌀 SUMMARY

- Organisational analysis is the process of analysing objectives and needs, considering alternatives and designing new forms of activity with consideration of the enabling role of information systems and information technology.

- We have considered two distinct approaches to organisational analysis: BPR and SSM.

- BPR – commercial genesis; emphasis on revolutionary change.
- SSM – academic genesis; emphasis on evolutionary change.
- Process re-engineering involves the following phases: process mapping, process selection, process redesign, process specification and process implementation.
- SSM uses the idea of a soft system to model alternatives to organisational activities.

33.8 QUESTIONS

(i) Define the term *organisational analysis*.

(ii) Describe the differences between BPR and SSM.

(iii) Describe the similarities between BPR and SSM.

(iv) List the key principles of process redesign.

(v) List the key activities of process redesign.

(vi) What is meant by a root definition in SSM?

(vii) Explain the acronym CATWOE.

33.9 EXERCISES

(i) Develop a process specification of both the before and after process for some other classic re-engineering exercise.

(ii) Consider the suitability of some organisation process known to you for re-engineering in terms of the three criteria listed in this chapter.

(iii) Think about which of the organisational analysis approaches – BPR or SSM – is most suited to application in business organisations. Why?

(iv) Produce a CATWOE definition for some organisational process from each stakeholder perspective.

33.10 PROJECTS

(i) Determine how often organisational analysis is conducted in organisations.

(ii) Conduct a small process re-engineering exercise in terms of a small business process.

(iii) Conduct a detailed analysis of the similarities and differences between business process re-engineering and soft systems methodology.

(iv) How many process re-engineering exercises rely on IT?

(v) BPR exercises have been seen as subject to high failure rates. Investigate why this is the case.

33.11 REFERENCES

Checkland, P. (1987). *Systems Thinking, Systems Practice*. John Wiley, Chichester.

Checkland, P. and Scholes, J. (1990). *Soft Systems Methodology in Action*. John Wiley, Chichester.

Hammer, M. (1990). Re-engineering work: Don't automate, obliterate. *Harvard Business Review*, July–August, pp. 18–25.

Hammer, M. (1996). *Beyond Re-engineering: how the process-centred organisation is changing our lives*. HarperCollins, London.

Hammer, M. and Champy, J. (1993). *Reengineering the Corporation: a Manifesto for Business Revolution*. Nicholas Brearley, London.

CHAPTER 34

INFORMATICS PLANNING

What business strategy is all about; what distinguishes it from all other kinds of business planning – is, in a word, competitive advantage. Without competitors there would be no need for strategy, for the sole purpose of strategic planning is to enable the company to gain, as effectively as possible, a sustainable edge over its competitors

Keniche Ohnae

LEARNING OUTCOMES

After reading this chapter, you will be able to:

● Define informatics planning and to consider its value to the organisation

● Describe three approaches to informatics planning

● Relate the phases of top-down informatics planning

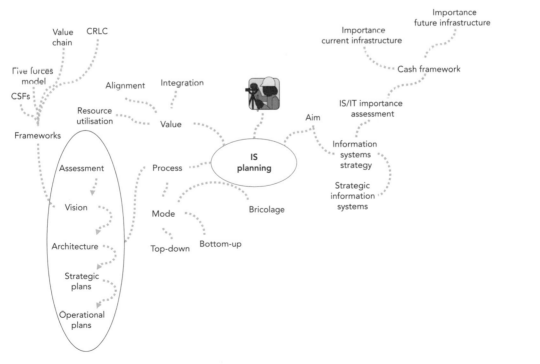

Informatics planning is the process of deciding upon the optimal informatics architecture (Chapter 21) for some organisation. Informatics planning is the process of planning the transformation of one informatics architecture into another. Informatics management is the process of putting plans into action and monitoring performance against plans. The informatics planning process is illustrated in Figure 34.1.

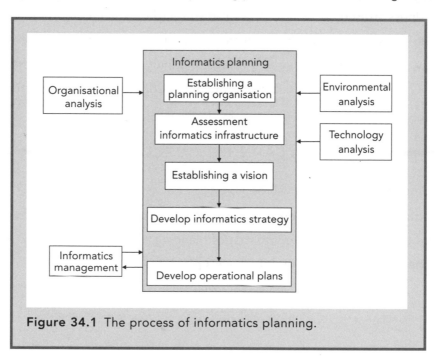

Figure 34.1 The process of informatics planning.

Three major forms of analysis have an input into the planning process. Organisational analysis feeds information concerning the shape of current organisational activities and plans for changes to such activities. An environmental analysis inputs information concerning current and future trends in the immediate environment of the organisation. A technology analysis will provide information concerning the trends in information technology that are likely to impact upon the organisation in the short to medium term future.

The objective of informatics planning is to develop an informatics strategy. The practical output of informatics planning is a document (or documents) which describes strategy in this area.

An informatics strategy can be described as being the structure within which information, information systems and information technology is applied within the organisation. Such a strategy should establish an organisation's long-term infrastructure that will allow information systems to be designed and implemented efficiently and effectively. An informatics strategy is particularly directed at avoiding fragmentation, redundancy and inconsistency amongst information systems in the organisation. The strategy should also be directed at ensuring an effective 'fit' between an organisation and its information systems.

34.2 THE VALUE OF INFORMATICS PLANNING

One of the inherent messages from work in this area is that informatics planning must take place within the context of general business planning. There are a number of advantages to effective informatics planning:

- *Closer alignment of information systems.* Informatics planning is important in ensuring that there is a close match between the proposed direction of an organisation and its information services. Informatics planning can be used to ensure that IS projects more clearly focus on business rather than purely technical objectives.
- *Better utilisation of informatics resources.* Planning facilitates effective resource allocation. It becomes easier to estimate the effect (risk) of proposed IS projects in terms of business objectives and evaluate current systems in terms of effectiveness. Planning should lead to greater integration of both current and future information systems.
- *More effective informatics management.* Good planning is a necessary part of good management of information systems. Planning is likely to improve the ability of an organisation to react better to unforeseen circumstances.

Having said this, the value of informatics planning varies in terms of the type of organisation. Cash *et al.* (1992) make the important point that the value of informatics planning varies with the type of organisation discussed in Chapter 21:

- Since *strategic* companies are critically dependent on smooth IS functioning, both now and in the future, such organisations benefit from considerable amounts of informatics planning.
- *Turnaround* companies also need a substantial informatics planning effort, since although current organisational effectiveness is not critically dependent on IS, future performance is critically dependent on future IS.
- In *factory* organisations mass effort in informatics planning is probably not needed, although year by year operational planning is still essential.
- In *support* organisations there is a tendency to assume that such organisations need little if any informatics planning. The danger, however, is that opportunities may arise in evolving technology that may be missed by such organisations.

34.3 APPROACHES TO INFORMATICS PLANNING

There are three major approaches to informatics planning:

- *Bottom-up*. Planning may be conducted in a bottom-up way on a needs basis. This is a bottom-up approach in the sense that when a specific organisational need calls for a new information system, some form of formal planning process is set in motion.

- *Top-down*. The classic literature on informatics planning emphasises the benefits of a top-down and corporate-wide approach. In this approach an informatics strategy is either produced in parallel with a business strategy, or becomes an inherent part of the business planning process.

- *Middle-out*. Recent work has suggested that while top-down approaches are valuable, they fail to take account of the informal/*ad hoc* nature of much informatics planning work. Ciborra and Jelassi (1994) have argued that this means that strategic information systems (Chapter 36) are unlikely to be created using top-down approaches. Effective IS must continually filter up from the bottom to the top layers of the organisation through a continuous process of bricolage – creative experimentation. This is similar to the conclusion of Currie (1994), who contrasts the formal models of the strategy planning process with what she calls the 'adhocracy' of actual informatics planning.

34.4 ⊚ THE PROCESS OF INFORMATICS PLANNING

The top-down approach to informatics planning is certainly the best documented and hence it is the approach to which we devote the most attention. Some generic phases for the informatics planning process are listed below and are illustrated in Figure 34.1. These phases can be adapted to bottom-up and middle-out approaches.

- Setting up an informatics planning organisation and method
- Assessment of the current informatics infrastructure
- Establishing a vision for organisational informatics
- Specifying the informatics strategy
- Developing strategic plans for informatics
- Developing operational plans for informatics

The form of an informatics strategy is discussed in Chapter 35. Therefore we devote most attention here to the remaining phases of planning.

34.5 ⊚ SETTING UP AN INFORMATICS PLANNING ORGANISATION AND METHOD

To develop an informatics strategy, an organisation first usually evaluates a number of existing planning methods, then generally selects a method for informatics planning or customises its own. The organisation then usually sets up a committee of users and IS specialists. It relies on the training provided by the method to guide the planning study. Next the committee carries out the multiple phases of the study, generally lasting several months, sometimes years. It uses existing documentation and interviews with organisational stakeholders to define its current business processes and data. It also studies how the current information systems support these processes and data. Using its documented understanding, the committee then identifies and prioritises its key IS for the future together with an implementation schedule. It prepares a report that includes a long-range plan with recommendations for hardware, software, data, communications and personnel support.

34.6 ASSESSMENT

Any planning process must begin with an assessment of the current situation. Current performance is compared with some set of objectives. Business and informatics objectives would be expected to result from both a business planning and an organisational analysis exercise (Chapter 33).

The informatics planning process should begin with an assessment of the use of information, information systems and information technology in the entire organisation as well as an assessment of the work of the informatics service. Such an assessment may be conducted by a committee composed of both informatics professionals and user-managers. Some representation may be provided by some outside organisation, particularly informatics consultancies.

An informatics assessment will probably document current levels of information, IS and IT use and compare them against some set of standards, perhaps produced as benchmarks of past performance or by analysing industry norms. A technical assessment of current information systems and technology infrastructure will also form part of the picture as well as an assessment of current attitudes to information systems and IT within the organisation.

Another important part of the assessment will be a review of the mission of the informatics service. This will address the important issue: what are the reasons for having an informatics service? Such reasons can be classified under three major headings: efficiency, effectiveness and competitiveness.

- *Efficiency*. Is the informatics service helping the organisation to remain active with the minimum of resources?
- *Effectiveness*. Is the informatics service helping the organisation to spend its time doing the right things?
- *Competitiveness*. Is the informatics service engaged in projects that will improve the position of the organisation in its environment?

Many organisations are clearly answering *no* to questions such as these and hence considering other options to an internal informatics service, such as facilities management and outsourcing (Chapter 40). Outsourcing is the idea of transferring the whole or part of the informatics service, particularly support activities, to outside suppliers. Facilities management is the idea of also transferring the management of the informatics infrastructure to outside contractors.

34.7 VISION

Establishing a vision normally involves assessing the competitive advantage (Chapter 20) that information systems may deliver. A number of frameworks have been proposed for assessing competitive advantage afforded by information systems such as:

- Critical success factors
- Five forces model
- Customer life cycle
- Value chain (the value chain has been discussed in Chapter 19)

34.7.1 CRITICAL SUCCESS FACTORS

Any organisation needs to identify areas in which it has relative superiority, and to use that superiority both to create barriers to entry as well as to launch strategic offensives. One popular method of doing this is the critical success factor concept, or CSF. A CSF is a factor which is deemed crucial to the success of a business. Consequently, CSFs are those areas that must be given special attention by management. They also represent critical points of leverage for achieving competitive advantage. There are normally only a few CSFs – perhaps between three and eight – for each organisation. CSFs follow the 80/20 rule – that only a few issues really count in terms of organisational effectiveness.

CSFs are usually contrasted with CFFs or critical failure factors. A CFF is an aspect of the organisation, the poor management of which is likely to precipitate organisational failure.

Example ▐▐▐▶ A CSF for a chain of high street jewellers is likely to be location of its outlets. A CSF for a health authority is likely to be the quality or standard of service it gives to its customers – patients.

A CFF for the high street jeweller chain is likely to be a high amount of shrinkage in consumer demand. A CFF for a health authority might be poor coordination of its staff, particularly subcontracted staff.

CSFs and CFFs are useful ways of identifying areas for the maximal application of information systems. A high street jeweller chain, for instance, would benefit from an information system which enabled managers to select optimal locations for their stores based on factors such as population density and the state of the local

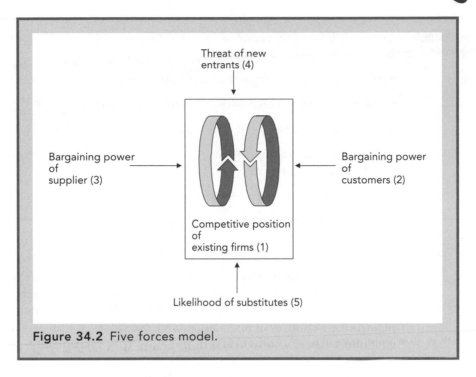

Figure 34.2 Five forces model.

economy. In contrast, a health authority would benefit from an information system which ensured the efficient work scheduling of nursing staff.

34.7.2 FIVE FORCES MODEL

Another framework for assessing competitive advantage is based on the work of Porter and Millar (1985). They argue that a successful firm shapes the structure of competition by influencing five primary forces (Figure 34.2):

- Industrial rivalry: the competitive position of rival organisations
- Customer bargaining power
- Supplier bargaining power
- Barriers to entry: threat of new entrants
- Threat of substitutes

Many combinations of these factors, such as low industrial rivalry, high barriers to entry, and low buyer bargaining power, can lead to sustainable, above-average, long-term profits. Information systems can be used to achieve such goals by:

- Changing the basis of competition
- Strengthening customer relationships
- Overcoming supplier problems
- Building barriers against new entrants
- Generating new products or services

> Example ‖‖➡ Customer information systems for marketing and sales can have a strategic impact by:
>
> - Winning customers from the competition by using a large customer database
>
> - Use of market research databases to target customer 'need'
>
> - Use of telemarketing and direct mailing to improve sales
>
> - The cost of setting up and maintaining an accurate customer database being a considerable barrier to entry
>
> - Introducing electronic shopping as a new service

34.7.3 THE CUSTOMER RESOURCE LIFE CYCLE

Ives and Learmonth (1984) define an information system as being strategic if it changes a company's product or the way a firm competes in its industry (Chapter 22). They use the idea of a customer resource life cycle to identify potential strategic information systems. This model considers a firm's relationship with its customers (the customer chain) and how this relationship can be changed or enhanced by the strategic application of IT.

The customer resource life cycle is discussed as a sequence of 13 stages:

- *Establish requirements*. To determine how much of a resource is required.
- *Specify*. To detail the attributes of the required resource.
- *Select a source*. Locate an appropriate supplier for the resource.
- *Order*. To order a quantity of the resource from the supplier.
- *Authorise and pay*. Before a resource can be acquired, authority for the expenditure must be obtained and payment made.
- *Acquire*. To take possession of the resource.
- *Test and accept*. The customer must verify the acceptability of the resource before putting it to use.
- *Integrate*. The resource must be added to an existing inventory.
- *Monitor*. Ensure that the resource remains acceptable while in inventory.
- *Upgrade*. If requirements change, it may be necessary to upgrade resources.
- *Maintain*. To repair a resource, if necessary.
- *Transfer or dispose*. Customers will eventually dispose of a resource.
- *Account for*. Customers must monitor where and how money is spent on resources.

> Example ‖‖➡ The idea of a customer resource life cycle is relevant to both private sector and public sector organisations, such as the UK National Health Service (NHS). In this

setting, the patient is the primary health service customer. The patient consumes a health service resource. A possible customer resource life cycle might then be:

- *Requirements specification*. IT can be used as a means to aid the general practitioner (GP) and the patient in establishing what health resource is required and what quantity of the resource is required.

- *Selection*. A series of options can be presented to the patient regarding, for instance, a number of hospitals able to offer a given treatment.

- *Order*. The GP would be able to query a hospital's elective admission system to find out when a stay is feasible at the hospital. If it suits the patient a provisional booking could be made on the system.

- *Authorise and payment*. Appropriate routines would update the treatment accounts of the hospital and the budget of the general practice.

- *Acquire*. When the patient arrives for a stay in hospital, his or her details would be transferred from the GP's system to the patient administration system of the hospital.

- *Test*. The patient would be given a listing of the proposed treatment and requested to sign it off.

- *Integrate*. The consumption of the health care resource would be added to the patient history held at the centralised register of the region.

- *Monitor and upgrade*. Preliminary investigation may change the initial prognosis leading to modification of the original health care plan. Any changes or additions to the plan would be recorded by hospital systems.

- *Maintain*. Regular checkups will be made of patients to ensure effective functioning. Such checkups will be notified to patients by the GP system, and the results recorded by the system.

- *Accountability*. The patient receives a report of every treatment concluded with the cost it has associated with the health service budget.

34.8 STRATEGIC PLANS

An informatics services strategic plan sets goals for this organisational function within some future time frame and will normally comprise:

- *A statement concerning the organisation of the informatics services function*. For instance, prior planning processes should have already established the basis for the financial control of the service. Two main options are normally considered: that of an unallocated cost centre in which a budget is delivered directly to the service and consequently user departments do not pay directly for informatics work; and that of an allocated cost centre and charge-out, in which informatics budgets are delivered to user departments and the service charges user departments for services.

- *An identification of how informatics can align itself with business strategy.* Cash *et al.* (1992) discuss the important difficulty of aligning informatics strategy with business strategy in that business strategy generally considers a 1 year frame for reference, whereas informatics strategy must consider a 3–5 year frame of reference. One attempt to improve the coupling between business and informatics is to create a seat on the board for a chief information officer or CIO.

- *A portfolio of development plans for IS.*

- *A portfolio of maintenance plans for IS.* Maintenance is a critical informatics activity that must be planned for.

- *A portfolio of operational and support plans for IS*, including training and help desks.

34.9 OPERATIONAL PLANS

Operational plans relate the activity of the informatics service with goals and budgets. Operational plans would normally include:

- A description of development projects with associated resource implications and costing

- A description of maintenance activity and associated resource implications and costing

- A description of operational effort and associated resource implications and costing

- A description of planning and management activity and associated resource implications and costing

34.10 SUMMARY

- Informatics planning is the process of formulating an optimal information systems strategy for some organisation.

- The value of informatics planning varies in terms of the type of organisation.

- Informatics planning can be conducted using a bottom-up, top-down or middle-out approach.

- Classic phases for informatics planning include setting up a planning organisation, assessing the informatics infrastructure, establishing a vision of how the organisation should use information systems, developing the information systems architecture, developing the information services strategic plan, and developing information services operational plans and budgets.

- Establishing a vision normally involves assessing the competitive advantage that information systems may deliver. A number of frameworks have been used for assessing competitive advantage such as the five forces model, the value chain, critical success factors and the customer resource life cycle.
- It is critical to assess the position of the informatics service in plans.

34.11 QUESTIONS

(i) Describe some of the key benefits of engaging in systematic informatics planning.

(ii) What sort of organisations will most benefit from informatics planning?

(iii) What are the three main ways of engaging in informatics planning?

(iv) Describe some of the key phases of conducting top-down informatics planning.

(v) List some of the major approaches to establishing a vision for informatics in some organisation.

(vi) Define what is meant by a critical success factor.

(vii) Describe the five forces in Porter's model.

(viii) List the major phases of the customer resource life cycle.

(ix) How do strategic plans differ from operational plans?

34.12 EXERCISES

(i) Assess the current state of information systems in some organisation known to you.

(ii) Develop a small analysis of how information systems might be used to improve the strategic position of some organisation using one or more of the frameworks discussed in the unit.

(iii) List two critical success factors for an organisation known to you.

(iv) Produce one other example of how information systems may impact upon Porter's five forces model.

(v) From the frameworks discussed, choose what you feel to be the most effective framework and briefly justify your choice.

34.13 PROJECTS

(i) Investigate the degree to which a limited sample of organisations conduct systematic informatics planning. Determine the forms of informatics planning undertaken.

(ii) Find an organisation that conducts informatics planning. Determine the key benefits experienced by this organisation.

(iii) The customer resource life cycle can be seen as a model of the customer chain. Determine its applicability for B2C e-commerce.

(iv) Analyse either B2B or B2C e-commerce in terms of Porter's five forces model.

34.14 ⊚ REFERENCES

Cash, J. I., McFarlan, F. W. and McKenney, J. L. (1992). *Corporate Information Systems Management*, 3rd edn. Richard Irwin, Homewood, IL.

Ciborra, C. and Jelassi, T. (1994). *Strategic Information Systems: a European Perspective*. John Wiley, Chichester.

Currie, W. (1994). The strategic management of a large-scale IT project in the financial services sector. *New Technology, Work and Employment*, **9**(1), 19–29.

Ives, B. and Learmonth, G. P. (1984). The information system as a competitive weapon. *Communications of the ACM*, **27**(12), 1193–1201.

Porter, M. E. and Millar, V. E. (1985). How information gives you competitive advantage. *Harvard Business Review*, **63**(4), 149–160.

CHAPTER 35

INFORMATICS STRATEGY

LEARNING OUTCOMES

After reading this chapter, you will be able to:

● Define the key elements of an informatics strategy
● Explain the links between an informatics strategy and informatics planning
● Relate the role of strategic information systems in an informatics strategy

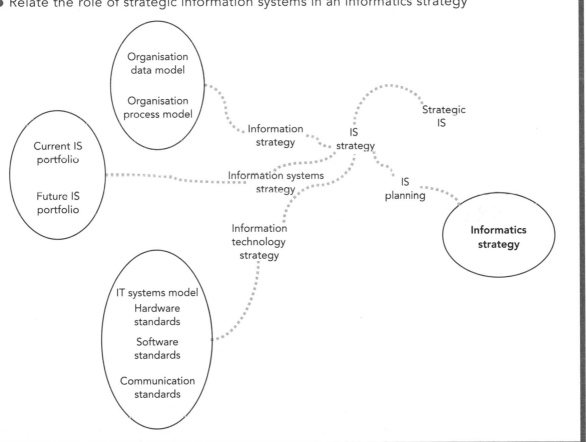

35.1 ⦿ INTRODUCTION

In this chapter we consider the issue of informatics strategy. We consider the key elements of such strategy and explain the links between an informatics strategy and informatics planning. We also consider the role of strategic information systems within an informatics strategy. Developing an informatics strategy is a key aspect of strategic decision-making (Chapter 6) in organisations.

35.2 ⦿ INFORMATICS STRATEGY

An informatics strategy defines the structure within which information, information systems and information technology is to be applied within an organisation over some future time frame. The term *strategy* implies a future reference. Informatics planning is the process of defining an informatics strategy. Organisation or business planning (the process of defining organisation strategy) drives informatics planning. Therefore, ideally, an informatics strategy should be closely aligned with an organisation strategy.

An informatics strategy will be constrained by an existing informatics architecture (Chapter 21). Very few organisations are able to build a 'clean slate' or a 'green field' strategy. Usually existing information needs, information systems and information technology have to be taken into account in terms of formulating strategy in this area.

However, an informatics strategy should be directed at ensuring an optimal 'fit' between an organisation and its information systems. Strategy implies the attempt to improve a current situation. An informatics strategy should define the future of both support and strategic information systems for some organisation.

35.3 ⦿ COMPONENTS OF AN INFORMATICS STRATEGY

An informatics strategy can be divided into three major layers:

- *Information strategy*. This details the information needs of the organisation and processes necessary to collect, produce, store and disseminate information.
- *Information systems strategy*. This consists of a specification of the information systems needed to support organisational activity in the areas of collection, storage, dissemination and use of information.
- *Information technology strategy*. This consists of a specification of the hardware, software, data, communication facilities and IT knowledge and skills needed by the organisation to support its information systems.

Ideally, each of these elements of strategy will support the other. The information needed by the organisation will determine the information systems it requires. In turn, the information systems needed will determine the information technology required.

The objective of informatics planning is to develop strategy in each of these three areas. The practical output of informatics planning is a document-set which describes strategy in these three areas. An informatics strategy can be described as being the structure within which information, information systems and information technology are intended to be applied within the organisation. Such a strategy should establish an organisation's long-term infrastructure that will allow information systems to be designed and implemented efficiently and effectively. An informatics strategy is particularly directed at avoiding fragmentation, redundancy and inconsistency amongst information systems in the organisation, whilst increasing the interoperability of such systems. The strategy should hence be directed at ensuring an effective 'fit' between an organisation and its information systems.

35.4 INFORMATICS STRATEGY AND ORGANISATIONAL FIT

One of the proposed benefits of having an explicit informatics strategy is to encourage a closer fit between an organisation's activities and its information systems. The question remains how do we measure this fit? Four aspects of an organisation's informatics infrastructure that may be measured and which can be used to determine elements of fit are the levels of fragmentation, redundancy, inconsistency and interoperability in the informatics infrastructure:

- *Fragmentation*. Poor fit is evident in the situation in which data is fragmented across information systems, usually because IS emulate structural divisions within the organisation and because organisational units put up barriers of ownership around data sets. Fragmentation may also be evident in processing where separate IT systems communicate through manual interfaces.

- *Redundancy*. Poor fit is evident when large amounts of data are unnecessarily replicated across information systems, usually because interfaces do not exist between systems, causing the same data to be entered many times. Redundancy may also be present when separate systems perform the same effective processing on data.

- *Inconsistency*. Poor fit is evident when the same data is held differently in different systems or processed differently by different systems, leading to inconsistencies in the ways in which information is produced, stored and disseminated.

- *Interoperability*. The property of interoperability is related to the other three. Generally speaking those systems that are fragmented, redundant and inconsistent are likely to suffer from poor levels of interoperability. This refers to the level to which systems communicate and cooperate within the infrastructure.

Situations subject to fragmentation, redundancy and inconsistency create a series of information 'islands' within the organisation. The existence of such islands makes it difficult to model the organisation in terms of its information. Hence operational managers find it difficult to plan effectively on a day-to-day basis and strategic managers (Chapter 6) find it difficult to plan for the medium and long-term future.

35.5 ⊚ INFORMATION STRATEGY

An information strategy details the information needs of the organisation and the processes necessary to collect, produce, store and disseminate information. However, there is no agreement as to the form an information strategy should take. As a minimum, Figure 35.1 details the three major elements of an information strategy:

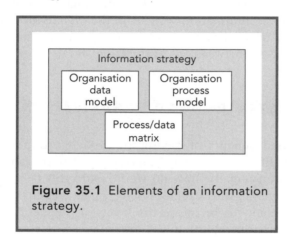

Figure 35.1 Elements of an information strategy.

- *Organisation data model.* An organisation data model details the structure of the major data elements used by the organisation plus the relationships between such data elements. For medium- to large-scale organisations, such a data model will necessarily be expressed at quite a high level.

- *Organisation process model.* An organisation process model details the necessary information collection, storage, dissemination and use activities within the organisation, again at a suitably high-level of generality. Such a process model corresponds closely to the idea of a process map discussed in Chapter 33, but focuses particularly upon information processes.

- *Process/data matrix.* This documents which data elements are used by which processes. It allows managers and developers to identify key clusters of common applications and databases. It can also be used to identify key business objects.

Alternatively one could document an information strategy using an object model, as discussed in Chapter 7.

Example ‖‖➡ The diagram in Figure 35.2 is a simplified example of an organisation data model for a UK university.

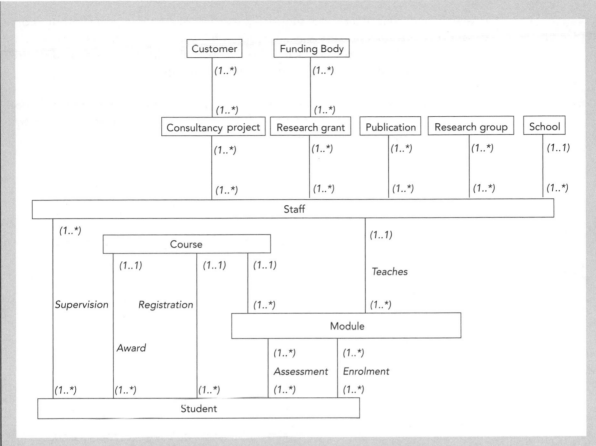

Figure 35.2 University data model.

Example ▶ Figure 35.3 provides an example of an organisation process model for a UK university. There are three main organisational processes in any university – teaching,

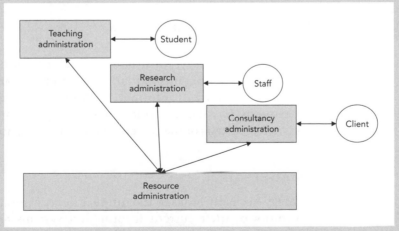

Figure 35.3 University process model.

research and consultancy. To support these we need three main information processes. One other process is included for administering the information needed to manage learning resources such as books, journals, CD-ROMs, and audio and video tapes, as well as other resources such as buildings and staff.

Example ▪▪▪▶ Figure 35.4 illustrates a simplified data/process matrix for a UK university. The shaded boxes indicate which entity on the organisation data model is used by which major organisational process.

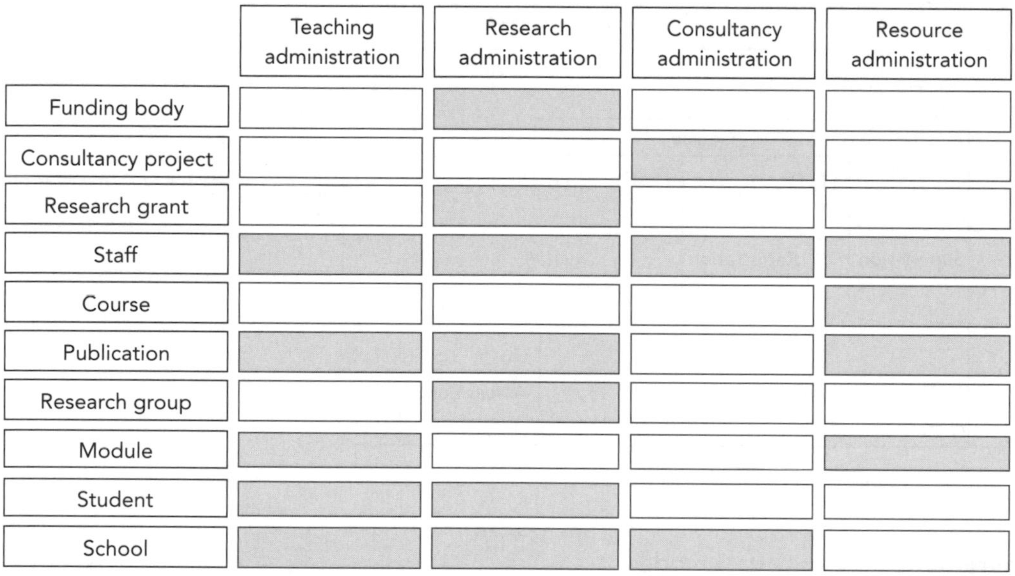

	Teaching administration	Research administration	Consultancy administration	Resource administration
Funding body		▓		
Consultancy project			▓	
Research grant		▓		
Staff	▓	▓	▓	▓
Course				▓
Publication	▓			
Research group		▓		
Module	▓			
Student	▓	▓		
School	▓	▓		

Figure 35.4 A process/data matrix for a university.

35.6 ⊚ INFORMATION SYSTEMS STRATEGY

An information systems strategy consists of a specification of the information systems needed to support organisational activity in the areas of collection, storage, dissemination and use of information. Informatics planning will collate and prioritise requests for new information systems. An information systems strategy should include details of the current and future IS portfolio (Figure 35.5).

35.6.1 CURRENT IS PORTFOLIO

Although a strategy normally looks to the future, most organisations need to build a detailed inventory of their current information systems and the links such systems have with organisation processes. This is a key element of the informatics

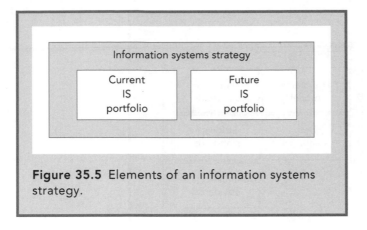

Figure 35.5 Elements of an information systems strategy.

infrastructure (Chapter 21) and should include documentation of non-computerised as well as computerised information systems.

35.6.2 FUTURE IS PORTFOLIO

This should detail the planned information systems projects for the organisation expressed against some reasonable future time frame (3–5 years is commonplace). A future IS portfolio may include projects such as:

- Corrections to existing information systems
- Enhancements to existing information systems
- Major new information systems development projects
- Major new infrastructure systems or technologies that attempt to integrate systems across the organisation
- Research projects investigating new possible information systems and technologies

An information systems strategy should also clearly state how information systems link to supporting current and future organisation processes. This linkage is clearly reliant on effective organisational analysis (Chapter 33) and the identification of core competencies/critical success factors for the organisation (Chapter 34).

35.7 INFORMATION TECHNOLOGY STRATEGY

An information technology strategy consists of the hardware, software, data, communication facilities and IT knowledge and skills needed by the organisation to support its information systems. Figure 35.6 details the five major elements of an information systems strategy:

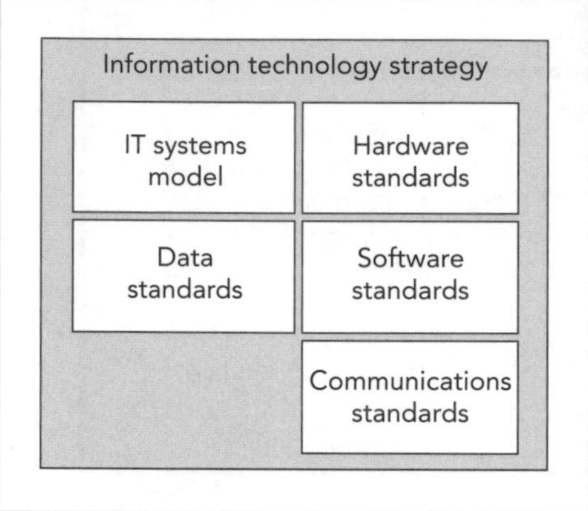

Figure 35.6 Elements of an information technology strategy.

- *IT systems model*. A detailed inventory of both current and future IT systems run by the organisation.
- *Hardware standards*. A listing of standards to be adopted in the areas of computers and peripheral devices.
- *Software standards*. A listing of standard system, communication and application software to be adopted throughout the organisation.
- *Communications standards*. Details of appropriate network standards.
- *Data standards*. Details of data representation and formats.

The major objectives of an IT strategy will be to reduce fragmentation, inconsistency and redundancy amongst information technology systems and improve levels of interoperability between systems. This may be achieved through the purchase of software packages (such as ERP) or the development of new bespoke information systems. Part of the IT strategy must also consider the needed support and maintenance required for both current and planned IT systems.

35.8 SUMMARY

- An informatics strategy defines the structure within which information, information systems and information technology is to be applied within an organisation. An informatics strategy should establish an organisation's long-term informatics infrastructure which will allow information technology systems to be designed and implemented efficiently and effectively.
- An informatics strategy is particularly directed at avoiding fragmentation, redundancy and inconsistency amongst information systems in the organisation. It is also

a key vehicle in promoting interoperability of systems. An informatics strategy should be directed at ensuring an optimal 'fit' between an organisation and its information systems.

- An informatics strategy comprises three levels: an information strategy, an information systems strategy, an information technology strategy.
- An information strategy comprises an organisation data model, an organisation process model and a data/process matrix.
- An information systems strategy comprises documentation of the current IS portfolio and future IS portfolio.
- An information technology strategy includes an IT systems model and standards for hardware, software, communications and data.

35.9 QUESTIONS

(i) Distinguish between an information strategy, an information systems strategy and an information technology strategy.

(ii) Explain the relevance of fragmentation, redundancy and inconsistency as measures of fit between the informatics infrastructure and an organisation.

(iii) Describe the main elements of an information strategy.

(iv) Describe the main elements of an information systems strategy.

(v) Describe the main elements of an information technology strategy.

35.10 EXERCISES

(i) Find one example of fragmented and redundant data in an organisation known to you.

(ii) Determine whether an organisation known to you has an organisation data model.

(iii) Determine whether an organisation known to you has an organisation process model.

(iv) Identify one example of a software standard.

(v) Identify one example of a hardware standard.

35.11 PROJECTS

(i) Collect data on a given organisation's informatics strategy. Does it distinguish between information, information systems and information technology strategies? How was strategy formulated? How is it used and maintained?

(ii) Develop an organisation data model, organisation process model and a data/process matrix for some organisation.

(iii) Develop an information systems strategy based on some established information strategy.

(iv) Develop an information technology strategy based on some established information systems strategy.

(v) Consider outsourcing as an informatics strategy. What are the critical success factors for successful outsourcing of IS?

STRATEGIC INFORMATION SYSTEMS

After reading this chapter, you will be able to:

- Define the concept of a strategic information system and distinguish it from a support information system

- Consider the relevance of a number of cases of strategic IS

- Discuss links between strategic IS, the informatics infrastructure and informatics planning

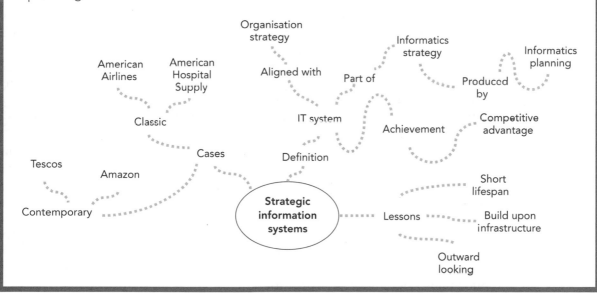

36.1 INTRODUCTION

In this chapter we consider a type of information system known as a strategic information system (SIS). Strategic information systems are IS that impact on the competitive position of the organisation. They are systems that directly support organisational strategy and are critical elements of an organisation's informatics strategy.

In this chapter we distinguish between support and SIS, consider cases of SIS in terms of some generic organisational strategies, discuss the key characteristics of SIS and the relationship of SIS to planning and infrastructure.

36.2 SUPPORT AND STRATEGIC IS

We may generally distinguish between two major types of information systems within organisations:

- *Support IS*. These are information systems which support current human activity systems within the organisation.
- *Strategic IS*. These are information systems which support new human activity systems for the organisation and which have a direct impact on the competitive advantage of the organisation.

Therefore a strategic information system might be defined as any information system that directly assists an organisation in achieving its strategy. In contrast, support IS are part of the current informatics infrastructure of an organisation.

Organisation strategy involves planning changes to the relationship of an organisation with its environment (see Chapter 20). Strategic decision-making involves determining what area of activity an organisation is in and what kinds of activity it will seek to enter. When an information system is used to achieve competitive advantage, it may be referred to as a strategic information system.

Competitive advantage may be defined as the market leverage afforded by some organisational innovation. In terms of information systems the innovation will be in new forms of human activity supported by IT. Hence, in information systems terms, competitive advantage might be defined as the value an information system provides in improving the position of an organisation in its environment.

Porter has argued that there are three major ways in which competitive advantage can be achieved by organisations: cost advantage, differentiation and location (Chapter 20). Strategic information systems are those systems that contribute to one or more of these generic organisational strategies.

36.3 CASES OF STRATEGIC INFORMATION SYSTEMS

In this section we briefly outline a number of information systems that proved successful in improving the competitive advantage of their respective companies.

We classify the examples under the forms of competitive advantage discussed in the previous section.

36.3.1 COST LEADERSHIP

A commercial organisation can gain competitive advantage or leadership by establishing itself as a low-cost leader in the market. Cost advantage is usually achieved by doing things more efficiently.

Food retail loyalty card ‖‖▶

The supermarket chain Tesco introduced a customer loyalty card that awarded discounts to customers on the basis of how much the customer purchased from the retail chain. Tesco used this to exercise a certain element of cost advantage over its competitors.

On-line banking ‖‖▶

A number of UK banks have set up on-line banking facilities. There are a number of reasons why on-line banking offers performance improvements for high street banks. One of the most significant is the low cost of banking transactions on-line as compared to traditional banking services. Hence on-line banking can be seen as a form of SIS for such businesses.

36.3.2 DIFFERENTIATION

A commercial organisation can gain competitive advantage by differentiating its product in the market-place. This generally involves attempting to establish within the market-place the perception that the organisation provides a superior product or service. This may be achieved through improving quality and reliability relative to price, better market understanding, image promotion etc.

American Hospital Supply (AHS) manufactures and distributes a broad range of medical products to doctors, laboratories and hospitals in the USA. Since 1976 it has used an order entry system that directly links its customers to AHS systems. Over 5000 terminals have been installed at customer sites. The system also allows customers to perform their own forecasting, planning and inventory control.

The key strengths of the system are: simplified order-processing for customers; reduced costs for customers and AHS; and the ability of AHS to manage price incentives across their product range. The result is increased customer loyalty and market share. The presence of AHS terminals on-site leads to a switching cost for customers.

American Airlines (AA) used computer and communications technology to build an entirely new business. It developed a reservation system that listed the flight schedules of every major airline on the world. Of the 24,000 automated travel agents in the USA, 48% use the system. The reservation system displayed AA flights on any particular sector on the screen before any other airline's flights. This took advantage of the reservation clerks' natural tendency to choose the first flight offered. This SIS proved so successful that an anti-trust case was brought against AA by other airlines.

Thomson Travel developed a communications network compatible with the British Videotex network (Prestel) for the purpose of providing direct reservations to its customers (travel agencies). As a direct result, Thomson's sales in a given product segment doubled in one year.

36.3.3   LOCATION

A commercial organisation can gain competitive advantage by finding a niche in the market-place for its product or service. This may be achieved in a number of ways. It may offer an entirely new product or service or offer its product or service to a previously untapped group of customers.

Amazon.com ‖‖▶

Internet-based retailing is an obvious area for establishing new ways of delivering products and services. The US-based company Amazon.com was one of the first to sell books and CDs on-line. As such it has established a certain dominance in this segment of e-tailing.

Tesco food retail ‖‖▶

Tesco has established itself as market leader in the electronic retail of foodstuffs. Customers may order foodstuffs over the Internet and have them delivered to their door the same day. This service has now become a key part of the company's future business strategy and has formed a critical part of its alliance with a major US food retailer.

36.3.4   CHARACTERISTICS OF A STRATEGIC IS

An analysis of cases like this provides us with a list of common characteristics of strategic information systems:

- *Integration of information and systems*. Many strategic information systems are built from an established informatics infrastructure. Organisational leverage may frequently be achieved merely by integrating systems and hence allowing more effective information flows in support of business processes.
- *Outward looking*. Many strategic information systems link the organisation more efficiently or effectively with its customers and suppliers. To be of benefit, strategic information systems must offer real value to the customer or supplier.
- *Technology edge*. A strategic information system must not be too easy to copy by competitors. The information system must be able to offer a medium to long-

term impact on organisational performance to justify the investment in its development.

- *New products or services.* A strategic information system must be capable of changing the market-place's perception of the firm. This it may do by enabling it to offer new products or services or offering such products and services in different ways.

- *Management information.* Many strategic information systems are strategic in the sense that they provide high-level management with better information about internal operations and/or the organisation environment, enabling them to plan strategically far more effectively.

36.5 THE CHANGING NATURE OF STRATEGIC IS

An IS is only likely to remain strategic for a limited period of time. Usually the competitive advantage afforded by a given information system will be eroded after a period of time because of emulation by competitors.

Example ‖‖➡ Most travel agents now have links to a range of travel companies through information technology. Also, most of the supermarket chains in the UK emulated the Tesco loyalty card within a matter of months.

However, the first entrant into an SIS area frequently determines standards in terms of technology and its use. Such standardisation normally means that there is usually a 'cost' involved in switching from a first entrant into some market-place for customers. An SIS will therefore offer a strategic advantage to an organisation in intangible as well as tangible ways.

Example ‖‖➡ Thomson's competitors developed similar networks and began operating reservation systems that were technologically superior to Thomson's. However, most travel agencies continued using Thomson's system, alleging they were already familiar with the Thomson system and did not wish to learn how to use the other systems. Thomson's competitors reacted by changing their reservation systems so that agencies could use them in exactly the same way as Thomson's.

36.6 STRATEGIC IS, PLANNING AND THE INFORMATICS INFRASTRUCTURE

A strategic information system cannot be produced from mid-air. Very few organisations are green field sites in the sense that they have no existing informatics infrastructure (Chapter 21). A strategic information system is normally built on top of an existing informatics infrastructure. Some would argue that for strategic systems to prove effective interaction is essential with the fundamental support IS of organisations.

Example ||||➡   A lot of so-called *dot com* companies appear to have failed because they invested too much effort into getting the customer interface right but not enough effort into having the infrastructure systems in place. A classic example here is an e-tailer who is able to take orders electronically, and consequently rapidly, but fails to meet specified delivery schedules because of a lack of good inventory control and distribution information systems.

The necessary linkage between strategic IS and support IS is only one of the reasons for having effective informatics planning within organisations. The vast range of literature on so-called strategic alignment of information systems emphasises the importance of planning for SIS.

However, a contrary theme is that strategic IS cannot be planned for in the traditional sense (Ciborra and Jelassi, 1994). They necessarily demand creative experimentation. To encourage this organisations are told to establish new technologies departments and look to technology champions within the organisation to stimulate innovation.

The management of innovation and the management of control demand two different sets of competencies. Cash *et al.* (1992) suggest setting up a specific group to address innovation issues. This should be separate from the normal development group. The main task of such a group is to be exploratory and experimental in the investigation of new technology applications within the organisation. Because of its very nature, the management of such a group must be more informal than development or maintenance groups.

36.7 ◉ SUMMARY

- Strategic information systems are those information systems that achieve competitive advantage for some organisation. They differ from support IS, which support current internal processes.
- Strategic information systems can be used to improve competitive advantage in terms of cost advantage, differentiation and location.
- Strategic information systems tend to be built on existing informatics infrastructure. They also tend to be outward looking, use innovative technologies and offer new products and services or more effective management information.
- Planning for strategic systems may be an important part of IS planning.
- Strategic information systems generally have a short lifespan. Competitors soon replicate systems.

36.8 QUESTIONS

(i) Distinguish between support IS and strategic IS.

(ii) List some of the major characteristics of strategic IS.

(iii) Distinguish between cost leadership, differentiation and niche positioning as approaches to focusing upon strategic IS.

(iv) Explain why strategic IS only remain strategic for a limited period.

(v) Explain how strategic IS link with informatics planning and the informatics infrastructure.

36.9 EXERCISES

(i) Find one example of a support IS.

(ii) Consider some information system known to you. In what respect would you define it as strategic and why?

(iii) Find one example of an SIS in the cost leadership, differentiation or niche strategy.

(iv) Find one example of a system which can be regarded as strategic but which is built on existing informatics infrastructure.

36.10 PROJECTS

(i) Develop case studies of strategic IS within the area of e-commerce.

(ii) Investigate the average length of time that an IT system remains strategic.

(iv) What consequences for informatics planning arise from the characteristics of strategic IS?

(v) In what respect are managed learning environments a strategic information system for universities?

36.11 REFERENCES

Cash, J. I., McFarlan, F. W. and McKenney, J. L. (1992). *Corporate Information Systems Management*, 3rd edn. Richard Irwin, Homewood, IL.

Ciborra, C. and Jelassi, T. (1994). *Strategic Information Systems: a European Perspective*. John Wiley, Chichester.

PART 8

MANAGEMENT

Technology is dominated by two types of people: those who understand what they do not manage, and those who manage what they do not understand.

Putt's Law

COVERAGE

- Informatics management
- Project management
- Knowledge management

- Informatics service
- IS evaluation

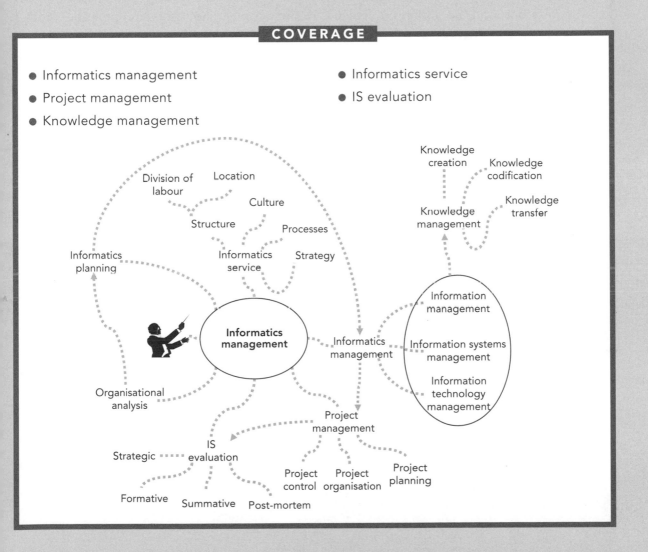

Informatics management is the process of putting information, information systems and information technology plans into action. Effective informatics management is critical to organisational success. We distinguish between three levels of informatics management corresponding to strategy and infrastructure in Chapter 37: information management, information systems management, information technology management.

Much of informatics work is project-based. Hence project management is a necessary part of informatics management concerned with the development of information systems. We distinguish between the important activities of project planning, project organisation and project control in Chapter 38.

In much of the recent management science literature there has been much emphasis on knowledge management. In Chapter 39 we portray knowledge management as reliant on information management. We also discuss the range of supporting information technology for knowledge management.

The informatics service is that specialist function of an organisation devoted to the planning, management, development and maintenance of information systems. We examine the forms that such a service may take in terms of the issues of structure, culture and processes in Chapter 40.

Information systems evaluation is a necessary but frequently forgotten part of informatics activity. Evaluation is important for demonstrating the worth of informatics to organisations. It is also critical to organisational learning about information systems. This is the topic of Chapter 41.

INFORMATICS
MANAGEMENT

So much of what we call management consists in making it difficult for people to work.

Peter Drucker

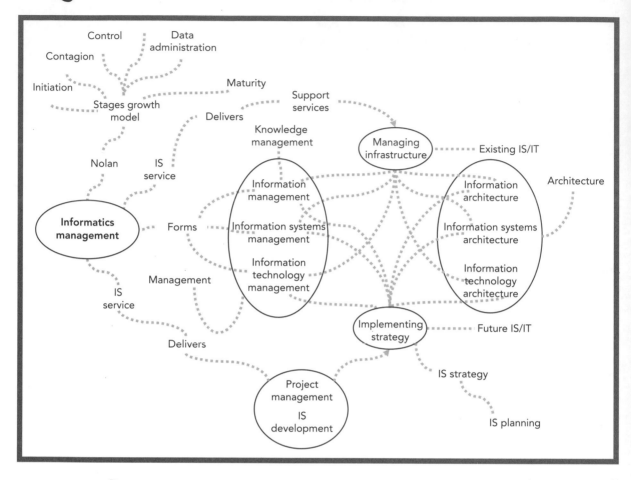

37.1 INTRODUCTION

Informatics management is the process of implementing the plans produced by informatics planning and monitoring the results of such plans. Informatics management is a key control for effective project management. In turn, informatics planning forms a control for informatics management. These relationships are illustrated in Figure 37.1.

Informatics management is one of the critical activities of the informatics service (Chapter 40).

37.2 INFORMATION, INFORMATION SYSTEMS AND INFORMATION TECHNOLOGY MANAGEMENT

Michael Earl (1989) has distinguished between three forms of management relevant to informatics: information management, information systems management and information technology management. These three forms are distinguished on

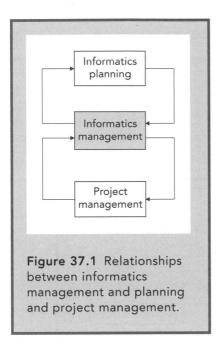

Figure 37.1 Relationships between informatics management and planning and project management.

the basis of the primary objective, the basis of management and the primary focus and responsibility:

- *Information management* is concerned with the general planning, regulation and coordination of information policies within the organisation. It is concerned with determining the overall strategic direction of the organisation in terms of its information. Earl suggests that it needs to be a role of senior management in organisations.

- *Information systems management* is concerned with the management of information handling applications in the organisation. It is concerned with the planning, execution and operation of these information systems to support organisational activities. As such, Earl suggests that it is a role for managers of business units within the organisation.

- *Information technology management* is concerned with the maintenance of the IT infrastructure of the organisation, developing new applications and maintaining existing IT applications. It is the concern of technical specialists within the organisation.

This framework is interesting in that it suggests that a range of competencies are required in the management of information, information systems and information technology, and that the locus of such forms of management should logically be sited at various levels within organisations. It presumes that business managers are given informatics knowledge, experience and responsibilities through some form of training. It also suggests that organisations need to have three levels of planning in place and also three consequent levels of informatics strategy (Chapter 35).

An informatics strategy is the major output of informatics planning. This acts as the major control input into the informatics management process. Informatics management is also constrained by the current informatics infrastructure. Hence this is also a key control input into the management process. Each element of informatics management takes responsibility for different aspects of both strategy and infrastructure. This is illustrated in Figure 37.2.

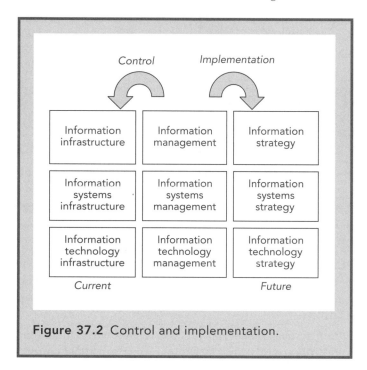

Figure 37.2 Control and implementation.

Hence we may suggest that there are two major aspects to informatics management:

- *Controlling the informatics infrastructure*. Essentially managing the current information, information systems and information technology in the organisation.

- *Implementing the informatics strategy*. Essentially managing the implementation of the future information, information systems and information technology in the organisation.

Ideally, information management should drive information systems management, which in turn drives IT management. An organisation first needs to identify its information needs then decide upon the information systems that will supply those needs and finally decide upon appropriate information technology for supporting its information systems.

37.4 INFORMATION MANAGEMENT ACTIVITIES

Information is a critical resource for organisations, particularly in modern information societies and economies. Hence the same disciplines that have been employed in managing other organisational resources such as people have to be applied in the area of information management. Information management activities consist of the two major processes of managing the current information architecture and implementing the future information strategy.

37.4.1 MANAGING THE INFORMATION ARCHITECTURE

The process of managing an information architecture includes activities such as:

- Continuously evaluating organisation information needs
- Identifying integration and interoperability opportunities
- Maintaining the organisation data model and process model
- Maintaining organisational standards for data and process representation

37.4.2 IMPLEMENTING THE INFORMATION STRATEGY

The process of implementing an information strategy includes activities such as:

- Enforcing data and process standards
- Re-engineering aspects of the data and process model
- Checking the conformance of new information systems with the information architecture

37.5 INFORMATION SYSTEMS MANAGEMENT ACTIVITIES

Information systems management is concerned with the management of information handling applications in the organisation. Such applications may be computerised or non-computerised. Information systems management activities include the following:

- *Managing the current information systems architecture.* This involves maintaining an inventory of the current information systems infrastructure and ensuring its effective operation. It also involves ensuring the effective maintenance of such systems.
- *Managing the development of IS planned in the information systems strategy.* This involves monitoring and controlling the range of development projects under way and planned in the organisation.

- *Controlling budgets for IS investment.* This involves strategically monitoring planned against occurred expenditure for IS investment within the organisation (Chapter 27).
- *Evaluating completed information systems.* This involves conducting rigorous summative (Chapter 41) evaluations of completed information systems to determine the levels of success achieved. For abandoned projects it also involves conducting a post-mortem analysis to ensure that the organisation learns from its mistakes.

37.6 ⊚ INFORMATION TECHNOLOGY MANAGEMENT ACTIVITIES

Information technology management is concerned with the maintenance of the IT infrastructure of the organisation, developing new applications and maintaining existing IT applications. Information technology management activities consist of the two major processes of managing the current information technology architecture and implementing the future information technology strategy.

37.6.1 MANAGING THE INFORMATION TECHNOLOGY ARCHITECTURE

- Maintaining organisation information technology system standards
- Maintaining organisation hardware standards
- Maintaining organisation software standards
- Maintaining organisation data standards
- Maintaining organisation communication standards
- Monitoring the total cost of ownership of IT networks

37.6.2 IMPLEMENTING THE INFORMATION TECHNOLOGY STRATEGY

- Managing the development of bespoke and package IT systems
- Managing the maintenance of existing IT systems
- Managing the purchase of hardware, software, data and communications technology
- Making sure IT systems match with corporate objectives established in organisation strategy

37.7 ⊚ THE MATURITY OF INFORMATICS MANAGEMENT

A number of attempts have been made to define the maturity of informatics management within an organisation. One of the most prominent is Nolan's stages of growth model in which he originally distinguished four phases or stages of IT assimilation within organisations. In a later paper, Nolan (1990) expanded this idea into a six-stage model. His model does not distinguish between information, IS and IT management but identifies the need for more sophisticated information and IS management on top of IT management:

- *Initiation*. This phase is characterised by the introduction of IT for cost savings, with IT belonging to business units. There is a lack of management and user interest in IT, but a steady expenditure growth on IT.
- *Contagion*. This phase is characterised by a blossoming of IT assimilation into new areas. However, this growth is unmanaged and management and control of IT is devolved to technologists. Consequently there is a steep rise in expenditure on IT.
- *Control*. This phase is characterised by senior management concern over the growth in IT spending. As a consequence, formalised control is introduced, and a concentration on information systems to save money not to make money is introduced. However, IT expenditure continues to rise.
- *Integration*. This phase is characterised by a gradual lowering of controls to encourage innovation, reorganisation of IS/IT to bring it closer to the business, and a steep rise in expenditure as the organisation attempts to implement infrastructure projects.
- *Data administration*. This phase is characterised by shared data and common systems across the organisation, business driven development, and a steady rise in expenditure.
- *Maturity*. This phase is characterised by the introduction of strategic planning of IS/IT, data resource management, and appropriate IS/IT expenditure.

Phases 1 and 2 of this model involve innovation, phases 3 and 4 involve control, and phases 5 and 6 involve strategic direction (illustrated in Figure 37.3). A given organisation may be at different levels in terms of different information technologies on this sequence. For instance, the organisation may be in phase 4 as far as relational database technology is concerned but only at phase 1 as far as object-oriented systems are concerned. It is therefore important that the informatics planning process (Chapter 34) takes these possible differentials into account.

37.8 SUMMARY

- Three forms of informatics management may be distinguished: information management, information systems management and information technology management.
- These three forms correspond to three levels of the information systems infrastructure of some organisation: information infrastructure, information systems infrastructure, and information technology infrastructure.

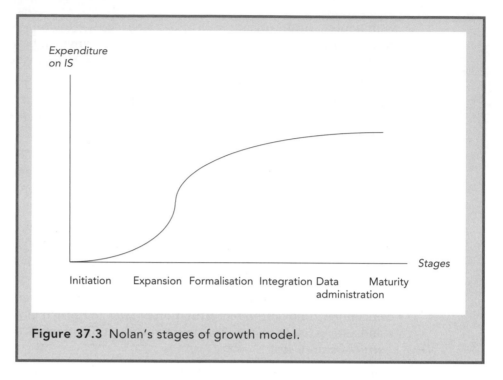

Figure 37.3 Nolan's stages of growth model.

- One side of information systems management corresponds to implementing strategy in each of these three areas – that is implementing future information systems that deliver new forms of information to support new forms of activity.

- The other side of informatics management corresponds to managing the existing informatics infrastructure. That is ensuring that current information systems work efficiently and effectively in support of current human activity.

- The informatics service delivers support services to support the current IS infrastructure.

- The informatics service delivers project management and development in support of developing the future informatics infrastructure.

- A number of attempts have been made to define the maturity of informatics management within an organisation. One of the most prominent is Nolan's stages of growth model.

37.9 ⊚ QUESTIONS

(i) Describe the distinction between information, information systems and information technology management.

(ii) List the activities of information management.

(iii) List the activities of information systems management.

(iv) List the activities of information technology management.

(v) What is meant by the maturity of informatics management?

(vi) Describe the key phase of Nolan's stages of growth model.

37.10 EXERCISES

(i) Give an example of each of the activities listed under managing the information, information systems or information technology architecture.

(ii) In terms of a new technology group, why do you think the management of such a group should be more informal than say an IS development or maintenance group?

(iii) Nolan's six stage model was developed a number of years ago. Discuss to what degree it is still relevant today.

(iv) Choose a market sector such as food retail, banking or manufacturing. Use Cash *et al.*'s framework to characterise the importance of IS/IT to the sector.

37.11 PROJECTS

(i) How is informatics management organised in a range of organisations? How closely do organisations distinguish between information, information systems and information technology management?

(ii) To what extent is the management of informatics distributed through the technical and business sides of the organisation?

(iii) Investigate the distinction between information management and knowledge management.

(iv) Determine the applicability of Nolan's model to the history of information systems and information technology innovation in some organisation.

37.12 REFERENCES

Earl, M. J. (1989). *Management Strategies for Information Technology*. Prentice Hall, Hemel Hempstead.

Nolan, R. L. (1990). Managing the crisis in data processing. In *The Information Infrastructure*. Harvard Business Review, Cambridge, MA.

CHAPTER 38

PROJECT MANAGEMENT

God is not dead but alive and well and working on a much less ambitious project.

Anonymous

LEARNING OUTCOMES

After reading this chapter, you will be able to:

- Define the process of project management in terms of planning, management and control
- Describe the process of project planning
- Explain the process of project organisation
- Outline the process of project control
- Discuss methods, techniques and tools available for project management

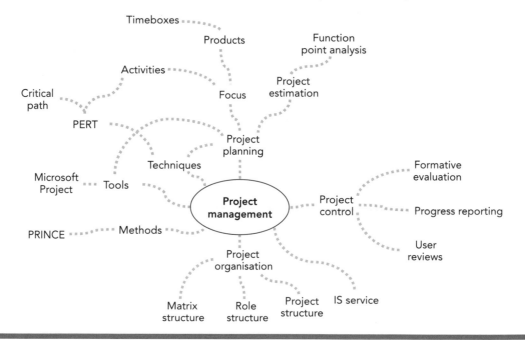

38.1 INTRODUCTION

A project is any concerted effort to achieve a set of objectives. All projects comprise teams of people engaging in the achievement of explicit objectives usually within some set duration. Most informatics work in organisations is structured in terms of projects. Hence planning, management and even organisational analysis will normally be conducted as projects. In this chapter we focus on development projects. A development project is any concerted effort to develop an information system.

The initiation of development projects will be done as part of an organisation's informatics planning and informatics management processes. Project management will interact with the development process in the sense that it acts as the major control process for development. This process is illustrated in Figure 38.1.

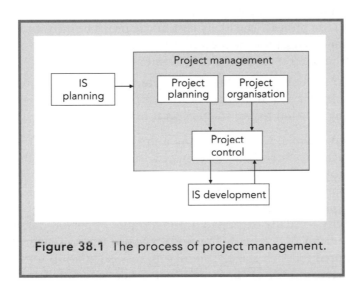

Figure 38.1 The process of project management.

The process of project management can be divided into three interrelated activities: project planning, project organisation and project control (O'Connell, 1996). Project planning involves determining as clearly as possible the likely parameters associated with a particular project. Project organisation concerns how to structure staff activities to ensure maximum effectiveness. Project control concerns ensuring that a project remains on schedule, within budget and produces the desired output.

38.2 PROJECT PLANNING

The classic questions of project planning are: What?, Who?, When?, How?, and Progress?

- *What?* The product or output of the project must be defined and the project must be broken down into a series of tasks. Adherence to a standard model of information systems development (Chapter 25) clearly aids this process. Standards to be used in the project, such as appropriate notations for the specification of requirements, must also be identified.

- *Who?* Staff must be assigned to the project and responsibilities identified. The most popular method of estimating the amount of staff needed for a project is to use experienced people who have conducted similar projects in the past. Another approach is to estimate the size of the proposed product and derive a staff estimate from this figure by the application of an appropriate formula.

- *When?* Milestones must be identified and schedules established. Many experienced project managers recommend that a software project be divided into sequential phases and a milestone or control point established at the end of each phase.

- *How?* A budget for the project must be constructed and resources must be allocated to the project. The likely cost of the project must be calculated and a case made for a budget for the project. This is a critical aspect of the systems conception (Chapter 27) phase of a development project.

- *Progress?* An effective mechanism for monitoring the progress of projects must be established. Milestones can be used as points of audit to ensure that standards are being adhered to and the project is on schedule.

The conventional way of planning a project is to segment it into a number of stages, each of which can be managed independently. Each of these stages is further broken down into a series of tasks or activities.

One popular method of representation is to lay out a project in diagrammatic form as a network. An estimate is then made of the resources required to achieve each activity – usually expressed in the number of person-days required. The sum of these person-days, plus a contingency factor for emergencies, is the estimated time required for each stage. Conducting this calculation for each stage will give the manager an idea of the overall person-days required for the project. Since person-time is also the most significant cost factor, this calculation will give the project manager an idea of total approximate cost for a project.

For each activity the earliest possible start date is calculated on the basis of a schedule assigned to predecessor activities. A latest completion date is also calculated for each activity on the basis of the scheduled start dates for each of the activity's successors and the target completion date for the overall project. The difference between the calculated time available to complete an activity and the estimated time required to complete it is known as an activity's float. If the float is zero, the activity is said to be critical, since any delay in completing it will cause a delay in completing the final project.

The process of project planning discussed above is focused around activities. Hence it is referred to as activity-based project planning. More recently there has been an emphasis on a form of project planning based around products rather than activities. This form of product-based planning is popular in approaches such as Rapid Application Development (RAD) (Chapter 25).

Fundamentally product-based planning works with two concepts: deliverables and timeboxes:

- A *deliverable* is a part of an information technology system agreed to be demonstrated at a review session by the development team to representatives of relevant stakeholder groups. A deliverable is normally expressed in terms of what the IT system module will be able to do.

- A *timebox* is an agreed period of time for the production of a deliverable. A timebox is normally expressed in terms of a fixed, immovable deadline. The timebox is never changed once established. However, the functionality of a deliverable may be renegotiated to fit the timebox.

38.3 PROJECT ORGANISATION

Project organisation concerns how to organise staff so that they produce the desired output. Essentially there are three alternatives in organising staff:

- *Organisation around projects*. In this form of project organisation, staff are organised within project boundaries. This form of organisation encourages quick decision-making, minimises interfaces between staff and generates high identification with projects among staff members. This is the style of project organisation promoted in RAD approaches. The disadvantages are that it works well only for small projects, the economies of scale are low, and the sharing of expertise across projects is minimal.

- *Organisation around roles*. In this form of project organisation, staff are organised according to development roles, each role supporting a number of different projects. This form of organisation generates economies of scale, promotes the growth of specialists, and reduces the effects of staff turnover. It is hence probably the most common type of project organisation used in large development centres. The disadvantages are that it generates lots of communication across projects, it decreases the number of people with a general feel for projects, and reduces the cohesion of given projects.

- *Matrix of projects and roles*. In this form of project organisation, staff are mixed across projects and roles. The basic organisation is based around development roles, but a project organisation is imposed under a series of project managers. The advantages of this approach are that short-term objectives (the success of a project) are maximised via the project organisation whereas long-term objectives (such as promoting specialism amongst developers) are maximised via division around roles. The major disadvantage is that the needs of a project and those of the developer roles may conflict in some organisations.

Project control is a type of formative evaluation (Chapter 41). The aim of project control is to ensure that schedules are being met, that the project is staying within budget and that appropriate standards are being maintained. The most important objective of project control is to focus attention on problems in sufficient time for something to be done about them. This means that continual monitoring of progress must take place.

Figure 38.2 illustrates the need for two major forms of information system in support of the development process. The actual process of development itself needs documentary support to enable collaboration between the development team. The process of managing a project also needs its associated information system. This will store not only project plans but data concerning progress against plans.

In activity-based project management the primary document used for the evaluation of progress is the progress report (Figure 38.2). This contains information on time estimated for each activity plotted against actual time spent. Another useful measure is an estimate as to the percentage of completeness of a project.

Time actually spent on a project is usually collected via weekly time sheets. Such time sheets normally indicate the tasks performed by development staff and their duration. They are also useful in highlighting time spent on unplanned work.

Progress reports can be used either by management reviews or project audits. Management reviews are scheduled opportunities for project managers to appraise

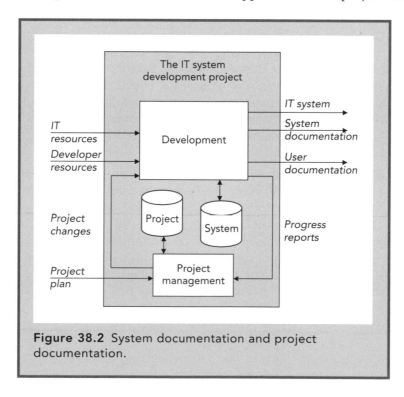

Figure 38.2 System documentation and project documentation.

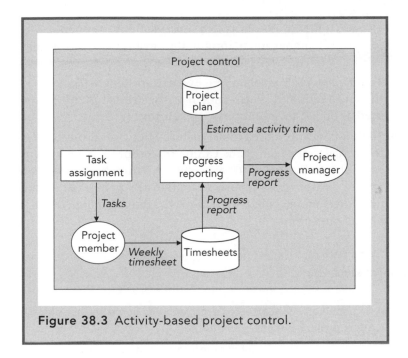

Figure 38.3 Activity-based project control.

themselves of the accomplishments and problems associated with a given project. Project audits are formal events scheduled into the life cycle of a given project in which an independent audit team examines the documentation associated with a given development effort and interviews key team members. The process of activity-based project control is illustrated in Figure 38.3.

In product-based project management project control is normally exercised through user review sessions. These are scheduled events at the end of each timebox at which versions of a developing IT system are demonstrated to representatives of the user community. At such sessions the parameters of the system may be renegotiated for the next timebox (Stapleton, 1997).

IT projects may also institute a change control mechanism. This involves setting up a systematic mechanism (sometimes known as configuration management) for handling all changes to a developing piece of software. Normally a change management committee is instituted for decision-making and a change management procedure is established. The essence of this procedure is to ensure that each version of a product can be uniquely identified and that time and money is not wasted on unimportant work.

38.5 METHODS, TECHNIQUES AND TOOLS

A number of different methods, techniques and tools exist for project management. For instance:

- *Methods*. PRINCE (PRojects IN Controlled Environments) is a structured method for project management originally developed from a government-sponsored initiative in the 1970s within the UK.
- *Techniques*. PERT (Programme Evaluation Review Technique) was developed in the late 1950s and is also known as the critical path technique. It is frequently used as an aid to activity-based planning.
- *Tools*. Many automated tools, such as Microsoft Project, are now available to aid the project manager. Plans can be represented using a graphical approach and estimates associated with each activity. Time sheet data can then be fed into the system and progress reports automatically generated. Some software packages for project management even allow the manager to perform 'What if?' reasoning on the project model.

38.6 ◎ SUMMARY

- A project is any concerted effort to achieve some set of objectives. Most informatics work is project-based.
- Project management involves project planning, project organisation and project control.
- There are two major project planning approaches based on focus. The traditional approach focuses on activities. More recent approaches focus on products or deliverables. Project planning involves project estimation.
- There are three main types of project organisation: focus around projects, roles or a combination of both.
- Project control is a form of formative evaluation. Configuration management is also important to project control.
- Methods, techniques and tools exist for project management: methods such as PRINCE; techniques such as PERT; tools such as Microsoft Project.

38.7 ◎ QUESTIONS

(i) Distinguish between project planning, management and control.

(ii) Describe the key questions of project planning.

(iii) List the key forms of project organisation.

(iv) Describe the process of project control.

(v) Distinguish between product-based and activity-based project management.

(vi) Distinguish between methods, techniques and tools available for project management.

38.8 EXERCISES

(i) At what point do you think a critical mass is reached in terms of project group size?

(ii) Discuss three of the main problems arising in the management of large project groups?

(iii) Which form of organisation do you think is most prevalent in information systems departments: project organisation, functional organisation or matrix organisation?

(iv) What sort of timings, effort and resource information should be kept in an organisation's project experience base?

(v) Even the most carefully planned of projects fail. Suggest some reasons.

38.9 PROJECTS

(i) Good project management practices have been around for many years, but IS projects still fail frequently. Investigate the limitations of project management with respect to this problem.

(ii) Investigate the range of project planning techniques and how frequently they are applied in information system projects.

(iii) Determine the prevalence of activity-based and product-based project management approaches in organisations.

(iv) Determine the forms of project organisation experienced.

(v) Determine the prevalence of use of the PRINCE project management method.

(vi) Investigate the suitability of project management tools for effective project management.

38.10 REFERENCES

O'Connell, F. (1996). *How to Run Successful Projects II: the Silver Bullet*. Prentice Hall, Hemel Hempstead.

Stapleton, J. (1997). *DSDM – Dynamic Systems Development Method: the Method in Practice*. Addison-Wesley, Harlow.

CHAPTER 39

KNOWLEDGE
MANAGEMENT

LEARNING OUTCOMES

After reading this chapter, you will be able to:

- Define knowledge and its relationship to information
- Discuss organisational knowledge and organisational learning
- Describe the relationship between information systems and knowledge management
- Relate the supporting role of knowledge management systems, data warehousing and data mining

39.1 INTRODUCTION

The word *knowledge* is derived from the Ancient Greek word *gignoskein*, which roughly translated means to decide upon, determine or decree. Epistemology, or the philosophical theory of knowledge (Chapter 49), is at least as old as the term itself, and knowledge, or the problem of knowledge, has been of intensive interest to sociologists and psychologists for a number of centuries. More recently the emphasis has been directed at the issue of organisational knowledge: how organisations learn and to what degree an organisation can manage its knowledge.

In this chapter we provide a brief review of such issues, but particularly focus on the contribution of informatics to knowledge management. To do this we establish a working definition of knowledge and demonstrate some of the linkages between information management and knowledge management. We also discuss a special class of information systems known as knowledge management systems – supporting technologies for knowledge management.

39.2 KNOWLEDGE AND INFORMATION

Acknowledging the vast amount of literature considering the question of what is knowledge, we provide a working definition of knowledge here for the purposes of explanation and relate it to a definition of information. Tsitchizris and Lochovsky (1982) define information as being 'an increment of knowledge which can be inferred from data'. Information therefore increases a person or group's knowledge of something. Note that this definition interrelates the concepts of data, information, knowledge and people:

- *Data is facts*. A datum, a unit of data, is one or more symbols that are used to represent something. We might represent this relationship as data = attribute + value.

- *Information is interpreted data*. Information is data placed within a meaningful context. This might be represented as information = object + attribute + value.

- *Knowledge is derived from information by integrating information with existing knowledge*. This may be represented as knowledge = object + relation + object. The relation in this definition may be expressed by a declaration or more efficiently by a rule.

Example ▐▐▶ Consider the string of symbols 43. Taken together these symbols form a datum, but by themselves they are meaningless. To turn these symbols into information we have to supply a meaningful context. We have to interpret them. This might be that they constitute an employee number. Employee constitutes the object, number the attribute and 43 the value. Information of this sort will contribute to our knowledge of a particular domain. It might add, for instance, to our understanding of the total number of products of a particular type sold. Here the relation is an aggregation of all the data on product sales for a particular product type.

39.3 WHY IS KNOWLEDGE IMPORTANT TO ORGANISATIONS?

Recently it has been argued that knowledge is a significant resource for organisations because:

- Increased knowledge leads to increased capability to perform effectively. Knowledge is one of the major assets of an organisation.
- Knowledge is complex and usually difficult to imitate. Therefore it has the potential to generate long-term and sustainable competitive advantage for organisations.
- Loss of personnel with significant amounts of knowledge through retirement, down-sizing etc. is a significant loss to the organisation. Hence there has been much emphasis on capturing, storing and sharing knowledge throughout the organisation to mitigate against staff turnaround.
- Knowledge must be created by organisations. Hence organisations need to invest in organisational learning – the processes by which organisations acquire new knowledge.

39.4 ORGANISATIONAL KNOWLEDGE

Individuals clearly acquire knowledge which improves their performance in specific fields. The question is to what degree is it appropriate to speak of human groups, and in particular organisations, as having knowledge. One useful concept is that of organisational memory being what an organisation knows about its processes and its environment. The knowledge in an organisation's memory is a critical resource for organisations in that it enables effective action within economic markets.

We may distinguish between three forms of organisational knowledge in terms of the accessibility of the knowledge (Liebowitz, 1999):

- *Explicit knowledge*. This is readily accessible, documented and organised knowledge.
- *Implicit knowledge*. Accessible through querying and discussion, but needing communication.
- *Tacit knowledge*. Accessible only with difficulty through elicitation techniques.

We may also distinguish between declarative knowledge (knowing what) and procedural knowledge (knowing how).

39.5 KNOWLEDGE MANAGEMENT AND INFORMATION MANAGEMENT

If knowledge is networked information, then information is clearly a prerequisite to effective knowledge. Knowledge management can be considered as being the topmost layer of management processes in organisations reliant on effective information management.

Knowledge management effectively consists of the following key processes:

- *Knowledge creation*. The acquisition of knowledge from organisational members and the creation of new organisational knowledge.
- *Knowledge codification/storage*. The representation of knowledge for ease of retrieval.
- *Knowledge transfer*. The communication and sharing of knowledge amongst organisational members.

Clearly the aim of such processes is to make as much tacit and implicit knowledge as possible explicit. It is also directed at formulating clear strategies for organisational learning.

39.6 ORGANISATIONAL LEARNING

The concept of organisational learning or the learning organisation, like many management science concepts, is one that seems open to many different interpretations. In recent times it has become particularly associated with the work of Peter Senge at the MIT Centre for Organisational Learning (Senge, 1990). In this section we particularly wish to utilise some of the concepts developed in the earlier work of Argyris and Schön (1978) on organisational learning and the related work of Zuboff (1988) on the informated organisation.

Argyris and Schön define organisational learning as occurring when: '...members of the organisation act as learning agents responding to changes in the internal and external environments of the organisation by detecting and correcting errors in organisational theory-in-use, and embedding the results of their inquiry in private images and shared maps of the organisation'.

Critical to this definition is the distinction made between espoused theories of action and theories-in-use. When someone is asked how she will behave under certain circumstances, the answer she usually gives is her espoused theory of action. However, the theory which actually governs her actions is theory in use, which may or may not be compatible with her espoused theory. Rules for collective decision and action in organisations often reflect an espoused theory that conflicts with the organisation's theory-in-use.

This has many similarities with Polanyi's concept of tacit knowledge. Tacit knowledge is the name given by Michael Polanyi (1962) to the ability of human beings to perform skills without being able to articulate how they do them. In this context, tacit knowledge seems to be used mainly to mean the unexplicated knowledge involved in enabling individuals to orient their own work to those of others in a particular work setting.

Argyris and Schön distinguish between organisational single-loop learning and double-loop learning. In single-loop learning, individuals respond to error by modifying strategies and assumptions within constant organisational norms. Such learning is directed at increasing organisational effectiveness. In double-loop learning, response to detected error takes the form of a joint inquiry into the

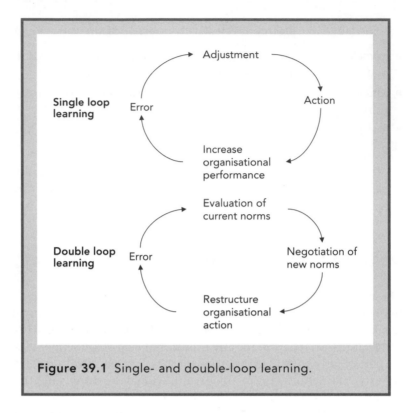

Figure 39.1 Single- and double-loop learning.

organisational norms themselves. The purpose is to resolve the inconsistency between existing norms and make a new set of norms realisable. In both cases, organisational learning consists of restructuring organisational action. This is illustrated in Figure 39.1.

This perspective on organisations treats them not as static entities but as collections of individuals that engage in the active process of organising. Individuals are continually engaged in the attempt to know the organisation, and to know themselves in the context of the organisation. The emphasis is on the process of organising not the entity of organisation. Organising is therefore essentially a continuous process of reflexive inquiry (Chapter 16).

There are clear links here between Argyris and Schön's account of organisational learning and Zuboff's (1988) account of the informed organisation. Zuboff makes a cogent argument for what she sees as a necessary form of new organisation needed in the information age: the learning or informed organisation.

> The informed organisation is a learning institution, and one of its principal purposes is the expansion of knowledge – not knowledge for its own sake, but knowledge that comes to reside at the core of what it means to be productive

Her theory is grounded in a number of ethnographic studies: two pulp mills, one paper and pulp mill, an operating unit of a telecommunications company, a drugs corporation, a dental claims operation of an insurance company, and the offices for stock and bond transfer of an international bank. The main argument of her book is that computer-based technologies are not neutral, '...they embody essential characteristics that are bound to alter the nature of work within our factories and offices, and among workers, professionals and managers'.

Information technology is frequently used to automate activities in organisations that were subject to tacit knowledge and skill. Such forms of knowledge were particularly subject to bodily performance in production – what she calls knowledge of 'acting-on'. Work, and the knowledge embodied in work, takes on a different form with computer-based technology; work is based on intellective skill, the ability to 'act-with'.

Intellective work has been traditionally the domain of management. With computer-based technology intellective skill becomes, or can become, the domain of the worker. This leads to a tension particularly in the role of middle managers that have informated in that their traditional authority was based on the distinction between the two forms of worker and managerial knowledge.

Much of Zuboff's case material is used to illustrate how middle management frequently reacts to this process by attempting to enforce greater imperative control via information systems. This is possible because IT 'textualises' work and hence makes it readable by the entire organisation. The electronic 'text' which IT provides is then used as a Panopticon, a means of continually monitoring the activities of the workforce and exercising authority and control in relation to the information provides by the system on worker performance. For instance, in the case of insurance clerks, decision-making which was previously only available to managers in terms of reciprocity on the part of the workforce was now visible to inspection by their supervisors. This means that:

> Managers can choose to exploit the emergent informating capacity and explore the organisational innovations necessary to sustain and develop it. Alternatively, they can choose to ignore or suppress the informating process.

39.7 SUPPORTING TECHNOLOGIES

Given the pyramid established for informatics management in Chapter 37, knowledge management will clearly rely on an effective information technology infrastructure within a particular organisation. Information technologies such as intranets, groupware, data warehousing and data mining are all much discussed as relevant technologies for knowledge management. In this section we discuss three technologies that directly support the knowledge management processes – knowledge management systems, data warehousing and data mining. Intranets are discussed in Chapter 44.

39.7.1 KNOWLEDGE MANAGEMENT SYSTEMS

Many of the contemporary knowledge management systems (KMS) have a history in a technology area known as knowledge-based Systems (KBS), or intelligent knowledge-based systems (IKBS). Such systems were much discussed in the literature during the 1980s and have become an accepted tool in the information systems developer's toolkit (Beynon-Davies, 1998). This section attempts to explain exactly what is meant by a knowledge management system.

The easiest way to approach the problem of defining a KMS is to contrast it with a database system (Chapter 10). Standard relational databases store facts about the properties of objects in some domain and some primitive information about the relationships between objects. However, facts can be said to come in five major forms, many of which cannot be handled conveniently in a relational database:

- ISA. Relationships between objects and object classes, sometimes referred to as ISA relationships. ISA is similar to set membership.
- AKO. Relationships between classes and other more general object classes, sometimes referred to as AKO (A Kind Of) relationships. AKO is similar to the idea of a subset.
- *Association*. Relationships between object classes that do not involve issues of generalisation, sometimes said to be relationships of association.
- *Attribution*. Relationships between an object and a property or attribute (HASA relationships).
- *Aggregation*. PARTOF relationships compose an object out of an assembly of other objects.

Examples ‖‖➡ When we state that:

- Paul Beynon-Davies ISA PolicyHolder we are defining a particular object as being a member of the set of policy holders.

- PolicyHolder AKO Customer we are defining the set of policy holders to be a subset of the set of customers.

- PolicyHolder Holds Policy, we are stating that there is an inherent link between policy holders and policies in the sense that data about policies is associated with data about policy holders.

- Policy HASA RenewalDate we are specifying that members of the class of policies have a renewal date attribute.

- railwayStation PARTOF railway and railwayLine PARTOF railway we are specifying a railway as being made up of an aggregation of stations and lines.

A knowledge base consists of a repository for knowledge. At its most basic it will represent information using the relations established above. At its most sophisticated it will utilise rules for generating new knowledge from existing knowledge.

Example ‖‖➡ Suppose we wish to build a knowledge base to store information on building society customers and the accounts they hold. We first need to create the object classes in the domain. This we do by inserting the following relations into the knowledge base:

```
Customer HASA Name
Customer HASA Branch
Customer HASA TelNo
BuildingAccount HASA StartDate
BuildingAccount HASA CurrentBalance
OrdinaryShare ISA BuildingAccount
```

The first few relations merely build the properties of objects. The last relation declares ordinary share accounts to be a subclass of building society accounts. In a true database system we would also probably need to provide a data type for each of the properties of an object. For example:

```
Name TYPE CHAR(20)
StartDate TYPE DATE
```

Data can then be recorded against each object:

```
4324 ISA OrdinaryShare
4324 StartDate 12/02/1997
4324 CurrentBalance 50
```

In its present form, the example could be implemented in a relational database, excepting the need to introduce primary keys. Suppose, however, we add the following relations to the knowledge base:

```
BuildingAccount HASA InterestRate
OrdinaryShare InterestRate 12
```

Here we have established a fact, an interest rate of 12%, relevant to all ordinary share accounts. Establishing this fact allows us to infer the following triple:

```
4324 InterestRate 12
```

Inference

The word *inference* is derived from the Latin words *in* and *ferre*, meaning to carry or bring forward. Inference is therefore the process of bringing forward new knowledge from existing knowledge. In the example above, the existing knowledge represented by the collection of relations in the knowledge base is turned into new knowledge, a new fact, by the application of inference. In our case, this is via the application of the following inference rule:

```
IF Object ISA ObjectClass
AND ObjectClass Property Value
THEN Object Property Value
```

Similar inference rules apply to AKO and PARTOF relations.

We can generalise the concept of a rule to include rules specific to the application domain – domain-specific rules. For instance, we might write the following rule into our building society system:

```
IF Object1 ISA Customer
THEN Object1 Holds Object2
AND Object2 ISA BuildingAccount
```

This statement is basically specifying the fact that all customers of the building society can be assumed to hold building society accounts. A rule such as this can be used in a number of ways. Probably the most relevant would be for the system to request details of a building society account after completion of customer entry, or to request details of a customer after entry of account details. This example is actually an instance of an integrity constraint, similar in nature to the entity and referential integrity constraints of the relational model (see Chapter 10).

39.7.2 DATA WAREHOUSING

Conventional database applications have been designed to handle high transaction throughput. Such applications are frequently called on-line transaction processing (OLTP) applications. The data available in such applications is important for running the day-to-day operations of some organisation. The data is also likely to be managed by relational DBMS (Beynon-Davies, 2000).

Contemporary organisations also need access to historical and summary data and to access data from other sources than that available through DBMS. For this purpose, the concept of a data warehouse has been created. The data warehouse requires extensions to conventional database technology and also a range of application tools such as those used for data mining.

A data warehouse is a type of contemporary database system designed to fulfill decision-support needs. However, a data warehouse differs from a conventional decision-support database in a number of ways:

- *Volume of data*. A data warehouse is likely to hold far more data than a decision-support database. Volumes of the order of over 400 Gbyte of data are commonplace.
- *Diverse data sources*. The data stored in a warehouse is likely to have been extracted from a diverse range of application systems, only some of which may be database systems. These systems are described as data sources.
- *Dimensional access*. A warehouse is designed to fulfil a number of distinct ways (dimensions) in which users may wish to retrieve data. This is sometimes referred to as the need to facilitate *ad hoc* query.

39.7.3 DATA MINING

Data mining is normally used in association with data warehouses. To gain benefit from a data warehouse or mart the data patterns resident in the large data sets characteristic of such applications needs to be extracted. As the size of a data warehouse grows the more difficult it is to extract such data using the conventional means of query and analysis. Data mining involves the use of automatic algorithms to extract such data.

Data mining is the process of extracting previously unknown data from large databases and using it to make organisational decisions (Beynon-Davies, 2000). There are a number of features to this definition:

- Data mining is concerned with the discovery of hidden, unexpected patterns of data.
- Data mining usually works on large volumes of data. Frequently large volumes are needed to produce reliable conclusions in relation to data patterns.
- Data mining is useful in making critical organisational decisions, particularly those of a strategic nature.

39.8 SUMMARY

- Knowledge is information in a network of relations with rules for the use of information.
- Organisations have knowledge stored in an organisational memory. Organisations may also learn.
- We may distinguish between explicit, implicit and tacit knowledge.
- Knowledge management relies on information management.
- Knowledge management processes include knowledge creation, knowledge codification and knowledge transfer.
- Supporting technologies include a range of knowledge management systems, data warehousing and data mining.

39.9 QUESTIONS

(i) Distinguish between data, information and knowledge.

(ii) Distinguish between implicit and explicit knowledge.

(iii) Distinguish between procedural and declarative knowledge.

(iv) Describe some of the reasons why knowledge is important to organisations.

(v) Distinguish between tacit, implicit and explicit knowledge.

(vi) Distinguish between information management and knowledge management.

(vii) Describe the three key knowledge management processes.

(viii) Distinguish between single-loop and double-loop learning.

(ix) Describe some of the supporting technologies for knowledge management.

(x) Describe what is meant by a knowledge base.

(xi) Explain how data warehousing and data mining may be used to support knowledge management.

39.10 EXERCISES

(i) Give an example which distinguishes between data, information and knowledge.

(ii) Provide some examples of procedural and declarative knowledge in an organisation known to you.

(iii) Provide some examples of tacit, implicit and explicit knowledge in an organisation known to you.

(iv) Classify an organisation, or part of, known to you as a single-loop learning organisation or a double loop learning organisation.

(v) Give an example of single-loop and double-loop learning.

(vi) Produce another example of a knowledge base using the notation discussed in the chapter.

(vii) Find an example of data warehousing.

(viii) Find an example of data mining.

39.11 PROJECTS

(i) How widely is tacit knowledge distributed within organisations?

(ii) Can information technology ever be used to store and disseminate tacit knowledge?

(iii) Investigate the applicability of knowledge management to the higher education sector.

(iv) Determine which of the supporting technologies for knowledge management is the most widely used.

(v) Investigate the consequences of organisational learning for information systems development.

39.12 REFERENCES

Argyris, C. and Schön, D. A. (1978). *Organizational Learning: A Theory of Action Perspective*. Addison-Wesley, Reading.

Beynon-Davies, P. (1998). *Information Systems Development: an Introduction to Information Systems Engineering*, 3rd edn. Macmillan, London.

Beynon-Davies, P. (2000). *Database Systems*, 2nd edn. Palgrave, London.

Liebowitz, J. (ed.) (1999). *Knowledge Management Handbook*. CRC Press, Boca Raton, FL.

Polanyi, M. (1962). *Personal Knowledge*. Anchor Day Books, New York.

Senge, P. M. (1990). *The Fifth Discipline: the Art and Practice of the Learning Organisation.* Doubleday, New York.

Tsitchizris, D. C. and Lochovsky, F. H. (1982). *Data Models.* Prentice Hall, Englewood Cliffs, NJ.

Zuboff, S. (1988). *In the Age of the Smart Machine: the Future of Work and Power.* Heinemann, London.

CHAPTER 40

INFORMATICS SERVICE

Quality in a product or service is not what the supplier puts in. It is what the customer gets out and is willing to pay for. A product is not quality because it is hard to make and costs a lot of money, as manufacturers typically believe. This is incompetence. Customers pay only for what is of use to them and gives them value. Nothing else constitutes quality.

Peter Drucker

LEARNING OUTCOMES

After reading this chapter, you will be able to:

● Define the concept of the informatics service

● Discuss the structure of the informatics service

● Consider the issue of culture in relation to the informatics service

● Describe the major processes of the informatics service

● Outline the issue of strategy in relation to the informatics service

● Discuss outsourcing of the informatics service

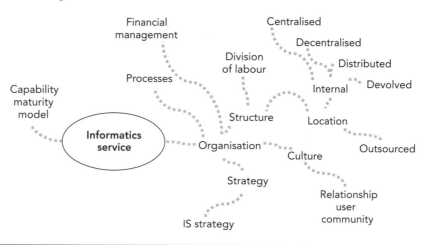

40.1 INTRODUCTION

Most medium- to large-scale organisations have people specifically employed in informatics work. In this chapter we consider a number of important issues in relation to how this sub-organisation is or should be organised. The name of such a unit will vary amongst organisations. In some organisations it may be called the IT or IS department, perhaps even the DP (data processing) department. In this chapter we refer to it generically as the informatics service, to emphasise that in most organisations information systems and technology is a critical supporting or strategic service supplied to the organisation.

The informatics service is an organisation and hence many of the concepts discussed in Part 4 are equally applicable to considering such a service. In this chapter we consider the informatics service in terms of possible structures, the issue of culture, its major processes and the importance of strategy.

40.2 STRUCTURE

In some organisations, particularly small organisations, there may be no actual section or department specialising in informatics. However, in most modern-day medium- to large-scale organisations some specialist structure is put in place for this service. Clearly there are a number of different ways in which such a service can be structured. In this section we consider structure in terms of the issues of division of labour and location.

40.2.1 DIVISION OF LABOUR

By division of labour we refer to the way in which various jobs or roles are delineated and structured within the informatics service. Traditionally, the division of labour of the informatics service has been one of quite rigid job specifications based around a hierarchy of control. Over the last twenty years or so a number of pressures for change have caused the gradual fragmentation of this structure and newer structures for the informatics service have emerged.

The traditional service
Because of the exigencies of building and running informatics on large, centralised mainframes, the traditional informatics services department was structured in a hierarchy of clearly delineated jobs:

- At the bottom of the hierarchy lay the operating staff. These staff were tasked with maintaining the operation of the centralised mainframe and the systems which run on it.

- Next in the hierarchy came the programmers. These were organised into groups such as maintenance programmers and development programmers. Development programmers constructed new applications. Maintenance programmers repaired and extended existing applications.

- Systems analysts were the next rung in the hierarchy. These were persons primarily involved in the analysis and design of IS. It is these persons who made contact with the business users.

- Many organisations segmented staff further in terms of project teams of analysts, programmers and sometimes operators (Chapter 25). Each such project team was normally headed by a project manager.

- The department was headed by one person probably called the data processing (DP) manager. In a large organisation there were frequently a number of middle-level managers such as operations managers, development managers and maintenance managers, each coordinating a particular aspect of informatics work.

Pressures for change

During the 1970s and 1980s a number of forms of pressure forced some radical changes upon many informatics departments. These changes accelerated during the 1990s.

- *The end-user movement.* The increasing infiltration of desktop computers into organisations meant that computing power could be sited wherever it is required. Desktop packages such as word-processing software and spreadsheets have been specifically written for the end-user. End-users have consequently gained much more experience of computing and have become much more confident in expressing their requirements, sometimes even building applications themselves.

- *The integration movement.* The developing use of databases and in particular the database approach has meant that organisations have to plan for and manage data at the corporate level. Organisations see key added value from integrating information systems across sectors.

- *The distribution movement.* Processing power and storage capacity no longer need to be centralised in organisations. Processing and storage can be distributed around the organisation on diverse sets of platforms and diverse software can be enabled to cooperate across local and wide area networks.

The information centre

In response to these pressures and others, the informatics service has recast itself in various different forms. One such form is the information centre: a corpus of informatics expertise whose role is to service other departments which are heavily involved in handling a large proportion of their IS/IT themselves. This is in marked contrast to the traditional department described above, which had a monopoly over organisational computing.

With the rise of different organisational structures for the service, such as the information centre, a greater diversification of informatics staff has ensued. We now have job titles such as Hybrid Managers, Analyst/Programmers, Database Administrators, Data Analysts, Business Analysts, and Systems Integrators, to name but a few. One particularly notable trend has been the growth in what might be called support staff: that is, those staff not directly tasked with developing any new systems directly but with installing and integrating existing information technology and helping end-users in the use of such technology.

The chief information officer

The recent literature has emphasised the important position of the chief information officer (CIO) to organisations. Following the terminology of the US chief executive officer (CEO) for the administrative head of a company, the CIO is tasked with maintaining the informatics activities of the organisation. Because of the perceived importance of informatics to organisational performance and the needed close integration of informatics strategy with business strategy, many have argued that the CIO must be at the executive or board level of businesses.

40.2.2 LOCATION OF INFORMATICS SERVICE

The rise of new organisational forms, such as the information centre, is partly a result of an increased number of options now open to the service in terms of its location. Below we list some of the dominant forms available:

- *Centralised*. This is the traditional model in which informatics provides one single service with single access provision. Hence the informatics service is located in one large facility with all other organisational units relying on this facility for all forms of informatics provision.
- *Decentralised*. Here the informatics service is structured around a number of smaller units each providing single access provision. Under this model the informatics service still forms a logical whole, but the various functions it provides, such as planning, management, development and maintenance, may be segmented off into separate organisational units.
- *Distributed*. In this model the informatics service is made up of a set of connected functions each providing a multiple of services. In particularly large-scale organisations, such as multinationals, it may prove impossible to provide any one function on a centralised basis. Hence, for instance, each country might have its own informatics services function providing all of the activities to their national units.
- *Devolved*. This model adheres to a distributed framework, but each informatics unit is not independent. Instead, the informatics service is made up of a matrix of units each sited close to the point of need and falling under direct business unit control.
- *Outsourced*. Frequently, because of a perceived dissatisfaction with many of the above forms of organisation for the informatics service on the part of the wider business, many organisations have recently pursued an outsourcing strategy. Here, the informatics service provision is sited either in whole or in part with external contractors. This issue is discussed in more detail below.

40.2.3   ADVANTAGES AND DISADVANTAGES OF CENTRALISATION

No one form of location for the informatics service is a clear winner. Each of these forms of location has its own advantages and disadvantages. To illustrate this we consider the advantages and disadvantages associated with the centralised versus decentralised dichotomy.

Advantages of a centralised informatics service

- Greater control can be exercised over the operation of IS resources.
- Recruiting and maintaining informatics skills becomes easier.
- Economies of scale can be achieved in the procurement of hardware and software.
- A centralised service is better able to consider issues of integration and the development of large infrastructure projects.
- Greater standardisation and compatibility of systems can be achieved.
- Duplication of effort is more easily avoided.
- Speedier and more consistent strategic decision-making is possible.

Disadvantages of a centralised informatics service

- The informatics service is more likely to be divorced from the 'coal face' of the business.
- Some diseconomies may be possible, e.g. high backup costs.
- Dissatisfaction is more likely concerning the level of personal attention given to business departments, particularly in terms of rapid response to needs.
- A large, centralised informatics resource may be less able to adapt quickly to changes in the business environment and technology.

40.3 ⊚ CULTURE

Some of the classic cultural dimensions of individualism/collectivism and risk-taking/risk aversion will equally apply to an informatics service. One key area of focus will be the degree to which the informatics service is focused on technical concerns or on business concerns. The culture of the informatics service will clearly influence its relationships with the organisation at large – what we might call the user community. The traditional relationship with the community has been one of dominance. Although being a service function, a 'wall' frequently existed between the technical and business functions.

In recent times more collaborative relationships have been fostered between technical and business functions. The informatics service has attempted to strike a more cooperative stance with its user community. Here we might distinguish a data management approach that defines the purpose of the service as being 'do it for them' from the project-based approach, where the purpose is 'do it with them'.

Also, we have the idea of information centres, in which the purpose of the service is to 'help them to do it for themselves'. Finally, there are externally focused departments where the purpose may be seen as maintaining the organisation's information warehouse.

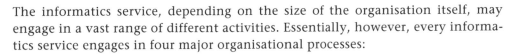

40.4 KEY PROCESSES

The informatics service, depending on the size of the organisation itself, may engage in a vast range of different activities. Essentially, however, every informatics service engages in four major organisational processes:

- *Planning*. Planning the strategy for information, information systems and information technology within some organisation. The strategy will include plans for changing aspects of the informatics infrastructure of the organisation.

- *Management*. The process of managing the existing informatics infrastructure: that is, controlling the process of supporting and maintaining existing IS and IT. This process will also frequently include issues of evaluating the investment in IS. Also, the management activities associated with individual IS projects as well as monitoring the success of IS projects and the service itself. Management will involve recruiting and organising informatics personnel and maintaining staff development programmes to ensure the professional service of staff.

- *Development*. The activity of constructing and delivering new application systems: analysing, designing, producing, testing and implementing systems.

- *Operations*. This area of the informatics service operates large, multi-user systems and/or supports the use of IS throughout the organisation. One crucial area of contemporary support is associated with the administration of corporate databases. Operations may also include the area of maintaining current information systems.

The interaction between these key processes is illustrated in Figure 40.1.

40.5 STRATEGY

An important part of any informatics strategy (Chapter 35) will be a strategy for the informatics service. For instance, outsourcing major parts of the processes of the service may be part of an informatics strategy for an organisation.

Each of the different possibilities for the organisation of the informatics service discussed in this chapter can be seen to be a historical reflection of features of the environment of commercial computing. In their global, historical study of the commercial information systems industry, Friedman and Cornford (1989) have proposed that three phases characterise the history of commercial computing up to the late 1980s, each phase dominated by a different set of constraints and hence determining a different strategy for the informatics service:

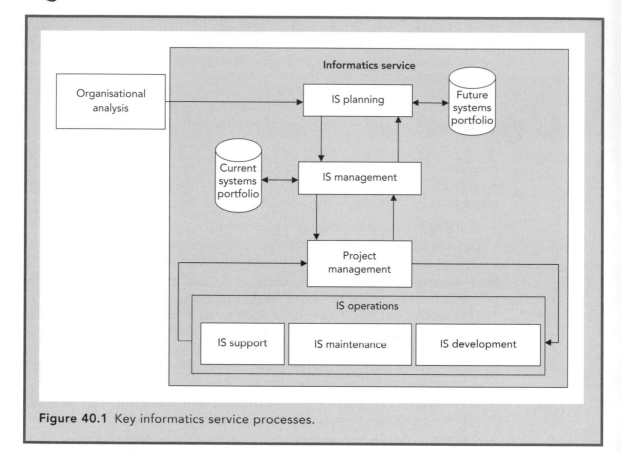

Figure 40.1 Key informatics service processes.

- *Hardware constraints* (before mid-1960s). The phase in which hardware costs and limitations of capacity and reliability dominated commercial computing. Not surprisingly, the shape of the informatics service reflected the need to maintain large corporate data centres. Much of the strategy for the informatics service in this phase was concerned with maintaining cost limitations on the computing resource.

- *Software constraints* (mid-1960s–mid-1980s). The phase dominated by the productivity of systems developers and difficulties of delivering systems on time and within budget. Here the emphasis shifts from strategies focused around hardware to strategies focused around the need to manage the information systems development process more effectively.

- *User relations constraints* (mid-1980s–early 1990s). The phase dominated by system quality problems, arising from an inadequate perception of user demands and an inadequate servicing of needs. In this phase the information centre was born as a way of attempting to satisfy concerns over the benefit the informatics service was providing to companies.

They also argue that since the early 1990s commercial computing has been entering a fourth phase dominated by organisational and environmental constraints. The particular focus of this phase is the search for ways in which IS can improve the position of the organisation in its environment. Some have argued that a key emphasis of this phase, which still continues, is the need for close alignment of business with informatics strategy. One way of encouraging this is to place the heads of informatics services (CIOs) at the executive level within companies.

A crucial feature of the strategy of the informatics service will be the development of its financial arrangements with the rest of the organisation. Informatics is normally a service function within organisations. Hence some way normally has to be found of funding such a service. A number of the possible options for schemes of financial management are listed below:

- *Free service*. Here an internal informatics service is farmed out free of charge to other departments. Some arrangement is formulated whereby each department or business unit has its budget top-sliced to finance informatics.
- *Profit centre*. Informatics bills other departments for its service using service level agreements (SLAs). An SLA specifies a fixed fee for a specified number of services for a given contract duration. An excess fee is usually negotiated for additional services.
- *Separate company*. One step removed from the profit centre is the concept of the informatics service converted into a separate company which contracts its services to the parent and potentially to external customers.
- *Outsourced*. The service is given over either in whole or in part to a different, specialist, company to perform for the organisation.

40.6 OUTSOURCING OF THE INFORMATICS SERVICE

Although informatics is now seen to be central to most organisations, the informatics service has traditionally experienced great difficulty in quantifying its benefits to the organisation. For this reason many organisations have decided to outsource their informatics service. Outsourcing might be defined as the use of external agents to perform one or more organisational activities. In the last decade or so there has been a trend, particularly among large-scale companies, to hand over either the whole or part of the IS function to external agents.

In general terms we may distinguish between a number of distinct types of informatics outsourcing:

- *Body shop*. This is the type of outsourcing in which contract programmers are brought in to supplement informatics personnel in the organisation.
- *Project*. Here outside vendors are used to develop a new system.
- *Support*. This is the type of outsourcing in which vendors are contracted to maintain and support a particular application system.
- *Hardware*. Organisations may choose to outsource hardware operations, disaster recovery and network management.

- *Total*. This is 'keys to the kingdom' outsourcing, implying outsourcing of the entire informatics service – the development, operation, management and control of informatics processes for a company.

The central focus of outsourcing is the contract negotiated with an external supplier. This contract is normally executed as a service level agreement.

There are a number of claimed benefits for outsourcing either the whole or a part of the informatics service:

- *Economy*. Scale and specialisation enables vendors to deliver the same value for less money than insourcing (20–40% reduction in costs is frequently claimed).
- *Quality*. More effective control of vendors leads to a better quality of service.
- *Predictability*. Fixed-price contracts and service level guarantees eliminate uncertainty.
- *Flexibility*. Business growth can be accommodated without quantum changes in infrastructure.
- *Making fixed costs variable*. Some agreements, such as running payroll, may be based on price per unit work done.
- *Freeing up human capital*. Scarce and costly IS talent can be refocused on higher value activity.
- *Freeing up financial capital*. Some agreements include the sale for cash of technology assets to the vendor.

Lacity and Hirschheim (1993) conducted major research into outsourcing strategies in the USA. They argue that much of the discussion of outsourcing in the literature has mythical qualities. In particular, they critique three dominant assumptions in this literature:

- *Organisations initiate outsourcing for reasons of efficiency*. Organisations may initiate outsourcing for a variety of reasons besides efficiency, such as to acquire or justify additional resources, to react to positive media reports of outsourcing, to reduce personal risk (management) associated with uncertainty, or to enhance the personal credibility of IS managers.
- *An outsourcing vendor is inherently more efficient than an internal informatics service* through economies of scale. An internal informatics service can frequently supply a service as efficiently as an external vendor.
- *Vendors are partners*. If a company decides to outsource, then the contract is the only mechanism to ensure that expectations are realised.

40.7 SUMMARY

- The informatics service is that part of the organisation tasked with supporting information, IS and IT within the organisation.
- Various forms of organisational structure are feasible for the informatics service.

- The informatics service can be seen to have four main processes: planning, management, development and operations.
- The informatics service needs to develop its strategy in alignment with the organisational strategy.
- Organisations are now choosing to outsource the informatics service either in whole or part. Outsourcing has to be carefully managed.

40.8 QUESTIONS

(i) Define the concept of the informatics service.

(ii) What is meant by the structure of the informatics service?

(iii) What is meant by the acronym CIO?

(iv) Describe some of the concerns of culture in relation to the informatics service.

(v) What major processes are present in the informatics service?

(vi) How is strategy important to the informatics service?

(vii) Describe the major forms of outsourcing of the informatics service.

40.9 EXERCISES

In terms of some organisation known to you find out whether it has an informatics services function. In what way is the service organised? Utilise the distinctions made in this chapter to help describe the organisation of this function:

(i) Does it conform to a traditional IT department or does it have a different structure?

(ii) How would you characterise the culture of the service?

(iii) Is the IT department seen purely as a service function or in a more strategic sense?

(iv) Is the service centralised, devolved or distributed?

(v) How does it conceive of its role in relation to the issues of innovation/control and IS/user dominance of IT?

(vi) How is the service funded?

40.10 PROJECTS

(i) Investigate two or more organisations. Consider differences in structure and function between their respective informatics services and why these differences have occurred.

(ii) How important is an 'open' culture to a successful informatics service?

(iii) Investigate the power that the informatics service has in modern organisations.

(iv) How prevalent is the pattern of placing CIOs on the board of companies?

(v) Determine the percentage and form of IS outsourcing experienced in a particular market sector.

40.11 REFERENCES

Friedman, A. L. and Cornford, D. S. (1989). *Computer Systems Development: History, Organisation and Implementation.* John Wiley, Chichester.

Lacity, M. and Hirschheim, R. (1993). *Information Systems Outsourcing: Myths, Metaphors and Realities.* John Wiley, Chichester.

CHAPTER 41

INFORMATION SYSTEMS EVALUATION

The life which is unexamined is not worth living.

Plato (428–348 BC): *Dialogues, Apology*

LEARNING OUTCOMES

After reading this chapter, you will be able to:

● Consider what we are evaluating in terms of some information system

● Distinguish between various types of IS evaluation

● Describe linkages between evaluation types and the IS development process

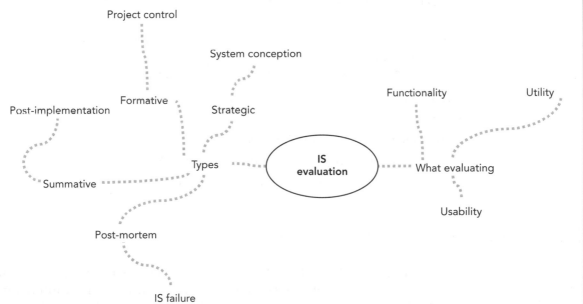

41.1 🌀 INTRODUCTION

In recent years a number of questions have been frequently voiced by general management within organisations in relation to information systems and information technology:

- Do we know how much is currently spent on IS and IT?
- What value results from this spending?
- How should IS/IT alternatives be justified/prioritised/financed?
- Why do we continually experience cost and time overruns in relation to IS/IT projects?
- Why do IS budgets continue to rise while IT unit costs continue to fall?
- How can we regain our belief in IS returns?

All such questions relate to the issue of evaluation. This chapter focuses on the evaluation of information systems by organisations and discusses the importance of this activity. We also highlight the different forms of evaluation and indicate some of the problems in the way in which organisations conduct evaluation. A model of IS evaluation linked to the IS development process (Chapter 25) is used to structure the discussion.

41.2 🌀 A MODEL OF IS EVALUATION

Figure 41.1 presents a model of IS evaluation fitted to the life cycle of information systems development. This illustrates the importance of evaluation to processes of organisational learning. Organisations need to conduct evaluation to:

- Assess and prioritise investment in IS and IT
- Control IS costs
- Determine the value arising from IS and IT
- Determine changes needed to the organisation's IS portfolio
- Learn successful strategies for IS management and development

41.3 🌀 WHAT ARE WE EVALUATING?

Conventional approaches to IS evaluation stress a product-based focus – the evaluation of information systems or components. However, in terms of information systems we can distinguish between three dimensions on which an IS should ideally be assessed (Chapter 13).

- *Functionality*. Does the information system do what is required? Assessing the degree to which a system is functionally complete and consistent is a classic concern of systems development.

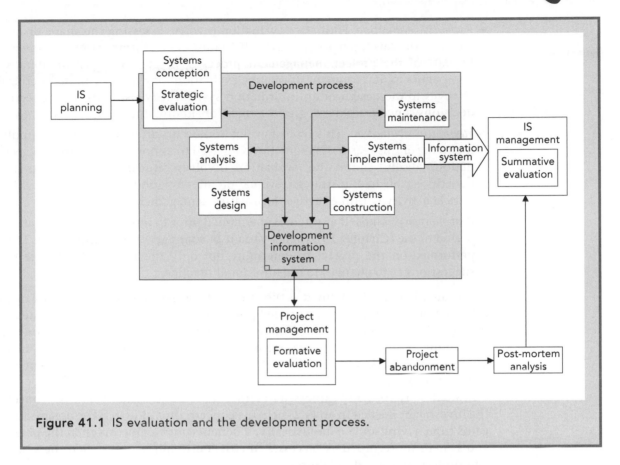

Figure 41.1 IS evaluation and the development process.

- *Usability*. Is the information system usable by its intended population? Assessing the usability of systems has become important with the continuing progress and use of graphical user interfaces and multimedia interfaces.
- *Utility*. Does the information deliver business benefit for the organisation? Assessing the utility of IS is something which most organisations conduct at the pre-implementation stage of a project, but seldom thereafter. However, this form of evaluation is becoming increasingly important because of the greater pressure being placed on the informatics service to account for its activities.

41.4   TYPES OF EVALUATION

Figure 41.1 makes a distinction between four types of IS evaluation activity:

- *Strategic evaluation*. Sometimes referred to as pre-implementation evaluation, this type of evaluation involves assessing or appraising an IS/IT investment in terms of its potential for delivering benefit against estimated costs. This is fundamentally part of the systems conception process (Chapter 27).

- *Formative evaluation*. Formative evaluation involves assessing the shape of an IS whilst in the development process itself. Traditionally, formative evaluation will be part of the project management process (Chapter 38). Within iterative approaches to development, formative evaluation may be used to make crucial changes to the design of an information system. It is also critical to effective decisions concerning the degree of project abandonment (Chapter 15).

- *Summative evaluation*. This type of evaluation occurs after an IS has been implemented. For this reason it is sometimes referred to as post-implementation evaluation. Ideally, summative evaluation involves returning to the costs and benefits established in strategic evaluation after a period of use of the IS. It is a critical activity within effective informatics management (Chapter 37).

- *Post-mortem analysis*. If a system is abandoned prior to implementation or after a period of use (Chapter 15), then a variant of summative evaluation needs to be performed on the project to determine not only the reasons for failure but suggestions as to changes to organisational practice.

IS evaluation may be defined as the attempt to assess the success or failure of an information system and the associated process by which the information system is developed and implemented. Although evidence suggests that organisations do not conduct evaluation of their systems and projects very effectively, the systematic evaluation of IS projects is critical to improvements in both development and organisational success.

Evaluation is normally expressed in terms of costs and benefits. IS costs concern the investment needed in an IS. IS benefits concern the value that the organisation gains from having an IS. Simplistically, if benefits outweigh costs then the project and system are regarded as successes. If costs outweigh benefits then the system and project are classed as failures.

It is useful to make the distinction between two types of costs and benefits associated with IS projects: tangible or visible costs/benefits and intangible or invisible costs/benefits. Tangible costs or benefits are frequently referred to as visible costs/benefits because they are reasonably straightforward to measure. Intangible costs or benefits are frequently referred to as invisible costs/benefits because most organisations experience difficulty in assigning actual measurable quantities to such costs and benefits (Chapter 27).

The important point to make is that the costs of an IS must be taken into account over its entire life, not solely in terms of its development cost. Frequently organisations forget that the initiation of an IS means a permanent commitment to costs in terms of continuing resources being committed to the running and maintenance of the IS.

41.5 THE MODEL EXPLAINED

Most organisations conduct some form of strategic evaluation of IS projects. Strategic evaluation is an activity that attempts to establish the balance of costs and benefits in terms of an intended IS project. It is normally used to initiate a go/no-go decision in terms of a given project. It may also be used to prioritise a number of IS investments. The most popular techniques applied in this process are *return on investment* and *payback period*. Such techniques are effective ways of evaluating tangible costs against tangible benefits. One of the most popular frameworks which includes facilities for an assessment of intangible costs and benefits is *information economics* (Parker *et al.*, 1988) (Chapter 27).

Formative evaluation should be an inherent part of the project management process (Chapter 38). Development projects should be continually assessed against objectives and careful attention should be paid to this activity to avoid project escalation. Project escalation is defined as the continued commitment to an IS project in the face of continual negative information from formative evaluation exercises. Major stakeholders in an IS project may be reluctant to withdraw support because of heavy investment in personnel and other resources devoted to a project.

At some point in this process a decision may be made to either wholly or partially abandon a project. In either case, the organisation should engage in another form of IS evaluation called here a post-mortem analysis. This should attempt to determine the key reasons for such total or partial failure. In a recent international survey, 60% of organisations internationally and 67% of organisations in the UK had suffered at least one systems project that had failed to deliver planned business benefits or had experienced significant cost and time overruns (Chapter 15).

The results of such an analysis are important in suggesting ways in which the organisation may improve its development practice. It is for this reason that the document produced from the post-mortem analysis needs to be disseminated to senior management, project management and members of the project team. This, of course, can only be done effectively if assurances of non-recrimination are given to all project participants. Ideally, this analysis should be conducted by a reputable senior executive not involved in any way with the project under consideration. Alternatively, it should be undertaken by an external body or consultant.

Wherever possible post-mortem information should be made public outside of the organisation. This is important in enabling the validation of IS development and management practice and the effective progression of the profession of informatics (Chapter 47).

The model also contains another important organisational learning feedback loop. Even if a project reaches completion, it may fail in some sense when it comes to be delivered. Therefore, at some suitable time after a system has been delivered the organisation should engage in a summative evaluation of the system and its project. One framework proposed for the summative evaluation of IS is *benefits management* (Ward *et al.*, 1996). Even at this point it is possible that the system may be wholly or partially abandoned, in which case it should also be the subject of a post-mortem analysis, as above.

It is important to emphasise that no system is ever complete. A summative evaluation is likely to suggest a number of ways in which the system may be modified or extended – normally both classed as systems maintenance (Chapter 32). This is the third feedback loop illustrated on the diagram. The conclusion is that effective evaluation leads to effective management of maintenance.

41.6 SUMMARY

- Evaluation involves assessing the worth of something.
- There are three types of information systems evaluation: strategic evaluation, formative evaluation and summative evaluation.
- Strategic evaluation involves assessing or appraising an IS/IT investment in terms of its potential for delivering benefit against estimated costs.
- Formative evaluation involves assessing the shape of an IS whilst in the development process itself.
- Summative evaluation involves returning to the costs and benefits established in strategic evaluation after a period of use of the IS.
- A variant of summative evaluation is post-mortem analysis. This involves the summative evaluation of some failed IS project

41.7 QUESTIONS

(i) Define the term *evaluation*.

(ii) Describe why evaluation is important to organisations.

(iii) Describe the four major types of IS evaluation.

(iv) What three dimensions are we evaluating in terms of some information system?

(v) Describe the linkages between types of IS evaluation and the IS development process.

41.8 EXERCISES

(i) Choose an information system known to you. Attempt to estimate the benefits associated with the IS and the costs associated with its development.

(ii) In terms of strategic, summative and formative evaluation what are we evaluating – usability/functionality/utility?

(iii) Provide an example of strategic evaluation.

(iv) Provide an example of formative evaluation.

(v) Provide an example of summative evaluation.

41.9 PROJECTS

(i) Determine appropriate approaches to assessing intangible costs and benefits within strategic evaluation.

(ii) Develop a natural history of some information systems project known to you. Attempt to determine whether strategic, formative and summative evaluation was performed on the project and to what extent.

(iii) There is a certain amount of evidence that evaluation is not treated seriously as an activity by most organisations. Investigate why this might be the case.

(iv) Investigate the importance of post-mortem analysis for organisational learning.

41.10 REFERENCES

Parker, M., Benson, R. and Trainor, H. (1988). *Information Economics: Linking Business Performance to Information Technology*. Prentice Hall, Englewood Cliffs, NJ.

Ward, J., Taylor, P. and Bond, P. (1996). Evaluation and realisation of IS/IT benefits: an empirical study of current practice. *European Journal of Information Systems*, **4**(1), 214–225.

PART **9**

E-BUSINESS

Worldwide networks will make certain types of competition brutally intense

James Martin

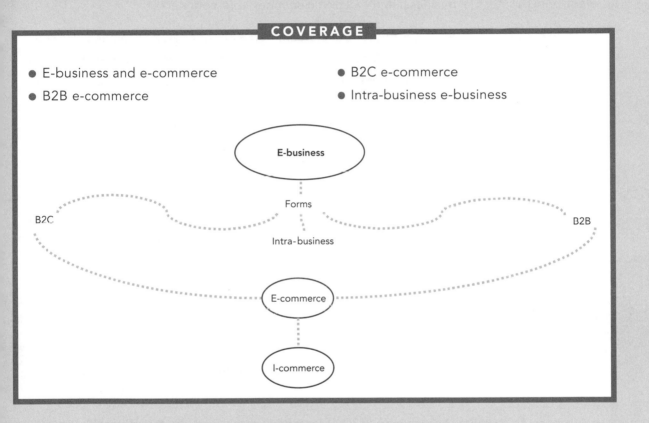

Business can be considered either as an entity or as the set of activities associated with a commercial organisation. Commerce constitutes the exchange of products and services between businesses, groups and individuals. Commerce can hence be seen as one of the essential activities of any business. This part is devoted to the consideration of the transformation in both business and commerce that has been effected by information and communication technology (ICT). Following the modern convention we call these phenomena electronic business (e-business) and electronic commerce (e-commerce).

Despite the recent obsession, e-business and e-commerce are not new phenomena. We shall argue that the use of ICT to transform internal and external business processes has been ongoing for at least three decades. Hence much of e-business and e-commerce is still based on the fundamental concepts and issues of informatics. One might argue that much of the discussion surrounding e-business and e-commerce is an acknowledgement of the centrality of information systems to the effective performance of the internal processes of modern business and the external processes of trading. Therefore, in this part we will utilise concepts established in previous chapters to elucidate key elements of the field.

In Chapter 42 we describe e-business as a superset of e-commerce. E-commerce is in turn a superset of Internet commerce (i-commerce). We particularly concentrate on Internet technologies because they are becoming key standards for inter- and intra-organisational communication. We also distinguish between:

- Business to business (B2B) e-commerce focused on the transformation of an organisation's supply chain (Chapter 43)

- Intra-business e-business focused on transforming the internal value chain of an organisation (Chapter 44)

- Business to customer/consumer (B2C) e-commerce focused on transformation of an organisation's customer chain (Chapter 45)

CHAPTER 42

E-BUSINESS AND E-COMMERCE

The power of technology as a competitive variable lies in its ability to alter competition through changing industry structure

Michael Porter

LEARNING OUTCOMES

After reading this chapter, you will be able to:

- Describe the concept of an e-market and explain some of the processes affecting e-markets
- Distinguish between generic forms of commerce
- Distinguish between e-business, e-commerce and i-commerce
- Define the major forms of e-business
- Explain the concept of an inter-organisational information system and distinguish it from a strategic information system
- List some of the major costs and benefits of e-commerce

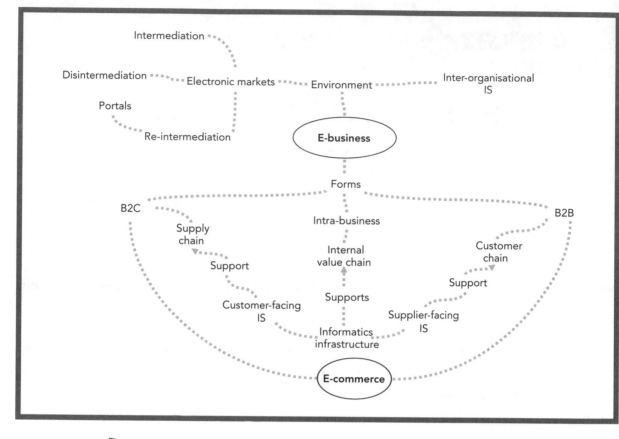

Over the last few years the terms *e-business* and *e-commerce* have become common-place. However, the terms have been used in a dazzling array of different senses. In this chapter we provide some order to the chaos by presenting some definitions and distinctions firmly based in the informatics concepts and frameworks discussed in previous chapters.

We first define the concepts of an electronic market and an inter-organisational information system (IOS). E-markets and IOS form the environment of e-business and have stimulated different and distinct forms of competition amongst companies. We then distinguish between e-business, e-commerce and i-business and discuss some of the forms in each of these areas. Finally, we consider some of the costs and benefits of conducting commerce electronically.

In Chapter 22 we defined a market as a medium for exchanges between buyers and sellers. Markets form the economic environment for most commercial organisations and are defined by activities and relationships between four main types of economic actors and the organisation: competitors, suppliers, customers and regulators.

Markets are about distributing value within and between organisations. From the position of any particular organisation (Chapter 19) a market can be seen as a series of value chains:

- *The internal value chain*. An organisation's internal value chain is a series of inter-dependent activities that produces a product or service for a customer/consumer.
- *The supply chain*. A series of interdependent activities by which an organisation sources products or services from other individuals, groups or organisations.
- *The customer chain*. A series of interdependent activities by which an organisa-tion sells its products or services to customers.

The supply and customer chain of an organisation constitutes its external value chains. A market can be seen as a complex network of such value chains. One company will be the supplier of another company and a customer of yet another. Commerce is clearly the trading of value along such chains.

Many contemporary markets are electronic markets or e-markets. By an e-market we mean one in which economic exchanges are conducted using information tech-nology and computer networks. In an e-market, electronic transactions between employees, buyers and sellers enable the efficient and effective flow of goods and services through internal, supply and customer chains.

The essential features of an e-market are illustrated in Figure 42.1. The e-market is the domain in which buying companies and selling companies meet. The exchange of goods and services is enabled through electronic transactions between both buyer and seller and the financial institutions of each. The market handles all the transactions between companies including the transfer of money between banks.

Aspects of the external value chains of organisations have been critically affected by the creation of electronic markets. The traditional retail chain is one of whole-salers, distributors and retailers. However, by using the Internet producers can now sell directly to their customers. This process is known as disintermediation in the sense that intermediaries are removed in the customer chain. But the Internet suffers from being a large and complex medium for supporting a market. Potential customers for particular products and services frequently find it difficult to find the precise company meeting their needs. Hence, in recent times, a new breed of intermediaries – electronic intermediaries – has emerged. Such organisations reim-pose middle-men between the producers of products and services and the consumers of such products and services. They supply a service to the consumer in locating companies fulfilling their needs and they supply a service to the producer in identifying potential customers. This process is known as reintermediation. Figure 42.2 illustrates these three processes of intermediation, disintermediation and reintermediation.

One of the most effective ways in which reintermediation has occurred is through the rise of Internet portals. A portal is designed to be an entry point for

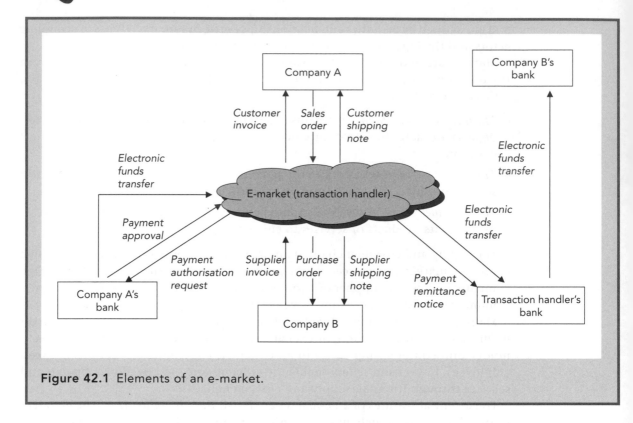

Figure 42.1 Elements of an e-market.

users into the Web. It tries to attract users to it, making it an anchor site for such users. We may distinguish between two major types of portal:

- *Horizontal portals.* These portals attempt to serve the entire Internet community, typically by offering search functions and classification for the whole of Web content. Typical examples of horizontal portals are Lycos and Yahoo!

- *Vertical portals.* These normally provide the same functionality as horizontal portals, but for a specific market sector. They attempt to target a niche audience. An example of a vertical portal is the one supplied by Dell.

42.3 E-BUSINESS, E-COMMERCE AND I-COMMERCE

The activity within electronic markets is generally referred to as electronic business (e-business) or electronic commerce (e-commerce) (Turban *et al.*, 2000). Electronic business is a superset of electronic commerce. In turn, E-commerce can be considered a superset of Internet commerce or i-commerce (Figure 42.3):

- *E-business.* Business can be considered either as an entity or as the set of activities associated with a commercial organisation. We treat e-business as the utilisation of information and communication technologies to support all the activities of business.

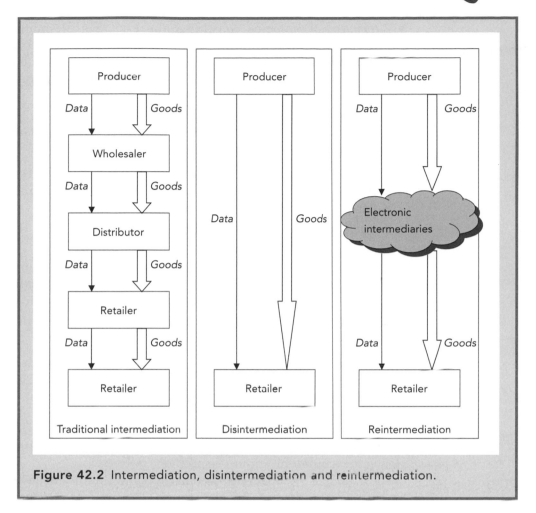

Figure 42.2 Intermediation, disintermediation and reintermediation.

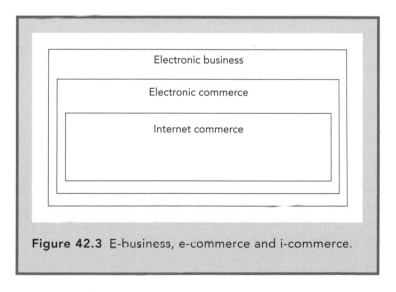

Figure 42.3 E-business, e-commerce and i-commerce.

- *E-commerce.* Commerce constitutes the exchange of products and services between businesses, groups and individuals. Commerce or trade can hence be seen as one of the essential activities of any business. E-commerce focuses on the use of ICT to enable the external activities and relationships of the business with individuals, groups and other businesses.

- *I-commerce.* Internet commerce is the use of Internet technologies to enable e-commerce. Such technologies are becoming the key standards for intra- and inter-organisational communication (Chapter 11).

Kalakota and Whinston (1997) define at least four perspectives on e-business:

- *Communications perspective.* The delivery of information, products/services, or payments via communications networks.

- *Business perspective.* The application of technology toward the automation of business transactions and workflows.

- *Service perspective.* A tool that addresses the desire of firms, consumers and management to cut service costs while improving the quality of goods and increasing the speed of service delivery.

- *On-line perspective.* Providing the capability of buying and selling products and information on the Internet and other online services.

In a sense these correspond to the distinctions between human activity system, information system and information technology system made in Chapter 4. Electronic business can be viewed in terms of the changes to organisational structures made possible by ICT (business/service perspective), in terms of the extension of information systems into the environment of organisations (on-line perspective) or in terms of innovations in technology making inter-organisational communication easier (communications perspective).

These perspectives demonstrate that, despite the recent obsession, e-business and e-commerce are not new phenomena. The trend to 'wire up' the corporation has been ongoing for a number of decades. Much of e-business and e-commerce is still based on the fundamental concepts and issues of informatics. However, the recent innovations in this area have undoubtedly been given new life by the use of Internet standards to enable the effective performance of the internal processes of modern business and the external processes of trading.

42.4 ⊚ FORMS OF E-BUSINESS

The importance of the Internet for business is that it provides new opportunities for conducting relationships with customers and suppliers. Some would argue that the Internet will eventually produce an electronic market-place that will largely replace existing forms of market economy. Generally we may distinguish between three major forms of e-business (Figure 42.4):

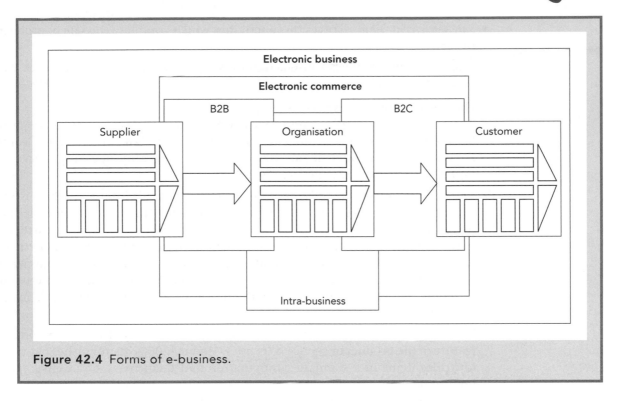

Figure 42.4 Forms of e-business.

- *Business to customer (B2C) e-commerce*. This invariably concerns the use of ICT to enable forms of cash and credit commerce between a company and its customers.

- *Business to business (B2B) e-commerce*. This invariably concerns the use of ICT to enable forms of credit and repeat commerce between a company and its suppliers.

- *Intra-business e-business*. This concerns the use of ICT to enable communication and coordination between the internal stakeholders of the business.

There are also other forms such as consumer/customer to consumer/customer and consumer to business e-commerce. However these are much lesser forms of e-business. Therefore we concentrate on the three major forms described above.

42.5 GENERIC PATTERNS OF COMMERCE

Commerce of whatever nature can be considered as a process with the following generic phases or states:

- *Pre-sale*. This involves activities occurring before a sale occurs.

- *Sale execution*. This comprises the activities of the actual sale of a product or service between economic actors.

- *Sale settlement*. This involves those activities which complete the sale of product or service.
- *After sale*. This involves those activities which take place after the buyer has received the product or service.

The precise form of this process will vary depending on:

- *The nature of the economic actors involved*. Generally speaking we may distinguish between organisational actors and individual actors. B2B commerce is clearly between organisational actors. B2C commerce generally speaking refers to exchanges between an organisation and individuals.
- *The frequency of commerce between the economic actors*. Whiteley (2000) distinguishes between three major patterns of frequency. Repeat commerce is the pattern in which regular, repeat transactions occur between trading partners. Credit commerce is where irregular transactions occur between trading partners and the processes of settlement and execution are separated. Cash commerce occurs when irregular transactions of a one-off nature are conducted between economic actors. In cash commerce the processes of execution and settlement are typically combined.
- *The nature of the goods or services being exchanged*. Generally the most important feature of the product or service is its price. Hoque (2000) distinguishes between low-price items in a standard configuration and quantity, such as envelopes, low- to medium-priced items, such as personal computers, medium- to high-priced items, such as office furniture, and high-price customised items such as bulk industrial components.

Cash commerce for low- and standard-priced goods typically follows the four stages of the generic commerce model quite closely. It typically involves a see/buy/get sequence. For medium- to high-priced items some form of credit commerce will operate. In other words, organisations will search for a product, negotiate a price, order a product, receive delivery of the product, be invoiced for the product, pay for the product and receive some form of after-sales service. For high-priced and customised goods traded between organisations some form of repeat commerce model operates. The same processes occur as for credit commerce, but the processes cycle around indefinitely in a trusted relationship between producer and consumer. These three models of commerce are illustrated in Figure 42.5.

42.6 B2B E-COMMERCE

B2B e-commerce has been undertaken for a number of decades in that businesses have used electronic records to transfer documentation in terms of standards in the area of electronic data interchange or EDI. More recently the Internet and its associated technologies have been used to transfer data between companies.

I-commerce is being used to impact upon the supply chain in ways that include:

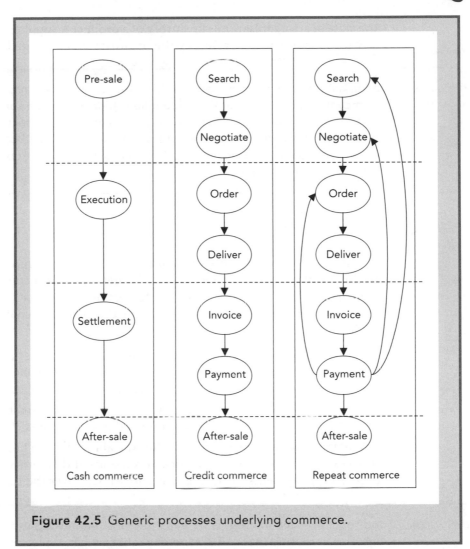

Figure 42.5 Generic processes underlying commerce.

- *Procurement*. Companies are setting up Web sites for suppliers to bid against particular requirements. Intermediary organisations are also offering supply-side services such as e-malls and Internet auctions.

- *Invoicing*. Extensible markup language (XML) – a version of HTML (Chapter 11) – is being piloted as a replacement to EDI standards for electronic document transfer between organisations. Using this technology standard documents such as invoices can be rapidly transferred between organisations and it is likely that it will provide a medium for organisations of all kinds to conduct their business transactions electronically in the near future.

- *Inventory*. Some companies have established a relationship with their supplier that provides them with a form of access to their extranet. An important application in this area is enabling suppliers to access up-to-the-minute information on the state of an organisation's inventory of a product it supplies. If stock levels are low it can automatically resupply the organisation concerned.

> Example — Traditionally, supply chain management has been conducted through specialised systems with limited sets of preferred suppliers. More recently a number of specialised e-markets have built up focused on particular industrial sectors. In these e-markets potential customers and suppliers can interact to conduct commerce in a far more dynamic way than in the past. Supply chains are likely to be far more fluid and temporary than in the past.

42.7 B2C E-COMMERCE

B2C is a relatively new feature of e-commerce. It is only comparatively recently, with the rise of such technologies as the Internet, that direct connections between customers and businesses have been made possible.

I-commerce is being used to impact upon the customer chain in ways which include:

- *Advertising*. Most medium to large companies now have a presence on the Internet. This ranges from merely putting up information about an organisation to more sophisticated versions of on-line product and service catalogues.
- *Marketing*. Companies are now contacting potential customers via email rather than the traditional forms of telephone and postal services.
- *Sales*. Organisations have begun to offer the ability to purchase their goods and services over the Internet. Sophisticated versions of this form of application will even accept payments for such goods and services over the Internet.

> Example — Food retail over the Internet is perhaps the most interesting example of B2C e-commerce in recent times. A UK supermarket chain has implemented a Web site that allows customers to order foodstuffs and other items from their local store for delivery the same day. Customer accounts with the store can be credited and debited to pay for such orders.

42.8 INTRA-BUSINESS E-BUSINESS

Intra-business refers to the changes to the internal value chain that may be affected by information and communication technology. Internet standards have been particularly used to:

- *Standardise interfaces*. Web browsers have now become one of the most popular ways of accessing interfaces to infrastructure information systems.

- *Share knowledge*. The creation and maintenance of corporate intranets have enabled organisations to share knowledge across the enterprise.
- *Integrate information systems*. Corporate intranets have been used as ways of integrating information across diverse infrastructure systems.

Example ||||➡ The public relations arm of a large telecommunications company uses the corporate intranet to make sure that its officers are all presenting a consistent message to the external world in relation to issues affecting the company. The intranet also contains 'best practice' for a number of public relations activities.

42.9 🌀 INTER-ORGANISATIONAL INFORMATION SYSTEMS

E-markets are founded on competition. A market is a network of interactions and relationships by which products and services are negotiated and exchanged. However, business can also be founded on cooperation and collaboration. A key way in which information systems may participate in business cooperation is through the concept of an inter-organisational information system (IOS) (Barrette and Konsynski, 1982). An IOS is an information system developed and maintained by a consortium of companies for the mutual benefit of member companies. Generally such systems provide an infrastructure for the sharing of an application. IOS are a form of organisational collaboration rather than competition and can prove a particularly effective way of sharing the costs of developing and maintaining large and complex information systems. Therefore an IOS is a type of information system directed at collaboration. This is in contrast to strategic information systems that are directed at competition. This distinction is illustrated in Figure 42.6.

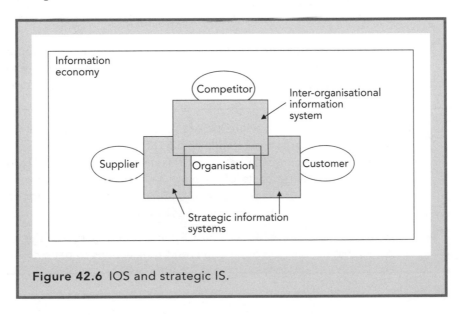

Figure 42.6 IOS and strategic IS.

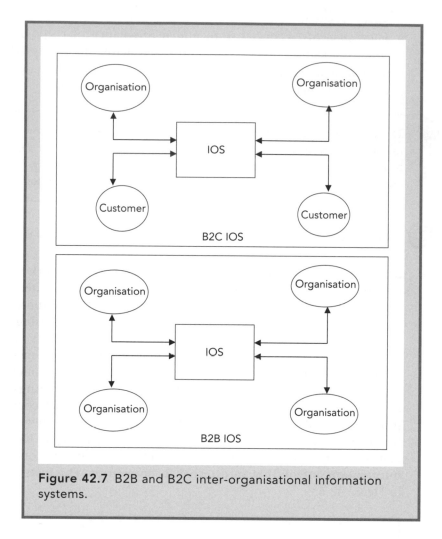

Figure 42.7 B2B and B2C inter-organisational information systems.

IOS can be used in B2C and B2B markets. A B2B IOS effectively supports the predetermined relationships of a supply chain. A B2C IOS supports the predetermined relationships of a customer chain. The concept is illustrated in Figure 42.7.

Examples ▌▌▌➡ The automatic teller machine (ATM) networks run by major building societies and banks in the UK are key examples of B2C IOS. These networks are constructed and maintained by consortia of these financial institutions. This enables them to distribute the large costs of running such networks amongst the participating members. Another example of a B2C IOS is the limited number of airline reservation systems run by the consortia of the major airlines.

A key example of a B2B IOS is BACS the clearing system of the major high street banks that handles the debit and credit transactions to bank accounts.

42.10 BENEFITS AND PROBLEMS OF E-COMMERCE

E-commerce, just like any informatics area, has a number of associated benefits and costs.

42.10.1 BENEFITS OF E-COMMERCE

The literature identifies a large volume of potential benefits from the adoption of e-commerce. These may be divided into five main areas:

- *Cost savings*, including lower logistic costs, lower postal cost, lower storage costs and lower personnel costs.
- *Time savings*, including quicker response time to markets, customers, suppliers, higher flexibility and a reduction in the delivery time and processing of payments.
- *Connection improvements* such as disintermediation. This is the process by which mediating organisations are removed in the customer chain.
- *Quality improvements*, such as access to new markets, new ways of marketing new products and services plus the general improvement in customer relations.
- *Strategic improvements* such as more efficient and effective organisational forms and doing business on the global scale.

42.10.2 PROBLEMS WITH E-COMMERCE

There are also a number of current problems and issues with e-commerce:

- *Security and privacy*. Many people do not trust e-commerce in the sense that they will refrain from purchasing large value goods or services using this medium. Such mistrust seems to be focused around issues such as the perceived difficulties of securing electronic transactions and the reluctance to release personal information over the Internet.
- *Reintermediation (brokerage)*. One of the problems with the Internet is the difficulty of finding exact/precise suppliers of goods and services. Organisations have arisen in electronic markets (frequently known as e-brokers) trying to satisfy this need.
- *Information rich and poor*. Concerns have been expressed over differential access to electronic markets afforded to different economic groups in society.
- *Technological standards*. Technological standards develop rapidly in support of electronic markets. Some of these standards are not particularly secure or have trouble integrating with standards in other areas.
- *Cost of computer-related mistakes and errors*. The visibility of mistakes made with customers and suppliers is much more prominent on electronic markets.

42.11 E-BUSINESS MODELS

Moore and Ruddle (2000) propose that companies may build e-businesses in a number of different ways:

- *Separate organisation.* This is where a firm packages its e-business activities as a separate organisation isolated from the parent firm. The separate organisation is expected to innovate with new products and services.
- *Semi-autonomous organisation.* A halfway house between a separate organisation and a fully integrated organisation.
- *Fully integrated organisation.* Here e-business is integrated into the conventional firm under control of specific business units.
- *Fully integrated within informatics service.* In this form e-business is run under control of the informatics service of some organisation.
- *Parallel organisation.* A sister organisation is created offering the same products or services as the parent company but through e-business channels.

42.12 E-BUSINESS ENVIRONMENT

Clearly, certain forms of business are more amenable to e-business than others. Some of the factors affecting the likelihood of success in this area include:

- *Type of commodity.* Companies supplying intangible commodities, particularly those subject to digitisation, such as music and programs, are likely to benefit greatly from e-business. Such products can be produced and distributed at very low cost via electronic channels.
- *Disintermediation.* Certain service industries such as travel agencies and high street banks are likely to be affected by processes of disintermediation. Customers can get fast and efficient service to travel services and financial services via the Internet.
- *Globalisation.* The Internet is a major force in the globalisation of markets. Certain industries, such as automobile sales, have been impacted by sites offering low-price cars delivered from the continent to the UK.

42.13 E-BUSINESS PLANNING

Issues for e-business planning include:

- *Organisational analysis.* Effective organisational analysis is a necessary prerequisite for effective e-business implementation. Organisational processes need to be mapped and new organisational processes have to be redesigned prior to investment in e-business systems

- *Strategic systems.* Many e-business systems are seen as strategic information systems. Organisations should be aware of the difficulties of maintaining competitive edge in such a volatile environment as the electronic market-place. Classic determination of the cost advantage, differentiation or niche strategies for such systems needs to be determined and a business case made for investment.

- *Strategy.* E-business strategy is a specialist form of informatics strategy. Key decisions have to be made as to the level of functionality to be provided in the B2B, B2C and intra-business areas. A key problem is the integration and interoperability of B2C and B2B systems with the existing informatics infrastructure. Considerable investment may be required to integrate the new Web-based interfaces with legacy information systems or existing exploitation of ERP systems.

42.14 E-BUSINESS MANAGEMENT

Issues for e-business management include:

- *Informatics infrastructure.* E-business initiatives become part of the informatics infrastructure of some organisation and have to be managed as such.

- *Maintenance.* In terms of e-business, one of the critical questions is the level of maintenance and support provided to the corporate Web site. Web sites have to be kept up to date both in terms of content and presentation to remain effective.

- *Content management.* E-business brings the issue of content and its management to the fore. An organisation will be judged on the content of its E-commerce sites. Systems have to be put in place to ensure that the information on the site is current and relevant.

42.15 E-BUSINESS DEVELOPMENT

Issues for e-business development include:

- *User involvement.* B2C systems have a high degree of interactivity. Most of the system is present in the interface. Hence it is important to build such systems with a high degree of user involvement.

- *Iterative development.* Iterative approaches to development appear most appropriate to B2C systems development. The development of Web sites normally demands extensive use of prototyping with associated configuration management.

- *Graphic design.* Web interfaces are multimedia interfaces. Hence media design issues such as graphic design come to the fore. Therefore, teams of multiple organisational stakeholders need to be involved in the design of such systems.

- *Systems integration*. The more complex forms of corporate Web site involve large amounts of systems integration work with existing systems. Technological issues can assume great significance. For example, the issue of response time between the front-end and back-end systems can be critical to making a sale.

42.16 SUMMARY

- E-business and e-commerce are features of e-markets. An e-market is one in which economic exchanges are conducted using information technology and computer networks.
- E-markets are subject to the processes of disintermediation and reintermediation.
- Reintermediation is evident in the rise of Internet portals.
- Three generic forms of commerce can be identified: cash commerce, credit commerce and repeat commerce.
- E-business is a superset of e-commerce. E-commerce is a superset of i-commerce.
- There are three major forms of e-business: B2C, B2B and intra-business.
- Inter-organisational IS are distinct from economic markets and enable collaboration between organisations in key areas.
- The benefits of e-commerce include cost savings and time savings.
- The costs of e-commerce include issues of security and technological standards.
- Planning, management and development are still critical activities for E-business as well as an analysis of the environment of E-business.

42.17 QUESTIONS

(i) Define the concept of an electronic market.

(ii) Explain the processes of intermediation, disintermediation and reinter-mediation.

(iii) Describe what is meant by an Internet portal and distinguish between a horizontal and vertical portal.

(iv) Explain what is meant by an inter-organisational information system.

(v) Distinguish between e-business, e-commerce and i-commerce.

(vi) Distinguish between cash commerce, credit commerce and repeat commerce.

(vii) What is meant by B2B e-commerce?

(viii) What is meant by B2C e-commerce?

(ix) What is meant by intra-business e-business?

(x) List some of the purported benefits of e-commerce.

(xi) List some of the problems experienced with e-commerce.

42.18 ⊙ EXERCISES

(i) Find one example of an e-market and describe its key stakeholders and features.

(ii) Find one example each of a vertical and horizontal Internet portal and describe their key features.

(iii) Choose an industrial or commercial sector. Investigate the degree with which B2B and B2C e-commerce has penetrated the sector.

(iv) Find one example of an inter-organisational information system and analyse some of the reasons for its creation.

(v) Consider whether the costs and benefits associated with e-commerce differ with the size of company.

42.19 ⊙ PROJECTS

(i) Investigate the take-up of e-business, e-commerce and i-commerce amongst companies in your local area.

(ii) Determine the levels of disintermediation and reintermediation amongst e-commerce conducted in a particular market sector.

(iii) Determine the costs and benefits associated with inter-organisational information systems.

(iv) In terms of a particular market sector, determine the most appropriate organisational form for e-business.

(v) Investigate whether conducting a systems conception exercise for either a B2B or B2C systems project differs substantially from traditional systems projects.

(vi) Investigate whether iterative approaches to development are the most commonly used on B2C systems development projects.

42.20 ⊙ REFERENCES

Barrette, S. and Konsynski, B. R. (1982). Inter-organisational information sharing systems. *MIS Quarterly*. Fall.

Hoque, F. (2000). *E-enterprise: Business Models, Architecture and Components*. Cambridge University Press, Cambridge.

Kalakota, R. and Whinston, A. B. (1997). *Electronic Commerce: a Manager's Guide*. Addison-Wesley, Harlow.

Moore, K. and Ruddle, K. (2000). New business models – the challenges of transition. In *Moving to e-Business: the Ultimate Practical Guide to E-business* (eds. L. Wilcocks and C. Sauer). Random House, London.

Turban, E., Lee, J., King, D. and Chung, H. M. (2000). *Electronic Commerce: a Managerial Perspective*. Prentice Hall, Upper Saddle River, NJ.

Whiteley, D. (2000). *E-commerce: Strategy, Technologies and Applications*. McGraw-Hill, Maidenhead.

CHAPTER 43

B2C E-COMMERCE

No one can possibly achieve any real and lasting success or 'get rich' in business by being a conformist.

J. Paul Getty

LEARNING OUTCOMES

After reading this chapter, you will be able to:

● Define the essential elements of B2C e-commerce

● Describe some of the major processes of the customer chain

● Distinguish between a number of distinct stages of growth in B2C e-commerce

● Explain some of the issues of security in relation to B2C e-commerce

● Relate some of the important lessons for B2C systems

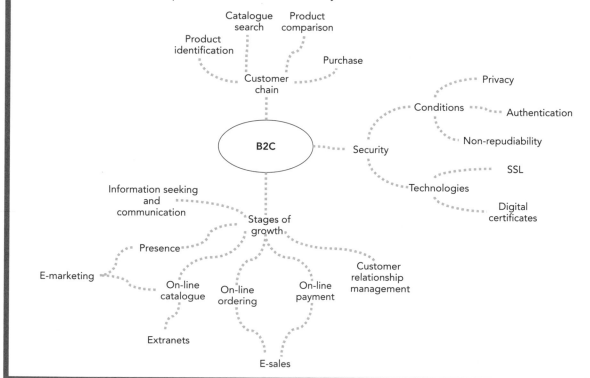

43.1 INTRODUCTION

B2C e-commerce (Figure 43.1) is the attempt to support the organisation's customer chain with ICT. B2C focuses on the IT-enablement of the key processes in the customer chain. Hence B2C systems are a natural extension of the customer-facing information systems described in Chapter 5. Typical customer-facing TPS include sales, customer relationship management, marketing and distribution systems.

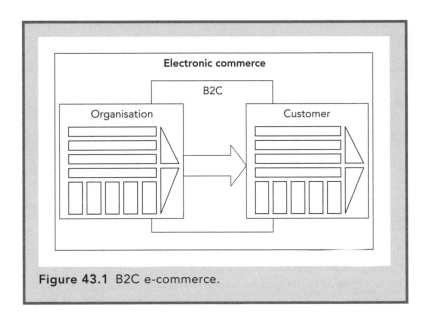

Figure 43.1 B2C e-commerce.

In this chapter we shall focus particularly on using Internet technology for B2C e-commerce. The important lesson we seek to establish is that B2C systems have to integrate with effective customer-facing IS for successful e-commerce.

43.2 THE CUSTOMER CHAIN

The customer chain generally uses either a cash or a credit model of commerce (Chapter 42). E-commerce applications can be used to support most of these stages of the customer chain (Figure 43.2):

- *Pre-sale.* On the Web, product identification can be enabled through banners on Web sites, inclusion in search engines and personalised marketing based on customer profiling. On-line catalogues and portals may also enable product comparison between vendors.
- *Sale execution.* Web sites permit on-line ordering of products and services.
- *Sale settlement.* On-line payment can be made through secure B2C sites and integration with back-end information systems such as accounting and distribution.

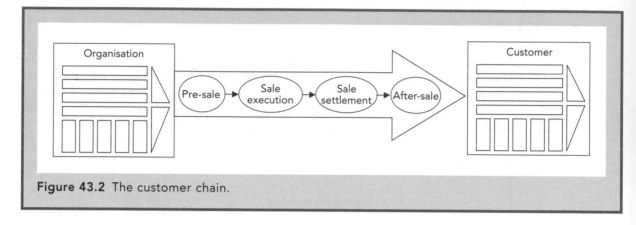

Figure 43.2 The customer chain.

- *After sale.* Various forms of customer profiling and preferencing systems may be used to encourage further purchases from customers.

This can be considered as a simplification of the Ives and Learmonth customer resource life cycle discussed in Chapter 34.

43.3 ⊚ STAGES OF B2C E-COMMERCE GROWTH

We may think of an organisation's experience of B2C e-commerce as moving through a number of distinct stages of increasing complexity. These stages can be considered as some typical scenarios of use (Chapter 28) for B2C e-commerce. The least complex of such systems involves using standard Internet technology for communication and information seeking. The most complex of such systems support the entire customer chain through integration of back-end information systems with front-end Web services. This has a resonance with the stages of growth model for ICT described in Chapter 40. The relationship between the stages of B2C growth and the cash and credit commerce models is illustrated in Figure 43.3.

43.3.1 INFORMATION-SEEKING AND COMMUNICATION

Here the company will be experimenting with the Internet, probably using it primarily for information seeking and communication via e-mail (Figure 43.4).

Example ▶ Many small and medium-sized enterprises (SMEs) are at this stage in the adoption of e-commerce. They use the Internet primarily as a tool for gathering information about organisations in the same market segment as themselves and e-mailing suppliers.

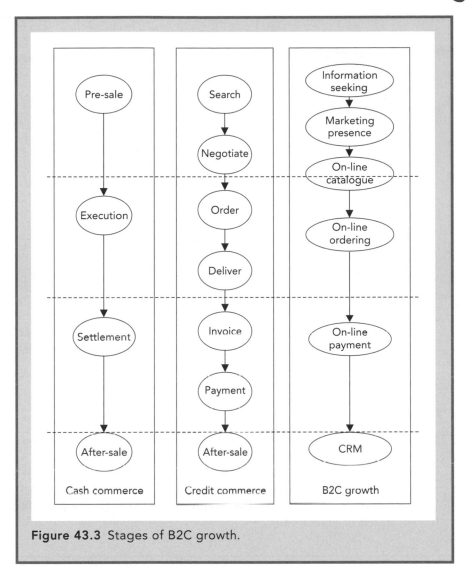

Figure 43.3 Stages of B2C growth.

43.3.2 MARKETING PRESENCE

Here the company will produce a corporate Web site and place details of the company profile on it. This will most likely include the main activities of the company, its location and some contact details. Potential customers may use the Web site only to contact the company. This scenario is illustrated in Figure 43.5.

Example ||||➡ Some SMEs have produced their own Web sites or have had a Web site produced for them. Within the UK a number of portals have been produced specifically to act as gateways to the Web sites of regional SMEs.

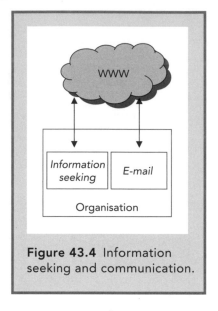

Figure 43.4 Information seeking and communication.

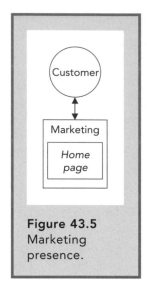

Figure 43.5 Marketing presence.

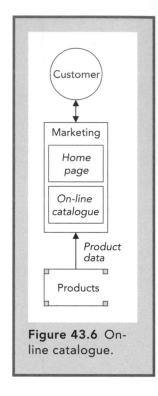

Figure 43.6 On-line catalogue.

43.3.3 ON-LINE CATALOGUE

Here the company provides an on-line catalogue of its products or services available for inspection by potential customers. The catalogue may amount to a series of static Web pages or may be dynamic in the sense that it is updated from a database of products. However, customers still have to place orders through traditional channels, such as over the telephone or through the post. This scenario is illustrated in Figure 43.6.

Example ||||➤ A specialist publisher produces an on-line catalogue of its limited range of specialist publications. The catalogue contains a cover image and a short synopsis of the contents of each publication, and details the cost of each publication and delivery charges. To order publications customers have to ring a telephone line or send an order form through the post with the appropriate payment.

43.3.4 ON-LINE ORDERING

The next logical step is to enable customers to place orders on-line for products or services. In a credit commerce model the company will then invoice the customer for payment after delivery. This demands integration between the Web site and the

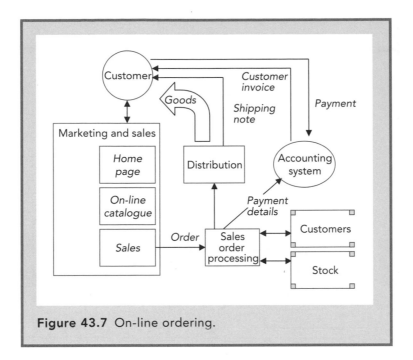

Figure 43.7 On-line ordering.

sales order information system (Chapter 5). The sales order information system will trigger the distribution information system that manages the delivery of goods and services. Payment details will also be passed to the organisation's accounting system that will send an invoice to the customer and receive payment from the customer. This scenario is illustrated in Figure 43.7.

Example ▌▌▌▶ A bulk supplier of stationery provides an on-line catalogue of its most popular range of office products. Certain volumes of this material can be ordered via the Internet site for established customers. The traditional distribution, invoicing and accounting systems of the supplier are used to support the B2C process.

An Italian motorcycle manufacturer decided to sell a new model motorcycle only through a special pre-sale Web site. The company pre-sold all of it first year's production of the product within 30 minutes of operation.

43.3.5 ON-LINE PAYMENT

In this scenario the customer can both order and pay for the goods using the Web site. This is more usual for cash commerce, in which the customer is an individual and the goods are standardised and relatively low in price, such as CDs or books. However, this form of B2C e-commerce demands close integration between an organisation's front-end and back-end information systems. The customer can first order goods using an electronic shopping trolley. The trolley calculates the total cost of the order for the customer and includes the delivery charge. The

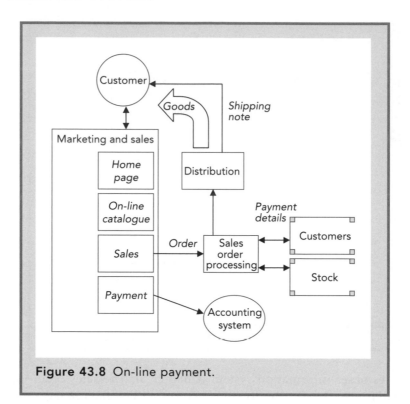

Figure 43.8 On-line payment.

customer enters her credit card details to complete the purchase. For such payment details to be entered the organisation supplies a secure site. This scenario is illustrated in Figure 43.8.

Example ⫸ A company supplies high-quality prints of works of art. The customer is able to search for prints by theme, period, artist and price, and images of selected prints can be displayed at various degrees of resolution. Prints are also offered in various sizes. The customer can add prints to a shopping trolley and pay on-line by credit or debit card. The site automatically confirms orders via e-mail.

43.3.6 CUSTOMER RELATIONSHIP MANAGEMENT

Customer relationship management has become a popular philosophy in the recent management science literature. Winning new customers and keeping existing customers happy is seen to be a key to organisational success. A customer relationship management system would ideally track all customer interactions with a company from initial enquiries through making orders to the whole range of after-sales services that might be offered to and consumed by the customer.

CRM will probably involve integration of the B2C systems with the addition of a customer profiling and preferencing system (Figure 43.9). This information system

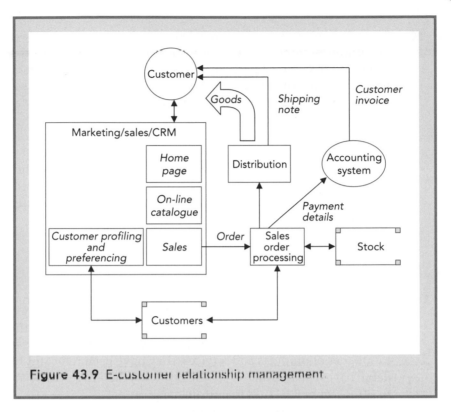

Figure 43.9 E-customer relationship management.

will dynamically build a profile of a customer and on the basis of this continuously adjust the profile to offer the customer individualised goods and/or services.

43.4 ⊚ THE CUSTOMER FOCUS

It might be argued that B2C systems are a natural extension of the increasing customer focus of organisations. Porter has argued that the value delivered to the customer is the primary feature of business. Hence it is not surprising to find a reorientation of information systems around the value chain of organisations. The push is for organisations to reorganise their information systems around a more overt customer focus.

However, for many organisations this demands a major reorientation of their informatics infrastructure. Traditionally, information systems within an infra-structure are organised around transactions or events such as invoices, payments,

> Example ▐▐▐▶ An insurance company runs a number of separate information systems for each of its insurance products. Hence if a customer takes out more than one insurance product with the company the customer is likely to receive a number of communications for each insurance policy. It is also difficult for the organisation to see which are its most valued customers and it is difficult to offer additional services to such customers easily.

orders. This makes it difficult to gain a precise picture of the objects or entities important to the business, such as customers. As part of e-business strategy, both back-end as well as front-end systems may need to be reconfigured around these key entities.

43.5 SECURITY AND B2C SYSTEMS

One of the major barriers to the utilisation of e-commerce by customers has been the expressed concern over the lack of security associated with such systems. This concern has meant that whereas customers might be prepared to inspect on-line catalogues of products and services, they have been reluctant to release credit card details over the Internet. Over the last few years there has been a growing attempt to offer secure B2C sites to customers.

To provide a secure environment for the conduct of e-commerce over the Internet, three conditions must be satisfied (Gloor, 2000):

- *Privacy*. Only the parties to the e-commerce transaction should have access to the information held.
- *Authentication*. Messages are exchanged between parties whose identity has been certified by a reputable organisation.
- *Non-repudiability*. A sender of a message cannot deny that they have sent the message.

Unfortunately, there is little agreement about the precise technological infrastructure for ensuring these different conditions. Different organisations tend to use different technological solutions to handling these problems. Here, we briefly consider two enabling technologies:

- *Secure socket layer*. SSL is Netscape's attempt to offer a secure channel of communication. It is a framework for transmitting sensitive information such as credit card details over the Internet. It involves using a sophisticated protocol between client and server systems, but is transparent to the user and provides a secure connection.
- *Digital certificates*. Digital certificates, sometimes called digital passports, are the means to authenticate users on the Internet. A digital certificate is issued by a trusted certification authority such as a government organisation, bank or chamber of commerce. Leading vendors of Internet browsers, such as Netscape

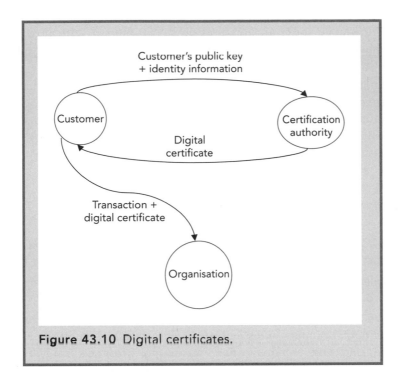

Figure 43.10 Digital certificates.

and Microsoft, use standards for digital certificates to implement SSL. Figure 43.10 illustrates the process of using digital certificates. The customer first has to request a digital certificate from the certification authority. She provides details of herself plus evidence of her identity to the certification authority. She also sends her public key to the certification authority (i.e. the key provided to her by the organisation she is trying to access). The certification authority produces a digital certificate and includes her public key within it. When she later wants to engage in e-commerce she uses her digital certificate to prove her authenticity to the participating organisation.

43.6 ◎ B2C INFORMATION SYSTEMS

B2C or customer chain systems are merely a special class of information system. Therefore, most of the material in the management, planning and development of information systems discussed in previous chapters is equally relevant to such systems. In particular, we must acknowledge that:

● Building B2C systems has increasingly become a core part of the informatics strategy for many contemporary businesses. B2C functionality in various forms such as those discussed in this chapter is seen as a form of strategic information system for many organisations.

- Knowledge about an organisation's customers is critical to that organisation's success. Hence effective knowledge management and systems to support it are critical to the success of many B2C initiatives.
- Evaluating B2C systems is critical for organisations. Evaluating Web sites is a specialist form of IS evaluation but the same principles apply. Organisations must assess functionality (a growth framework, such as the one discussed above, is useful for this), usability and utility. An assessment of the value a Web site provides to the business is essential.

43.7 SUMMARY

- B2C e-commerce focuses on the IT-enablement of the key processes in the customer chain.
- Customer chain processes include product identification, catalogue search, product comparison and purchase.
- We may think of an organisation's experience of B2C e-commerce as moving through a number of distinct stages of increasing complexity including information seeking and communication, marketing presence, on-line catalogue, on-line ordering, on-line payment and customer relationship management.
- Effective B2C e-commerce will involve the reorientation of the informatics infrastructure around a customer focus.
- A secure environment for B2C e-commerce should ensure privacy, authentication and non-repudiability.
- B2C systems demand the same disciplines as conventional information systems.

43.8 QUESTIONS

(i) Explain some of the major activities within the customer chain.

(ii) Describe some of the major stages of growth organisations may experience in relation to B2C e-commerce.

(iii) Why is a customer-focused information systems infrastructure important for B2C e-commerce?

(iv) Describe the three conditions necessary for a secure B2C system.

(v) Explain how SSL and digital certificates can contribute to greater security of B2C systems.

43.9 EXERCISES

(i) Use the customer resource life cycle as a model of the customer chain. Follow through its consequences for B2C e-commerce.

(ii) Take one company known to you and place it relative to the stages of growth model for B2C e-commerce.

(iii) Describe the customer relationship management system utilised within a company known to you.

(iv) Describe the technologies used to secure a B2C system known to you.

43.10 PROJECTS

(i) Study the take-up of B2C e-commerce amongst a limited range of companies. Discover the degree to which the evolution of e-commerce in these companies corresponds to the growth model discussed.

(ii) Investigate the degree of disintermediation and reintermediation in a particular industry sector in terms of i-commerce.

(iii) Investigate the issue of trust in relation to the growth of B2C e-commerce.

(iv) Determine the degree to which organisations now have effective customer relationship management systems.

(v) Consider the most effective ways of evaluating B2C systems.

43.11 REFERENCES

Gloor, P. (2000). *Making the e-Business Transformation*. Springer-Verlag, London.
Hoque, F. (2000). *E-enterprise: Business Models, Architecture and Components*. Cambridge University Press, Cambridge.

CHAPTER 44

INTRA-BUSINESS E-BUSINESS

Managers should map and comprehend the corporation in terms of its value streams and understand that most value streams need radical re-inventing

James Martin

LEARNING OUTCOMES

After reading this chapter, you will be able to:

- Distinguish between the Internet, an intranet and an extranet
- Explain some of the key components of a corporate intranet
- List some of the key benefits of intranets
- Describe some of the key application areas for corporate intranets

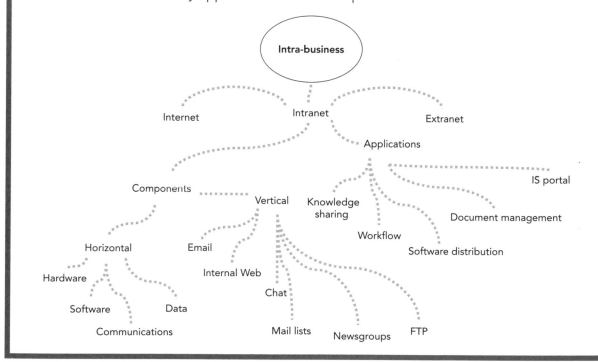

44.1  INTRODUCTION

Intra-business e-business is the use of ICT to support an organisation's internal processes. In a sense, all the material we have covered in the previous chapters of this work is relevant to successful intra-business e-business. Of particular relevance is:

- The focus on organisational processes and the importance of re-engineering such processes with the support of ICT to achieve improvements in efficiency and effectiveness.
- The way in which organisations have developed integrated and interoperable information systems architectures in an attempt to improve organisational performance.
- The recent concentration of IT systems architectures around the utilisation of mega-packages.
- The importance of developing strategy for information, information systems and information technology in organisations.

In this chapter we focus particularly on the issue of corporate intranets as key tools for improving organisational performance.

44.2 INFORMATION SYSTEMS AND THE INTERNAL VALUE CHAIN

The traditional structure of organisations is founded in a functional model. Organisations are structured in terms of functions such as marketing, finance and manufacturing and information systems have been designed to emulate this organisational structure. Each functional unit tends to have its own information system to service its needs. Martin (1996) calls this type of organisational model a functional silo, and the information systems architecture associated with it one of stovepipe systems. Stovepipe systems frequently use incompatible data, making it difficult for communication across functional silos. They are also systems that are likely to suffer from redundancy and fragmentation (Chapter 35). This situation is illustrated in Figure 44.1.

Value chain models of organisations stress the importance of cross-organisational processes. The emphasis is on designing efficient and effective cross-organisational processes that deliver value to the customer. This model of the organisation encourages the design of integrated information systems to support key organisational processes. Martin argues that this form of information systems architecture not only provides more utility for organisations, it enables the organisation to more easily adapt to changing environmental influences. This is similar to Hoque's (2000) idea of building dynamic business models on the foundation of reusable process and application models. This value chain perspective is illustrated in Figure 44.2.

Internet technologies have been used to restructure not only the external value chains of business but also the internal value chain. Of particular relevance here is the concept of an intranet.

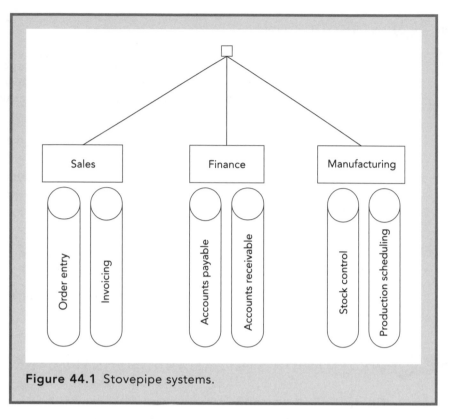

Figure 44.1 Stovepipe systems.

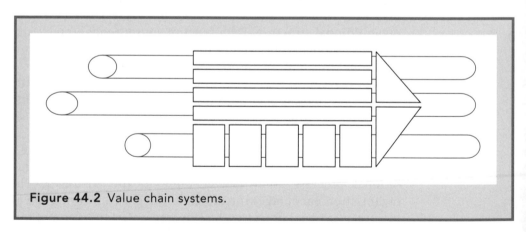

Figure 44.2 Value chain systems.

44.3 @ INTERNET, INTRANET AND EXTRANET

The Internet, an intranet and an extranet can be distinguished in terms of the type of user, the level of access and the type of information supplied. The main differences are summarised in Table 44.1.

The Internet is a public and global communication network that provides direct connectivity to anyone who has access to a local access provider, such as through a

Table 44.1 Differences between the Internet, intranets and extranets.

Network type	Users	Access	Information
Internet	Any external actor with access	Unlimited; no restrictions	General
Intranet	Authorised employees only	Private and restricted	Specific/corporate
Extranet	Authorised external actors	Private and authorised partners only	Shared partnership information

LAN or ISP. The local access providers are connected to Internet access providers and eventually to the Internet backbone. The control of information and access to such information of the Internet is unrestricted.

An intranet is a corporate LAN or WAN that uses Internet technology and is secured behind firewalls. The intranet links various clients, servers, databases and applications together. While using the same technology as the Internet, the intranet is run as a private network. Only authorised users from within the company are allowed to use it.

An extranet is an extended intranet. It uses Internet technology to connect together a series of intranets, in the process securing communications over the extranet. This it does by creating tunnels of secured data flows using cryptography and authorisation algorithms. The Internet with tunnelling technology is known as a virtual private network (VPN). Data on the extranet is shared between partners and enables collaboration between such partners. Access to the extranet is therefore restricted by agreements amongst the parties to the extranet. The concept of an extranet is illustrated in Figure 44.3 and is discussed in Chapter 45.

44.4 THE CORPORATE INTRANET

Martin (1996) refers to a corporate intranet as the internal nervous system of the cyber-corporation. An intranet can be considered as a special type of information technology system. As such, we can consider it in terms of its horizontal components or in terms of its vertical components. Horizontally, an intranet will be made up of (Figure 44.4):

- *Hardware.* Computers acting as both clients and servers will be required as well as communication lines between such machines.
- *Software.* Web browser software will be required on client machines and Web server software on server machines. The role of the Web server software involves processing requests from the client browser software and returning documents to the clients. An intranet may also have a domain server. This system translates between the numeric addresses assigned to each machine in the network under TCP/IP and more meaningful names for servers.

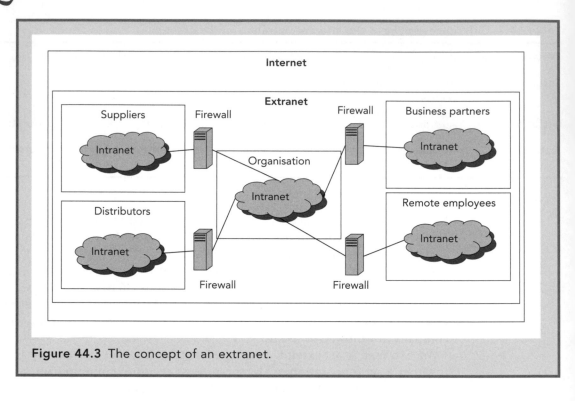

Figure 44.3 The concept of an extranet.

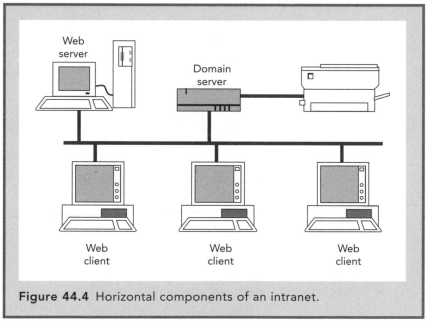

Figure 44.4 Horizontal components of an intranet.

- *Communications*. An intranet relies on some form of communications infrastructure. This may be a LAN, WAN or a combination of both. Hardware and software will be required to run the TCP/IP communications protocol.

- *Data*. Data will primarily be held in the form of HTML documents held on the servers in the network. Some data may be held in database systems accessible from the Web pages.

Vertically, we can consider an intranet in terms of a series of typical applications such as:

- *E-mail*. Most intranets utilise both e-mail servers and e-mail software to enable organisational members to communicate.
- *Internal web*. An intranet will use Internet technology such as browsers, HTML and TCP/IP (Chapter 11) to produce and disseminate information throughout the organisation.
- *Mail lists and list servers*. A mail list is a collection of e-mail addresses. Using this technology the same message can be distributed precisely to the persons that need the information. List servers permit the easy maintenance of mail lists.
- *Newsgroups*. Newsgroups consist of threaded discussions. Participants can post messages onto the newsgroup using e-mail.
- *Chat*. This enables people to communicate in approximate real time using Internet technology.
- *FTP*. File transfer protocol enables users to download large files from servers.

44.5 BENEFITS OF INTRANETS

Companies have implemented intranets with some of the following expected benefits in mind:

- *Better communication*. Email, chat and newsgroups may enable more effective communication between organisational members.
- *Access to more accurate information*. Information can be kept more up-to-date on central servers.
- *Better coordination and collaboration*. Workflow can be incorporated into intranets enabling structured coordination of activities between dispersed organisational stakeholders.
- *Easy to implement and use*. Establishing an intranet is relatively straightforward technologically speaking. Most people are relatively familiar with using the concept of a Web browser.
- *Cheap to implement and use*. The hardware, software and communication facilities required for constructing a corporate intranet are relatively inexpensive.
- *Scalable*. A corporate intranet is easily grown with changes in demand and use.
- *Flexible*. Adaptations in an intranet are relatively easy to achieve.

44.6 ORGANISATIONAL ACTIVITIES AND INTRANETS

Intranets have been used to support the following organisational activities:

- Enhanced knowledge sharing through Web pages. For instance, companies are using intranets to disseminate information in the form of manuals for various company practices.
- Enhanced group decision-making through the use of Web-based groupware and workflow systems. Intranets can be used to foster communication and debate on key organisational issues. They may also incorporate business rules that aid the flow of work between dispersed groups in the organisation.
- Distributing software around the organisation from an intranet server. The informatics service may find an intranet an invaluable tool for managing the software inventory of a company. Upgrades to clients can be managed more effectively and efficiently from central servers.
- Document management. An intranet may provide a repository for users to access pictures, photographs or text. The intranet can be used to manage key organisational resources such as manuals, news feeds, directories, organisation charts, corporate logos and reports.
- Providing a common organisational portal to key information systems. Intranets can offer organisations the possibility of building cross-organisational and uniform access to key organisational systems. Access to the launching of key applications can be more easily controlled.

Intranet examples ||||➡

Coopers and Lybrand developed an intranet to share knowledge amongst its consultancy employees in the taxation area.

Many newspapers utilise an intranet to make the archive of previous stories available to its journalists.

Compaq uses part of its intranet to allow staff to access human resources information such as retirement accounts.

44.7 SUMMARY

- Intra-business e-business involves refocusing the information systems architecture around a process model of the organisation.
- The distinction between the Internet, an intranet and an extranet can be made in terms of type of user, the level of access and the type of information supplied.
- Intranets are used by authorised internal users for specific organisational tasks and to access specific organisational information.

- An extranet uses Internet technology to connect together a series of dispersed intranets. Extranets are particularly used to establish links between an organisation and key stakeholders such as suppliers.
- On a horizontal level an intranet comprises a network of client and server machines running client and Web server software and storing HTML documents.
- Intranets are used for knowledge sharing, document management, distributing software and as organisational portals to key systems.

44.8 QUESTIONS

(i) Describe why a model of the organisation based around processes leads to a more effective information systems architecture.

(ii) Distinguish between the Internet, an intranet and an extranet.

(iii) List some of the major component elements of an intranet.

(iv) Describe some of the main benefits of intranets.

(v) List some of the major applications of intranets.

(vi) In what ways do organisations use intranets?

44.9 EXERCISES

(i) Try to identify any information silos and consequent stovepipe systems in an organisation known to you.

(ii) Build a case study of Internet, extranet and intranet usage in an organisation known to you.

(iii) Study one chosen intranet and identify the applications used.

(iv) Produce a detailed list of the expected benefits of intranets. Classify the benefits as tangible and intangible.

(v) Develop a case study of the organisational activities associated with an organisation's intranet.

44.10 PROJECTS

(i) Build two case studies of intra-business e-business and its linkage to knowledge management.

(ii) Survey a range of companies to determine the main uses of corporate intranets.

(iii) Conduct an investigation into the likely growth of intranets in an industrial sector.

(iv) In what respect is the corporate intranet an effective knowledge management tool?

44.11 © REFERENCES

Hoque, F. (2000). *E-enterprise: Business Models, Architecture and Components.* Cambridge University Press, Cambridge.

Martin, J. (1996). *Cybercorp.* American Management Association, New York.

B2B E-COMMERCE

Any business arrangement that is not profitable to the other person will in the end prove unprofitable for you. The bargain that yields mutual satisfaction is the only one that is apt to be repeated.

B. C. Forbes

LEARNING OUTCOMES

After reading this chapter, you will be able to:

- Describe some of the major processes of the supply chain and how these can be enabled through Internet-based information systems
- Define the relevance of vertical portals, Internet auctions and e-malls for B2B e-commerce
- Explain the enabling technologies of extranets, EDI and XML

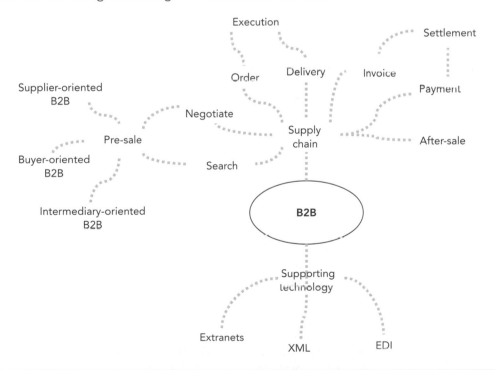

45.1 INTRODUCTION

B2B e-commerce (Figure 45.1) represents the attempt to use ICT to improve elements of the supply chain of organisations. Traditional aspects of the supply chain such as the execution and settlement of sales have been conducted electronically for a number of decades using technologies such as electronic data interchange. Much of the current interest in this area has been in the use of Internet technologies to enable the pre-sale activity within the supply chain. Enabling technologies in this area include the concept of an extranet and the recent interest in extensible markup language (XML).

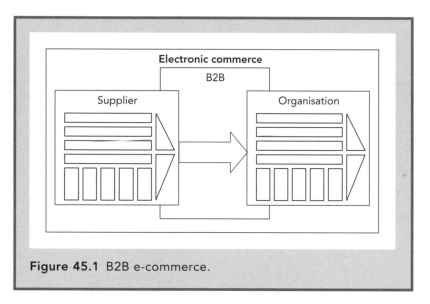

Figure 45.1 B2B e-commerce.

45.2 SUPPLY CHAIN PROCESSES

Most discussion of B2B e-commerce is directed at supporting the repeat commerce model (Figure 42.5). Here a company sets up an arrangement with a trusted supplier to deliver goods of a certain specification at regular intervals. Each of the phases of the repeat commerce model may be impacted upon by B2B e-commerce (Figure 45.2):

- *Search*. On-line forms will be filled out by buyers within organisations detailing features of the product or service required. This may then be submitted via the corporate intranet for requisition approval. After requisition approval the purchasing department will issue a request for quote to potential suppliers. Nowadays this may be conducted on an on-line bulletin board that connects buyers and sellers.

- *Negotiate*. After all bids have been received, a vendor is selected, probably using some software which ranks bids on the basis of chosen key features of the bid.

- *Order*. The supplier is notified of a successful bid and a purchase order is electronically transmitted to the chosen supplier.
- *Delivery*. After delivery of goods the stock control system is automatically updated.
- *Invoice and payment*. After receiving the invoice from the supplier the company arranges an electronic funds transfer with the supplying company.
- *After sale*. Supplier relationship management systems monitor all interactions with suppliers and can be used to check on the performance of particular suppliers.

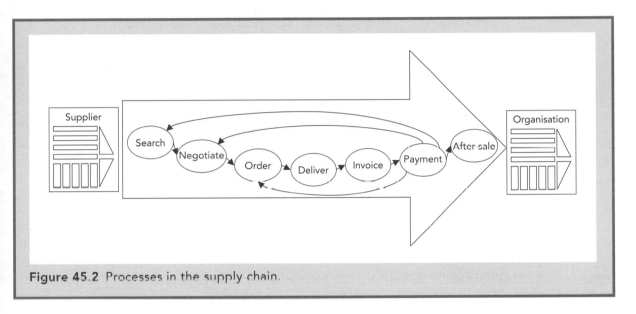

Figure 45.2 Processes in the supply chain.

45.3 B2B E-COMMERCE AND INFRASTRUCTURE SYSTEMS

B2B e-commerce is a natural extension of the informatics infrastructure of commercial organisations. In Chapter 5 we referred to such information systems as supplier-facing information systems.

The settlement and execution stages of the commerce cycle are normally handled by purchase order processing and payment processing systems. Such information systems are an established part of the information systems architecture of most medium to large organisations. Such systems have used standards for the electronic transfer of documentation with suppliers. Electronic data interchange (EDI) is a technology that has been used for B2B e-commerce for a couple of decades. More recently, extensible markup language (XML) has been proposed as a replacement technology for EDI.

The pre-sale and after-sale stages of the commerce cycle have been the most open to innovation in B2B e-commerce. Requisitioning, request for quote and vendor selection are part of what we previously called a supplier relationship management

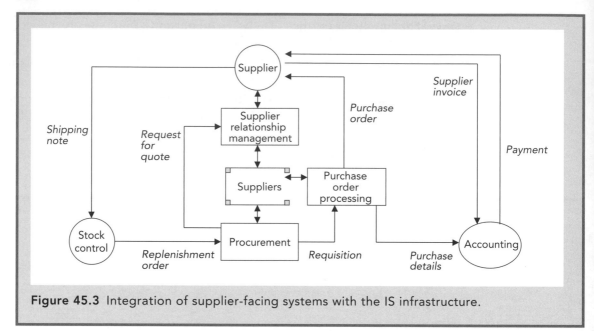

Figure 45.3 Integration of supplier-facing systems with the IS infrastructure.

information system. It is in this area that most of the discussion of B2B e-commerce occurs.

Figure 45.3 illustrates the relationships between the supplier-facing systems of supplier relationship management, procurement and purchase order processing and other infrastructure systems such as accounting and stock control. This emphasises that successful B2B e-commerce relies on integration with back-end information systems.

45.4 ⊚ PRE-SALE ACTIVITY

In terms of pre-sale activity the Internet has enabled three distinct models for B2B e-commerce to occur (Turban *et al.*, 2000):

- *Supplier-oriented B2B*. In this model, producers and consumers use the same market-place. Effectively, this is essentially the same as B2C e-commerce. One of the most popular forms of supplier-oriented B2B is the e-shop – the promotion of the supplier's products or services through the Internet.

- *Buyer-oriented B2B*. In this approach a consumer opens an electronic market on its own server. It then invites suppliers to bid on the supply information displayed on the site. This scenario can be expanded into e-procurement in which the later stages in the supply chain are handled electronically.

- *Intermediary-oriented B2B*. In this model an intermediary runs effectively a subset of some electronic market where buyers and sellers can meet and exchange products and services.

Intermediary-oriented B2B can be conducted in a number of ways, including:

- *Vertical portals*. Vertical portals aggregate buyers and sellers around a particular market segment. They produce revenue through subscription, advertising, commission and transaction fees.
- *Internet auctions*. B2B auction sites enable buyers and sellers to negotiate the price and terms of sales. Inventory is held by the seller but the auction site handles fulfilment of goods and the exchange of payment.
- *E-malls/e-stores*. These are general portals run by third parties offering a range of products/services from suppliers for customers. An e-mall is effectively a collection of e-shops.

45.5 THE BENEFITS OF B2B E-COMMERCE

B2B E-commerce has been driven by potential benefits that include (Turner, 2000):

- *Lower purchasing costs*. Traditionally purchasing is a complex, multi-layered process. E-commerce promises lower costs by lowering the costs of transactions and through economies such as the consolidation of purchases
- *Reduced inventory*. Through just-in-time initiatives, e-commerce allows companies to lower their levels of inventory, thus reducing the costs of warehousing.
- *Lower cycle times*. Cycle time is the time it takes to build a product. Electronic links between companies enables partners to have lower lead times, speedier product design and development, and faster ordering of components.

45.6 ENABLING TECHNOLOGIES

B2B e-commerce is built on a number of enabling technologies. We briefly review three such technologies here – extranets, EDI and XML.

45.6.1 EXTRANETS

An extranet is an extended intranet. Extranets can be considered as a series of connected intranets between the organisation and important stakeholders such as suppliers, distributors, business partners and remote employees. Martin (1996) refers to an extranet as the external nervous system of the cyber-corporation. The links between the elements of the extranet constitute direct leased lines or virtual private network (VPN) lines.

- *Suppliers*. Trusted suppliers may be given access to a company's inventory through an extranet. The supplier may then be alerted of falling stock levels and will be better able to plan its own production on the basis of predicted demand.

- *Distributors*. These stakeholders may be able to query warehouse databases directly via an extranet. This will enable the distributor to better plan the fulfilment of orders to customers.

- *Remote employees*. Salespeople of a company may be able to query the company's stock while on the road through an extranet. They are then able to determine precise delivery times for customers. This may be achieved through traditional connections between laptop computers and telephone lines or through the new generation of Internet-enabled mobile phones. Predictions are that this area of mobile-commerce, or m-commerce, will be a growth area over the next decade.

Extranet examples |||➡

FedEx maintains an intranet that tracks the packages of customers. A limited part of this intranet is made available to the customer, thus avoiding the company from engaging in time-consuming enquiry-handling.

General Motors has placed information kiosks in some of its major dealerships allowing customers to check on new automobile products.

45.6.2 EDI

EDI (Electronic Data Interchange) provides a collection of standard message formats and an element dictionary for businesses to exchange data through an electronic messaging service (Whiteley, 2000). EDI mainly supports the execution and settlement phases of the repeat commerce model. Four main flows of documentation occur in support of these phases:

- The customer sends an order to the supplier.
- The supplier sends the goods and a delivery note.
- The supplier follows up the delivery note with an invoice.
- The customer makes payment against the invoice and sends a payment advice.

Each piece of documentation, such as order, delivery note, invoice and payment advice would be coded up as EDI messages. Each message would be made up of a number of data segments and each data segment is made up of a tag and a number of data elements. The tag identifies the data segment and the data elements include the codes and values required in the message.

EDI has been in existence for over twenty years and has been used by major companies such as Ford to tightly link suppliers into their business processes. There is also a UN/EDIFACT standard that provides standard data formats for different application areas within business. The main problems with EDI are that standardisation has never been sufficiently broad and technical implementation has proved expensive. For this reason organisations are looking to the next generation of business documentation standards based on Internet technology.

45.6.3 X M L

XML (eXtensible Markup Language) is an extension of HTML (Chapter 11). It has been defined by the W3 consortium (the consortium formed to determine standards for the WWW) with the participation of prominent software companies such as Microsoft and Oracle. The fundamental difference between HTML and XML is that, whereas in HTML users use a set of pre-defined tags to define the makeup of Web pages, in XML tags can be defined by the users themselves for different application areas. XML can thus be used in a wide range of ways. For instance:

- Because the format of data can travel with the data itself in an XML document this language can be used to mediate between databases of various forms.
- XML allows customisation of content such as presentations and guides tailored to the particular needs of the user.
- XML can be used to specify standard templates for business documents such as invoices, shipping notes and fund transfers. Hence XML has been seen as a major way in which EDI may be replaced for electronic document transmission between organisations.

45.7 SUMMARY

- Most discussion of B2B e-commerce is directed at supporting the repeat commerce model. Here a company sets up an arrangement with a trusted supplier to deliver goods of a certain specification at regular intervals.
- Pre-sale activity can be conducted using vertical portals, Internet auctions or e-malls.
- An extranet is a series of connected intranets between the organisation and important stakeholders such as suppliers, distributors, business partners and remote employees.
- The benefits of B2B e-commerce include lower purchase costs, lower cycle times and reduced inventory.
- EDI or XML can be used as standards for the electronic transmission of documentation such as orders, invoices and payments.

45.8 QUESTIONS

(i) Explain some of the major activities within the supply chain.

(ii) Why is repeat commerce the most important model of commerce for B2B e-commerce?

(iii) Explain the differences between supplier-oriented, buyer-oriented and intermediary-oriented B2B.

(iv) Explain how Internet portals, auctions and e-malls are relevant to B2B e-commerce.

(v) Define the concept of an extranet and explain its relevance to B2B e-commerce.

(vi) Explain what is meant by EDI.

(vii) Explain what is meant by XML.

45.9 EXERCISES

(i) Find one example of an e-mall/e-store and analyse its key features.

(ii) Find one example of the use of EDI by a company and determine its key application.

(iii) Describe one key example of B2B e-commerce.

(iv) List some of the key problems associated with the take-up of XML.

45.10 PROJECTS

(i) Investigate the degree to which EDI is exploited in a particular industrial sector.

(ii) Survey a range of companies to determine the prevalence and main uses of corporate extranets.

(iii) Determine the level of usage of intermediary-oriented B2B.

(iv) Those companies that survive in the e-conomy will be those that integrate effectively their B2B systems with their existing information systems infrastructure – investigate.

(v) Determine the degree to which XML is replacing EDI as a standard for inter-business communication.

45.11 REFERENCES

Martin, J. (1996). *Cybercorp*. American Management Association, New York.

Turban, E., Lee, J., King, D. and Chung, H. M. (2000). *Electronic Commerce: a Managerial Perspective*. Prentice Hall, Upper Saddle River, NJ.

Turner, C. (2000). *The Information E-Conomy*. Kogan-Page, London.

Whiteley, D. (2000). *E-commerce: Strategy, Technologies and Applications*. McGraw-Hill, Maidenhead.

PART **10**

DISCIPLINE

The computing field is always in need of new cliches.

Alan Perlis

- Practice
- Profession
- Field
- Research

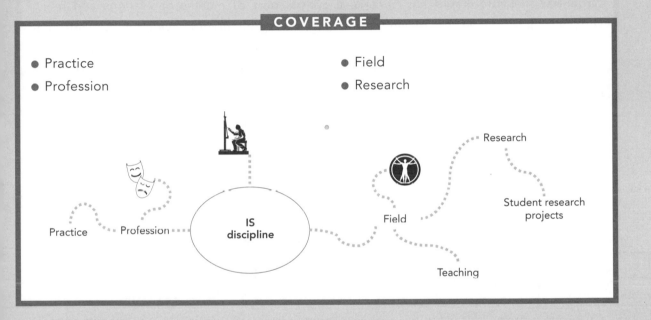

A discipline is an area of concern that encompasses an area of industrial practice, an area of study and an area of potential self-regulation. In the final part of the book we examine the discipline of organisational informatics in these different ways. As we mentioned in the Preface, organisational informatics is often referred to simply as the IS discipline. Since informatics is both an area of industrial practice and an academic field, we devote two chapters each to considerations of practical experience and academic endeavour.

Organisational informatics has become a central part of most organisations and many specialist jobs are now available in the planning, management and development of information systems (Chapter 46). In terms of practice there has been a substantial debate about whether the vast array of jobs and roles available in the area can reasonably be considered a profession (Chapter 47).

In Chapter 48 we consider the issue of whether organisational informatics forms a coherent academic field. The major question here is what makes it distinctive from other fields such as computer science and software engineering. It might be argued that it is impossible to build a well-founded academic field without a coherent body of well-established research. In Chapter 49 we consider appropriate ways of conducting research in the informatics area.

PRACTICE

Practice yourself what you preach.

Titus Maccius Plautus (254–184 BC)

LEARNING OUTCOMES

After reading this chapter, you will be able to:

● Describe some of the structure of the informatics industry

● Discuss the issue of careers in informatics

● Consider the crisis in recruitment within informatics practice

46.1 INTRODUCTION

Information systems and their associated technologies are essential for the effective working of modern economies, societies and polities (Part 5). Therefore, not surprisingly, a vast industry has developed worldwide servicing the IS and IT needs of organisations, groups and individuals. Informatics is a practical discipline. Many people are now employed in information-rich industries. Such information industries are heavily reliant on efficient and effective information systems.

In this chapter we consider some of the structural issues of such an industry and particularly focus on the issues of careers and skills. It is certainly true to say that something of a gap has emerged within recent times between the demand for and the supply of informatics workers in Western economies.

46.2 THE SHAPE OF THE INDUSTRY

Informatics is primarily part of the service sector of the economy. One of the notable facets of the change in employment patterns over the last forty years amongst Western countries has been the rise in the service sector. Within this sector the most rapid growth in employment has been in office-based private services such as financial, business and professional services.

Informatics personnel either work for one of the providers of IS and IT or for an established user of IS and IT, what we might call IS/IT consumers. Providers produce component elements for IT systems. Consumers will utilise such component elements for organisational purposes.

46.2.1 PROVIDERS

Informatics providers may be divided into:

- *Hardware providers*. These organisations are producers of computing devices, input devices, output devices, storage devices and communication devices (Chapter 8). Representative organisations include Dell, Intel and Apple.
- *Software providers*. These organisations are producers of software (Chapter 9), such as office software and enterprise software. Representative organisations include companies such as Oracle and Microsoft.
- *Applications providers*. These are a special type of software provider offering integrated package solutions to informatics infrastructure problems (Chapter 21). Representative companies include SAP and Baan.
- *Communications infrastructure providers (ISP)*. These are companies/organisations building, maintaining and supporting the physical telecommunications infrastructure of organisations, regions and countries (Chapter 11). Representative companies include companies such as BT and NTL.

- *Internet service providers*. ISPs are companies providing access to the Internet for individuals, groups and organisations. Representative companies include America Online (AOL) and BT Internet.

- *Application service providers*. These are companies that are able to operate and maintain aspects of an organisation's informatics infrastructure. They are similar in nature to what used to be known as service bureaux. Representative companies include Storagetek.

- *Informatics consultancies*. These companies provide information systems services to companies, particularly in the areas of planning, management and development. Representative companies include PricewaterhouseCoopers.

- *Outsourcing vendors*. These companies offer informatics outsourcing solutions (Chapter 37) either in whole or in part to companies. Representative companies include EDS and Oracle.

46.2.2 CONSUMERS

Informatics consumers may be divided in terms of industrial sector, such as:

- Manufacturing
- Agriculture
- Process industries, such as petrochemical industries
- Transport
- Financial services
- Retail
- Local and central government

Certain industrial sectors are much more advanced in terms of information technology than others. For instance, the financial services sector continues to invest heavily in information technology within the UK. In comparison the agriculture sector continues to be a poor investor in IT.

Another division of informatics consumers is in terms of large, medium, small and micro-enterprises. In recent years within the European Union particular focus has been placed on the small and medium-sized enterprises, or SMEs for short. SMEs are those companies with fewer than 250 employees. They are seen as the major seedbed for innovation in industrial economies. Hence major initiatives have attempted to stimulate adoption of information technology amongst such businesses.

46.3 INFORMATICS CAREERS

Informatics or information systems professionals work for either informatics providers or informatics consumers. Such workers have become an increasing part of the workforce of developed countries such as the UK. This is clearly an indicator of the growth in the information society, economy and polity (Part 5).

However, informatics is a relatively young industrial area. It is also an area that is subject to rapid change. Recruitment patterns in the industry tend to be driven by short-term technological skills such as the ability to program in Java rather than longer-term transferable skills such as the ability to design effective and efficient programs. This has made it difficult to establish coherent and consistent career patterns across the industry.

Professional bodies such as the British Computer Society (BCS) have attempted to develop a clear specification of careers in the industry. The BCS has developed what they call an industry structure model. This classifies some 200 roles within the area into nine broad functional areas:

- Management
- Policy, planning and research
- Systems development and maintenance
- Service delivery
- Technical advice and consultancy
- Quality
- Customer relations
- Education and training
- Support and administration

Ten levels of autonomy, accountability and responsibility are defined across these nine functional areas ranging from 0 – unskilled entry through 5 – experienced practitioner to 8/9 – senior manager/director/consultant. Not all functions are performed across all levels of responsibility. Programming as a role, for instance, will only be performed across the lower levels of responsibility, whereas management will only be performed across the higher levels of responsibility. For each role the ideal background is specified, as well as a range of activities expected to be undertaken by the role.

46.4 SKILLS CRISIS

Because informatics is now central to most organisations the demand for skilled informatics staff has grown steadily. This has caused a skills crisis both in the UK and worldwide. For example, at the time of writing there is an estimated shortfall of 300,000 such staff in the UK.

There are a number of factors that have contributed to such a skills crisis:

- The supply of qualified people in this area from sources such as further and higher education has remained relatively constant within Western countries such as the UK for a number of years.

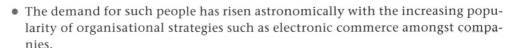

- The demand for such people has risen astronomically with the increasing popularity of organisational strategies such as electronic commerce amongst companies.

- Traditionally there has been a heavy gender imbalance within this area of work. This seems to have had something to do with the 'nerdish' image of practice in this area, which has discouraged women from training and establishing a career in informatics.

- Employers typically take rather short-term views in informatics recruitment. The focus of many organisations is on the latest IT skills rather than industrial experience and transferrable skills such as analysis, design and communication skills.

This shortage has persuaded many Western economies to look to third world countries to supply people with the requisite skill to address this demand/supply gap. Many US companies, for instance, have undertaken outsourcing of development phases to the Indian subcontinent. Also, countries such as the UK have included informatics workers in their list of preferred occupations, thus reducing entry requirements for foreign workers in this area.

46.5 SUMMARY

- Informatics is primarily part of the service sector of the economy. It is an increasingly prominent part of the makeup of most Western economies.

- The informatics industry can be divided into the producers of informatics products and services and the consumers of such products and services.

- Informatics suffers from a lack of clear career paths for workers in this area. Professional bodies such as the BCS have attempted to address this problem.

- Demand for informatics workers has outstripped supply in recent years. The skills crisis in informatics is due to a number of factors, such as image and gender imbalance.

46.6 QUESTIONS

(i) Distinguish between informatics producers and consumers.

(ii) Describe some of the major informatics producers.

(iii) How much of an informatics career structure is there?

(iv) Describe the key elements of the BCS's industry structure model.

(v) Why is there a crisis in recruitment in the informatics industry?

46.7 EXERCISES

(i) Search the Internet for companies in each of the producer areas identified in this chapter.

(ii) Discuss the importance of regulation to developing clear career paths for IS professionals.

(iii) Develop a brief policy statement indicating possible strategies for addressing the skill crisis in information systems.

46.8 PROJECTS

(i) Determine the precise makeup of informatics in a nation – determine the percentage in each producer area and the major consumers of informatics.

(ii) Investigate the utilisation of the BCS professional development scheme in an organisation known to you.

(iii) Investigate the skills shortage in informatics and develop policy guidelines for its solution.

(iv) Why is there a gap between informatics practice and informatics academia?

CHAPTER 47

PROFESSION

To become an able and successful man in any profession, three things are necessary, nature, study and practice.

Henry Ward Beecher (1813–1887)

LEARNING OUTCOMES

After reading this chapter, you will be able to:

- Define the concept of a profession
- Consider whether informatics work constitutes a profession at the current time
- Describe some models of the professionalisation process
- Discuss why professionalism is important for informatics

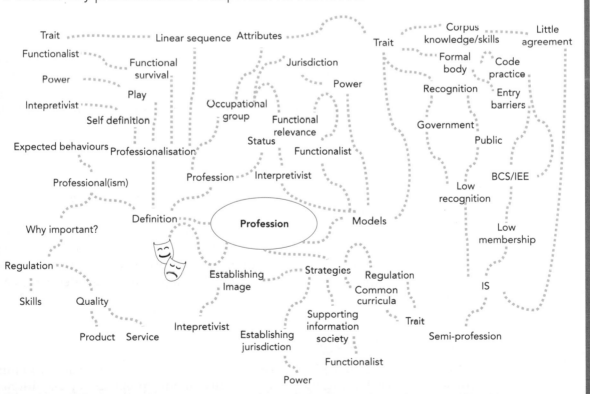

47.1 ⊚ INTRODUCTION

The ubiquity of modern information systems has caused a debate within the community involved in their development about the status of their work. Societies like the British Computer Society (BCS) and the Institute of Electronic Engineers (IEE) within the UK have attempted to cast informatics or information systems work as a true profession in much the same guise as lawyers, accountants, architects and the medical profession (Beynon-Davies, 1996).

In this chapter we consider the domain of informatics or IS as an area of practice and discuss the key issue of whether IS constitutes a profession. From this analysis we conclude that IS displays some characteristics of a profession but does not match the features of occupational groups such as medical doctors and lawyers. The issue of whether IS is a profession is important in ensuring that appropriate skills are imparted to practitioners in this area and also that their activities are suitably monitored and regulated.

47.2 ⊚ THE DEFINITION OF A PROFESSION

Many occupational groups have sought professional status. However, there is little agreement about what constitutes a profession. Elliot (1972) discusses how the term *profession* is widely and imprecisely applied to a variety of occupations. The adjective *professional* is even more overworked, extending to cover the opposite of amateur and the opposite of poor work, two concepts which need not be synonymous. Some sociologists disillusioned somewhat with the hazy nature of the term, have concluded that the concept of a profession is of little scientific value. They therefore cast the term *profession* merely as a symbolic label for a desired status.

We turn to the sociological literature for a number of models of a profession and the process by which occupational groups attain professional status – the process of professionalisation.

47.2.1   TRAIT MODEL

The traditional model of professionalism in the literature might be referred to as the trait model (Johnson, 1982). Trait models of professionalism present a list of attributes that are said to represent some common core of professional occupations. In this model the process of professionalisation is portrayed as a process made up of a determinate sequence of events. An occupation is seen as passing through predictable stages of organisational change, the end-state of which is professionalism.

47.2.2   FUNCTIONALIST MODEL

In the functionalist model a profession is an occupational group that have a functional relevance for society. A functionalist model proposes an evolutionary account of the professionalisation process. Those occupational groups that can clearly demonstrate their contribution to the 'health' of society in providing expert services in critical areas of human life are the most likely to succeed to professional status.

47.2.3 POWER MODEL

In terms of a power model, a profession is considered merely as a powerful occupational group in the sense that has achieved a certain dominance in terms of the claims made to practice in particular industrial areas. According to a power model, professionalisation is a process of power-play between occupational groups in their attempts to establish jurisdiction over expert work.

47.2.4 INTERPRETIVIST MODEL

The interpretivist model is less interested in defining an ideal-type of what a profession constitutes and more interested in the question of how persons in different occupational groups define themselves as professional. In this model the concept of a profession is a folk concept. Likewise, professionalisation is a process of interpretation by human actors. A process by which some degree of consensus emerges amongst groups of people about using the label professional to describe their work practices.

Table 47.1 summarises the four definitions of a profession described above.

Table 47.1 Definitions of profession.

Model	Definition of profession
Trait	Ideal-type of occupational grouping defined in terms of a series of traits
Functionalist	Occupational group that contributes to the 'health' of society
Power	Dominant occupational group that claims jurisdiction in an area of expert work
Interpretivist	Occupational grouping that defines itself as professional

47.3 TRAIT MODEL OF PROFESSIONALISM

In this section we focus on the trait model and then apply it to informatics work. Trait models are normally constructed by defining some common features from occupational groups with a readily agreed professional status, e.g. law and medicine. A feature analysis of such occupations leads to the development of the following 'ideal-type' (Jackson, 1970).

A profession might be defined as a group of persons with:

- An accredited corpus of specialist knowledge and skills.
- One or more formal bodies involved in organising the profession. In particular, the formal body will be involved in: maintaining a code of conduct/practice and monitoring adherence to the code(s); ensuring that only suitably 'qualified' persons enter the profession.
- Some form of recognition of the professional status of members.

47.3.1 AN ACCREDITED CORPUS OF SPECIALIST KNOWLEDGE AND SKILLS

To be a profession, some agreement has to have been reached in the occupational group regarding the content of theoretical knowledge and practical expertise demanded of members of the profession.

A profession normally sees itself as having an essential underpinning of abstract principles which have been organised into some theory. Alongside the set of basic principles are various practical techniques for the recurrent application of at least certain of the fundamental principles.

47.3.2 ONE OR MORE FORMAL BODIES INVOLVED IN ORGANISING THE PROFESSION

Established professions such as medicine have longstanding bodies such as the British Medical Association (BMA) which organise professional activities within the UK. Such bodies maintain a code of conduct defining the limits of medical practice. The BMA also accredits recognised medical schools and ensures that only suitably qualified persons enter the medical profession.

Most professions build an ideology based around notions of professional behaviour. This usually includes aspects such as:

- An orientation to the community interest
- An internalised code of ethics
- Rewards based primarily in symbolic work achievement

47.3.3 SOME FORM OF RECOGNITION OF THE PROFESSIONAL STATUS OF MEMBERS

Recognition is usually a critical aspect of professionalisation. Such recognition can take two forms: state recognition and public recognition. In the UK, Bott *et al.* (1991) discusses state recognition as being embodied in the assignment of a Royal Charter to a collective body. This charter defines the extent of the profession's authority and requires it to undertake certain duties and responsibilities. A profession also needs public recognition, particularly from its potential customers. Only with such recognition does the status of a profession act as a useful lever in the market-place.

47.4 INFORMATICS AS A PROFESSION

In this section we shall discuss whether information systems work in the UK constitutes a profession at the present time.

47.4.1 CORPUS OF KNOWLEDGE AND SKILLS

There is little agreement concerning the corpus of knowledge and skills constituting informatics work. In the UK, a number of standards have been developed for such work in the public sector, the most notable being the systems development methodology SSADM and the project management methodology PRINCE. However, it is still not true to say that an informatics specialist has an agreed body of transferable knowledge and skills that he can take with him when moving between positions.

There is also a big question about whether purely technical knowledge is sufficient. Friedman and Kahn (1994) have discussed the importance of including material on social and ethical issues within standard computer science curricula. Also, institutions like the British Computer Society have recently become interested in broadening the skills expected of information systems engineers. Within this debate the idea of a hybrid manager has been much discussed. The term *hybrid manager* was coined by Michael Earl to define a manager who combines information systems and business skills (Earl, 1989):

> People with strong technical skills and adequate business knowledge, or vice versa... hybrids are people with technical skills able to work in user areas doing a line or functional job, but adept at developing and supplementing IT application ideas.

47.4.2 FORMAL BODY

A number of bodies are competing to represent work within commercial computing in the UK. The main practical problem in turning informatics or information systems work into a profession is the fact that as little as 20% of the persons involved in IS belong to bodies like the BCS.

The BCS lays down a code of conduct and a code of practice. The code of conduct is concerned with questions of ethics and standards of behaviour. A member breaching these principles is said to be guilty of professional misconduct. The code of practice lays down, in very general terms, the way in which members shall approach the development of information systems.

The BCS has a number of routes to membership: a person can apply for membership after a certain number of years experience in the field, a person can pass the BCS Part 1 and Part 2 examinations, or a person can pass a degree in computer-oriented courses at an accredited university and obtain exemptions from Part 1 and/or Part 2 exams.

47.4.3 RECOGNITION

The British Computer Society attained chartered status in 1984, but there is some debate about the public recognition of the BCS. For instance, during the highly public systems failure at the London Ambulance Service the BCS was not reported in the general press (Chapter 15). Most of the statements made by the BCS were made in the computing press.

The main arguments for professional status are that in a time of increasing disquiet over the quality of information systems, a body such as the BCS can guarantee persons able to build quality systems. This can quite clearly be seen as an attempt to promulgate an ideology of public service in information systems work. It is clearly one manifestation of the attempt to link issues of accountability with good practice in systems development.

47.4.4 SEMI-PROFESSION

The key conclusion is that informatics constitutes at most a semi-profession at the present time. Etzioni (1969) defines a semi-profession as being an occupational group in which 'their training is shorter, their status is less legitimated, their right to privileged communication less well established, there is less of a body of specialist knowledge, and they have less autonomy from supervision or societal control than "the professions"'. Teachers, nurses and social workers are given as three prime examples of the semi-profession.

47.5 WHY IS PROFESSIONALISM IMPORTANT FOR IS?

There are clearly a number of benefits for organisations, economies and societies that may arise from the professionalism of IS. For instance, it is a truism at the current time that any person with a PC and an interest in computing can develop and sell software. Hence there is very little regulation in place to ensure that software developed is of a sufficient quality and standard to meet the needs of industry and the economy. Also, there is concern that there is little recourse to the purchaser of such software in terms of the market.

Professionalism implies regulation usually by some professional body. Such regulation is important to:

- *Ensure effective codes of conduct*, particularly focused on ensuring ethical conduct of informatics workers
- *Ensure effective quality of informatics work*, particularly offering forms of clear control of informatics workers

47.6 MODELS OF THE PROFESSIONALISATION PROCESS

Each of the models discussed above offers strategies for improving the professional status of a particular occupational group. We might therefore formulate some of the possible strategies in relation to information systems as an occupational group.

47.6.1 TRAIT MODEL

The trait model tends to portray the process of professionalisation as a determinate sequence of events. An occupation is seen as passing through predictable stages of change, the end-state of which is professionalism. Features of exemplar occupational groups such as medical doctors and lawyers are used to represent the end-state of the professionalisation process.

A trait model is implicitly applied in much of the IS and software engineering literature. As evidence of this, frequent statements are made portraying the relative youth of computer-related work as compared to, for instance, work in medicine or the law. Conventionally, a route is portrayed to professionalism which involves aspiration to the status of an engineering profession (Bott *et al.*, 1991). What is interesting is that although information systems work has used engineering as a professional status symbol, there may be problems embodied in the professionalisation of engineering disciplines.

However, the trait model does provide a template of professional status to aim towards. It indicates which areas of the current profile of informatics work need strengthening. Clearly, improving the strength of professional bodies is important. Having one professional body rather than a plethora would help. Organisational and governmental recognition of the importance of professional accreditation and regulation is perhaps even more important.

47.6.2 FUNCTIONALIST MODEL

A functionalist model proposes an evolutionary account of the professionalisation process. Those occupational groups that can clearly demonstrate their contribution to the 'health' of society in providing expert services in critical areas of human life are the most likely to succeed to professional status. As societies change different occupational groupings may be able to demonstrate their functional relevance.

The functionalist model indicates the need to focus on demonstrating the contribution IS makes to society and consequently the importance of IS workers to the 'health' of a nation's economy and society. The current prominence of the issue of the information society may help here in that it focuses on the information revolution and the importance of information technologies and the people who maintain them.

Hence there is a key need to demonstrate to the general public and to external regulatory agencies, particularly government, the necessary reliance on information systems in the modern world. Y2K and project failures have indicated the cost of IS/IT when it goes wrong. Better ways of justifying the expenditure on IT and demonstrating value would help. Also there is a need to demonstrate the importance of good practice to the production of good systems which in turn contributes to the health of the economy.

47.6.3 POWER MODEL

According to a power model, professionalisation is a process of power-play between occupational groups in their attempts to establish jurisdiction over expert work. Abbot's (1988) systems theory of professions provides a way of understanding the dynamics of professionalisation. Abbot's theory suggests that members of occupational groups formulate ideas of important tasks and of the expert knowledge needed to address these tasks. Each occupational group then competes with other groups in the same or similar domains of work for jurisdiction, or the legitimation of their view of both tasks and the expert work necessary to undertake them. Competition between occupational groups in one domain constitutes a system which achieves a temporary balance through what Abbot calls 'negotiated settlements', or temporary agreements on who does what in what territory. These temporary settlements are always subject to disturbance from factors both internal and external to the system of professions, resulting in jockeying for position until a new temporary settlement is reached. Typical disturbances result from technological change, organisational change, and the actions of legal or regulatory bodies.

The power model indicates the importance of gaining jurisdiction over information systems work. Ways need to be sought of establishing effective jurisdiction over information, information systems and information technology problems. Claims need to be established over claims by other occupational groups such as librarians, accountants and management consultants. This constitutes the need to focus on external power struggles. Informatics internally has traditionally been in a low power position due to its service role in most organisations. The expressed need to get more IS/IT managers onto the boards of the major companies is clearly part of this process of establishing jurisdiction.

47.6.4 INTERPRETIVIST MODEL

In the interpretivist model professionalisation is a process of interpretation by human actors. A process by which some degree of consensus emerges amongst groups of people about using the label *professional* to describe their work practices. It is also the process by which external agencies recognise the validity of applying the label *professional* to a particular occupation.

The interpretivist model focuses on the image and self-awareness of the occupational group. Professionalisation involves a process of building consensus about appropriate definitions both within and without the occupational group.

Clearly there is some interest from within the occupational group in defining IS work as professional work. An interpretivist model would emphasise ways of promoting the image of information systems as a profession. This would include promoting self-awareness within the profession and establishing better links between IS academia and practice with clearer definitions of core knowledge and skills. Some progress has been made in combatting the image of computing as a *macho* and *nerdish* profession. This may have some impact on the traditionally low recruitment of women into IS work.

Table 47.2 summarises the various models of the professionalisation process and possible professionalisation strategies for informatics.

Table 47.2 Models of the professionalisation process.

Model	Definition of professionalisation and strategies for informatics
Trait	Movement towards traits of ideal-type
	Strengthening and unifying formal bodies – increasing membership
	Clearer definitions of key knowledge and skills
	Stronger mechanisms of accreditation
	Improving external recognition of IS work
Functionalist	Evolution in terms of changing societal needs
	Demonstrating the value of IS work to organisations and society
	Encouraging more IS leadership within organisations
Power	Power-play between occupational groups
	Developing clearer notions of jurisdiction
	Lobbying the regulators for rightful jurisdiction
Interpretivist	Process of building consensus of definitions and attitudes
	Improving image of IS work
	Developing stronger internally consistent definitions of IS
	Promoting self-awareness within occupational groupings

47.7 SUMMARY

- Four major models of what constitutes a profession and the process of professionalisation exist: trait model, functionalist model, power model and interpretivist model.
- An analysis of established professions gives us the following key features as defining an ideal-type of profession: an agreed corpus of knowledge and skills; a collective body; and recognition.
- Assessing informatics work against each of these features leads us to conclude that at present it is at most a semi-profession. The trade has many of the trappings of a

profession such as a formal body. However, such a body presently suffers from low membership and diffuse public opinion.

- Each model of a profession suggests a distinct set of strategies for informatics or IS to achieve professional status.

47.8 QUESTIONS

(i) Define the key features of the concept of a profession in terms of a trait model.

(ii) What other ways are there for defining a profession?

(iii) In what respect does IS work constitute a profession at the current time?

(iv) Why is professionalisation important for IS?

(v) What strategies are available to informatics to improve the professional status of this form of work?

47.9 EXERCISES

(i) In an organisation known to you find out:
  - How many people see themselves as professionals.
  - How many belong to an organisation such as the BCS or IEE.
  - Ask some of the members and non-members about their attitudes to the BCS/IEE. What do they see to be the key benefits and disadvantages of BCS membership?

(ii) Discuss briefly what you feel are the main advantages of having a professional development scheme in place across the UK, and perhaps Europe.

47.10 PROJECTS

(i) Investigate the importance of professionalism to the informatics industry.

(ii) Consider two or more countries' experiences of the professionalisation of IS work.

(iii) How likely is informatics to become a true profession?

(iv) Many people have attempted to equate informatics work with engineering work. Investigate the advantages and disadvantages of this idea as a professionalisation strategy.

(v) Investigate the concentration of informatics skills in a limited number of outsourcing suppliers. What consequences does this trend have for the informatics profession.

47.11 ◎ REFERENCES

Abbot, A. (1988). *The System of Professions: an Essay on the Division of Expert Labour*. The University of Chicago Press, London.

Beynon-Davies, P. (1996). *Professionalism and Information Systems Failure*. Professional Awareness in Software Engineering, London.

Bott, F., Coleman, A., Eaton, J. and Rowland, D. (1995). *Professional Issues in Software Engineering*, 2nd edn. Pitman, London.

Earl, M. J. (1989). *Management Strategies for Information Technology*. Prentice Hall, Hemel Hempstead.

Elliot, P. (1972). *The Sociology of the Professions*. Macmillan, London.

Etzioni, A. (1969). *The Semi-Professions and their Organisation: Teachers, Nurses and Social Workers*. Free Press, New York.

Friedman, B. and Kahn, P. (1994). Educating computer scientists: the social and the technical. *Communications of the ACM*, **37**(1), 65–70.

Jackson, J. A. (ed.) (1970). *Professions and Professionalisation*. Cambridge University Press, Cambridge.

Johnson, T. J. (1982). *Professions and Power*. Macmillan, London.

CHAPTER 48

FIELD

An expert is a person who has made all the mistakes that can be made in a very narrow field.

Niels Bohr (1885–1962)

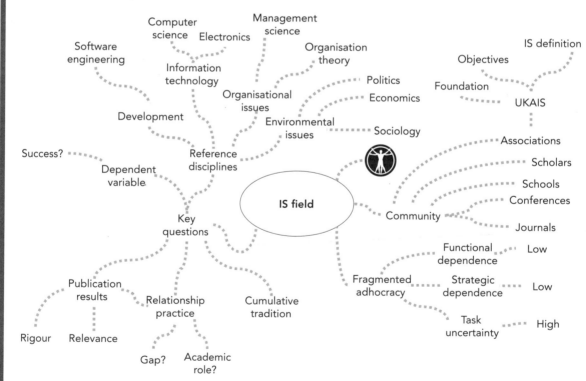

48.1 INTRODUCTION

In this chapter we consider the issue of whether organisational informatics is truly a valid field of academic endeavour. We first consider some of the classic questions which informatics seeks to answer. Then we compare this field to other academic disciplines and conclude it is something known as a fragmented adhocracy, a discipline in the very early stages of development. After considering the relationship between theory and practice in informatics we provide some concrete reasons for considering this field as an important area of study. Finally, we consider one attempt to define the structure of informatics or information systems as a valid field of study.

48.2 KEY QUESTIONS

Peter Keen (1980) identified five issues that he felt needed to be resolved in order for organisational informatics to establish itself as a coherent discipline:

- What are the reference disciplines?
- What is the dependent variable?
- How does informatics establish a cumulative tradition of knowledge?
- What is the relationship of research to practice?
- Where should researchers in this area publish their findings?

In this chapter we shall provide some preliminary answers to these questions. We shall describe informatics as being a fragmented adhocracy, a discipline in the very early stages of development. Part of the reason for it being a fragmented adhocracy is that it is by its very nature an interdisciplinary and multi-faceted discipline interested in the linkage between information technology and organisations. This defines the key independent variable as being information systems success. We will argue that informatics is necessarily a practice-led discipline. It seeks to provide theory for emerging practice. Because of its practice-led nature, focused around organisational and technological innovation, it is difficult to build cumulative knowledge in this area. The linkage between academia and practice within the domain of informatics is also subject to some strain.

48.3 A FRAGMENTED ADHOCRACY

Banville and Landry (1989) utilise a model due to the sociologist Whitley to examine the state of information systems or organisational informatics as a discipline. Whitley defines intellectual fields in terms of three variables:

- *Functional dependence* refers to the degree to which specific researchers in a field have to use results, ideas and procedures of fellow researchers in order to make knowledge claims. As functional dependence increases in a discipline there is evidence of greater specialisation of research topics, procedures and forms of communication.

- *Strategic dependence* refers to the extent to which researchers have to persuade colleagues of the importance of their problem and approach in order to gain a high reputation. High strategic dependence means a greater need to coordinate research strategies and goals with colleagues.

- *Strategic task uncertainty* refers to the degree to which hierarchies of problems are stabilised in a field. Low task uncertainty indicates tight control over research goals and minimal local autonomy amongst research groups. High task uncertainty is associated with loosely coupled schools of thought.

Their analysis of the informatics or IS field using these variables leads them to propose that informatics is a 'fragmented adhocracy' in that strategic dependence is low, task uncertainty is high and functional dependence is low. This means that IS is a discipline which has characteristics such as:

- Weak barriers to entry into the field
- Standards which can be affected by 'amateurs'
- 'Common-sense' language rather than well-defined terms
- Fluid reputations, often based on narrowly specific work
- Personal, weakly coordinated research agendas

One of the common responses to this analysis is that informatics is in this state because it is an immature discipline. It is proposed that with time it will mature and will occupy positions such as the discipline of physics that Whitley classifies as a conceptually integrated bureaucracy since it has low task uncertainty, high functional dependency and high strategic dependence. However, this response is open to some debate since management science, a cognate or reference discipline for informatics, is also classed by Whitley as a fragmented adhocracy and has been in existence for much longer.

48.4 TECHNOLOGY-DRIVEN FIELD

Clearly informatics is both a practical area of work and an area of academic endeavour and hence the relationship between the practice and theory of informatics is a defining characteristic of the field. However, there are a range of opinions as to whether this relationship is strengthening or weakening.

Senn (1998), for instance, has argued that a gap has opened up between the practice of IS and the theory of IS in the sense that practitioners see little if any relevance in the research produced by the academic community.

Holwell and Checkland (1998) argue that there will always be a gap between theory and practice within informatics because of its very nature as a technology-driven field. This relationship is illustrated in Figure 48.1.

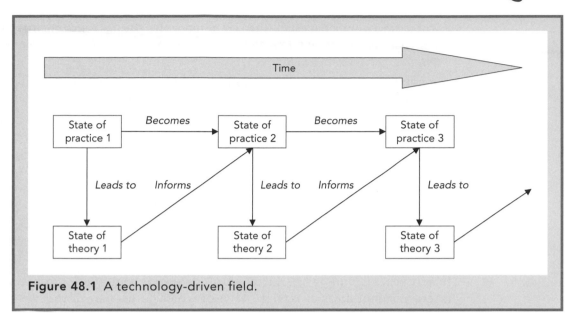

Figure 48.1 A technology-driven field.

In any field in which technology is important there will be a relationship between the investigation and exploitation of technical possibilities and the development of thinking which gives sense to the happenings within practice. However, in a domain in which the technology changes rapidly the investigation and exploitation of technical possibilities will happen prior to any developed theory of their application. Hence practice will always tend to outrun theory in such fields of study.

48.5 HOW DO WE KNOW THAT INFORMATICS IS AN ACADEMIC FIELD?

If organisational informatics or IS is a relatively young discipline striving currently for a distinctive face as compared to older more established disciplines such as computer science and management science, how do we know it constitutes a distinct discipline? Some of the reasons are provided below:

- There are currently a substantial community of scholars both within the UK and throughout the world who label themselves as IS academics.

- Within the UK there are some 20 plus departments/schools which either call themselves Information Systems departments, or have the term somewhere in their title. There are many more such departments worldwide. IS people can also be found in Computer Science/Studies departments and Information Science/Library Studies departments, as well as in Business Studies departments and Business Schools. The UK Academy of Information Systems lists some 85 departments in the UK that run Information Systems courses.

- There are a number of established conferences for the discipline such as the *International Conference on Information Systems* (ICIS) and the *European Conference on Information Systems* (ECIS).
- A number of journals exist for publishing the results of research in this area such as the *Information Systems Journal*, *European Journal of IS*, and *MIS Quarterly*.
- A number of bodies exist to foster communication, cooperation and collaboration for IS academics, such as the Association of IS and the UK Academy of IS.
- Professional bodies exist which support the work of IS practitioners. Within the UK, for instance, the British Computer Society (BCS) sees itself as the professional society for Information Systems Engineering.

48.6 COMPOSITION AND REFERENCE DISCIPLINES

In very general terms it is useful to see informatics as being made up of a number of interdependent areas of interest, each of which forms part of this work (Figure 48.2):

- *Environment.* This constitutes the economic, social and political environment within which the IS domain takes place.

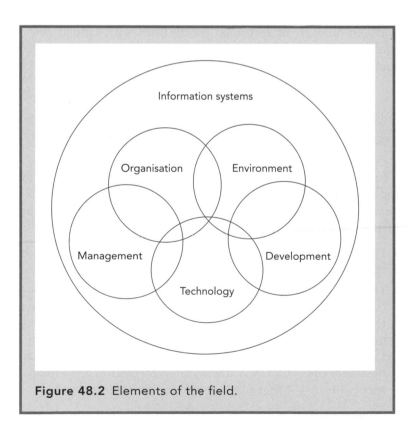

Figure 48.2 Elements of the field.

- *Organisation.* This area is interested in the ways in which modern information systems can support traditional and newer organisational forms. It is also interested in the link between IS and organisational effectiveness.

- *Management.* Here the interest is in effective ways of managing information, information systems and information technology within organisations.

- *Technology.* Information technology is an important component of IS work. However, informatics takes a balanced interest in both the use of technology and the principles underlying technology.

- *Development.* Here the concern is with appropriate ways of constructing information technology systems that support human activity, particularly decision-making. This means that certain classes of software system, such as real-time process control, are not seen as areas of concern.

In terms of the division of informatics detailed above, it can be seen to overlap with five other established disciplines (Figure 48.3). These are called reference disciplines because they provide major frames of academic reference for the domain of organisational informatics:

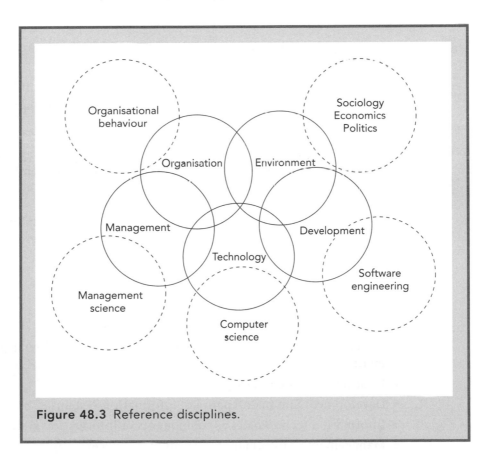

Figure 48.3 Reference disciplines.

- Through its emphasis on context, particularly the social and economic effects of IS/IT, it overlaps with the disciplines of economics, politics and sociology.

- Through its emphasis on organisational issues, there is a clear overlap with organisational theory as well as business studies.

- Its interest in appropriate management clearly references work in the area of management science.

- In its interest in computing and communications technology, there is a clear overlap with many of the issues underlying computer science.

- In terms of its interest in the development process there is clear overlap with the best practice described in software engineering principles.

IS is therefore a multi-faceted and potentially a multidisciplinary endeavour. But what defines the core essence or mission of IS? To risk over-simplifying we might argue that the concern is with the necessary interaction between information systems and organisations. Traditionally this has been described as an interest in information technology applications within organisations. This central theme is evident in a recently published definition for IS.

48.7 UKAIS DEFINITION OF INFORMATION SYSTEMS

The UK Academy of Information Systems has proposed a definition for the discipline of information systems in terms of product, domain and scope.

Product
Information systems are the means by which organisations and people, utilising information technologies, gather, process, store, use and disseminate information.

Domain
The domain of information systems requires a multidisciplinary approach to studying the range of socio-technical phenomena which determine their development, use and effects in organisation and society.

Scope
- Theoretical underpinnings of information systems
- Data, information and knowledge management
- Integration of information systems with organisational strategy and development
- Information systems design
- Development and maintenance of information systems
- Information technologies as components of information systems
- Management of information systems and services

- Organisational, social and cultural effects of technology-based information systems
- Economic effects of technology-based information systems

48.8 SUMMARY

- Organisational informatics is multi-faceted and multidisciplinary. There are a number of reference disciplines for organisational informatics or IS, including computer science, software engineering, management science, sociology, economics and politics.
- In a practical sense, informatics constitutes a field of study in that it has a community of scholars devoted to its study and a community of practitioners undertaking its practice. Informatics is a practice-led discipline.
- As an academic field of study informatics is a relatively immature discipline. It has many of the characteristics of a fragmented adhocracy.
- Because of its technology-driven nature there is always likely to be a gap between theory and practice in informatics.
- A number of definitions exist for informatics or information systems as a field of study including the UKAIS definition.

48.9 QUESTIONS

(i) List the fundamental questions of IS as an academic field.

(ii) In what way is IS a form of fragmented adhocracy?

(iii) In what way is informatics a practice-led discipline?

(iv) Describe the composition of IS as a field.

(v) What are the major reference disciplines for organisational informatics?

48.10 EXERCISES

(i) Prioritise the importance of Keen's key questions for information systems.

(ii) Search the Internet to determine how many actual UK universities use the term *information systems* to describe a department, faculty or school.

(iii) Conduct a search to see how many journals use the term *information systems* somewhere in their title.

(iv) Develop a SWOT analysis of information systems as an academic field of study. From such an analysis determine its likely potential for growth.

(v) Map the UKAIS scope of information systems onto the five-fold areas of information systems described in this chapter.

48.11 PROJECTS

(i) Replicate Banville and Landry's study some 12 years on and confirm or otherwise their key conclusions. Has information systems become less of a fragmented adhocracy during the intervening period?

(ii) Assess the likelihood of informatics or information systems becoming an established academic discipline such as physics.

(iii) Investigate the gap between academic knowledge and industrial practice in informatics.

(iv) Investigate in more detail why is it difficult to accumulate knowledge in a discipline such as informatics.

48.12 REFERENCES

Banville, C. and Landry, M. (1989). Can the field of MIS be disciplined? *Communications of the ACM*, **32**(1), 48–60.

Holwell, S. and Checkland, P. (1998). *Information, Systems and Information Systems*. John Wiley, Chichester.

Keen, P. G. W. (1980). Reference disciplines and a cumulative IS tradition. *Proc. 1st International Conference on Information Systems*, Philadelphia, PA, pp. 9–18.

Senn, J. (1998). The challenge of relating IS research to practice. *Information Resources Management Journal*, **11**(1), 23–28.

49

R E S E A R C H

If we knew what it was we were doing, it would not be called research, would it?

Albert Einstein (1879–1955)

LEARNING OUTCOMES

After reading this chapter, you will be able to:

- Consider organisational informatics as an area of research
- Discuss the importance of informatics research
- Relate various approaches to conducting informatics research
- Describe the nature of student research projects in organisational informatics

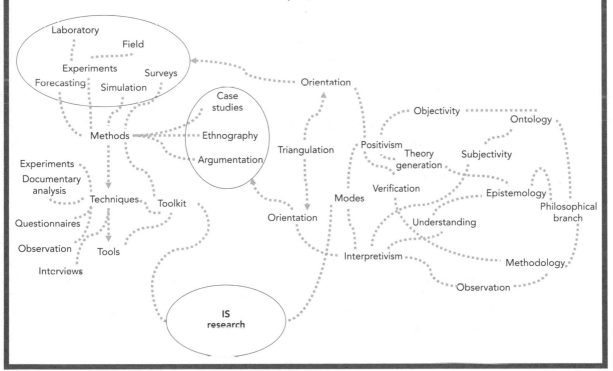

49.1 INTRODUCTION

In this chapter we consider organisational informatics or information systems as an area of research. The domain of informatics was considered in terms of its area of interest in Chapter 1. In this chapter we first discuss the importance of informatics research and consider appropriate ways of conducting informatics research. Much of this material builds upon the established traditions of social science research. We first consider two opposing traditions founded in alternative philosophies of social scientific enquiry. Then we consider some appropriate methods for use in organisational informatics research projects. We conclude with a discussion of some issues relating to student-based projects in this tradition.

49.2 THE IMPORTANCE OF INFORMATICS RESEARCH

Much of the material published in informatics or IS traditionally has been normative or prescriptive in flavour. For example, the empirical study of IS development methods (ISDMs) is a much neglected area of informatics research. Wynekoop and Russo (1997) conducted a systematic survey of the existing literature on ISDMs. They found that over half of the 123 research papers examined consisted of normative research in which concept development was not based on any empirical grounding or theoretical analysis, but merely on the authors' speculations and opinions. Of those that constituted empirical research, almost half were undertaken to evaluate ISDMs or parts of ISDMs. Few studies were undertaken to identify how ISDMs are selected or adapted or how they are used.

One characteristic of the informatics industry is that new tools, techniques, methods and managerial approaches tend to arise out of the practitioner community with very little empirical validation. Hence much of the industry tends to take on board such new tools, techniques, methods and managerial approaches largely on the basis of blind faith. Harel (1980), usefully characterises much of the knowledge underlying informatics as being based on what he calls folk theory. a collection of accepted wisdom that has three major characteristics: popularity, anonymous authorship, and apparent age.

It seems to us that it is essential to the practice of informatics that this cycle of generating folk theory is broken. Only if a true discipline of organisational informatics is created based upon the systematic investigation of this activity and the construction of best practice on the basis of empirical evidence will this area of work achieve anything like the degree of professionalisation it desires and produce anything like the products to which it aspires.

A large debate has occurred in social science generally and more latterly within informatics about what we would call an appropriate philosophy for research in this area. In general this philosophical debate has occurred along three main dimensions: ontology, epistemology and methodology (Orlikowski and Baroudi, 1991):

- *Ontology* constitutes that branch of philosophy concerned with theories of reality. Ontological assumptions concern the essence of phenomena. Generally speaking there are two main ontological positions: that the empirical world is assumed to be objective and hence independent of humans, or subjective and hence having an existence only in the sense that humans create and re-create reality through their actions.

- *Epistemology* constitutes that branch of philosophy concerned with theories of knowledge. Epistemological assumptions concern the criteria by which valid knowledge about phenomena may be constructed and evaluated. One popular epistemological position popular in the natural sciences is that a theory of the world (knowledge) is true only in so much as it is not falsified by empirical events.

- *Methodology* constitutes assumptions about which research approaches are appropriate for generating valid evidence. Certain approaches to collecting and analysing data, as we shall see, have a natural affinity with certain epistemological and ontological assumptions.

All of these dimensions are important for any research in that they define fundamental assumptions or pre-suppositions about how reality exists and appropriate ways of building knowledge of reality. In broad terms there are two philosophical positions that package together ontological, epistemological and methodological assumptions. These are known as positivism and interpretivism. These two positions are plotted against the dimensions of ontology, epistemology and methodology in Table 49.1. We have, of course, greatly over-simplified these positions for the purposes of explanation here.

Orlikowski has argued that the positivist tradition has dominated research in organisational informatics for a number of decades. She argues for a more balanced research programme that accepts the validity of interpretivist approaches to conducting informatics research. Generally speaking, acceptance of an interpretivist stance has been more popular in Europe than in the USA in recent times (Walsham, 1993).

From a pragmatic point of view both positivism and interpretivism are valid positions. This is of course why attempts like structuration theory as discussed in Chapter 16 have received such backing.

It is undoubtedly true to say that positivism has proven extremely successful as an approach for understanding the physical world. The physical world does demonstrate many features of independent existence and laws have been constructed which better enable us to understand the physical, chemical and biological processes underlying the universe. The social world, however, is a far

Table 49.1 Alternative modes of enquiry.

Philosophical position	Ontology	Epistemology	Methodology
Positivism	Reality has an objective existence independent of the observer. Reality is made up of objectively given, immutable objects and structures	The appropriate way to generate knowledge is to develop theories of reality, to test these theories against reality using structured instrumentation	Law-like generalisations about the working of reality can be constructed independent of time and context. Such laws can be constructed through the formulation of hypotheses and the verification or falsification of hypotheses in controlled tests
Interpretivism	Reality is an inter-subjective experience. Socially created and transmitted concepts direct how reality is perceived and structured	Knowledge of reality can only be generated in the process of attempting to understand phenomena through the meanings that people assign to them	Since an objective account of reality independent of social context is infeasible, interpretive researchers seek to develop context-sensitive accounts of social process by getting inside the world of those generating it

different phenomenon. Social processes are much more variable in terms of time and context. For social phenomena an interpretivist position appears much more tenable.

Organisational informatics or information systems bridge the physical world and the social world. Organisations are clearly part of the social world. Information technology is clearly part of the physical world. Hence both these positions are valid within informatics research.

49.4 RESEARCH METHODS, TECHNIQUES AND TOOLS

Because the discipline of informatics is interested in the question of the benefit of information, information systems and information technology, and because answers to this question demand multiple viewpoints, informatics has generally utilised research methods from the social sciences to gather data (Galliers, 1992). In a similar way to the distinctions employed between IS development methods, techniques and tools we may distinguish between research methods, techniques and tools:

- *Research methods* are general approaches to conducting research. Normally any given research project will utilise one particular research method.

- *Research techniques* constitute ways of collecting, analysing and representing data. A given research method may use a number of particular research techniques, although many will focus around one particular research technique.
- *Research tools* constitute 'technology' for conducting research. This may comprise video/audio recorders, statistical packages or simple pencil and paper.

49.4.1 RESEARCH METHODS

Table 49.2 indicates some, but not all, of the research methods currently being used in IS research and is based on one provided in the article by Galliers. Note that each research method has inherent strengths and weaknesses and that some constitute compound research methods in that they utilise a number of lower-level research methods. It is also useful to categorise methods in terms of whether they assume a positivist or interpretivist philosophy. Generally speaking, positivism tends to utilise quantitative approaches to collecting and analysing data while interpretivism tends to use qualitative data and analysis.

49.4.2 RESEARCH TECHNIQUES

In Table 49.3 we list some of the key features of some of the most popular research techniques. We also indicate their applicability in terms of particular research methods.

In terms of any one particular research project, one or more of these research techniques may be used in combination. This is frequently known as 'triangulation' of data collection, and is intended to provide a more complete picture of some phenomenon through exploiting the inherent strengths of each technique. Hence, if we were studying a phenomenon such as the contemporary practice of object-oriented programming, we probably would first wish to conduct a survey to gain an appreciation of the scale of adoption of this practice. We would then wish to interview staff at a number of organisations that had indicated adoption to gain an in-depth understanding of their utilisation of this approach. Finally, we would probably wish to observe one or more development projects utilising object-oriented programming to perceive some of the strengths and weaknesses of this development paradigm in practice.

49.5 STUDENT RESEARCH PROJECTS IN IS

On most undergraduate and masters programmes in the UK students will be required to conduct a piece of independent research on a chosen topic (Smithson, 1992). This is normally a requirement because:

- It is an effective vehicle to assess a student's ability to manage and conduct a piece of independent investigation in which a substantial amount of analytical and/or critical thinking can be demonstrated.

Table 49.2 Major research methods.

Research method	Key features	Strengths	Weaknesses	Philosophy
Laboratory experiments	Identification of precise relationships between variables in a designed laboratory situation with the aim of making generalisations applicable to real-life situations	The intensive study of a small number of key variables	The limitations of generalisations made due to the over-simplification of the laboratory situation as compared to the real situation	Positivist
Field experiments	Extension of the experimental method into real-life situations within organisations and society	Greater realism and consequently a greater confidence in generalisations made	Achieving sufficient control of variables to enable replication of experiments; Difficulty of finding organisations to participate	Positivist
Surveys	Obtaining snapshot data on phenomena through questionnaires and/or interviews; inferences are made from this data about relationships that exist between elements of the real-world situation	Greater number of variables may be handled than with experimental approaches; well-established protocols for making appropriate generalisations	Difficulty of controlling for biases such as respondent bias or that due to the time at which the survey is made; Little insight may be gained into the causes or processes of phenomena being studied	Positivist
Case studies	An attempt to develop a detailed account of some group or organisation's experience of a phenomenon	Ability to handle a large number of variables; provides a rich description of some phenomenon within its context	Restriction to a single instance or organisation; difficulty of controlling for variables and different interpretations; Difficulty in generalising from one case	Positivist/interpretivist
Forecasting, futures research	Use of techniques such as regression analysis and time series analysis to deduce future events	Provision of useful insights into future situations	Complexity of variables and relationships under study; dependent on the quality and relevance of past data and expertise of researchers	Positivist

Table 49.2 *(continued)*

Research method	Key features	Strengths	Weaknesses	Philosophy
Simulation, game/role playing	An attempt to emulate the behaviour of some system which would normally be difficult to study	Opportunities to study situations normally not amenable to study	Similar to the experimental method particularly in the validity of generalising from simulations to real-world situations	Positivist/ interpretivist
Subjective, argumentative	Creative research based on informed argument and/or speculation; particularly used as a means of synthesising knowledge by reviews of existing material	Useful in building theory or formulating new insights	Increased likelihood of bias in terms of researcher prejudices or time in which the research is conducted	Positivist/ interpretivist
Action research	Applied research where the researcher is allied to the group under study and attempt to both contribute practical value to the group and to develop theoretical knowledge	Practical as well as theoretical outcomes; frequently aimed at emancipatory outcomes; Biases of the researcher made known	Similar to case study research, but placing an increasing burden on the researcher to balance research with practical objectives; the ethics of this particular form of research may prove problematic	Interpretivist
Ethnographies	A style of research in which the researcher immerses him or herself in the life of some social group, both participating in and observing upon group activities	Potential to provide deep and rich accounts from the position of group participants	Problems of researchers becoming too closely involved in group life; difficulties of generalising from ethnographies in terms of theoretical and practical implications	Interpretivist

- It provides an opportunity for the student to integrate material from other modules of study.

The term *research* can prove quite daunting for many students. Here, we define research as a form of activity in which:

- The aim is to explore a problem or issue and to discover some interesting things about some phenomenon.

Table 49.3 Major research techniques.

Research techniques	Key features	Use
Experiments	Experiments are normally designed in terms of hypothesised relationships between independent variables (those presumed to cause certain phenomena) and dependent variables (those presumed to indicate the presence of certain effects). To study these relationships closely all other variation in the environment has to be controlled.	Laboratory and field experiments
Documentary analysis	A form of research which relies on the collection and analysis of written documents or other forms of artefacts produced by organisations and groups	Case studies, action research, ethnographies, subjective/ argumentative
Questionnaires	A questionnaire is a set of formulated questions on some topic. The answers to questions in a questionnaire may be either predetermined or open. Questionnaires may be used in association with interviews or sent to a group of respondents to be filled in independently.	Surveys, forecasting/ futures research
Interviews	This research technique is frequently used as a means of gaining an in-depth appreciation of some phenomena. Interviews essentially involve either a structured or unstructured discussion with some person(s) on a certain topic.	Surveys, case studies, action research, ethnographies
Observation	This research technique is important as a means of gaining detailed data on what people actually do. The observer may participate in the activities of the observed group or be independent of these activities. Observation may also be explicit or illicit.	Case studies, action research, ethnographies

- The process of exploration or discovery is approached in a methodical and systematic manner.
- Part of being methodical includes an assessment of appropriate methods of investigation.
- Both the process of discovery (the research method) and the results of the investigation (the research findings) are communicated to other persons.

The expectations as to the deliverables expected from an undergraduate or masters research project vary between higher education institutions. Typically a student is expected to choose an issue or problem relevant to the domain of informatics, to formulate a plan of research relevant to the chosen topic, to execute the research plan in a systematic manner and to effectively report on what is discovered. Typically on taught courses the student will be expected to spend between 30 and 60 person-days on the project and the final report or thesis will be expected to be between 6500 and 10,000 words long. On some undergraduate and masters courses the student may also be expected to give a presentation on his or her work.

Master of Philosophy (MPhil) and Doctor of Philosophy (PhD) research projects clearly fall into a different category. Students conducting full-time MPhil projects would normally be expected to take between 18 and 24 months to complete them. Students undertaking full-time PhDs would normally take between 36 and 48 months to complete their research.

Both MPhil and PhD theses will be expected to demonstrate some contribution to knowledge in the area of informatics and typically will be examined by eminent academics in the field at a *viva voce* – a spoken defence of the thesis by the student.

The contribution to knowledge does not, however, need to be ground-breaking. An MPhil, and more particularly a PhD, must demonstrate that the student has built upon previous work and added in some way to the sum total of knowledge in an area. However, the knowledge accrued does not need to be large. The important emphasis is that the results of the research project represented in some thesis must demonstrate that the student has received a satisfactory research training in its undertaking.

49.6 THE PHASES OF A STUDENT RESEARCH PROJECT

A typical student research project will involve the following phases.

49.6.1 CHOOSING A PROJECT

The student will be involved in generating ideas, briefly reviewing them and discarding those that prove infeasible or undesirable.

49.6.2 REVIEWING THE SELECTED AREA

Once a topic area has been chosen, literature in the area needs to be reviewed and a clear scope for the project defined.

49.6.3 PRODUCING THE PROJECT PROPOSAL

It is good practice for the student to generate a project proposal that should include the following elements:

- A project title.
- A brief description of the aims of the project.
- A limited number of specified objectives (no more than 6–8). It is useful to phrase these objectives in terms of clear deliverables.

Project proposals may also include:

- Some indication of what previous course/modules have been taken by the student that are expected to prove relevant to the project
- A brief list of references which are considered important
- Some indication of what resources such as IT, access to people etc. are seen as critical to a successful project

49.6.4 PLANNING THE PROJECT

A plan should be formulated for the project which includes some indication of how the objectives are to be achieved and by when. The project plan should ideally be included in the project proposal.

49.6.5 MANAGING THE PROJECT

The student needs to continually monitor progress against the plan and to revise the plan in the face of contingencies. To aid the student in this task some form of project supervision by experienced academics is normally provided.

49.6.6 DATA COLLECTION

A critical aspect of many informatics research projects will be a data collection stage. This may involve use of one or more methods, techniques and possibly tools from those discussed above.

49.6.7 ANALYSING THE DATA

Given research methods will determine particular ways of analysing data. For instance, collecting data using questionnaires will normally involve some form of statistical analysis.

49.6.8 WRITING THE PROJECT REPORT

The structure of the project report should address how each of the specified objectives have been achieved.

49.7 SUMMARY

- There are two main philosophical positions: positivism and interpretivism. Each position is defined in terms of ontology, epistemology and methodology.
- Ontology concerns the definition of reality.
- Epistemology concerns the definition of knowledge

- Methodology concerns the definition of appropriate ways of studying reality and generating knowledge.
- Generally speaking, interpretivism maintains that reality is inter-subjective, that knowledge involves interpretation and that appropriate ways of studying reality are through gathering context-sensitive accounts from actors in the social situation.
- Generally speaking, positivism maintains that reality is objective, that knowledge consists of theories and that hypothesis testing is the most appropriate approach to studying reality.
- The two philosophical positions determine a range of research methods, techniques and tools.
- Research projects of whatever level tend to be composed of a number of inherent features and go through a set sequence of phases.

49.8 QUESTIONS

(i) Define organisational informatics as an area of research.

(ii) Describe the fundamental differences between positivism and interpretivism as philosophies for research.

(iii) Why is informatics research important?

(iv) Describe some of the major research methods.

(v) Describe some of the major research techniques.

(vi) Describe some research tools.

(vii) Outline the nature of student research projects in organisational informatics.

49.9 EXERCISES

(i) Discuss the importance of documentary analysis to good information systems research.

(ii) Take one information systems paper and determine whether it uses a positivist or interpretive research approach.

(iii) Choose one information systems journal. Take the papers in one issue and produce a table of the research methods, techniques and tools were used in each paper.

(iv) Produce a project proposal for one of the projects listed in the projects section.

(v) Produce a plan of work for the chosen project.

(vi) Plan a research method for your chosen project.

49.10 ❀ PROJECTS

(i) Consider the interpretive/positivist debate within IS. Which research approach is likely to generate the most usable results for informatics practitioners?

(ii) How do we distinguish between good informatics research – is rigour or relevance the most important criterion?

(iii) Investigate the role of ethnography as a practicable research method – what advantages does it have and what problems does it generate?

(iv) What type of information system is needed to support informatics research.

49.11 ❀ REFERENCES

Galliers, R. (1992). *Information Systems Research: Issues, Methods and Practical Guidelines.* Blackwells, London.

Harel, D. (1980). On folk theorems. *Communications of the ACM,* **23**(7), 379–389.

Orlikowski, W. J. and Baroudi, J. J. (1991). Studying information technology in organisations: research approaches and assumptions. *Information Systems Research,* **2**(1), 1–28.

Smithson, S. and Cornford, T. (1992). *Project Research in Information Systems.* Macmillan, London.

Walsham, G. (1993). *Interpreting Information Systems in Organisations.* John Wiley, Chichester.

Wynekoop, J. L. and Russo, N. L. (1997). Studying system development methodologies: an examination of research methods. *Information Systems Journal,* **7**(1), 47–65.

BIBLIOGRAPHY

Abbot, A. (1988). *The System of Professions: an Essay on the Division of Expert Labour*. The University of Chicago Press, London.

Ansoff, H. I. (1965). *Corporate Strategy*. McGraw-Hill, New York.

Argyris, C. and Schön, D. A. (1978). *Organizational Learning: a Theory of Action Perspective*. Addison-Wesley, Reading.

Auramaki, E., Hirschheim, R. and Lyytinen, K. (1992). Modelling offices through discourse analysis: the SAMPO approach. *The Computer Journal*, **35**(4), 342–352.

Backhouse, J., Liebenau, J. and Land, F. (1991). On the discipline of information systems. *Journal of Information Systems*, **1**(1), 19–27.

Banville, C. and Landry, M. (1989). Can the field of MIS be Disciplined? *Communications of the ACM*, **32**(1), 48–60.

Barrette, S. and Konsynski, B. R. (1982). Inter-organisational information sharing systems. *MIS Quarterly*, Fall.

Bell, D. (1972). *The Coming of the Post-industrial Society*. Addison-Wesley, Reading, MA.

Benbasat, I., Goldstein, D. K. and Mead, M. (1987). The case research strategy in studies of information systems. *MIS Quarterly*, **4**, 368–386.

Bertalanffy, L. V. (1951). General Systems Theory: a New Approach to the Unity of Science. *Human Biology*, **23**(Dec.), 302–361.

Beynon-Davies, P. (1995). Information systems 'failure': The case of the London Ambulance Service's Computer Aided Despatch System. *European Journal of Information Systems*, **4**, 171–184.

Beynon-Davies, P. (1996). *Professionalism and Information Systems Failure*. Professional Awareness in Software Engineering. London.

Beynon-Davies, P. (1998). *Information Systems Development: an Introduction to Information Systems Engineering*. 3rd edn. Macmillan, London.

Beynon-Davies, P. (2000). *Database Systems*, 2nd edn. Palgrave, London.

Boehm, B. W. (ed.) (1989). *Software Risk Management*. IEEE Computer Society Press, Washington.

Bott, F., Coleman, A., Eaton, J. and Rowland, D. (1995). *Professional Issues in Software Engineering*, 2nd edd. Pitman, London.

Boulding, K. E. (1956). General systems theory – the skeleton of a science. *Management Science*, **2**(Apr.), 197–208.

Brynjolfson, E. (1993). The productivity paradox of information technology. *Communications of the ACM*, **36**(12), 67–77.

Burnham, D. (1983). *The Rise of the Computer State*. Random House, New York.

Burns, T. and Stalker, G. M. (1961). *The Management of Innovation*. Tavistock, London.

Button, G. and Harper, R. H. R. (1993). Taking the organisation into accounts. In *Technology in Working Order: Studies of Work, Interaction and Technology* (ed. G. Button). Routledge, London.

Buzan A. (1982). *Use Your Head*. BBC Books, London.

Carroll, J. M. (ed.) (1995). *Scenario-Based Design: Envisioning Work and Technology in Systems Development*. John Wiley, New York.

Cash, J. I., McFarlan, F. W. and McKenney, J. L. (1992). *Corporate Information Systems Management*, 3rd edn. Richard Irwin, Homewood, IL.

Castells, M. (1996). *The Rise of the Network Society*. Blackwell, MA.

Channel 4 (1999). *Station X*. Channel 4 programmes.

Checkland, P. B. (1978). The origins and nature of 'hard' systems thinking. *Journal of Applied Systems Analysis*, **5**(2), 99–110.

Checkland, P. (1987). *Systems Thinking, Systems Practice*. John Wiley, Chichester.

Checkland, P. and Scholes, J. (1990). *Soft Systems Methodology in Action*. John Wiley, Chichester.

Chin, J. P., Diehl, V. A. and K, N. (1988). Development of an instrument for measuring user satisfaction of the human–computer interface. *CHI'88 Conference on Human Factors in Computing Systems*. New York, ACM, pp. 213–218.

Churchman, C. W., Ackoff, R. L. and Arnoff, E. L. (1957). *Introduction to Operations Research*. Wiley, New York.

Churchman, C. W. and Verhulst, M. (1960). *Management Science, Models and Techniques*. Pergamon, New York.

Ciborra, C. and Jelassi, T. (1994). *Strategic Information Systems: a European Perspective*. John Wiley, Chichester.

Coopers (1996). *Managing Information and Systems Risks: Results of an International Survey of Large Organisations*. Coopers and Lybrand.

Currie, W. (1994). The strategic management of a large-scale IT project in the financial services sector. *New Technology, Work and Employment*, **9**(1), 19–29.

Currie, W. (2000). *The Global Information Society*. John Wiley, Chichester.

Davenport, T. H. (1993). *Process Innovation: Re-engineering Work Through IT*. Harvard Business School Press, Cambridge, MA.

Davenport, T. H. (1998). Putting the enterprise into the enterprise system. *Harvard Business Review*, July/Aug, pp. 121–131.

DeLone, W. H. and McLean, E. R. (1992). Information systems success: the quest for the dependent variable. *Information Systems Research*, **3**(1), 60–95.

Drucker, P. F. (1994). The theory of the business. *Harvard Business Review*, **72**(5), 95–104.

Drummond, H. (1994). Escalation in organisational decision-making: a case of recruiting an incompetent employee. *Journal of Behavioural Decision-Making*, **7**, 43–55.

Durkheim, E. (1936). *The Rules of Sociological Method*. The Free Press, Glencoe.

Earl, M. J. (1989). *Management Strategies for Information Technology*. Prentice Hall, Hemel Hempstead.

Eason, K. D. (1988). *Information Technology and Organisational Change*. Taylor & Francis, London.

Elliot, P. (1972). *The Sociology of the Professions*. Macmillan, London.

Ellis, W. D. (1938). *A Source Book of Gestalt Psychology*. Routledge & Kegan Paul, London.

Emery, F. E. and Trist, E. L. (1960). Socio-technical systems. In *Management Science, Models and Techniques* (eds. C. W. Churchman and M. Verhulst). Pergamon, New York.

Etzioni, A. (1969). *The Semi-Professions and Their Organisation: Teachers, Nurses and Social Workers*. Free Press, New York.

Ewusi-Mensah, K. and Przasnyski, Z. H. (1994). Factors contributing to the abandonment of information systems development projects. *Journal of Information Technology*, **9**, 185–201.

Ewusi-Mensah, K. and Przasnyski, Z. H. (1995). Learning from abandoned information system development projects. *Journal of Information Technology*, **10**, 3–14.

Fitzgerald, G. (2000). *IT at the Heart of Business*. BCS, Swindon.

Fitzgerald, G. (2000). Adaptability and flexibility in IS development. In *Business Information Technology Management: Alternative and Adaptive Futures* (eds. R. Hackney and D. Dunn). Macmillan, London, pp. 13–24.

Flowers, S. (1996). *Software Failure, Management Failure: Amazing Stories and Cautionary Tales*. Chichester, John Wiley.

Friedman, A. L. and Cornford, D. S. (1989). *Computer Systems Development: History, Organisation and Implementation*. John Wiley, Chichester.

Friedman, B. and Kahn, P. (1994). Educating computer scientists: the social and the technical. *Communications of the ACM*, **37**(1), 65–70.

Galliers, R. (1992). *Information Systems Research: Issues, Methods and Practical Guidelines*. Blackwells, London.

Giddings, R. V. (1984). Accommodating Uncertainty in Software Design. *Communications of the ACM*, **27**(5), 428–434.

Gladden, G. R. (1982). Stop the lifecycle I want to get off. *Software Engineering Notes*, **7**(2), 35–39.

Gloor, P. (2000). *Making the e-Business Transformation*. Springer-Verlag, London.

Goffman, E. (1990). *Stigma: Notes on the Management of Spoiled Identity*. Penguin, Harmondsworth.

Goodhue, D. L., Wybo, M. D. and Kirsch, L. J. (1992). The impact of data integration on the costs and benefits of information systems. *MIS Quarterly*, **16**(3), 293–311.

Hackney, R. and Dunn, D. (eds.) (2000). *Business Information Technology Management: Alternative and Adaptive Futures*. Macmillan, London.

Hammer, M. (1990). Re-engineering work: Don't automate, obliterate. *Harvard Business Review*. July/August, pp. 18–25.

Hammer, M. and Champy, J. (1993). *Reengineering the Corporation: a Manifesto for Business Revolution*. Nicholas Brearley, London.

Hammer, M. (1996). *Beyond Re-engineering: How the Process-centred Organisation is Changing Our Lives*. HarperCollins, London.

Harel, D. (1980). On folk theorems. *Communications of the ACM*, **23**(7), 379–389.

Hirschheim, R. A. (1983). Assessing participatory systems design: some conclusions from an exploratory study. *Information and Management*, **6**, 317–327.

Hirschheim, R. and Newman, M. (1988). Information systems and user resistance: theory and practice. *Computer Journal*, **31**(5), 398–408.

Hirschheim, R. and Newman, M. (1991). Symbolism and IS development: myth, metaphor and magic. *IS Research*, **2**(1), 29–62.

Hofstede, G. (1991). *Cultures and Organisations*. McGraw-Hill, New York.

Holwell, S. and Checkland, P. (1998). *Information, Systems and Information Systems*. John Wiley, Chichester.

Holwell, S. and Checkland, P. (1998). An information system won the war. *IEE Proceedings Software*, **145**(4), 95–99.

Hoque, F. (2000). *E-enterprise: Business Models, Architecture and Components*. Cambridge University Press, Cambridge.

Ives, B. and Learmonth, G. P. (1984). The information system as a competitive weapon. *Communications of the ACM*, **27**(12), 1193–1201.

Jackson, J. A. (ed.) (1970). *Professions and Professionalisation*. Cambridge University Press, Cambridge.

Johnson, T. J. (1982). *Professions and Power*. Macmillan, London.

Johnson, G. and Scholes, K. (2000). *Exploring Corporate Strategy: Text and Cases*. 2nd edn. Prentice Hall, Englewood Cliffs, NJ.

Kalakota, R. and Whinston, A. B. (1997). *Electronic Commerce: a Manager's Guide*. Addison-Wesley, Harlow.

Katz, D. and Kahn, R. L. (1966). *The Social Psychology of Organisations*. Wiley, New York.

Keen, P. and Gerson, E. M. (1977). The politics of software systems design. *Datamation*, November.

Keen, P. G. W. (1980). Reference disciplines and a cumulative IS tradition. *Proc. 1st International Conference on Information Systems*, Philadelphia, PA, pp. 9–18.

Keen, P. (1981). Information systems and organisational change. *Communications of the ACM*, **24**(1), 24–33.

Klein, H. K. and Hirschheim, R. A. (1987). A comparative framework of data modelling paradigms and approaches. *The Computer Journal*, **30**(1), 8–14.

Kling, R. and Scaachi, W. (1982). The Web of computing: computer technology as social organisation. *Advances in Computers*, **21**, 1–90.

Kling, R. and Iacono, S. (1984). The control of IS developments after implementation. *Communications of the ACM*, **27**(12), 1218–1226.

Kling, R. and Allen, J. P. (1996). Can computer science solve organisational problems? The case for organisational informatics. In *Computerisation and Controversy: Value Conflicts and Social Choices* (ed. R. Kling). Academic Press, San Diego, CA.

Kumar, K. (1990). Post-implementation evaluation of computer-based information systems: current practices. *Communications of the ACM*, **33**(2), 236–252.

Lacity, M. and Hirschheim, R. (1993). *Information Systems Outsourcing: Myths, Metaphors and Realities*. John Wiley, Chichester.

Landauer, T. K. (1995). *The Trouble with Computers: Usefulness, Usability and Productivity*. MIT Press, Cambridge, MA.

Lewis, P. (1994). *Information Systems Development: Systems Thinking in the Field of Information Systems*. Pitman, London.

Liebenau, J. and Backhouse, J. (1990). *Understanding Information: an Introduction*. Macmillan, London.

Liebowitz, J. (ed.) (1999). *Knowledge Management Handbook*. CRC Press, Boca Raton, FL.

Lucas, H. C. (1975). *Why Information Systems Fail*. Columbia University Press, New York.

Lyytinen, K. J. (1985). Implications of theories of language for information systems. *MIS Quarterly*, **9**(March), 61–74.

Lyytinen, K. (1988). The Expectation Failure Concept and Systems Analysts View of Information Systems Failures: results of an exploratory study. *Information and Management*. 14.45-55.

Lyytinen, K. and Hirschheim, R. (1987). Information systems failures: a survey and classification of the empirical literature. *Oxford Surveys in Information Technology*, **4**, 257–309.

Malone, T. W., Crowston, K. G., Lee, J. and Pentland, B. (1999). Tools for inventing organisations: toward a handbook of organisational processes. *Management Science*, **45**(3), 425–443.

Martin, J. (1996). *Cybercorp*. American Management Association, New York.

Maurer, J. G. (1971). *Readings in Organisation Theory: Open Systems Approaches*. Random House, New York.

Mayo, E. M. (1933). *The Human Problems of an Industrial Civilisation*. Macmillan, New York.

McGregror, D. (1960). *The Human Side of the Enterprise*. McGraw-Hill, New York.

McKenzie, D. (1994). Computer-related accidental death: an empirical exploration. *Science and Public Policy*, **21**(4), 233–248.

Moore, K. and Ruddle, K. (2000). New business models – the challenges of transition. In *Moving to e-Business: the Ultimate Practical Guide to e-Business* (eds. L. Wilcocks and C. Sauer). Random House, London.

Morgan, G. (1986). *Images of Organisation*. Sage, London.

Mumford, E. (1983). *Designing Participatively*. Manchester Business School Press, Manchester.

Mumford, E. (1996). *Systems Design: Ethical Tools for Ethical Change*. Macmillan, London.

Newman, M. and Sabherwal, R. (1996). Determinants of commitment to information systems development: a longitudinal investigation. *MIS Quarterly*, **20**(1), 23–54.

Nielsen, J. (1993). *Usability Engineering*. Academic Press, Boston.

Nolan, R. L. (1990). Managing the Crisis in Data Processing. In *The Information Infrastructure*. Harvard Business Review, Cambridge, MA.

O'Connell, F. (1996). *How to Run Successful Projects II: the Silver Bullet*. Prentice Hall, Hemel Hempstead.

Orlikowski, W. J. (1996). *Realising the Potential of New Technologies: an Improvisation Model of Change Management*. Business Information Technology, Manchester Metropolitan University.

Orlikowski, W. J. and Baroudi, J. J. (1991). Studying information technology in organisations: research approaches and assumptions. *Information Systems Research*, **2**(1), 1–28.

Orlikowski, W. T. and Gash, T. C. (1994). Technological frames: making sense of information technology in organisations. *ACM Trans. on Information Systems*. **12**(2), 174–207.

Oz, E. (1994). When professional standards are lax: the confirm failure and its lessons. *Communications of the ACM*, **37**(10), 29–36.

Parker, M., Benson, R. and Trainor, H. (1988). *Information Economics: Linking Business Performance to Information Technology*. Prentice Hall, Englewood Cliffs, NJ.

Polanyi, M. (1962). *Personal Knowledge*. Anchor Day Books, New York.

Porter, M. E. and Millar, V. E. (1985). How information gives you competitive advantage. *Harvard Business Review*, **63**(4), 149–160.

Porter, M. E. (1985). *Competitive Advantage: Creating and Sustaining Superior Performance*. Free Press, New York.

Public Accounts Committee (1993). *Wessex Regional Health Authority Regional Information Systems Plan*, HMSO.

Robey, D. and Markus, M. L. (1984). Rituals in information systems design. *MIS Quarterly*, **8**, March, 5–15.

Sachs, P. (1995). Transforming work: collaboration, learning and design. Communications of the ACM, **38**(9), 36–45.

Salabert, D. and Newman, M. (1995). Regaining control: the case of the Spanish air traffic control system – SACTA. *European Conference on Information Systems* (ed. G. Doukidis), Athens, Greece, pp. 1171–1179.

Sauer, C. (1993). *Why Information Systems Fail: A Case Study Approach*. Alfred Waller, Henley-On-Thames.

Scott-Morton, M. S. (ed.) (1991). *The Corporation of the 1990s: Information Technology and Organisational Transformation*. Oxford University Press, New York.

Senge, P. M. (1990). *The Fifth Discipline: the Art and Practice of the Learning Organisation*. Doubleday, New York.

Senn, J. (1998). The challenge of relating IS research to practice. *Information Resources Management Journal*, **11**(1), 23–28.

Shannon, C. E. (1949). *The Mathematical Theory of Communication*. University of Illinois Press, Urbana.

Silver, M. S., Markus, M. L. and Beath, C. M. (1995). The Information Technology Interaction Model: a foundation for the MBA core course. *MIS Quarterly*. **19**(3). 361-390.

Silverman, D. (1982). *The Theory of Organisations*. Macmillan, London.

Simon, H. (1960). *The New Science of Management Decisions*. Harper & Row, New York.

Simon, H. A. (1976). *Administrative Behavior: A Study of Decision-making Processes in Administration*, 3rd edn. Free Press, New York.

Singh, S. (2000). *The Science of Secrecy*. Fourth Estate, London.

Smithson, S. and Cornford, T. (1992). *Project Research in Information Systems*. Macmillan, London.

Sommerville, I., Bentley, R., Rodden, T. and Sawyer, P. (1994). Cooperative systems design. *The Computer Journal*, **37**(5).

Sowa, J. F. (1984). *Conceptual Structures: Information Processing in Mind and Machine.* Addison-Wesley, Reading, MA.

Stamper, R. K. (1973). *Information in Business and Administrative Systems.* Batsford, London.

Stamper, R. K. (1985). Information: mystical fluid or a subject for scientific enquiry? *The Computer Journal.* **28**(3).

Stamper, R. and Liu, K. (1991). From database to normbase. *International Journal of Information Management*, **11**, 67–84.

Stapleton, J. (1997). *DSDM – Dynamic Systems Development Method: the Method in Practice.* Addison-Wesley, Harlow.

Swanson, E. B. (1992). *Maintaining Information Systems in Organisations.* John Wiley, Chichester.

Taylor, F. W. (1911). *Principles of Scientific Management.* Harper & Row, New York.

Tsitchizris, D. C. and Lochovsky, F. H. (1982). *Data Models.* Prentice Hall, Englewood Cliffs, NJ.

Turban, E., Lee, J., King, D. and Chung, H. M. (2000). *Electronic Commerce: a Managerial Perspective.* Prentice Hall, Upper Saddle River, NJ.

Turner, C. (2000). *The Information E-Conomy.* Kogan Page, London.

US (1979). US Government Accounting Office Report FGMSD-80-4. Reported in *ACM Sigsoft Software Engineering Notes*, **10**(5), October.

Walsham, G. and Han, C.-K. (1991). Structuration theory and information systems research. *Journal of Applied Systems Analysis*, **17**, 17–85.

Walsham, G. (1993). *Interpreting Information Systems in Organisations.* John Wiley, Chichester.

Ward, J., Taylor, P. and Bond, P. (1996). Evaluation and realisation of IS/IT benefits: an empirical study of current practice. *European Journal of Information Systems*, **4**(1), 214–225.

Weber, M. (1946). *Essays in Sociology.* Oxford University Press, Oxford.

Whiteley, D. (2000). *E-commerce: Strategy, Technologies and Applications.* McGraw-Hill, Maidenhead.

Wiener, N. (1948). *Cybernetics.* Wiley, New York.

Wilcocks, L. and Margetts, H. (1994). Risk assessment and information systems. *European Journal of Information Systems*, **3**(2), 127–138.

Wynekoop, J. L. and Russo, N. L. (1997). Studying system development methodologies: an examination of research methods. *Information Systems Journal*, **7**(1), 47–65.

Zuboff, S. (1988). *In the Age of the Smart Machine: the Future of Work and Power.* Heinemann, London.

GLOSSARY AND INDEX

Term	Definition	Pages
A		
Acceptance testing	Conducting any tests required by the user to ensure that the user community is satisfied with the system	366, 373, 374
Action perspective	The perspective on organisations that focuses on the process of organising	219, 224–6
Activity-based project management	A form of *project management* in which planning and control is conducted in terms of project activities	444–5
Adaptive maintenance	Changes made to the information system to provide a closer fit between an information system and its environment, the human activity system	203, 379
Agent	An agent is something (usually a person, group, department or organisation but possibly some other information system) that is a net originator or receiver of system data	48, 101–2
Aggregation	This type of relationship serves to collect together a set of different classes into one unit or aggregate.	106–7, 449, 454
Analysis	*See* Systems analysis	–
Application	A term generally used as a synonym for an IT system or some other piece of software designed to perform a particular function	128, 131
Application service provider	A company supplying a software service as an application	533
Application software	Software designed for a particular set of tasks in an organisation	131
Assembly language	A second generation programming language, above machine code	126
Association	An association relationship establishes a connection between the instances of classes and is defined by cardinality and optionality	103, 106, 107, 454
Authority	Authority is legitimated power in that those over whom it is exercised accept the exercise of power	36–7, 229

Term	Definition	Pages
B		
B2B	Business to business. *See* Supply chain	–
B2B e-commerce	The use of e-commerce in the supply chain	488–90
B2B IOS	An inter-organisational information system used to connect businesses together	492
B2C	Business to customer. *See* Customer chain	–
B2C e-commerce	The use of e-commerce in the customer chain	490
B2C IOS	An inter-organisational information system used to connect businesses to customers	492
Behavioural modelling	That form of information systems modelling concerned with specifying the behaviour of the information system	100–2
Bespoke development	In bespoke development an organisation builds an information system to directly match with the requirements of the organisation	317
Bit	An abbreviation of binary digit – one of the two digits (0 and 1) used in binary notation	120
Business case	The case made for the utility of some information system	315, 329–32
Business process	*See* Organisational process	–
Business process re-engineering	An organisational analysis approach to redesigning business processes	245–6, 388–94
Business strategy	*See* Organisation strategy	–
Buyer-oriented B2B	Consumer opens electronic market on its own server and requests bids	522
Byte	A set of eight binary digits/bits	120
C		
CAISE	*See* Computer-Aided Information Systems Engineering	–
Cardinality	Cardinality establishes how many instances of one entity are related to how many instances of another entity	103–4
CATWOE	A framework for specifying root definitions in soft systems methodology	395–6
Chain of command and control	This refers to the relationships of power and authority established in the organisation between its members	229
Character set	A scheme for representing symbols in binary notation	125
Chief information officer	A term for executive level manager in the organisation responsible for informatics	408, 463
CIO	*See* Chief information officer	–
Class	*See* Object class	–

Term	Definition	Pages
Client–server	An applications architecture in which the processing is distributed between machines acting as clients and machines acting as servers	161–3
Communication channel	The medium along which messages travel	40–1, 147–9
Communication software	Software enabling the interconnection of computer systems	129–30
Communication subsystem	That part of an IT system enabling distribution of the processing around a network	121, 161
Communication technology	Technology used for communication	146–57
Competitive position	An organisation takes up a particular position in a market defined by its activities and relationships with its competitors, suppliers, customers and regulators	260, 285–6
Computer-aided information systems engineering	Information technology has been used to aid automated aspects of the development process	325–6
Concept	The idea of significance. The collection of properties that in some way characterise the phenomena	98–9
Conception	*See* Systems conception	–
Conceptual model	A conceptual model represents some Universe of Discourse, but contains little or no implementation detail	100
Configuration management	The process of controlling the changes made to an information system over time	380–1
Consensus participation	A design group is formed as in representative participation, but representatives are elected by staff and given the responsibility to communicate group decisions back to staff	359
Construction	*See* Systems construction	–
Consultative participation	Decision-making is still in the hands of systems analysts and systems designers, but there is a great deal of staff at every level consulted about such decision-making	359
Control	Control is the mechanism that implements adaptation in most systems	49–50
Corrective maintenance	Changes made to correct previously unidentified system errors	379
Correspondence failure	Lack of correspondence between objectives and evaluation	204
Cost advantage	This essentially aims to establish the organisation as a low-cost leader in the market	260–1, 423
Cost–benefit analysis	Cost–benefit analysis is critical to assessing whether or not the process of developing an IS is a worthwhile investment	332–5
Critical success factor	A factor which is deemed crucial to the success of a business	404–5

Term	Definition	Pages
Culture	The set of behaviours expected in some social group	12, 35, 235–42
Customer chain	The chain of activities that an organisation performs in the service of its customers	22, 248–50, 499–500
Customer relationship management	The set of activities devoted to managing the customer chain	82, 504–5
Customer resource life cycle	A strategic planning framework due to Ives and Learmonth. Also useful in defining elements of the customer chain	406–7
Customer-facing TPS	Transaction processing systems that interface with the customer	82
D		
Data	Sets of symbols	134–43
Database	An organised pool of logically related data	139
Database management system (DBMS)	A suite of computer software providing the interface between users and a *database* or databases	140
Data flow	A data flow is a pipeline through which packets of data of known composition flow	101
Data management	The set of facilities needed to manage data	139
Data management layer	That part of an IT system concerned with data management	139
Data mining	Data mining is the process of extracting previously unknown data from large databases and using it to make organisational decisions	456–7
Data model	An architecture for data or a blueprint of data requirements for some application	140–1
Data privacy	Ensuring the privacy of personal data	296–8
Data protection	The activity of ensuring data privacy	296–8
Data store	A data store is a repository of data	76, 101
Data subsystem	*See* Data management layer	–
Data type	A categorisation of data defining the format and operations for data	138
Data warehouse	A data warehouse is a type of contemporary database system designed to fulfil decision-support needs. It utilises large amounts of data from diverse data needs to fulfil multi-dimensional query	142, 456–7
Datum	A unit of data	4
DBMS	*See* Database management system	–
Decision-support database	Databases used to support organisational decision-making	142
Decision support system	DSS. *See* Executive information system	–

Term	Definition	Pages
E-market	An e-market is a market in which economic exchanges are conducted using information technology and computer networks	482–4
Empirics	Branch of semiotics concerned with the physical characteristics of the communication channel	35, 40–2, 147–8
Employee-facing TPS	Transaction processing systems that interact with employees of an organisation	83
End-user	That stakeholder group which uses an information system to conduct work	183, 342, 462
Enterprise resource planning system	A software package consisting of a set of IT systems which integrate to form an infrastructure for some company	166, 269
Entity	Some aspect of the 'real world' which has an independent existence and can be uniquely identified	103
Entity model	A model of the entities, relationships and attributes pertaining to some application	103
Entity modelling	*See Entity-relationship diagramming*	–
Entity type	*See Entity*	–
Entity-relationship data model	A data model, originally propose by P. P. S. Chen, which utilises three primary constructs: entities, relationships and attributes	322, 324
Entity-relationship diagramming	A technique for graphically representing a conceptual model using constructs from the entity-relationship data model	322, 324
Environment	Anything outside the organisation from which an organisation receives inputs and to which it passes outputs	14–15, 47, 281–307
Epistemology	The theory of knowledge	559–60
E-R diagramming	*See Entity-relationship diagramming*	–
ETHICS	Mumford's socio-technical design method	356–8
Executive information system	EIS. That type of information system designed to support high-level, strategic decision-making in organisations	69, 92–3
Expectation failure	The inability of an IS to meet a specific stakeholder group's expectations	204
Explicit knowledge	This is readily accessible, documented and organised knowledge	450
Extension	*See Referent*	–
External tele-democracy	Used to refer solely to the enablement of democratic processes between members of some political grouping and their governmental representatives	304–6
Extranet	Allowing access to aspects of an organisation's intranet to accredited users	155–6, 512–13, 523–4

Term	Definition	Pages
HTML	Hypertext Markup Language. A standard for marking up documents to be published on the WWW	154, 525
HTTP	Hypertext Transfer Protocol. An object-oriented, stateless protocol that defines how information can be transmitted between client and server	153
Human activity system	A human activity system is a logical collection of activities performed by some group of people	4–5, 66, 84–5, 348–51, 354–6, 367
Human activity system design	Design which includes job design, team design and procedure design	361–8
Hybrid implementation	This form of implementation phases in particular components as replacements or pilots major modules of the system	373

I		
I-commerce	The use of Internet technologies in support of e-commerce	484–6
Illocutionary act	A type of speech act that expresses intention	240–1
Implementation	*See* Systems implementation	–
Implicit knowledge	Knowledge accessible through querying and discussion but needing communication	450
Inconsistency	A measure of the degree to which data is held or processed differently across information systems	413
Informatics	Informatics is the study of information, information systems and information technology applied to various phenomena.	1–27
Informatics architecture	A specification of the information, information systems and information technology needed by some organisation	264–74
Informatics field	The academic study of informatics issues and problems	548–56
Informatics infrastructure	An informatics infrastructure consists of the sum total of information, information systems and information technology resources available to the organisation at any one time	264–74
Informatics management	The process of putting information, information systems and information technology plans into action	20–1, 431–9
Informatics planning	The process of defining the optimal informatics architecture for some organisation	18–20, 399–410
Informatics practice	The practical application of informatics knowledge and skill within organisations	531–6
Informatics profession	The bodies exercising control over informatics practice	537–47
Informatics research	Appropriate ways of creating new knowledge in the area of informatics	557–8
Informatics service	That organisational function devoted to the delivery of informatics services	460–70

Term	Definition	Pages
Informatics strategy	A definition of the structure within which information, information systems and information technology is to be applied in some organisation	19–20, 261, 411–20
Information	Information is data interpreted in some meaningful context	4
Information architecture	This consists of definitions of information need and activities involved in the collection, storage, dissemination and use of information within the organisation	19, 267, 435
Information centre	A structure for the informatics service in which the service acts as a centre of expertise for other business units	462–3
Information economics	Information economics attempts to include the evaluation of intangible as well as tangible benefits into the process of IS evaluation	334–5
Information economy	An economy in which information is both important and essential to effective performance	287–90
Information infrastructure	*See Information architecture*	–
Information management	That part of informatics management concerned with the management of information	431–9
Information security	The process of protecting information systems from criminal or unwanted activity	294
Information strategy	That part of an informatics strategy concerned with specifying the information need for the future within some organisation	412, 414–16
Information system	An information system is a system of communication between people. Information systems are systems involved in the gathering, processing, distribution and use of information.	4
Information systems architecture	This consists of the information systems needed to support organisational activity in the areas of collection, storage, dissemination and use	19, 267
Information systems development	The process of developing some information system	15–17, 311–20
Information systems infrastructure	*See Information systems architecture*	–
Information systems management	The process of managing the current information systems architecture and implementing the information systems strategy	20, 432–7
Information systems planning	The process of defining some information systems architecture	399–410
Information systems portfolio	A list of current systems in the information systems architecture or future systems in the information systems strategy	416–17
Information systems strategy	That part of an informatics strategy concerned with specifying the future control of an information systems infrastructure and implementation of new elements of this infrastructure	261, 412, 416–17

Term	Definition	Pages
Information technology	Information technology is any technology used to support information gathering, processing, distribution and use. Information technology consists of hardware, software, data and communications technology.	113–170
Information technology architecture	This consists of the hardware, software, data and communication facilities as well as the IT knowledge and skills available to the organisation	19, 267
Information technology infrastructure	*See* Information technology architecture	–
Information technology strategy	The process of managing the current IT architecture and implementing the IT strategy	261, 412, 417–18, 436
Information technology system	An information technology system is a technical system sometimes referred to as a 'hard' system. An information technology system is an organised collection of hardware, software, data and communications technology designed to support aspects of some information system	5–6, 158–170, 365–7
Input	The elements that a system takes from its environment	4, 48, 118
Input device	A device concerned with the input of data	118
Input subsystem	That part of a computer system concerned with the input of data	118
Institutional perspective	That perspective on the organisation that treats them as wholes or units	219–24
Instruction set	A list of instructions understood by the processor of some computer system	125
Integration testing	At some point the system has to be assembled as a complete unit and testing conducted of all related systems together	366
Intension	*See* Concept	–
Interaction failure	The argument is that if a system is heavily used it constitutes a success; if it is hardly ever used, or there are major problems involved in using a system then it constitutes a failure	204
Interface subsystem	That part of an IT system concerned with managing the user interface	160
Intermediary-oriented B2B	Intermediary runs an electronic market for buyers and sellers in a specific area	522–3
Internal tele-democracy	The way in which information and communications technology (ICT) can be used to improve internal democratic processes within government.	304–5
Internet	A set of interconnected computer networks distributed around the globe	152–5, 481–526
Internet service provider	ISP. A company supplying connections to the Internet	150, 533

Term	Definition	Pages
Interoperability	A measure of the degree to which information systems are able to coordinate and collaborate	413
Inter-organisational information system	That form of information system that is developed and maintained by a consortium of companies in some cognate area of business for mutual benefit	491–2
Interpretivism	A philosophical position which assumes a subjective reality that should be studied through interpretive immersion and description	559–60
Intra-business e-business	The use of ICT to enable the internal business processes of the firm	487, 490–1, 510–18
Intranet	The use of Internet technology within a single organisation	155–6, 512–16
IS development method	These constitute frameworks which prescribe, sometimes in great detail, the tasks to be undertaken in a given development process	322–7
IS evaluation	The process of evaluating the worth of some information system	471–7
Iterative development	In this model systems conception triggers an iterative cycle in which various versions of a system (prototypes) are analysed, designed, constructed and possibly implemented	495

J

Term	Definition	Pages
Job analysis	Job analysis involves the analysis of the content and relationships of current jobs in terms of both organisational and individual objectives	349–51

K

Term	Definition	Pages
Kilobyte	Approximately 1000 bytes	120, 137
Knowledge	Knowledge is derived from information by integrating information with existing knowledge. This may be represented as knowledge = object + relation + object	449
Knowledge codification	The representation of knowledge for ease of retrieval	451
Knowledge creation	The acquisition of knowledge from organisational members and the creation of new organisational knowledge	451
Knowledge management	Knowledge management consists of knowledge creation, knowledge codification and knowledge transfer	448–59
Knowledge management systems	A group of information technologies used for managing knowledge within organisations	453–6
Knowledge transfer	The communication and sharing of knowledge amongst organisational members	451

L

Term	Definition	Pages
Language action approach	An approach to information systems specification based on the concept of speech acts	239–40

Term	Definition	Pages
Linear development	The phases of development are strung out in a linear sequence with outputs from each phase triggering the start of the next phase	317–18
Local area network	LAN. A type of communication network in which the nodes of the network are situated relatively close together	151
Location strategy	A location strategy involves the organisation attempting to find a niche market to service	260
Logical data representation	The form of data representation primarily used by computer software	135–6
Logical model	An implementation-independent model	100
Logical modelling	The process of producing logical models	100
M		
Machine code	The lowest level of programming language	126
Main memory	*See* Primary storage	–
Maintenance	*See* Systems maintenance	–
Management information system	MIS. A type of information system supporting the tactical decision-making of managers	69
Market	A market is a medium for exchanges between buyers and sellers	283–6, 482–4
Mass deployment database	Databases used on the desktop	143
Megabyte	Approximately 1,000,000 (million) bytes	120, 137
Mega-package	*See* Enterprise resource planning system	–
Message	An object-oriented mechanism for activating methods	33, 40–1, 152–3
Method	A defined operation associated with an object. *See also* IS development method	17, 105, 108
Methodology	Constitutes assumptions about which research approaches are appropriate for generating valid evidence	559
MIS	*See* Management information system	–
Modelling approach	A modelling approach consists of constructs, notation and principles of use	98
N		
Negative feedback	The monitoring subsystem monitors the outputs from the system and detects variations from defined levels of performance. If the outputs vary from established levels then the monitoring subsystem initiates some actions that reduce the variation	51–2
Norm	An expectation of human behaviour	35, 236

Term	Definition	Pages
Organisational learning	Organisational learning occurs when members of the organisation respond to changes in the internal and external environments of the organisation by detecting and correcting errors in organisational theory-in-use, and embedding the results of their inquiry in private images and shared maps of the organisation	451–3
Output	The elements that a system passes back to its environment	120–1, 148
Output device	A device that outputs data	120–1
Output subsystem	That part of a computer system that outputs data to the user or to some other device	120–1
Outsourcing	The strategy in which the whole or part of the informatics service is handed over to an external vendor	467–8

P

Term	Definition	Pages
Package development	In package development an organisation purchases a piece of software from a vendor organisation and tailors the package to a greater or lesser extent to the demands of a particular organisation	317, 366
Parallel implementation	An implementation approach in which two systems, the old and the new system, run in parallel for a period	373
Payback period	Payback is then calculated on the basis of: Payback = Investment – cumulative benefit (cash inflow)	334
Perfective maintenance	Changes made to the information system which make improvements but without affecting its functionality	379
Physical data representation	The form of data representation primarily used by computer hardware	136–7
Physical design	The process of detailing the major elements of how a system will work on some computer system	359, 361
Physical flow	This represent the flow of tangible or physical goods and services such as foodstuffs and automobiles	251
Physical model	A model close to a description of reality and containing detailed plans for implementation	100
Physical store	This represents a place in which collections of physical artefacts accumulate such as warehouses	251
Political environment	The external environment of the organisation concerned with power and its exercise	15, 301–7
Portal	A portal is designed to be an entry point for users into the WWW	483–4
Positive feedback	Positive feedback involves the monitoring subsystem increasing the discrepancy between desired and actual levels of performance	52–3

Term	Definition	Pages
Positivism	A philosophical position which assumes an objective reality which should be studied through systematic theory-testing in order to generate law-like generalisations	559–60
Post-mortem evaluation	That variant of summative evaluation concerned with assessing the reasons for and lessons from information systems failures	436–74
Power	Power is the ability of a person or social group to control the behaviour of some other person or social group	36–7
Pragmatics	The study of the general context and culture of communication	34, 35–7
Preventative maintenance	Changes aimed at improving a system's maintainability such as documentation or improving the flexibility of some information technology system	379
Primary storage	Primary storage includes media that can be directly acted upon by the central processing unit (CPU) of the computer, such as main memory or cache memory. Primary storage usually provides fast access to relatively low volumes of data	120
Process	Some transformation of input into output. In behavioural modelling a process is a transformation of incoming data flow(s) into outgoing data flow(s).	244–54
Process failure	This type of failure is characterised by unsatisfactory development performance	204
Process map	See Organisation process model	–
Process mapping	The activity of analysing and specifying major organisational processes	393
Process redesign	See Process re-engineering	–
Process re-engineering	The process of analysing, redesigning and implementing organisational processes	245–6, 389–92
Process/data matrix	A matrix which relates entities on an organisation data model against processes on an organisation process model	414
Product-based project management	A form of project management in which project planning and control is focused around information systems products	445
Production database	A type of database designed to support standard organisational functions	142
Productivity paradox	The paradox that those organisations that have invested significantly in IT do not appear to have experienced significant improvements in productivity	195–6
Programming language	A language for instructing some computer system	126–7
Project control	Project control concerns ensuring that a project remains on schedule, within budget and produces the desired output	444–5
Project escalation	The process in which decision-makers become locked in an irrational course of action	210, 275
Project management	The process of planning for, organising and controlling projects	21, 440-7

Term	Definition	Pages
Project organisation	Project organisation concerns how to structure staff activities to ensure maximum effectiveness	443
Project planning	Project planning involves determining as clearly as possible the likely parameters associated with a particular project	441–3
Prototyping	The development approach in which prototypes are produced	325, 346

R

Term	Definition	Pages
Record	A physical data structure composed of fields	137
Redundancy	A measure of the degree to which data is unnecessarily replicated across information systems	413
Referent	That which is being signified. The range of phenomena referred to	37
Reintermediation	The process in electronic markets of new intermediaries developing between buyers and sellers	483, 493
Relationship	An association between entities or objects	103
Representation formalism	A set of syntactic and semantic conventions that make it possible to describe things	394
Representative participation	A design group is formed made up of representatives of all grades of staff with systems analysts. The representatives however are selected by management	359
Requirements analysis	The stage in the database development process involved in the elicitation of data requirements	346–8
Requirements elicitation	See Requirements analysis	–
Research method	A general approach to conducting research	560–1
Research technique	A way of collecting, analysing and representing data	560–1
Research tool	'Technology' for conducting research	560–1
Return on investment	The return on investment (RoI) associated with an IS project is calculated using the following equation: RoI = average (annual net income/annual investment amount)	333
Risk analysis	The identification, estimation and assessment of risk	335–6
Role	A package of behaviour associated with particular social situations	36
Root definition	A way of specifying organisational processes in soft systems methodology	395–6
Rules subsystem	That part of an IT system concerned with application logic	160

S

Term	Definition	Pages
Satisficing	The term used by Herbert Simon to describe the characteristics of human decision-making	91–224

Term	Definition	Pages
Scenario	A narrative description of what people do and experience as they try to make use of computer systems and applications	324, 347
Scientific management	An approach to management thinking created by Frederick Taylor	221
Secondary storage	Secondary storage cannot be processed directly by the CPU. It hence provides slower access than primary storage but can handle much larger volumes of data. Two of the most popular forms of secondary storage are magnetic disk and magnetic tape	120
Semantics	The study of the meaning of signs	34, 37–9
Semiosis	The process of using signs	39
Semiotics	The study of signs and sign-systems	32–5
Sign	Anything that is significant. Normally made up of symbol, concept and referent	33–5
Social environment	The external environment of the organisation concerned with society	292–300
Socio-technical design	The parallel design of both technical and social systems	356–8
Socio-technical system	A socio-technical system is a system of technology used within a system of activity.	6
Soft system	Collections of people undertaking activities to achieve some purpose	56
Soft systems methodology	The approach to organisational analysis created by Peter Checkland	394–6
Speech act	An action of speech. See also Illocutionary act	221, 240–1
Stages of growth model	A model which defines some key phases in the life of informatics management for some organisation	436–8
Stakeholder	The group of people to which an information system is relevant	5, 179, 183–4, 209
Stakeholder analysis	Analysing the types of and impact of stakeholders on information systems	196–7
Stakeholder involvement	Involvement of stakeholder representatives in the development of an IT system	179, 184–5
Stakeholder participation	Involvement of stakeholders both in the development of the IT system and the work surrounding its use	358–9
Stakeholder resistance	The resistance of stakeholder groups to the introduction of some information system	185–6
Stakeholder satisfaction	The state of satisfaction expressed by some stakeholder group in an information system	179, 184
State	The state of a system is defined by the values appropriate to the system's attributes or state variables	49
Storage	That part of a system concerned with the representation of data	119–20

Term	Definition	Pages
Storage device	A device that persistently represents data	119–20
Storage subsystem	That part of the computer system concerned with the persistent representation of data	119–20
Strategic analysis	Strategic analysis involves determining the organisation's mission and goals	258
Strategic choice	This involves generating strategic options, evaluation of such options and the selection of a suitable strategy to achieve the selected option	258
Strategic evaluation	That form of IS evaluation concerned with assessing the utility of some information system prior to development	21, 473
Strategic implementation	Strategic implementation comprises determining policies, making decisions and taking action	258
Strategic information system	An information system that delivers competitive advantage	19–20, 421–7
Strategic management	The top level of management concerned with making unstructured decisions with heavily summarised data	91–2
Strategy	Strategy is the art of a commander-in-chief; the art of projecting and directing the larger military movements and operations in a campaign	256–7
Structural modelling	That form of IS modelling concerned with representing the structure of data in the system	103–5
Structuration	The process by which human action both produces and reproduces social structure and also how social structure both informs and constrains human action	220–1
Subculture	The set of behavioural expectations associated with some part of a larger social grouping	237
Subsystem	A subsystem is some coherent part of a system	48–9
Summative evaluation	That form of IS evaluation that assesses the worth of some system after implementation	21, 198, 374–5
Supplier-facing TPS	Transaction processing systems that interface with the supplier	82
Supplier-oriented B2B	Producers and consumers use the same electronic market-place. Essentially the same as B2C e-commerce	522
Supply chain	The chain of activities that an organisation performs in relation to its suppliers	22, 248–50, 483
Supply chain management	The collection of an organisation's activities devoted to the management of the supply chain	490
Symbol	That which is signifying something	37–8
Syntactics	That part of semiotics devoted to the study of the structure of signs and sign-systems	34, 39–40
Syntax	The operational rules for the correct representation of terms and their use in the construction of sentences of the language	40

Term	Definition	Pages
System	A coherent set of interdependent components which exists for some purpose, has some stability, and can be usefully viewed as a whole	4
System documentation	This describes the structure and behaviour of the IT system for developers	367
System lag	Lag is a delay between the issuing of a control signal and the adjustment of the system process to the signals	53–4
Systems analysis	That part of the development process devoted to eliciting and representing the requirements for systems	55–6, 339–52
Systems conception	That part of the development process devoted to assessing the investment potential and feasibility of systems	328–38
Systems construction	That part of the development process devoted to constructing systems	364–70
Systems design	That part of the development process devoted to designing the functionality of systems	353–63
Systems engineering	A systems discipline concerned with the production of large, complex physical artefacts	55
Systems implementation	That part of the development process devoted to delivering the system into its context of use	371–6
Systems maintenance	That part of the development process devoted to maintaining systems	377–83
System software	That collection of programs which coordinates the activities of hardware and all programs running on a computer system	128–9
Systems thinking	*See* General systems theory	–
System testing	Testing of an entire system as a unit	366
T		
Tacit knowledge	Knowledge accessible only with difficulty through elicitation techniques	225, 450, 451
Tactical management	Middle management which interfaces between strategic and operational management	91–2
Tactics	Tactics belongs only to the mechanical movement of bodies set in motion by strategy	256–7
Task analysis	Specifying the precise organisation of tasks associated with the use of some computer system	348–9
Technique	Some systematic activity within the development process	17, 322, 324
Technological frame	A technological frame is a collection of underlying assumptions, expectations and knowledge that people have about technology and its use.	183–4
Telecommunication carrier	An organisation which provides the infrastructure for telecommunications	150

Term	Definition	Pages
Telecommunication device	A piece of hardware that permits electronic communication to occur	150
Telecommunication media	Media used for the transmission of data in communication networks	149
Telecommunication service	*See* Telecommunication carrier	–
Tele-democracy	The use of IS and IT to improve democratic processes	304–6
Tele-government	*See* Electronic government	–
Teleology	The study of the purposes of systems	47
Terabyte	Approximately 1,000,000,000,000 (trillion) bytes	120, 137
Testing	Part of systems construction. Ensuring that an information system is working effectively	366–7, 373
Theory X	According to this theory the average human being is perceived as disliking work and hence avoiding it wherever possible. The average human being avoids responsibility and has little ambition	361–2
Theory Y	According to this theory physical and mental effort are important and natural human functions. If humans are committed to certain objectives they will exercise self-direction and self-control. The capacity to exercise imagination, ingenuity and creativity are widely distributed in the population	361–2
Third generation programming language	Also known as high-level language. A programming language one further step removed from assembly language	325, 366
Tool	Some software used to aid the development process	325
TPS	*See* Transaction processing system	–
Transaction processing system	TPS. A type of information system supporting the operational activities of some organisation	69, 81–4
Transaction subsystem	That part of an IT system concerned with communicating between the interface and rules subsystem and the data subsystem	160
Transactional data	Transactional data is data that records events taking place between individuals, groups and organisations	289, 294, 295
Turing machine	An abstract machine, created by Alan Turing, that proposed the essential features of the modern computer	116–17

U

UKAIS	UK Academy of Information Systems. An academic group attempting to press for the position of information systems as a distinctive discipline within the UK and Eire	554–5
Unit testing	Testing of individual programs or software modules	366

Term	Definition	Pages
Usability	An information system's usability is how easy a system is to use for the purpose for which it has been constructed	8, 178–9, 182, 210, 473
Use case	A use case model provides a high-level description of major user interactions with some information system	324, 346–8
Use failure	Failure of an information system after a period of use	203
User documentation	A source of reference for users to turn to when puzzled about aspects of use	367
User interface	That part of an IT system which allows the end-user to use the system	180–2
Utility	Utility refers to the worth of an information system in terms of the contribution it makes to its human activity system and to the organisation as a whole	8–9, 178, 210, 473

V		
Value added network	VAN. A type of communication network in which a third-party creates and maintains a network for other organisations	151
Value chain	An organisation's value chain is a series of interdependent activities that delivers a product or service to a customer	22, 247–8, 483, 511–12
Vertical portal	These normally provide the same functionality as horizontal portals but for a specific market sector	484, 523
Virtual organisations	Also referred to as network organisations. Organisations characterised by flat organisational hierarchies, formed around projects and linked together by information technology	232
Vocabulary	A complete list of the terms of a language. See Syntactics	40
Volume testing	Testing the application with large amounts of data and use	366

W		
Wide area network	WAN. A type of communication network in which the nodes of the network are geographically remote	151
Word	One or more bytes treated as a unit	120
WWW	World Wide Web. A set of standards for hypermedia documentation. It now has become synonymous with the Internet	153–6